A Search for Solvency

A Search for Solvency

Bretton Woods and the
International Monetary
System, 1941–1971

Alfred E. Eckes, Jr.

University of Texas Press   Austin

The publication of this book was assisted by a grant from the Andrew W. Mellon Foundation.

Library of Congress Cataloging in Publication Data

Eckes, Alfred E   1942–
    A search for solvency.

    Bibliography: p.
    Includes index.
    1. International finance.   2. Foreign exchange.
    3. United States—Foreign economic relations.
    I. Title.
    HG3881.E26   332.4'5   75-14433

    ISBN: 978-0-292-74083-9

First paperback printing 2012

For My Mother and Father

Contents

Contents

Preface

War dominated the public consciousness in July 1944 as it had for over four years since the beginning of the world's most destructive military and political struggle. Bold headlines recorded a dazzling series of Allied military triumphs in Europe and Asia. Gen. Dwight Eisenhower's troops entered Normandy and penetrated German defenses on the Cherbourg Peninsula. In Eastern Europe a massive Soviet army continued to push back Hitler's forces. Simultaneously, B-29 superfortresses pounded Japanese military installations on Kyushu, and American ground troops captured Saipan and invaded Guam. The shifting fortunes of war encouraged an unsuccessful attempt to assassinate Hitler, forced resignation of the Japanese Imperial Cabinet, and ensured President Franklin Roosevelt's renomination at the Democratic Convention.

Diverted by dramatic military and political events, few Americans realized the significance of an international conference being held at Bretton Woods, a mountain resort in the White Mountains of New Hampshire far from the battle zones. But there United Nations experts were completing plans for a world monetary and financial system that they hoped would create a prosperous efficient global economy and avert the economic causes of another world war.

Three weeks after it began, Bretton Woods concluded with a forty-four–nation agreement on the outlines of a postwar money system. Secretary of the Treasury Henry Morgenthau, who presided over the deliberations, halted proceedings briefly during the final plenary session on July 22 so that he could describe the results in a nationwide radio broadcast. Recalling how economic nationalism had turned prewar neighbors into enemies and ultimately brought ruin to all, Morgenthau explained the rationale for this experiment in world monetary organization. "We have come to recognize that the wisest and most effective way to protect our national interests is through international cooperation." Understanding, too, that peace and prosperity were interrelated and attainable only within the framework of international agreements, the delegates had proposed two new institutions, the International Monetary Fund and the International Bank for Reconstruction and Development.[1]

These arrangements concerned international payments and investments, not trade, commodities, or relief, which required separate consideration. In brief, the fund, designed to help alleviate those balance-of-payments difficulties that periodically afflicted nations in a world with minimal barriers to trade and capital movements, would have an $8.8 billion pool of currencies and gold to assist its members. They, in turn, would maintain relatively stable exchange rates among national currencies and remove, as soon as possible, the network of exchange restrictions that hampered prewar trade. To complement the fund Bretton Woods delegates also proposed an international bank, with $9.1 billion in subscriptions. This companion agency, considered indispensable in promoting a balanced world economy in which the fund could function effectively, would provide and guarantee loans to war-devastated and underdeveloped lands for economic restoration and development.

Morgenthau and other officials recognized the historic significance of their deliberations. For the first time in peace preparations, governments had acted on the assumption that economics must serve as a handmaid for international politics if victors were to overcome the dislocations of war and establish a durable framework for lasting peace. As Morgenthau observed, the conference erected a signpost "pointing down a highway broad enough for all men to walk in step and side by side. If they will set out together, there is nothing on earth that need stop them."[2]

At the concluding session Norwegian delegate Wilhelm Keilhau contrasted the apparent success of Bretton Woods to disasters of the post–World War I period when "politicians" tried to promote narrow national interests while "disregarding the interdependence of the ex-

changes, disregarding the interdependence of national economies."
This time, he added, if postwar planners failed to create "something
new and unique," there was only the consolation that "it would inspire my world-famous friend Lord Keynes" to write "a second brilliant volume of 'The Economic Consequences of the Peace.' "[3]

John Maynard Keynes, who led the British delegation, did not anticipate having to write another biting indictment of peacemaking
follies. Despite some harsh public criticism of Bretton Woods, he was
optimistic that the "amity and unbroken concord" of these sessions
augured well for the international community. "If we can . . . continue," he said, "this nightmare, in which most of us . . . have spent too
much of our lives, will be over. The brotherhood of man will have become more than a phrase."[4]

A generation later the fears and hopes of Morgenthau, Keynes, and
other founding fathers have new relevance as nations struggle with
the difficulties of replacing Bretton Woods with a more flexible
regime, better suited for the needs of the late twentieth century. The
current quest is more truly a multinational effort than the Bretton
Woods deliberations were. At the conclusion of World War II the
United States occupied a dominant position in the global economic
hierarchy. This country held nearly two-thirds of all monetary gold
and produced about 50 percent of the world's gross domestic product.
Without American assistance and leadership, there was little prospect
that other nations could act independently to reconstruct world
finance and create institutions and rules for an open global economy—one in which trade and capital movements link the domestic
economies of politically sovereign nations.

Accordingly, this volume concentrates on American planning for
the postwar monetary order, emphasizing the efforts of Treasury
policymakers, particularly Morgenthau and his talented deputy Harry
Dexter White, to formulate and effect the Bretton Woods system.
While necessarily considering at length complex economic issues and
concepts—liquidity, adjustment, and confidence, in particular—this
study examines foreign-policy implications as well. Archival documents indicate, for instance, that to Treasury officials Bretton Woods
was the economic foundation for continuing collaboration with both
the Soviet Union and the United Kingdom in the postwar era.

From another perspective, this work shows how an international
elite of economists—"service intellectuals"—approached global prob-

lems from a common theoretical perspective and labored to reconcile the requirements of economic internationalism with the realities of a nation-state political system. In concentrating on these themes, I have avoided a lengthy legal and diplomatic analysis of the Bretton Woods system as it evolved in the generation after World War II. First, both the International Monetary Fund and the World Bank Group have undertaken detailed self-examinations of their birth certificates and experiences. Second, and more important, official documentation is not yet available to allow comprehensive historical research by the outside scholar, nor has adequate time elapsed to give these events sufficient perspective. Nevertheless, the magnitude of monetary convulsions in the last decade and the gradual breakdown of the Bretton Woods monetary mechanism and rules warrant tentative assessment, and I have relied here extensively on contemporary writings, interviews with policymakers in the United States and abroad, and my own observations as a journalist covering some international monetary meetings in 1971 and 1972 for the *Columbus Dispatch*.[5]

Like others involved in historical research and writing, I have accumulated many debts to former teachers, other scholars, and archivists and librarians who contributed directly or indirectly to the evolution of this study. At Washington and Lee University, John M. Gunn first initiated me into the exciting world of international economics, and later at the University of Cambridge members of the economics faculty sharpened and refined my perception of these issues. Robert A. Divine, who supervised my graduate work in history at the University of Texas, first saw the opportunity for combining my interests in diplomatic history and international economic relations in a study of the Bretton Woods system and its origins. I am deeply indebted to him for many perceptive suggestions and patient counsel. Other Texas faculty members, including R. Conrad Doenges, Thomas F. McGann, and H. Wayne Morgan, graciously read early drafts and suggested refinements in argument and writing style.

More recently, conversations with a number of scholars and former policymakers have influenced versions of this manuscript. John Gaddis of Ohio University and my former colleague Robert Gates of the Social Science Research Council have both read and advised me on portions of the draft. I am also grateful for discussions with Edward M. Bernstein, Henry Bittermann, and the late Ansel Luxford, who all generously recounted their memories of Bretton Woods.

Preston Wolfe and editors of the *Columbus Dispatch* made it possible for me to follow and report on the 1971 monetary crisis and thus gain a firsthand perspective on events leading to the breakdown of the Bretton Woods currency arrangements. A summer research grant from Ohio State University also aided research and writing.

While it is impossible to acknowledge the many librarians and archivists who assisted my research, I want to single out for special praise the staffs of the Franklin D. Roosevelt Library, the Library of Congress, the National Archives, the University of Texas and the Ohio State University libraries, and the U.S. Department of State Historical Office, who located long-retired manuscripts in obscure government depositories.

Finally, I wish to thank Margaret Kalatta, Donald McElwee, Betsy Manton, and Phyllis Tietzel for assistance in preparing this manuscript for publication.

The Quest for a Durable Global Monetary System

"Those who cannot remember the past are condemned to repeat it," George Santayana wrote in 1905. For the generation of American leaders who held power during World War II no epigram had more relevance. For President Franklin Roosevelt, Secretary of State Cordell Hull, and other officials, the memory of World War I mistakes, culminating with the defeat of the Treaty of Versailles, provided a vivid, and haunting, reminder of how previous leadership had tried and failed to create a permanent peace. The shadow of ill-fated experiences touched many dimensions of military and foreign policy—including the decisions to cooperate with the Soviet Union and to press for unconditional surrender—but it was particularly evident in postwar planning. As Franklin Roosevelt told a group of school children: "We have profited by our past mistakes. This time we shall know how to make full use of victory."[1]

The most conspicuous imprint of the past was on preparations for a postwar international organization, a second League of Nations, that would replace the unstable balance of power with collective security. But lessons of the past also shaped international economic preparations. Here, unlike the political plane where global political integration had been largely a vision before World War I, planners had a rich legacy of systematic thought and accomplishment reaching back through the nineteenth century. The most important lessons came from three separate bands of economic experience: the nineteenth-

1

century international economy, attempts to rehabilitate the global economy after World War I, and the economic anomie of the 1930's.[2]

That policymakers sought to avoid the mistakes of the past is not to argue that they sought to restore blindly a golden age or that they obdurately attempted to pour new wine into old bottles. There was recognition, especially during the 1930's, that the international environment had changed and that policy objectives had shifted. Britain, for instance, no longer dominated world trade and finance, and full employment had replaced stable currencies as the most urgent economic priority. Yet, in each of the three critical periods, earlier policymakers faced similar tasks—how to reconcile national self-determination with the widely understood advantages of international economic collaboration. On a technical level, the economic policymakers faced the vexing tasks of adjusting imbalances in trade and payments without discouraging an international division of labor and an unrestricted flow of trade and capital, on the one hand, and without disturbing domestic prices and employment, on the other hand. These goals, the economic planners learned from experience, were not always compatible.

An international economy emerged for the first time during the century of comparative peace lasting from Napoleon's defeat at Waterloo in 1815 to the outbreak of World War I. It was international in the sense that trade, capital, and people moved with relative ease between countries, especially between the industrializing nations of Western Europe and the peripheral suppliers of raw materials and foodstuffs. During the century global exports multiplied from $550 million to $19.8 billion. In the fifty years before World War I it is believed that the value of world trade rose an average of 34 percent per decade and the volume of trade climbed 36–37 percent each decade. The flow of international investments contributed to the rapid growth of trade, as the industrializing nations of Western Europe and North America invested approximately $44 billion abroad. The result was a new pattern of economic interdependence that linked nations together through trade and finance at a time when nationalism was strengthening countries politically.[3]

This first international economy was comparatively unstructured, emerging as the result of private, not governmental, initiatives. Except for adherence to the gold standard, which made national currencies stable and convertible, there were no rules of the game, negotiated by governments and maintained by international sanctions.

A number of factors, some unique to the nineteenth century, contributed to the evolution of this international economic system. The absence of war and the widespread belief that governments had few responsibilities for economic management or social welfare allowed private activity to expand with few impediments. Also, the rapid pace of European industrialization, the pressures of growing population, and new technological developments—especially the railroad and the steamship—encouraged and made possible the outward thrust of Europe and invited that continent to rely on low-cost foreign suppliers. Thus, during a period when the advanced countries were completing the process of national, political, and economic unification, their citizens were already looking elsewhere for profit, adventure, and service. The result, ironically, was a thriving, but unstructured, international economy that loosely tied citizens of many countries together economically at a time when political forces continued to accentuate the nation-state.

The first world economy evolved slowly and haphazardly, but not irrationally. Classical economists, including Adam Smith, David Ricardo, David Hume, and John Stuart Mill, supplied the intellectual foundation in their writings, and some battled in the political marketplace to translate their ideas into public policy. These political economists, many of them amateurs and not professional academicians, first posed rigorously the basic questions of international economics and offered answers based on their careful analyses of abstract models that seemed to resemble the world in which they lived. Because these doctrines provide the basis for nineteenth-century activity as well as the core of twentieth-century international economic thought, they require a brief summary.[4]

One question that bothered the early economists was why nations should exchange products. Taking issue with the seventeenth- and eighteenth-century mercantilists who advocated trade principally to dispose of exports and to acquire gold, the classical economists stressed how trade contributed to efficiency and growth. Certainly, as Adam Smith himself recognized, trade did permit a nation to market its surplus production, but trade also brought the benefits of imports. Clearly two countries could gain from exchanging products in which each had a natural advantage, such as coffee or bananas. In

Smith's words, "If a foreign country can supply us with a commodity cheaper than we ourselves can make it, better buy it of them with some part of the produce of our own industry, employed in a way in which we have some advantage."[5]

But trade could also be advantageous for two countries who produced the same two products. In a famous abstraction, David Ricardo demonstrated that if Portugal produced both items more efficiently than Britain, the two countries could still benefit from trade. Because Portugal was relatively more efficient in the production of wine than cloth, it should specialize in wine making and allow Britain to concentrate on cloth manufacture. Specialization according to comparative advantage, then, would permit workers in both countries to hold the most remunerative jobs, allow capitalists to obtain the highest return from production, and bring consumers lower prices. The economic case for trade rested in part on these static gains and also on the indirect benefits of commerce acting as an engine of development, expanding and improving production facilities.[6]

Some nineteenth-century political economists also emphasized the noneconomic benefits. John Stuart Mill, for instance, stressed an important theme of international economic thought: economic interdependence fostered world peace. "It is commerce," Mill asserted, "which is rapidly rendering war obsolete, by strengthening and multiplying the personal interests which are in natural opposition to it. And it may be said without exaggeration that the great extent and rapid increase of international trade, in being the principal guarantee of the peace of the world, is the great permanent security for the uninterrupted progress of the ideas, the institutions, and the character of the human race."[7]

A second issue that concerned the political economists was how nations, in the absence of a universal currency, balanced their accounts from private trade. For instance, if costs were lower in one country than in another, how could the two nations continue to trade if consumers behaved rationally and bought from the least expensive supplier? The price-specie-flow theory, which David Hume first employed and others elaborated, provided an answer. In a world with national currencies, two or more countries could trade indefinitely if they played by the widely understood rules of the gold standard. The rules were not difficult. Participants simply had to define their domestic currencies—francs, marks, dollars, and others—in terms of gold, thereby establishing a fixed relationship among the currencies that were anchored to gold. Each player must also permit the free conversion of its currency into gold and gold into national monies. Each must allow gold to move freely between countries. And, finally, each player must maintain a fixed relationship between the quantity of gold in its banking reserves and the amount of domestic money in circulation. Under these conditions, trade-and-payments imbalances induced gold transfers, and gold flows automatically altered internal prices and incomes so as to restore payments equilibrium.[8]

An example illustrates the balancing process. If Portugal and Britain accepted the informal rules of the gold standard, and then Portugal imported more from Britain than it sold, Portuguese traders would settle their accounts with British exporters by buying gold and shipping it to Britain. In the deficit country, Portugal, a gold loss would reduce the quantity of money in circulation, increase interest rates, and eventually cut prices and incomes. These internal adjustments would cause Portugal to import less and export more. Conversely, in Britain the arrival of gold would soon swell banking reserves, reduce interest rates, and trigger an upward adjustment of incomes and prices. As a result, Britain would export less and import more, and adjustments in both countries would move each toward equilibrium.

Before World War I the gold-standard adjustment mechanism linked all major commercial countries, except China. It was, of course, not the only way to remove payments imbalances, but other choices, which depended either on controls on trade and currencies or on fluctuating exchange rates, had little support. Controls and fluctuating currencies both increased uncertainty, interfered with trade and capital movements, and seemed to require more government intervention than did the self-adjusting gold standard. Provided central banks and governments observed the rules of the game, the gold standard assured that market forces would remove payments imbalances, and before World War I countries generally accepted these obligations. As it was widely understood then, the gold standard maintained stable currencies necessary for export expansion and increasing capital movements by shifting the burden of adjustment to domestic economies. A payments imbalance was automatically corrected by expansion in the surplus country and contraction in the deficit country. For this reason the gold standard achieved stable currencies and an open global economic order by compelling nations to sacrifice an independent domestic monetary policy.[9]

Much of the mystique of the prewar gold standard rested on the notion that it was a self-operating adjustment system that responded to market forces, not human management. After World War I, however, economists began increasingly to realize that the system functioned rather differently from what was supposed. Studies showed that, contrary to legend, gold had not moved in great quantity and that advanced countries often moved along parallel, not divergent, internal paths of expansion and contraction. The revised explanation emphasized that the prewar monetary system had been managed from London and that short- and long-term capital movements from the British financial center, then the capital of global finance, had provided a breathing space, or a cushion, for underlying payments adjustments to occur more gradually.[10]

Whatever their deficiencies for explaining events, the twin theories of comparative advantage and price-specie flow offered an abstract model for a self-regulating, efficient world economy of independent nation-states. And these ideas, as well as the conditions they supposedly produced, had a pervasive impact on policymakers who tried to rehabilitate the international economic system after World Wars I and II. At the beginning of the Second World War, State Department economist Herbert Feis acknowledged this legacy from the past. "If thoughts, like flowers, grew in beds, it could be said that up until recent years almost all thoughts upon international economic relations grew in a neatly planted and attractive bed. The seeds," Feis wrote, "had been planted long ago by the great economists of the classical tradition. Hume, Adam Smith, Ricardo, John Stuart Mill, Alfred Marshall, Frank W. Taussig, were among the great gardeners. This bed," he added, "had a fine pattern and order, and to the sunny intellect, glowing colors. It made the world a pleasant place to live in."[11]

World War I shattered the unique multilateral trade-and-payments system that evolved in the late nineteenth century and forced the victors to cope with reconstruction problems for which there were no precedents. But policymakers, unaccustomed to peacetime economic planning and unaware of how seriously the conflict had disrupted prewar relationships, underestimated the difficulty of reconstructing an open, stable world economy. Anxious to return to the prewar norm, officials thought that automatic market forces would restore equilibrium if governments removed wartime controls and indicated their determination to play according to gold-standard rules. Reconstruction of the monetary system, however, defied quick prescriptions, and the subsequent experience provided object lessons for a later generation of planners.

Several factors doomed immediate attempts to restore the pre-1914 world. For one thing, the conflict hastened underlying forces that were altering the foundation of the prewar system even before the outbreak of war. The war provided the occasion for an expansion of government activities, not merely over trade and payments, but over all aspects of economic activity. Moreover, the war weakened the appeal of nineteenth-century ideology and established a precedent for government involvement in domestic economic and social regulation.[12]

Suspension of the gold standard and currency convertibility during the war removed the outside discipline that had previously harmonized the price structures of independent countries. Freed from gold-standard discipline, governments printed inconvertible paper money to mobilize domestic resources, and inevitably inflation advanced unevenly, distorting the relative values of national currencies. By 1919, for example, wholesale prices had increased approximately 200 percent in the United States, 300 percent in Britain, and 430 percent in France. This rate of inflation imperiled a quick return to the gold standard, partly because it stretched existing gold reserves and threatened to drain Europe of gold, precipitating a serious bout of deflation.[13]

In addition, when the war concluded, the world's stock of monetary gold was inadequate and unevenly distributed. While other prices jumped upward, the value of gold fixed by monetary authorities did not, and, as a consequence, the world output of gold actually declined about one-third between 1915 and 1922. What gold was in official reserves was redistributed, and the United States emerged with 34 percent of all the monetary gold, compared to 27 percent before the war. With inadequate gold reserves countries could not accept the obligations of fixed parities, unless outside assistance was available.[14]

Perhaps the most significant economic consequence of the war was Europe's decline from its unchallenged position in the world trading-

and-payments system. The war, by dislocating European domestic economies, damaged that continent's competitiveness on world markets and, by disrupting traditional trading patterns, temporarily impaired Europe's capacity to sell on world markets. Without a continuing flow of European products many overseas markets turned during the war to American or Japanese producers. Others fostered their own import substitutes and later resisted a return to the prewar distribution of international production. Furthermore, the war left Germany with a heavy reparations debt and France, as well as other allies, with sizeable war-loan repayments. These transfers, because they depended on a revival of European exports, complicated a swift return to multilateral trade and payments.[15]

One of the most difficult adjustments, hastened by the war, was the decline of Britain as the dominant trade and financial center and the rise of the United States as a global economic power. World War I turned the United States from a debtor to a creditor, and, as the leading source of long-term capital in the 1920's, the United States had to adjust its economic policies to the new role. Before the war England had maintained the financial system by importing more than it exported and by paying for the import surplus from its "invisible" earnings—banking, insurance, and shipping—as well as its earnings on overseas investments. If the new order was to adjust smoothly, permitting both victors and vanquished to make debt payments, the United States would have to relax tariffs, reverse its export surplus, and invest more abroad.[16]

When President Woodrow Wilson, British Prime Minister David Lloyd George, French Premier Georges Clemenceau, and other Allied leaders met in Paris to settle peace terms, international monetary issues were not on their agenda. Instead, peacemakers concentrated their intellectual energies on such urgent, immediate problems as boundaries, colonies, security, indemnities, and relief. Even when the victors debated how to reconstruct a vanquished Germany and reintegrate it into a prosperous European economy, leaders took a narrow perspective. They did not grapple systematically with an array of permanent economic problems—such as currencies, trade, and raw materials—crucial to rehabilitation of Europe within a healthy global economy. There were several reasons for these glaring omissions. For one thing, officials did not have a clear or common perception of underlying changes and maladjustments brought by World War I, nor could they agree on how to establish the economic foundations for peace. For instance, France, having suffered physically and psychologically from Germany's efforts to dominate the continent, sought in the exuberance of victory to impose a Carthaginian peace on her old enemy, and that approach required heavy reparations payments. Preoccupied with the German problem, French leadership gave little attention to global rehabilitation. Britain, however, had a different set of interests. Eager to escape crushing debt burdens and excessive German competition in foreign markets, London hoped the United States would cancel war debts, underwrite intergovernmental reconstruction credits, and concert measures to facilitate recovery and financial stabilization. Finally, Woodrow Wilson, unwilling to place the burden on American taxpayers already suspicious of protracted entanglement in Europe's internal problems, hoped a lenient reparations settlement, coupled with diligent steps by European governments to put their domestic finances in order, would prove sufficient incentive for private lending and trade to rehabilitate Europe and establish a new global equilibrium.

Other factors discouraged a comprehensive approach to economic peacemaking. Not only did laissez faire philosophy and custom place some topics—including international lending—outside the pale of legitimate government concern, except in wartime, but also Wilson and his fellow peacemakers felt more comfortable deliberating political and security issues than intricate points of high finance. Crossing the Atlantic on his way to Paris, Wilson confided he was "not much interested in the economic questions."[17]

Ironically, then, President Wilson, the individual so often lauded for his single-minded commitment to a permanent mechanism of collective security for achieving a just and durable peace, underestimated the need for parallel economic and financial collaboration as a pillar for successful political cooperation. Part of the problem was that the American chief executive, a talented student of political history, simply did not conceptualize easily in economic terms. On an abstract plane he recognized that the United States' economic well-being was inextricably linked to a revival of Europe along liberal-capitalist lines and sensed intuitively that tariff reduction and equal access to raw materials tightened the bonds of national interdependence. Uninterested in technical details, he assumed that experts could resolve issues if he gained a lenient reparations settlement and won European support for a League of Nations. Unfortunately for Wilson, and perhaps world stability, France insisted on burdening Germany with war costs, and the U. S. Senate turned its back on the League of Nations.

Retrospectively it is easy to blame the World War I peacemakers for yielding to popular passions and short-sightedly imposing a punitive settlement on defeated Germany without at least making some provision for rehabilitation credits. But elected leaders are often prisoners of circumstance and rigid political constituencies, and these poisoned the discussions of victory in 1919. Certainly public pressure reduced British and French flexibility on the crucial reparations issue, and, similarly, domestic opinion militated against cancellation of European war debts or postwar lending, as some bankers favored. Nevertheless, had Wilson displayed the same vigorous leadership on economic reconstruction that he provided in behalf of the League of Nations, the peacemakers would at least have discussed in a comprehensive and systematic way how to cope with interrelated trade, reparations, investments, and currency dislocations before new tensions reduced the prospects for unified action. As it happened, the world's dominant economy, then producing about half of the world's industrial product and holding a third of the monetary gold, declined to supply leadership commensurate with its new role as a world creditor.

In 1920, as President Wilson lay paralyzed in the White House, the Treasury Department repeatedly advised Europeans to put their domestic finances in order so as to pay back governmental debts and attract private capital for reconstruction. Dissatisfied with the lack of direction and vision, bankers and businessmen in Europe and the United States encouraged the League of Nations to sponsor an international financial conference in Brussels for a wide-ranging discussion of economic issues. Although the United States wanted to restore European stability and promote a healthy trade-and-payments system, it elected to send only an unofficial observer, hoping this way to avoid embarrassing political ties to the League of Nations and additional pressure to wipe away the slate of war debts.[18]

Experts from thirty-nine countries came to Brussels in September 1920, and, after two weeks of talks, they recommended a number of financial remedies, including restrictive measures to curb internal inflationary pressures and adoption of a new international standard of value—though gold was not specifically mentioned. Delegates heard a Belgian proposal for an international bank, but they endorsed the Ter Meulen Plan for making long-term commercial credits available to needy European nations. These recommendations, however sound and well-intentioned, were poorly timed. A postwar depression, fluctuating currencies, and unsettled economic conditions doomed international cooperation.

Eighteen months later the British government, having made an initial decision to reconstruct the gold standard, offered leadership, and delegates met again in Genoa under League of Nations auspices for what Prime Minister David Lloyd George called the "greatest gathering of European nations which has ever assembled in this continent." This time participants—again without formal American participation—openly pledged to recreate the gold standard, and, more importantly, they approved a program to achieve that goal. First, nations should restore internal stability by reducing budgetary expenditures, ceasing unproductive borrowing, and halting inflationary monetary policies. Then, after ways were devised to economize on monetary gold, countries should declare currency values at either old or new parities. Also, since governments themselves were presumably too sensitive to political pressures, central banks should cooperate to implement the stabilization program under direction of the Bank of England. Finally, after internal and external currency stabilization were achieved, delegates expected private international capital flows to revive, satisfying the urgent need for outside assistance.[19]

Representatives of thirty-three trading nations agreed in Genoa to restore the gold standard, but they did not propose simply to rehabilitate the self-adjusting, invertebrate prewar regime. Instead, authorities believed a new gold system should operate within a more structured set of rules than existed previously. Accordingly, they proposed an international convention to centralize and coordinate the demand for gold. This arrangement never materialized, but, in looking forward to a more structured monetary system, based on clearly stated obligations and close central bank cooperation, the Genoa experts sought to rationalize and improve the world monetary system. Fundamentally, however, Genoa preserved a vital link with the prewar system, for nations were expected to subordinate internal economic policy to the requirements of maintaining exchange-rate stability. In the last analysis, international equilibrium depended, the delegates assumed, on the willingness of sovereign government to stabilize internal conditions, reduce trade and exchange barriers, and to use gold and key currencies, such as the dollar and pound sterling, as reserves.[20]

At Brussels and Genoa, experts considered some of the same issues debated at Bretton Woods during World War II, but, unlike the latter conference, the two post–World War I sessions accomplished too little and came too late. Genoa and Brussels took place after conclusion of hostilities and after the wartime harmony of interests ceased to exist. Partly because recommendations preceded a settlement of vexing war-debt and reparations questions, governments generally chose to ignore the resolutions. Without a formal American commitment to reconstruction, European nations lacked the monetary resources to undertake global monetary stabilization alone.[21]

While the United States government remained outwardly aloof, an informal coalition of central and commercial bankers took charge of monetary reconstruction and proceeded to stabilize European economies. With encouragement from central bankers—especially Benjamin Strong of the New York Federal Reserve Bank and Montagu Norman of the Bank of England, private bankers quietly cooperated to work out in 1924 a German reparations settlement—the Dawes Plan —recognizing that the recovery of Europe and Germany were interrelated. Then, Strong and Norman took over to stabilize the world's two most important trading currencies—the dollar and the pound. These two central bankers recognized that simultaneous stabilization of all currencies was hazardous, perhaps impossible, and they wisely concentrated on the crucial sterling-dollar relationship. Justifying this approach, Strong said: "We must not turn a twelve-inch gun on a sparrow. The great problem is sterling; the others will come along easily enough if sterling could be dealt with."[22]

Determined to maintain London's position as a world banking center and to restore the pound's prestige, British authorities embarked on a controversial austerity program designed to wring out wartime inflation and appreciate sterling. Austerity at home, combined with a $200 million gold credit from the New York Federal Reserve Bank, set the stage for Britain's fateful decision to restore sterling convertibility at the prewar gold parity in April 1925. Unfortunately, British policymakers underestimated the difficulties. For, at the old par value, sterling was overvalued, perhaps between 10 and 11 percent, and, as a result, British manufactures, already becoming technologically obsolete, experienced added difficulty competing in world markets. Unemployment mounted and public protests grew as the authorities doggedly pursued stringent domestic policies so as to reduce wages, prices, and profits in order to maintain gold convertibility.[23]

Britain's unlucky experience with stabilization vividly demonstrated the difficulty of achieving stable exchange rates, unrestricted trade and capital movements, and common domestic policies in an unbalanced world. No longer, it seemed, would domestic opinion tolerate sharp, unpleasant internal adjustments to support exchange-rate stabilization. Moreover, the British experiment appeared to demonstrate that economic structures in advanced democracies were now less flexible than previously. Trade union resistance to wage cuts, government social welfare policies, and business reluctance to slash prices all impeded domestic price and income adjustments. Hereafter, it appeared that international economic policy would have to harmonize with domestic policies rather than the reverse.

After Britain anchored sterling to gold, France stabilized the franc—at an undervalued level—and more than thirty other nations made similar decisions. Strong, Norman, and other central bankers supervised, and aided, this piecemeal stabilization process. To facilitate internal economic adjustments they often provided a gold credit to the local central bank and obtained, in return, assurance that the borrowing country would play according to the rules of responsible financial conduct outlined at Genoa. The beneficiary pledged to maintain a balanced budget, follow noninflationary monetary policy, and preserve central bank independence from political interference. These conditions established, the central bankers provided credit references enabling local governments to borrow additional sums from private bankers to undertake specific internal reconstruction programs. While this procedure involved some sacrifice of national sovereignty over the home economy to achieve a return to the gold standard, the conditions encountered little resistance in the 1920's until the lessons of Britain's ruinous stabilization experience became clear. Only later was there a general awareness that a decision to support stable currency rates might conflict with domestic policies to boost employment or achieve more rapid economic growth.[24] ·

The Quest for a Durable Global Monetary System

From 1925 to 1929 the world economy regained its prewar momentum. Except for overvaluation of sterling and undervaluation of the French franc, this first experiment with general stabilization appeared successful. Once more currencies became relatively stable and convertible. Despite the distortions of protective tariffs, commerce flourished and goods once again flowed through the pre-1914 multilateral channels. In 1927, for instance, the volume of world trade was approximately 20 percent higher than in 1913. While Europe's share of world exports had fallen, the overall pattern still resembled older arrangements. The United States, now the leading exporter and capital supplier, continued to generate a trade surplus with Canada and Europe but an import surplus from the rest of the world. Continental countries, especially Germany and France, imported more than they sold to non-European countries, and they offset this deficit with a trade surplus on European transactions. Finally, Britain, while remaining the world's largest single importer, consumed larger quantities of goods from Europe and North America than it exported. London offset this deficit with a favorable balance on transactions with Latin America, Africa, and Asia. Revival of this flourishing triangular trade depended in no small way on currency stabilization. Stable and convertible currencies enabled trading nations to balance their earnings from one region with payments to other areas, thus lubricating the way for an effective international division of labor.[25]

Currency stabilization also established a favorable climate for capital movements. The flow of long-term capital rose steadily from 1919 to 1929, especially after 1925. Whereas London supplied the bulk of investment capital before World War I, New York emerged as the principal capital exporter in the 1920's. In 1928, for instance, the United States invested $1,099 million abroad; Britain, $569 million; and France, $237 million. During the decade before the 1929 collapse, the United States supplied about $7 billion of the approximately $10 billion invested overseas.[26]

The United States' rise to financial preeminence came without adequate preparation or public understanding. Lacking extensive experience in international banking, American underwriters sometimes ignored the canons of successful lending in the 1920's. During the nineteenth century, for instance, British investors insisted on sound, self-liquidating projects, but in the exuberance of financial adolescence competitive American underwriters frequently failed to examine carefully the character and purpose of a loan proposal or prospects for repayment. As a result, both creditors and borrowers suffered. Some Latin American governments took advantage of New York's inexperience to borrow irresponsibly for financing internal corruption or subsidizing never-completed public works projects. On other occasions the lenders set excessive interest rates and inappropriate repayment schedules and thus created conditions conducive to default in hard times. There was another serious shortcoming in lending practice. A high proportion of American portfolio capital—80 percent—went to governments or received host-government guarantees, but instead of enhancing repayment prospects these loans contained their own perils. Because the servicing of public debts depended on the ability of government officials to collect taxes, these loans proved increasingly unsound as the world depression depressed government revenues and disrupted government budgets.

Before World War I, London's lending facilitated international payments, and now in the 1920's New York capital markets assumed that function. For a time the United States supplied the critical margin of liquidity required to sustain a high level of international transactions and to facilitate repayment of war debts and reparations. This system might have survived and prospered had the United States, like prewar Britain, removed trade barriers and reinvested investment earnings to finance an import surplus, but the inexperienced nation did not. With a Congress and a public unsophisticated in the harsh realities of global finance, this country failed to assume the obligations of a mature creditor. Instead, it tried to lend abroad and protect a balance of trade surplus simultaneously. This was possible as long as capital flowed abroad in sufficient volume to cover debt repayments and to provide the dollars other countries needed to continue buying American exports.

Expanding trade, increasing investments, and general prosperity temporarily concealed the perils. Soon, however, a severe world depression and related currency collapse exposed the fundamental weaknesses of the new gold-standard system: inappropriate currency rates, a crisis-prone gold-reserve network, an inadequate adjustment mechanism, and an unstable source of international liquidity.

Experienced central bankers helped major and minor nations establish new gold parities, but too often officials selected exchange rates without giving adequate attention to the market value of currencies or differences in national price levels. As a result, stabilization was piecemeal, uncoordinated, and often inappropriate. Britain, for instance, selected an overvalued parity, thus exposing her domestic market to more intensive import competition, reducing export competitiveness, and compelling monetary authorities to maintain artificially high interest rates to protect that country's gold reserve. France, on the other hand, selected an undervalued rate. This permitted France to gain an export surplus and accumulate gold. French gold reserves increased from $954 million in 1927 to $1,633 million in late 1932, and the flow of gold to Paris placed added strain on London and other monetary centers. As a League of Nations study concluded later, this uncoordinated piecemeal currency reconstruction "sowed the seeds of subsequent disintegration."[27]

The restored gold standard also proved crisis prone, particularly when occasional crises of confidence precipitated mass transfers of gold and currencies from one monetary center to another. The problem stemmed from the need to economize on the use of gold, which was scarce and unevenly distributed after the war, and from the decision to try what was a gold-exchange standard. Under the rules of the new system participants could keep their reserves either in gold or in gold-convertible currencies, such as dollars or pounds. The willingness of nations to keep reserves in certain currencies depended on their confidence in the capacity of the key country to redeem its currency into gold upon demand. Actually, this reserve-currency system had emerged before World War I, but at that time paper money accounted for only a small percentage of total reserves. In 1928, however, twenty-four European countries kept an average of 42 percent of their reserves in foreign currencies.[28]

That the gold-exchange standard was less stable than the old gold standard became known in the 1920's when political unrest, uncoordinated currency alignments, and divergent interest rates in major money centers encouraged periodic movements of hot capital from one country to the next. To control these disruptive capital movements required more monetary coordination than central banks had developed. In brief, institutions and procedures had not evolved quickly enough to cushion operations of the new exchange system. No incident dramatized how accident prone the gold-exchange system was better than the sterling crisis of September 1931. Withdrawal of foreign funds from London threatened to exhaust British gold reserves and compelled the United Kingdom, once the pillar of international finance, to close its gold window and float the pound.[29]

Unlike the prewar gold standard, which was largely self-operating (except for occasional Bank of England intervention), the gold-exchange standard of the 1920's was generally managed. No longer were monetary authorities ready to tolerate an equilibrium achieved from gold movements or exchange-rate fluctuations. During the 1920's they increasingly sought to insulate home economies for the internal adjustments required to operate a gold-standard regime. And, while they succeeded in neutralizing gold movements and in cushioning the home market from unpleasant, but necessary, adjustments, these policies did not contribute to a positive solution for the problems of restoring balance-of-payments equilibrium. As long as deficit countries did not exhaust their supplies of gold or gold-convertible currencies and surplus countries continued to accumulate reserves, an imbalance could continue indefinitely. Without sanctions on either surplus or deficit countries, the system postponed symmetrical or asymmetrical adjustments and made currency realignments larger and more difficult when they ultimately came. In the unbalanced world of the 1920's, then, countries sought the best of two systems—they wanted the benefits of fixed currency rates and open markets, but they also wanted the advantages of economic self-determination. This conflict, a basic one between the requirements of international and internal stability, became critical when the world plunged into the great depression.[30]

Finally, international lending posed a danger to the gold-exchange standard. For one thing, since there was no international agency to extend emergency reserves, a number of small countries had obtained gold and hard currencies from private lenders. But these short-term borrowings often were withdrawn hastily when confidence declined, and as a result the borrowing country often found itself without sufficient reserves to maintain its exchange rates at critical moments. While much of the lending in the 1920's was short-term fixed-interest lending, susceptible to capital flight or to difficult servicing in the event of an economic collapse, there was another basic weakness. The availability of capital depended on the economic health of the United States. If American lending declined, as it did shortly before the stock market collapse, other countries found it increasingly difficult to generate the export earnings from sales to the United States that would meet debt-service requirements. The restored gold standard was, in short, a fair weather system. It could function satisfactorily as long as members retained confidence in reserve currencies, payments imbalances remained small, and the United States continued to invest abroad. These conditions prevailed for a short time in the late 1920's until the 1929 New York stock market crash disturbed business confidence and ushered in a world depression.[31]

During the turbulent 1930's it became fashionable to blame central bankers for blithely imposing a defective currency system on an unstable world and mismanaging the results. In fact, while the bankers occasionally erred and underestimated danger signals, they labored conscientiously to rationalize and extend international monetary cooperation. Eager to strengthen the gold-exchange standard, they proposed a common gold pool to economize on clearing operations and provide short-term payments assistance to gold-standard countries experiencing temporary deficits in their international accounts. Thus, while the United States government declined to collaborate with League of Nations activities or to consider reparations and war debts as a single problem, American bankers and businessmen took a leading role in early efforts to establish the World Bank, officially designated the Bank for International Settlements.[32]

An opportunity came in 1929 as technical experts drew up the Young Plan for a final settlement of German reparations payments. To facilitate and monitor these transfers the technicians recommended an international agency that would also serve as a permanent mechanism for monetary collaboration. Though German central banker Hjalmar Schacht favored an international credit-creating authority, a consensus emerged in behalf of an institution that would serve as a center for central bank collaboration and as a mechanism for cooperation to improve international payments, but that lacked substantial powers. Initially, the Bank for International Settlements (BIS) could not issue its own currency or supervise a pool of national monies for short-term payments aid. Some founders hoped, however, that the BIS would gradually evolve as an international central bank when it gained experience and inspired confidence.

Established primarily to handle European reparations, the BIS emerged as an instrument for central bank collaboration, but not as a truly international bank. Aside from Japan, the BIS membership did not include smaller non-European countries, and its line of communication with the United States remained ambiguous. Determined to avoid foreign pressure designed to link delicate reparations and war-debts settlements—and thereby offend congressional and public opinion opposed to debt cancellation—the Hoover administration forbade direct Federal Reserve participation, but not close informal ties. As a result, private American banks, not the Federal Reserve, subscribed shares in the Bank for International Settlements to avoid an embarrassing formal connection, but President Hoover had no objection to a former chairman of the New York Federal Reserve Bank, Gates McGarrah, becoming president of the new banking agency. This decision mirrored the ambiguity of American financial policy. Washington officials desired to strengthen international monetary relations, but they could not assume formal commitments that might compromise the United States' freedom of action.

Like World War I, the Great Depression marked a turning point in global economic history as deflation shattered fragile international economic ties and forced governments to sacrifice the advantages of interdependence in order to shelter home economies from the world hurricane. The contraction disrupted trade and capital movements, destroyed the gold-exchange system, and ignited a cycle of economic anarchy and nationalism.

Statistics compiled by the League of Nations measure the depression's crippling impact on world and national economies. Between 1929 and 1932 world prices dropped 47.5 percent, and the value of world trade declined over 60 percent. The volume of world trade fell about 25 percent. This commercial collapse hammered both developed and underdeveloped countries, but it fell with particular severity on the advanced countries, where an estimated 25 million industrial workers lost their jobs. In the twenty-four countries for which statistics were available, the total income lost reached $60 billion in 1932. This figure was "approximately equal to the total income of all these countries, exclusive of the United States and the United Kingdom, in 1929."[33]

Many underlying structural imbalances undoubtedly contributed to the crisis, but the American contraction quickly spread far and wide, afflicting the global economy. The drop in American lending and the decline in import purchases meant that the United States no longer provided the dollars other countries required to meet their debt and reparations obligations. It was estimated that other countries needed $900 million annually simply to service their debts. And, during the four years preceding the New York Stock Exchange collapse, this country had supplied approximately $7.5 billion annually to other countries, allowing them to meet debt and import requirements. The depression reversed this trend, shutting off the flow of investment capital, reducing American import demand, and strengthening domestic protectionists. The pressure for tariff shelter led to the Hawley-Smoot Tariff Act of 1930, which increased duties on eight hundred agricultural and industrial items.[34]

As a result, the quantity of dollars available to other nations declined 68 percent, or $5 billion, in three years, presenting what American officials later described as a "readjustment problem of unparalleled dimensions." In little more than three years the world's largest economy collapsed and transferred its deflation outward to its trading partners. What emerged in this chaotic period was what economists would later describe as a "dollar shortage." The United States was not generating enough dollars to permit others to meet debt obligations, maintain levels of current transactions, and defend exchange parities.[35]

As the depression widened and deepened, other nations confronted the dilemma: how were they to keep the advantages of open trade and stable currencies without exposing home markets to the American deflationary hurricane? A number of small primary-product exporting nations, including Argentina, Brazil, Paraguay, and Uruguay, soon chose one course. Lacking adequate foreign reserves, they opted to abandon the gold standard and to float their currencies, hoping to shift the burden of adjustment from home economies to exchange rates. Others, such as Turkey and Iran, elected to sacrifice not stable currencies or stable home economies but the flow of trade and capital. They imposed exchange controls. Major powers at first shunned both of these expedients and attempted to ride out the contraction without experimenting with currency depreciation or controls. Instead, their central bankers worked together with unusual harmony to reduce interest rates and to encourage domestic and international investment. Cooperation appeared partially successful as the decline halted, briefly, and American lending revived in 1930, but the advanced countries could not reverse the declines of prices and incomes that continued to erode confidence and to unsettle currencies.[36]

In 1931 the depression entered a second phase: the great contraction brought a global currency crisis. The currency disorder, which demonstrated the inherent weakness of the gold-exchange standard, actually began as a confidence crisis. A banking failure in Austria sent shock waves into the German financial community, and anxious foreign creditors desperately tried to withdraw their short-term capital. But foreign withdrawals placed pressure on German currency reserves and soon prompted Germany and eleven other countries to clamp controls on outward capital movements. Soon the spotlight turned to Britain, where heavy French withdrawals of short-term capital also drained Britain's gold reserves and forced Parliament on September 21 to suspend gold payments and float the pound.

The collapse of sterling, like the fall of the dollar in 1971, had enormous psychological and economic implications. For countries that kept large portions of reserves in sterling, the suspension of convertibility was equivalent to a default. These countries found that their sterling balances lost a portion of their gold value. And, within several weeks of the British decision, the Bank of France, the Bank of the Netherlands, and several other central banks lost 30 percent of their holdings. Also, by cheapening British exports and pricing up imports, sterling depreciation encouraged other nations to impose retaliatory tariffs, quotas, and exchange restrictions to offset Britain's new trade advantage. Moreover, because Britain allowed the pound to fluctuate over a wide range, uncertainty about future currency values depressed trade and discouraged foreign investments.[37]

After the United Kingdom abandoned the gold standard, the world monetary system disintegrated into rival blocs and autarkic units. England's principal trading partners and her Commonwealth allies also left the gold standard, pegged their currencies to sterling, and depreciated against gold. Fifteen countries followed Britain off gold in 1931, and another nine did so in 1932. Britain and her smaller allies devised an imperial preference system that sheltered Commonwealth trade from outside competition. Nazi Germany went a step farther along the path toward controls and inaugurated a bilateral trading system that allowed Berlin to manipulate its trade for maximum economic and political advantage. Only five major countries remained on the gold standard: the United States, France, Switzerland, Belgium, and the Netherlands. The others, forced to choose between stable currencies and stable domestic economies, erected a labyrinth of economic controls that hindered trade and capital movements. From the ruins of the old multilateral trading-and-currency system emerged a more effective form of economic nationalism than even seventeenth- and eighteenth-century mercantilists had devised.[38]

When Franklin Roosevelt took the oath of office in March 1933, the United States and other nations looked for new leadership to reverse the economic decline. But there was disagreement as to whether Roosevelt and his advisers should press for international accords to stabilize currencies and resuscitate trade and investments, or whether they should concentrate on domestic recovery. While the two options were not necessarily contradictory—currency stabilization would, for instance, help restore business confidence—officials in the Hoover administration and the banking community generally favored presidential initiatives to strengthen currencies, reduce the debt and reparations burden, and liberalize international trade.[39]

Roosevelt, however, rejected this option and issued his famous "bombshell message," shattering the World Economic Conference that was meeting in London to consider the interlocking economic issues. In his statement he announced his conviction that domestic recovery should take priority over global stabilization. "The sound internal economic system of a nation," he said, "is a greater factor in its well-being than the price of its currency in changing terms of the currencies of other nations." Placing domestic recovery ahead of international stability, Roosevelt chose to follow the British example. Thus, during the first months of his administration the new president barred gold shipments, allowed the dollar to fluctuate uncertainly in world currency markets, and soon obtained authority to devalue the dollar formally in terms of gold.[40]

Why did Roosevelt reject the advice of experienced bankers and businessmen and proceed with dollar devaluation? Personal pique and an impulse to experiment with untested ideas for reviving the home economy seem to have shaped the decision more than rational calculation. The new chief executive was not knowledgeable in economics, and he did not devalue the dollar for the respectable reason that stabilization was then impracticable unless the United States conceded other countries the competitive advantage gained from their own devaluations. This would likely have handicapped

American exporters and exposed American workers to more competition from foreign goods.[41]

Recognizing that some of his political opponents in the international banking community, such as Thomas Lamont of J. P. Morgan and Company, were urging stabilization, the president concluded that a cabal of bankers and European governments anxious to sustain the gold standard were conspiring to effect an agreement that would prevent the New Deal from reflating domestic prices. Roosevelt interpreted this disagreement not as a conflict between two respectable schools of economic thought but as a continuation of the historic struggle between private and public power. As he stated in a letter to Woodrow Wilson's adviser Col. Edward M. House, "the real truth of the matter is . . . that a financial element in the larger centers has owned the Government ever since the days of Andrew Jackson. . . . The country," he continued, "is going through a repetition of Jackson's fight with the Bank of the United States—only on a far bigger and broader basis."[42]

Always the experimenter, Roosevelt saw the magical formula for prosperity in the novel, but specious, theories of Professor George Warren, a Cornell University agricultural economist. The professor insisted that gold purchases would artificially increase the price of gold and boost the prices of other commodities as well. This notion, based as it was on the then discredited bullionist theory, held that commodity prices moved proportionately to the price of gold, and higher prices clearly meant higher incomes. The idea appealed to Roosevelt's friend and unofficial adviser Henry Morgenthau, who helped persuade the administration to try Warren's approach.[43]

Like Britain, the United States chose, when confronted with seemingly incompatible goals of promoting stable exchange rates or stable home economies, to cut the golden knot. The two great financial powers devalued, but not for identical reasons. Britain depreciated its currency when an outflow of gold threatened to exhaust reserves. If British leaders faced the cruel choice of devaluation or domestic deflation, American leaders faced no similar outside pressure. The New Deal leadership resorted to devaluation not to protect the balance of payments but to induce domestic expansion, or reflation.

Both devaluations, however, had similar consequences. As the currency depreciated, altering the exchange values of currencies, other nations reciprocated with competitive devaluations or controls.

The cumulative effect was to further disrupt monetary relations. After the United States adjusted its gold parity, Argentina, Brazil, Canada, and Mexico promptly devaluated their currencies. The cycle of devaluations did nothing to restore business or political confidence and, in fact, did little to improve the devaluing nation's competitive position. After the gold-bloc nations in Europe succumbed in 1935 and 1936, the pattern of exchange relationships among major currencies was not significantly different from the pattern that had prevailed in 1929.[44]

What had changed, however, was the quantity and distribution of gold. Higher gold prices stimulated gold production, and, in the ten-year period from 1929 to 1939, annual output doubled from 19.2 million ounces to 39.5 million ounces. The new monetary gold eased the shortage that had prompted nations to experiment with the gold-reserve system in the 1920's. But during the devaluation cycle monetary gold flowed to the United States, and European political distress added to that flow in the late 1930's. Between 1928 and 1938 American gold reserves increased from 37 percent to 56 percent of the world's supply. This mounting maldistribution of gold had serious implications for American policymakers because, if other nations lacked gold to use as backing for their home currencies or to make international settlements, they might seek a substitute for gold. In that event the United States might awaken to discover that its mountain of monetary gold had no more international value than several tons of pyrite. In contrast to the situation after World War I, when an inadequate supply of gold distributed unevenly sparked discussion of ways to economize on gold, policymakers in the late 1930's sought to shut off the golden avalanche and to restore balance in reserve holdings.[45]

An important result of Roosevelt's experiment with monetary nationalism was the concentration of authority over international monetary matters in the Treasury Department. When his early appointees, including Under Secretary Dean Acheson, opposed devaluation, Roosevelt appointed his old friend Henry Morgenthau, the individual most responsible for the gold purchase program, as secretary of the treasury. Morgenthau now took charge of the administration's efforts to establish public control over international finance. The Gold Reserve Act of 1934, which authorized the president to fix the gold value of the dollar between 50 and 60 percent of its pre-1933 value, enhanced the Treasury's jurisdiction. The treasury secretary gained authority to buy and sell gold, foreign exchange, and government securities in such quantities as regulation of the currency required. To fulfill this mandate Morgenthau's agency utilized an exchange stabilization fund, containing $2 billion of the $2.8 billion "profit" from revaluation of the Federal Reserve's gold stock.[46]

Morgenthau presided over the Treasury's climb to preeminence in international monetary matters, but he was an unlikely secretary of the treasury. Morgenthau was a gentleman farmer, not a banker, and he knew little about economics. But he was the president's friend. The new cabinet official, whose father once served as Woodrow Wilson's ambassador to Turkey, was of German-Jewish extraction. His friendship with Franklin Roosevelt flowered during the latter's gubernatorial days, when he often turned to Morgenthau for advice and assistance. The two, who were neighbors in Dutchess County, New York, had complementary personalities and common interests. Both, for instance, enjoyed experimentation, ranging from schemes to grow squash as a cash crop to plans for manipulating gold prices. Yet, Morgenthau had several shortcomings. He was not Roosevelt's most cerebral adviser nor was he particularly tactful in dealing with Congress. But Morgenthau was loyal and devoted—and these qualities assured him the president's ear and confidence. The new secretary, unlike his predecessors William Woodin and Dean Acheson, stood ready to implement the president's programs as he understood them.[47]

Initially, Roosevelt probably wanted a rubber stamp to carry out his antidepression policies, and Morgenthau satisfied this need. But, as time passed, Morgenthau increasingly became the vehicle for advancing the bureaucratic interests of the Treasury officialdom. Following a practice already established in other agencies, such as Agriculture, Commerce, and the Federal Reserve, Morgenthau recruited a staff of expert technicians from the universities who were capable of applying abstract theories to practical problems in research, analysis, and policy formulation. Because Morgenthau lacked finance experience and economic insight, these technical advisers enjoyed more influence in the Treasury than in other agencies. For, while Morgenthau held Roosevelt's confidence, Morgenthau needed sharp-minded advisers to serve up the ideas and devise the bureaucratic tactics that would sustain his position against the competing interests of other empire builders in Roosevelt's cabinet. More than most Treasury secretaries, Morgenthau depended on the quality of advice his subordinates supplied, and others noticed this weakness. Arthur Krock observed that in congressional hearings Morgenthau referred even the easiest questions to his technicians. He was, as Democratic presidential nominee Alfred Smith reportedly quipped, "just an echo."[48]

Once Roosevelt and Morgenthau completed dollar devaluation, they became more receptive to international stabilization. The Treasury, anxious to cushion devaluations of gold-bloc countries and halt the cycle of competitive currency realignments that prolonged uncertainty and stifled international trade, cautiously opened negotiations with Britain and France. Soon these three powers, along with future members Belgium, the Netherlands, and Switzerland, worked out a tripartite agreement to employ their respective national stabilization pools to buy each other's currencies at a price guaranteed in gold for twenty-four hours. This pact assured convertibility of foreign currency holdings, but it did not establish a pool of credit that would help deficit countries sustain fixed parities for extended periods of time. Neither did the tripartite pact formally bind members to consult or obtain the consent of the others on exchange-rate adjustments. Implicitly, however, there was an obligation to consult about currency revaluations. Even so, the pact had limited scope. It did not establish international procedures for controlling disruptive short-term capital movements or for removing persistent payments imbalances.[49]

Under the Tripartite Agreement the United States acquired the dominant position in international monetary relations that it held until August 1971, when President Nixon suspended the convertibility of dollars and gold. Of all the participants, only the United States announced its intention to buy and sell gold at the newly established prices. The other powers, having chosen new exchange values, employed controls to regulate their payments. To sustain the convertibility pledge when the dollar was strong, as it was in the 1930's, the Treasury's stabilization fund acted in a passive way to support the new rates. It bought foreign currencies and gold, and with few exceptions it did not sell foreign currencies to prop up the dollar.[50]

Despite the one-sided adjustment procedure and the limited obligations, the Tripartite Agreement marked an important accomplishment in reconstructing the global monetary system. Governments, operating through their finance ministries, displayed an unprece-dented determination to collaborate and intervene in private currency markets so as to stabilize currency values. By 1936 there was dawning recognition that stable currencies were required to boost confidence and encourage world commerce. In the broad chain of monetary cooperation the pact was a critical link in the process of reversing autarky and in restructuring a multilateral trading-and-currency sys-tem. It was a giant stride toward Bretton Woods eight years later.[51]

Economists justified the pact in terms of expanding trade, restoring confidence, and stabilizing currencies, but Morgenthau emphasized the political advantages. With France weakened from internal defla-tion and political strife and with nazism threatening European security and ideals, Morgenthau defended his diplomatic triumph, privately, as a measure to strengthen Western Europe against German intimida-tion.[52]

Late in the 1930's, as Germany, Italy, and Japan continued to flout the League of Nations and calculate political and military action to achieve prestige, revenge, and security, the international climate was hardly conducive to new forms of economic collaboration. The world was too unbalanced—economically, politically, and psychologically—for concerted negotiations to repeal autarky and to erect a new frame-work of rules for a stable, open world economy. Yet, at the same time that Congress resisted political involvement in the problems of Eu-rope and that isolationism held grass-root support, the United States and Western Europe cautiously probed for interim arrangements that would arrest currency anarchy and prepare for more effective rules at a more propitious time. The Tripartite Agreement reflected this current on the monetary plane; the Reciprocal Trade Agreements programs marked a parallel concern for commercial agreements that would remove the economically dysfunctional autarkic barriers to international specialization.[53]

During the second decade of the interwar period, economic policymakers grappled with seemingly insoluble problems, and they sought guidance from both theory and experience. As in the past, the ideal international economy consisted of relatively stable ex-change rates and relatively unrestricted movements of goods and capital. No longer, however, could realistic policymakers single-mindedly promote these foreign economic objectives without regard to the internal implications of external stability in an open world.

Their problem was how to reconcile the advantages of specialization and efficiency in an open world with the requirements of internal stability of prices and employment.

A number of second-best solutions circulated, but each had serious disadvantages. In some quarters, especially the international banking community, support ran strong for a return to some version of the gold standard, perhaps accompanied by greater coordination of internal monetary and fiscal policies to ease the internal adjustments of a fixed exchange system. However desirable this option was for stimulating trade and capital movements, it still depended on successfully subordinating domestic policies to the requirements of external stability. In the United States, the United Kingdom, and other industrial countries, this basic solution, which underlay post–World War I reconstruction efforts, was now generally discredited in pure form.[54]

Fluctuating exchange rates appealed to some economists. If national currencies adjusted in the marketplace in response to supply-and-demand pressures, it was argued, countries could initiate whatever internal monetary and budgetary policies circumstances required without concern for exchange-rate stability. While variable exchange rates have gained wide support among economists in the 1970's, this solution seemed unsuited to the disturbed economic circumstances of the interwar period. Floating rates, it was argued, would increase the uncertainty of international transactions and impede trade and capital movements necessary for an efficient utilization of world resources. Also, frequently fluctuating rates would, it was believed, bring wasteful and costly internal adjustments as the changing price of currency encouraged nations to shift production to and from export-oriented production. Experience with the fluctuating pound and other currencies after 1931 suggested that frequent exchange-rate variations would encourage speculative short-term capital movements from one currency to another. Finally, this alternative appeared likely to encourage "competitive exchange depreciations" and "beggar-thy-neighbor" economic policies. A country facing domestic unemployment might be tempted to depreciate its currency, perhaps unjustifiably, to stimulate exports and discourage imports. Other nations might then retaliate, and the net result would be a series of disruptive exchange-rate depreciations.[55]

A more reliable method for maintaining balance-of-payments

equilibrium, which gained support in theory and practice during the interwar period, was reliance on exchange and trade controls. Proponents of this course, especially in centrally planned economies, were prepared to sacrifice the benefits of international specialization for stable currencies and internal economies. But experience in the 1930's discredited exchange controls, particularly because they were associated with Nazi Germany's policy of national expansion and military preparation. Also, bilateral trading arrangements, disrupting as they did the intricate network of multilateral trade and payments, seemed to replace orderly and mutually beneficial trade with a chaotic and unregulated form of economic warfare. In a world with unevenly distributed resources and ecorfomic progress, controls distorted the flow of resources, reducing economic welfare and creating frictions that threatened civilization everywhere.[56]

Each of these fundamental solutions—fixed rates under a gold standard, flexible paper currencies, and controls—provided a different answer to the basic question: how can nations with divergent price structures and currency systems maintain balance-of-payments equilibrium and obtain the benefits of specialization in a world economy? Basically, adherence to the gold standard required sacrificing domestic stability for maximum gains from trade, capital, and currency movements. Both flexible rates and controls tended to subordinate international gains to the need for a booming home economy. One subjected the burden of adjustment to the free market—permitting currencies to adjust imbalances—and involved minimum government intervention and interference with movements of goods and capital. The other, controls, was dependent on extensive official management of international economic contacts and seemed certain (assuming effective government management) to prevent destabilizing fluctuations of currencies and domestic economies. While it provided greater security, it seemed to reduce unnecessarily the gains from economic efficiency and to disrupt multilateral trade and payments for the self-interest of one country.

As a result, while the debate continued in academic circles, officials searched for the least harmful way of achieving maximum trade, balance-of-payments equilibrium, and domestic stability. The consensus that seemed to emerge, before World War II disrupted progress, centered on a return to fixed, but not unadjustable, currency values anchored to gold; continued restrictions on short-term capital movements; and more vigorous, and coordinated, government management of domestic economies through the continuous application of monetary and fiscal tools. The new emphasis was on coordinated national management to even out business cycles, regulate capital movements, and adjust currency values; but this management, it was understood, would have to take place, at least in the short run, without formal infringement on the sovereignty of each nation to regulate its own destiny. The Tripartite Agreement indicated that in the future monetary managers would not be quasi-autonomous central bankers but treasury ministers and experts who were presumably more responsive to national interests.[57]

Had war not erupted, the world monetary system might have evolved, according to League of Nations experts, in the following manner: Gold would continue as the principal medium for international settlements, and major powers would mutually consult over their exchange values. However, exchange rates would continue, without formal commitments, and gradually the various currency areas would amalgamate into a single global system with relatively stable exchange rates. International cooperation would develop to "reduce the amount and mitigate the effects of abnormal transfers of liquid private funds," and the major powers would gradually coordinate their domestic fiscal and monetary policies to combat violent fluctuations of income. The immediate problems, then, were how to establish, maintain, and alter exchange rates without disrupting other currencies, how to make available an adequate supply of gold or other reserves to finance temporary payments imbalances in an open world, how to coordinate domestic policies to prevent serious depressions, and how to prevent disruptive capital movements from straining the system. These fundamental issues of adjustment, liquidity, and stability were, as they continued to be later, the chief obstacles to a durable global monetary system. But, assuming nations were willing to cooperate, the economic managers were confident that they had the experience and technical expertise to avoid the perils of the past.[58]

Hence, by the late 1930's economists had gained substantial experience in the problems of establishing and sustaining a viable international monetary system. In the Western world, the legacy of the unstructured first international economy that flowered before World War I and the economic doctrine that explained these developments continued to provide a guide for policymakers. But experience in reviving this order after World War I indicated that at least equal weight had to be assigned to measures that would insulate home economies from global depression, unstable currencies, and economic warfare. What was required was early preparation of a comprehensive code—perhaps expressed informally—that would guide economic relations in the future. Most of all, the interwar breakdown, leading to disruptive monetary nationalism and economic warfare, indicated that governments, while retaining sovereignty, must subordinate narrow conceptions of national advantage for the creation of a mutually beneficial system.

America's Global
Monetary Design

The Second World War, like the depression and the currency crisis, interrupted the efforts of finance ministers and economists to create a durable international monetary system. This new setback, which brought another network of emergency controls over trade and capital movements, shattered piecemeal attempts to reweave the torn fabric of international economics and offered the victors a second opportunity to redesign global economic rules and mechanisms.

Had Nazi Germany and her allies sustained the military momentum of 1940 and 1941 and defeated the major English-speaking powers, undoubtedly the Axis would have promulgated and imposed their world economic order. Though Axis leaders were too concerned with achieving victory to draft specific proposals, they held out the promise of far-reaching changes that would provide employment and economic security to downtrodden peoples. The Germans, in particular, seemed to think of a European trading and currency bloc directed from Berlin, not London. These promises, though ambiguous and open to later interpretation, nevertheless encouraged hope of sweeping reforms at a time when British and American leaders avoided stating their postwar objectives.[1]

Before the United States became a full-fledged belligerent in late 1941, American leaders generally avoided carefully reasoned discussions of this country's postwar economic interests and objectives. However, in his statement of the famous "four freedoms" in January 1941, President Roosevelt hinted that political and economic security were interrelated. He listed "freedom from want" among his basic principles for postwar order. Vice-President Henry Wallace elaborated this theme several months later. "The next peace," Wallace said, "must take into account the facts of economics; otherwise, it will serve as the seedbed for aggression."[2]

As pressure mounted for a more concrete statement that would undercut enemy propaganda and direct postwar preparations, administration officials and outside advisers turned their attention to the fundamental principles of global economic organization. And, despite the mistakes and reverses of the interwar period, the old vision of an open world economy in which private trade, capital movements, and stable currencies provided harmony and a rational allocation of world resources continued to burn brightly. Herbert Feis, the State Department economic adviser, had predicted the triumph of this system when the prospects seemed dim. In 1939 he forecast that "in those imbued with the pattern for which reason reached, faith will sustain itself, and from them effort will be forthcoming. For they had graven on their minds, despite deficiency and inelasticity of doctrine, a vision in which economic activity united the world into a society of independent and equal nations, serving both strong and weak."[3]

In Washington the driving force behind the move for a statement of liberal economic principles was Feis's boss, Secretary of State Cordell Hull. This silver-haired Tennessee internationalist understood only the outlines of economic theory, but he, more than any other cabinet-level official, was persuaded that economics was the key to peace. As he said later: "To me, unhampered trade dovetailed with peace; high tariffs, trade barriers, and unfair economic competition, with war. Though realizing that many other factors were involved, I reasoned that, if we could get a freer flow of trade—freer in the sense of fewer discriminations and obstructions—so that one country would not be deadly jealous of another and the living standards of all countries might rise, thereby eliminating the economic dissatisfaction that breeds war, we might have a reasonable chance for lasting peace."[4]

Persuaded that his great political mentor, Woodrow Wilson, had inadequately considered the economic foundations of peace at Versailles, Hull resolved to avoid that mistake. Early in 1940, while the United States was still neutral, the secretary ordered his deputy Leo Pasvolsky to formulate economic peace proposals that the belligerents might incorporate into an early settlement. Alternatively, the liberal economic principles—especially nondiscriminatory trade—would help unify the rest of the world against the autarkic Axis, Hull thought. Emphasizing the propaganda value of liberal economics in his instructions to Pasvolsky, Hull asserted, "Moses never could have gotten his followers to go into the Red Sea if he had not promised them something to look over to over the other side of the mountain."[5]

Hull's discussions seldom ventured beyond abstract commercial principles—like nondiscriminatory trade or equal access to raw materials—but other Washington officials moved beyond these general objectives to consideration of mechanisms and methods that would initially strengthen the non-Axis powers and would later afford a working basis for long-term collaboration. As early as November 1939, for instance, Treasury experts considered ways to utilize the United States' mounting gold holdings in economic warfare and postwar reconstruction. Another scheme for an inter-American bank flowered in the State Department. Sumner Welles, the undersecretary of state, supervised this draft, which was prepared by experts from several agencies, including the Treasury, to facilitate the flow of long-term investment funds, to assist in stabilizing currencies, and to operate as a clearing house for inter-American payments. Essentially, the proposal combined the functions of an intergovernmental bank, an international stabilization fund, and an ordinary commercial bank, and this broad mandate aroused concern in New York banking circles, where private financiers questioned New Deal motives and feared the emergence of a government-sponsored competitor. A convention for the bank, approved by Latin American nations at Rio de Janeiro in 1941, languished in Congress, but it did at least demonstrate that American planners sought to link wartime assistance to the long-term evolution of international monetary institutions.[6]

The great imponderable in all discussions of postwar economic and political commitments was political acceptability. Would Congress and the American people shoulder international responsibilities or would they shun this second chance to erect a permanent peace structure?

Before the Japanese attack on Pearl Harbor compelled Americans to consider postwar goals, a number of individuals and interest groups sought to awaken general interest in distant objectives and to elicit support for political and economic internationalism. Most of these efforts concentrated on the so-called attentive public—that minority of citizens who deliberated public problems and alternatives but did not directly formulate policy. Enlightened analysis of these inter-related issues, the internationalists thought, would produce a con-sensus in support of American participation in world institutions.

Much discussion centered on proposals for an international or-ganization, or a second League of Nations as it was often described. In this area, dedicated individuals like Professor James Shotwell, Clarke Eichelberger, and John Foster Dulles worked to promote public backing for global peacekeeping. Simultaneously, other opinion molders—including publicists Otto Mallery and Lewis Lorwin, as well as economists Jacob Viner and Alvin Hansen—sparked discussion of parallel economic agencies.[7]

Like those who espoused political security arrangements, the eco-nomic internationalists often phrased their appeals in oversimplified and highly emotional rhetoric to spur awareness of postwar national interests and the interdependence of political and economic security. At least in the economic area such approaches were probably de-fensible, because trade and monetary issues were too confusing for all but the specialists.

Mallery, an old-Wilsonian internationalist and former government economist, effectively employed a biblical parable to hammer home his message that another League of Nations could not function suc-cessfully without a complementary economic union. Once upon a time, he claimed, an investigator died and went to Heaven. Before settling down he asked to satisfy his curiosity by visiting Hell. There he found a circle of hungry-looking cadaverous individuals sitting around a banquet table spread with a large feast. Each man had a long metal spoon strapped to the inside of his arm, like a splint, so that he could not bend his elbow. No one could feed himself. There they sat, all hungry and disconsolate. On his return to Heaven the investigator found a similar scene, but this time he found fat and happy people. Although each had a spoon strapped to his arm, all were using it to feed their neighbors. So that the most undiscerning listener might grasp the moral, Mallery emphasized: "In this parable you, the reader, are the investigators. The great empires are the hungry, cadaverous people. The people of the United States would like to be the fat and happy ones.

"The great empires have strapped splints onto their trade arms and have bound themselves so they cannot be prosperous and cannot trade freely with others.

"These great empires had their millions of hungry unemployed while waging economic war for years before the first bullet was fired." Like nineteenth-century liberals, Otto Mallery believed that free trade was the panacea for economic nationalism and great power rivalries. "If soldiers are not to cross international boundaries," he said, "goods must do so."[8]

More influential in shaping elite and official opinion were specialist groups organized to examine all phases of international collaboration —including political, economic, military, and territorial issues. Their broad-gauged investigations indicated that the World War II internationalists were determined to avoid the lapses of those who conceived the League of Nations but failed to make adequate preparation on the economic plane.

While the Commission to Study the Organization of the Peace sought to expose community leaders across the country to these interrelated problems, the Council on Foreign Relations attempted to crystallize thinking within the government hierarchy. With funding obtained from the Rockefeller Foundation, the council established four committees, including a panel on economic and financial issues under the supervision of two prominent former presidents of the American Economic Association. One was Alvin Hansen, the most distinguished American advocate of Keynesian economic analysis, and the other was Jacob Viner, widely regarded as the most influential international economist.[9]

In the spring of 1941 the Hansen-Viner group, reporting confidentially to government policymakers, urged a concrete statement of American economic objectives, stressing the benefits of world economic cooperation and the importance of economic harmony for political liberty and national security. William Diebold, the secretary, drafted a preliminary statement of economic war aims that would serve propaganda needs and would provide a guide for future technical assessments. Diebold defined the nation's postwar economic interest as follows: "(1) the full use of the world's economic resources—implying full employment and a reduction in business cycle fluctuation; and (2) the most efficient use of the world's resources—implying an interchange of goods among all parts of the world according to the comparative advantages of each part in producing certain goods." The American interest, he added, did not require "a specially privileged position in the world." On the contrary, the "long-run interests of the United States are identical with those of all other countries." While some would interpret this statement as an endorsement of free trade, Diebold understood that this concept was no longer politically practicable. Future policies, he indicated, should not be phrased in terms of past slogans. Instead, a statement of economic objectives should emphasize the mutually advantageous cooperation that all countries could share from new mechanisms to increase trade, revive international lending, stabilize currencies, and combat depressions.[10]

Under pressure to announce its support for liberal economic objectives, so as to undercut the appeal of Hitler's "new economic order" and to establish the direction of America's postwar preparations, the Roosevelt Administration contracted with Britain to work jointly toward a multilateral economic solution. This mandate appeared in two declarations of intent—the Atlantic Charter and the Master Lend-Lease Agreement.

The first, the outcome of bilateral talks between President Roosevelt and Prime Minister Winston Churchill in August 1941, was actually a broad statement of the two English-speaking countries' war aims. At their meeting off the coast of Newfoundland the two leaders pledged to work for national self-determination, freedom of the seas, and a "wider and permanent system of general security." They also renounced territorial expansion, agreeing that territorial changes should "accord with the freely expressed wishes of the peoples concerned." On economic matters, Roosevelt and Churchill promised, "with due respect for existing obligations," to promote access on equal terms for all nations to the trade and raw materials of the world. In addition, the president and the prime minister announced a "desire to bring about the fullest collaboration between all nations in the economic field with the object of securing, for all, improved labor standards, economic advancement, and social security."[11]

Although the Atlantic Charter contained a declaration of economic neighborliness, it did not satisfy Secretary of State Hull, who wanted an unambiguous Anglo-American commitment to the principles of nondiscriminatory trade. "Keenly disappointed" because Churchill had insisted on an escape clause—"with due respect of existing obligations"—that would apparently exempt Britain's system of imperial preferences, Hull determined to extract a more precise commitment to nondiscrimination in future negotiations over the settlement of lend-lease obligations.[12]

Hull's single-minded quest for a British pledge to abandon restrictive trade practices was more than an effort to open the British Empire to American exports—though it would have that effect. For Hull, restrictive trade practices, whether they were employed by the British or the Nazis, were artificial impediments to peaceful commercial competition as well as instruments of the economic nationalism that contributed to World War II. If the United States' economic strength allowed Hull the luxury of pursuing principles, Britain's balance-of-payments weakness, as well as her declining export competitiveness, compelled her negotiators to insist on safeguards.[13]

John Maynard Keynes, England's leading financial negotiator, realized that, without parallel arrangements to assure an expansionary world economy, to reconstruct war-debilitated nations, and to erase currency imbalances, Britain could not adjust to the cold shower of American competition. Thus, on one visit to Washington in 1941, Keynes bluntly dismissed the "lunatic proposals of Mr. Hull," and warned that without American financial assistance Britain might be compelled to select an autarkic course in the postwar period. Of course, more than economic considerations shaped the British position. Advocates of imperial preference argued vigorously that nondiscrimination spelled the death of Britain's historic empire and England's decline as a world power.[14]

However, the State Department advocates of nondiscrimination persisted and eight months later gained a second, more precise definition of Anglo-American economic objectives in the lend-lease agreement. Article VII stated that a final lend-lease settlement would contain "provision for agreed action by the United States of America and the United Kingdom, open to participation by all other countries of like mind, directed to the expansion, by appropriate international and domestic measures, of production, employment, and the exchange and consumption of goods . . . ; to the elimination of all forms of discriminatory treatment in international commerce, and to the reduction of tariffs and other trade barriers." This clause, though it did seem to provide for abandoning imperial preferences, was not simply a British concession to American strength, for it also bound the United States to cooperate with Britain, and other countries, on proposals to promote a high level of employment and production. Even though the terms were sufficiently ambiguous to permit divergent interpretations, the lend-lease agreement indicated that the two major allies had agreed on a set of common principles to guide their technical negotiators, who were to begin their work at an "early convenient date." As Hull wrote later, "the foundation was now laid for all our later postwar planning in the economic field."[15]

Interestingly enough, the Master Lend-Lease Agreement, which provided the direction for future initiatives, was an executive agreement, not a treaty subject to Senate approval. In international economic planning, as in other areas of wartime diplomacy, the Roosevelt administration frequently resorted to expedients that circumvented Congress but that nonetheless created binding obligation. While it is true that Congress would later have the opportunity to pass on specific mechanisms, the Anglo-American pact, like the Atlantic Charter before it, channeled American thought to a multilateral economic solution and established a moral obligation that Congress could not easily ignore.[16]

Now that Britain and the United States had determined their economic objectives, a host of procedural, jurisdictional, and technical questions competed with more immediate problems of economic warfare for the attention of overburdened policymakers. Should London and Washington press forward together and translate these principles into more specific rules and mechanisms—perhaps an Anglo-American blueprint? Or should they postpone action to encourage the wider participation of other members of the United Nations coalition and await a more favorable political and military situation than existed in 1942, when the Allies were on the defensive? If the two countries opted to move forward, should they consider financial, trade, and commodity problems jointly or separately?

On these matters London and Washington had sharp differences. Essentially, the British, anxious to obtain a firm assurance of future American assistance to ease their transitional balance-of-payments difficulties before London had to relax controls, urged immediate, comprehensive bilateral negotiations. This procedure appealed to John G. Winant, the American ambassador to Britain, and to some Anglophiles, such as influential publisher Henry Luce, who wanted to strike a "fatal blow at the whole system of economic nationalism and regimentation."[17]

But President Roosevelt and Secretary Hull, having established basic goals, preferred to wait until other nations were consulted, the mood of domestic public opinion was favorable, the military situation was improved, and technical assessments were available. Moreover, Roosevelt and Hull both feared that further negotiations with Britain would raise fears, at home and abroad, that the two countries were devising a bilateral great-power settlement without giving proper attention to smaller nations, who would then have little practical alternative but to accept these terms. A precipitate move might revive charges of Anglo-American imperialism and jeopardize unity of the war effort. Also, because 1942 was a congressional election year when the American people would have their first opportunity to comment on Roosevelt's policies at the ballot box and to indicate whether the war had shaken isolationist sentiment, the two American leaders were anxious to avoid unnecessary controversy and to await a clear indication of popular sentiment. Undoubtedly, memories of the brutal debate over the United States' objectives in World War I also dictated political caution to officials determined to avoid Woodrow Wilson's mistakes. Other practical considerations reinforced this position. Policymakers in Hull's State Department had not yet formulated precise proposals and discussed them with other agencies.[18]

At this point the State Department understandably wanted to direct and coordinate all aspects of postwar planning, and Hull, anticipating this assignment, had established, with President Roosevelt's approval, an interagency advisory committee on postwar foreign policy in December 1941. On paper Hull's initiative seemed sound, but unfortunately for the State Department the committee was ineffective. Not only did personal frictions between Hull and Welles and among the assistant secretaries impede decision making, but the agency also lacked technical personnel to frame concrete recommendations and to advance the State Department's position against other bureaucratic empires determined to press their points of view. At this critical procedural juncture the State Department stood, according to Dean Acheson, "breathless and bewildered like an old lady at a busy intersection during the rush hour."[19]

As the State Department dawdled, organizing layers of committees, Vice-President Henry Wallace, who supervised the Economic Defense Board, attempted to seize the initiative. In a speech apparently intended both to inform and test the public, Wallace called for plans to expand and regularize world trade, production, and consumption so that the economic foundations for democracy could be established "while the war is still in progress." Wallace's call reflected the direction of technical work under way in the Economic Defense Board, but politically it served only to exacerbate relations with the State Department and Hull. Hull did not like Wallace, and he interpreted the vice-president's public diplomacy as further evidence of opportunism and demagoguery.[20]

But, while the old Tennessee veteran of the New Deal bureaucratic infighting took aim at Wallace, Henry Morgenthau successfully wrested responsibility for financial planning away from Hull. Like Wallace, Morgenthau had a reputation as a bureaucratic empire builder, and after he became secretary in 1934 the Treasury quickly established jurisdiction over international monetary matters. Not only did the Treasury administer the stabilization fund and supervise gold purchases, but it also created an overseas network of Treasury officials who negotiated directly with foreign finance ministries. After carving out this role, Morgenthau had no intention of relinquishing authority to Hull; if the administration were to prepare a coherent international economic program, Morgenthau and his aides were determined to draft it, or at least frame the monetary provisions.[21]

More than interagency competition shaped Morgenthau's decision. He regarded his Treasury as the most reliable pro–New Deal agency in Washington and suspected that private bankers might recover some of the power and influence they had wielded before the depression, if the State Department prevailed. Private bankers, Morgenthau believed, had mishandled monetary affairs in the 1920's, precipitating the Wall Street collapse and the currency crisis, and he resolved to prevent private interests from again subordinating national interests to private benefit.[22]

Anticipating that the Treasury would have a critical role in wartime monetary matters, Morgenthau had streamlined his department's operations after Pearl Harbor, consolidating responsibility for foreign economic matters in the hands of Harry Dexter White, his assistant. "I want it in one brain," Morgenthau said, "and I want it in Harry White's brain." It was White, the short, stocky economist with a bristling mustache and distinctive bow tie, who would take charge of the Treasury's postwar planning.[23]

White's background and career conformed to the American dream: he was a poor boy from immigrant stock who through sheer persistence, intelligence, and ambition blazed his way up the ladder to a responsible position and public view. Born in 1892 to Jewish parents who had immigrated from Lithuania in the 1880's, White served in World War I and then directed an orphanage. At age thirty he returned to college, earning two degrees from Stanford before completing his doctorate in 1930 at Harvard. His dissertation on the French international accounts pleased Professor Frank Taussig, the distinguished international economist, and won the coveted Wells prize for the best essay in economics.[24]

After a brief stint teaching in a small Wisconsin college, White came to Washington in 1934 to participate in a Treasury currency study. Quickly impressing senior officials with his diligence, reliability, administrative skill, and capacity to apply current economic theories to practical problems, White was invited to remain and in 1938 was appointed director of the recently formed division of monetary research. Morgenthau organized this unit to prepare research analysis and recommendations related to Treasury currency and customs policies.[25]

As a result, White soon emerged as Secretary Morgenthau's top adviser on international monetary matters. Morgenthau chose to rely on White and other experts in related areas because he had neither the inclination nor the training to assimilate the complexities of international finance. Of course, even if Morgenthau had shown more interest, the pressures of his responsibilities required delegating authority to talented subordinates. Morgenthau liked White and overlooked his aide's hot temper, occasional rudeness, and vaingloriousness because White seemed competent and dependable.[26]

Morgenthau and White had occasional frictions, but they worked well together. White, drawing on the talents of his technical staff, produced imaginative proposals, and Morgenthau took many of these directly to Roosevelt, simultaneously currying presidential favor and advancing Treasury interests. By 1941 Harry Dexter White was so irreplaceable that Morgenthau hesitated to let his assistant lead a monetary mission to Cuba. "You do beautiful jobs, both of you," Morgenthau told White and tax economist Roy Blough, "and I leave it to you up to the point I have got to sign, and then I am completely in ignorance, and I have got to spend two days finding out what you fellows can tell me in fifteen minutes. If you weren't so indispensable," Morgenthau added, "I would say, 'Go and good riddance,' but I am very sincere, you have made yourselves indispensable."[27]

White's subordinates also had a deep loyalty and affection for their sometimes blunt boss, who could be "arrogant to his intellectual inferiors." While White was a good economist, but not the most creative in his division, he recruited top-caliber economists for the Treasury—more than a hundred during the war years—established tough professional standards, and proved himself an able bureaucratic infighter when Treasury interests were involved.[28]

Technicians from other government agencies, particularly the State Department and Federal Reserve, respected the economic competence of White and his assistants but sometimes complained bitterly of the "viciously-assertive" Treasury experts. On one occasion E. A. Goldenweiser, director of Federal Reserve research, became so irritated when White broke an oral understanding that he grumbled, "This convinces me that one cannot depend on Harry White's word and one cannot make agreements with him."[29]

Secretary Morgenthau apparently never had any reason to question White's integrity or loyalty, and after the war he expressed astonishment when rumors circulated that White had been a central figure in a Soviet espionage ring operating in the Treasury. The charges against White, made by Elizabeth Bentley and Whittaker Chambers, two refugees from the Soviet intelligence apparatus, brought a full-scale investigation, but the government failed to gather enough evidence to obtain a grand jury indictment in 1947. Nevertheless, the investigation and other testimony to the House Un-American Affairs Committee in 1948 raised a cloud of controversy and cast an ugly shadow over all of White's wartime activities, including monetary planning.[30]

Was White a Soviet espionage agent, a misguided fellow traveler, or merely a loyal official framed in an anti-Communist witch hunt? Available evidence does not permit a final historical judgment, but it does show that White, like many young New Deal liberals, was an ardent friend of the Soviet Union. Like a number of liberals whose loyalty was never questioned, White publicly expressed a romantic enthusiasm for Soviet experiments in economic planning, wanted the Roosevelt administration to employ more economic planning at home, and hoped that Soviet-American wartime collaboration would provide the basis for a peaceful world order. Soon after finishing his doctorate, White wanted to visit Russia to assess how a nation could benefit from comprehensive state planning without sacrificing the advantages of international exchange. But opportunity drew White to Washington, where he soon encountered other young intellectuals who thought Roosevelt should rely on Keynesian economic prescriptions and more actively employ the government as an instrument of social reform. Although principally concerned with global financial problems, White had occasion to express his views on domestic topics in top-level Treasury strategy sessions. In September 1941, during a discussion of social-security modifications, the monetary expert urged basic reforms because the United States was "already fifty years behind any other nation." He predicted that, after nazism was defeated, domestic reform would have wide popular appeal. At the moment of victory "there will be only one other 'ism' that will compete and it will be an 'ism' which will be an increased danger unless we go a whole lot further in the direction of providing security for all classes than we have done in the past."[31]

White, according to former associates, had Communist friends and occasionally sought to shield subordinates and friends from loyalty tests and security investigations that he considered an impingement on civil liberties. But, it is said, White could never have been a party member—he simply was too independent to accept party discipline. Instead, Harry Dexter White "enjoyed the sense of being in touch with the party, but not in it, courted by it, but yielding only so much as he chose."[32]

If Harry White's political predilections and affiliations remain mysterious after twenty-five years, his economic interests and recommendations place him firmly in the mainstream of contemporary thought. He and his contemporaries gradually accepted the Keynesian emphasis on deficit spending and government planning to correct internal deflation, and he saw more extensive government intervention as a way to redistribute excessive wealth and remove social injustice. At times White may have had private doubts about the durability of the private enterprise system, but his concern as a Treasury economist was to salvage the inherent dynamism of the market system and to make it more responsive to the public interest. His confidence in planning mirrored the exuberance of other young economists who, having read Keynes, thought they had found a magical formula for prosperity and full employment. On the international front White also wanted to reconcile planning with the dynamic of market forces, and that interest attracted him to Soviet economic experiments. There is no evidence, however, that White found autarky an acceptable second-best alternative to multilateralism. Certainly, his doctoral dissertation, an inductive case study to verify an aspect of orthodox international trade theory, accepted the value of international trade, though it did conclude that regulation of capital exports might be desirable for the exporting country.[33]

White's responsibility for international monetary policy, as well as his involvement in discussions of the proposed inter-American bank, undoubtedly directed his attention to long-term solutions for currency and financial problems. In the spring of 1941, as economists outside the government sought to spark official thought on these topics, White began to consider a comprehensive program of institutional reforms. Secretary Morgenthau heard of this work, and on Sunday, December 14, formally directed his aide to draft an Inter-Allied Stabilization Fund that would provide monetary assistance to wartime allies, promote postwar international monetary stabilization, and establish an "international currency." With this broad and somewhat ambiguous directive, White and his aides ambitiously completed a draft of a "single-package" plan to rebuild the world economy.[34]

As the "starting point for intelligent discussion" of methods to move the world from "shortsighted disastrous economic nationalism to intelligent international collaboration," the Treasury economists proposed two institutions: a United Nations Stabilization Fund and a Bank for Reconstruction. These plans evolved through successive modifications, and soon the second institution was a Bank for Reconstruction and Development of the United and Associated Nations, a title that emphasized the collateral importance of development.[35]

On one level the fund was little more than a lineal extension of the Tripartite Agreement, for it was an international agency designed to supply emergency reserves, or aid, to members with balance-of-payments deficits so that they could intervene directly in the foreign exchange markets to support currency values at official levels. The lack of an available, assured pool of outside assistance had been an important shortcoming of the tripartite arrangements, which made no provision for international assistance. The objective was to enable deficit countries to maintain stable exchange rates and convertible currencies for longer periods of time without resorting to what White called the "law of the jungle"—discriminatory controls and competitive depreciations.[36]

As it was conceived in April 1942, the fund would have at least a $5 billion pool of currencies, gold, and securities contributed by members, all of whom were associated in the war effort. Of the total resources 25 percent of each member's quota was payable in cash—at least half in gold—and another 25 percent was payable in interest-bearing securities redeemable in gold or its equivalent. To meet a need for additional reserves growing out of a balance-of-payments deficit, a member could sell the fund its currency—up to 100 percent of its contribution—for other national currencies. And, if members with four-fifths of the total votes approved, the fund might agree to purchase more of a deficit country's currency provided it accepted fund recommendations on how to correct the deficit.[37]

Either way the American proposal gave the fund authority to evaluate the reasons for an adverse balance of payments and to determine whether a member had legitimate reason for drawing on the pool of currencies. Transactions with the international agency, then, were privileges, not rights. White wanted some restriction on access to the currency pool, because he suspected that some members might utilize their quotas to finance "illegitimate" flows of investments abroad. Certainly the fund would need to examine each request individually, but White emphasized that his "fund could not . . . supply an unlimited amount of foreign exchange to any country which might not wish to adopt the proper measures to correct a prolonged disequilibrium in its transactions with foreign countries."[38]

Up to this point the fund was little more than a multinational stabilization pool equipped to bail out members whose foreign expenditures exceeded earnings. Outside support, it was thought, would temporarily enable members to avoid having either to deflate the domestic economy or to improve the external position through exchange regulations or currency depreciations. But the fund was also an extensive international code of monetary conduct that would restrict national sovereignty over some economic matters and vest unprecedented authority in a world agency controlled by the United States and administered by a board of economists. These technicians, White thought, would share a "comprehensive experienced world outlook and tenacity of social purpose." Among the membership conditions was a requirement that participants abandon all exchange controls within a year of joining the fund or the cessation of hostilities, whichever was later. Signatory states must also eschew bilateral clearing arrangements and embark upon a program of gradual tariff reduction. Moreover, they must agree not to adopt internal monetary or price policies that would bring about a serious balance-of-payments disequilibrium, if four-fifths of the fund's voting membership disapproved. Finally, members must agree to alter exchange rates only with the fund's permission. These membership obligations involved an unprecedented surrender of sovereignty to an international agency. No modern state had ever voluntarily surrendered authority over trade, currency, and internal economic policies to outside authorities, but this was exactly what White and his aides proposed for the future.[39]

White also wanted the fund to assume some banking functions and to exercise authority over world currency relationships. This organization would not create money, but it would act as a depository for gold and as a clearing house for intergovernmental transactions. Specifically, the fund could "buy, sell and hold gold, currencies, foreign exchange, bills of exchange and government securities of the 'member' countries and act as a clearing house for international movements of gold and balances." To avoid the patchwork quilt of inappropriate rates that would likely develop if each nation selected its own exchange rate, White proposed that the fund establish stable rates of exchange for converting one member's currency into another and for buying and selling gold. Here the guiding principle was a stable pattern of exchange rates, but stability did not imply rigid rates. White recognized that "there are occasions when it may be economically wise for a country to increase or decrease the value of its currency in terms of other currencies." But, because currency adjustments necessarily affect the interests of other countries, White wanted to obtain advance approval from the fund before taking action to modify currency values. Under the Treasury proposal the fund could, with the approval of members having four-fifths of the votes, authorize a currency variation to remove a "fundamental disequilibrium," an elusive phrase that apparently defied technical definition. In brief, the American experts proposed to sanction periodic currency realignments, provided these had fund approval, as the ultimate solution for payments difficulties. But currency realignments would come only after members utilized fund resources and attempted to remove the payments imbalance with less drastic internal measures. Nowhere in the American proposal was there a hint that countries with a favorable balance of payments had a parallel obligation to revalue their currencies in order to help remove a "fundamental disequilibrium." White seemed to accept the conventional wisdom that deficit, not surplus, countries were responsible for chronic payments imbalances.[40]

In joining the fund, countries nominally ceded portions of their economic sovereignty to the monetary league of nations; but in practice this meant deferring not to the fund but to the United States, for this country would have a veto over exchange-rate variations and access to international reserves. As it was conceived in early 1942, participants would each appoint one representative to sit on the board of directors, but individual directors cast weighted votes, roughly proportional to that member's financial contribution. Thus, if total fund assets approximated $5.25 billion, the United States would subscribe about $3.2 billion, according to an illustrative formula that took into account such diverse factors as gold holdings and production, national income, foreign trade, population, foreign investments, and foreign debts. The American contribution, roughly 61 percent of the total pool, would allow the United States 25 percent of the votes. In addition, Latin American countries would contribute 4.6 percent of the monetary resources and hold nearly 35 percent of the votes. This division of voting power left the Western Hemisphere bloc with a controlling interest, while the other two postwar economic powers, the British Empire and the Soviet Union, gained only 17.6 percent and 2.85 percent of the votes. This preliminary formula suggested that the Treasury intended to hold out for a system in which a member's contribution (for instance, the United States) was loosely proportional to the combined voting strength of that major power and its client supporters. Thus, the Western Hemisphere would contribute about 66 percent of the money and hold 60 percent of the votes. On this point the American technicians were not inflexible; they considered the proposed allocation merely a "pattern of quotas for discussion." They recognized that a "more appropriate formula could be worked out if several minds focused on the problem."[41]

Determined to remodel the world monetary system in a way that would encourage international transactions and protect American interests, White and his aides recognized that the success of this new monetary order hinged on the participation of all major nations, including the Soviet Union. White, in discussing the fund, argued that policymakers should not again succumb to fear or prejudice and exclude Russia from postwar arrangements, as they had after World War I. Such a policy would be an "egregious error" because in denying the Soviet Union an opportunity to participate nations would "repeat the tragic errors of the last generation" and introduce discord at a time when millions of people hoped for a new era. If Russia did not participate, the Soviet government might employ its foreign trade monopoly to disrupt global trading relationships. For these reasons, "if the Russian government is willing to participate, her counsel in the preliminary negotiations should be as eagerly sought as that of any other country, and her membership in both Fund and Bank equally as welcome." The Soviet Union "could both contribute and profit by participation," White added without elaboration.[42]

With a broad mandate of authority and intelligent leadership, the Treasury experts expected the fund to make a major contribution to postwar economic order. Among the many advantages, White stressed stable exchange rates, which, by reducing the risk of exchange fluctuations to traders and investors, would help revive the flow of goods and capital among nations. "If the Fund were successful in bringing about a much greater degree of stability in foreign exchange relationships than existed during the 'twenties and 'thirties," White said, "it will have justified its existence on that score alone." Moreover, having assurances that the fund stood ready to provide temporary assistance, members could dismantle exchange controls, reduce trade barriers, and eliminate all of the multiple-currency rates and bilateral-clearing arrangements that had stifled trade and payments since 1929. No longer would nations have to subordinate international economic harmony to the immediate imperative of halting a currency outflow. Also, White believed the fund would contribute to price stability, sounder national monetary and banking policies, and easier servicing of international debts.[43]

According to its authors, the fund would also promote a more equitable distribution of global gold reserves and ease the settlement of Britain's sterling debts, two problems that seemed likely to disturb postwar monetary cooperation. The maldistribution of gold reserves was a serious problem for the United States, which held the largest share of monetary gold, and the American experts naturally favored a postwar system that gave the auric metal a central role. Because their fund would hold, buy, and sell gold, presumably it would encourage members to accumulate larger gold reserves and lessen the volume of hectic gold flows that had disrupted monetary relations before the war. White also thought that the fund could encourage the return flow of gold from the United States by providing strength to countries with weakened monetary systems. While Washington experts had not explored all aspects of the gold problem, their proposals for the fund signalled America's intent to restore gold, at least temporarily, as reserve currency and *numéraire* for the postwar monetary system.[44]

If America's problem was too much gold, Britain's concern was too little gold and too many sterling debts. Anticipating that the United Kingdom might end the war with $5 billion in sterling debts and anxious that a strong Britain provide monetary leadership in the future, the Treasury technicians offered a complicated procedure for funding this external debt through the fund. It would absorb a proportion of the blocked sterling if Britain agreed to repurchase the sterling over a twenty-three–year period. This procedure, White stated, would restore confidence in sterling and in the effectiveness of monetary collaboration. "Probably," he added, "no single action would do more to stimulate world trade, prevent pressure on numerous exchanges, and reduce the probability of widespread depreciation of currencies." For this reason, "if the Fund can eliminate that danger spot it will have justified its existence—even were it to accomplish little else."[45]

This first segment of the Treasury plan was a tentative draft, and its writers realized it would be modified in talks with other American and foreign officials. That the United States stood to benefit more from currency stabilization than many countries—though proportionately other nations, except the Soviet Union, were more dependent on world trade—does not suggest that only self-interest and a desire to extend the capitalist system dictated the American position. It is true that American experts could not devise a plan for state trading, even if they had desired. Not exaggerated self-interest but enlightened understanding, based on a knowledge of economic doctrines and interwar experiences, motivated the American technicians to prepare a program that harmonized the monetary interests of all nations. In White's words, both large and small nations had a common interest in devising a flexible, mutually beneficial framework. "The lesson that must be learned is that prosperous neighbors are the best neighbors; that a higher standard of living in one country begets higher standards in others; and that a high level of trade and business is most easily attained when generously and widely shared."[46]

The stabilization fund, designed to strengthen national monetary systems and to prevent international currency disorders, might have functioned successfully in a balanced, prosperous world economy. But after a decade of war and economic disruption had destroyed confidence and halted long-term capital flows, economists anticipated a need for international mechanisms to supply the large volume of capital required for reconstruction, relief, and economic recovery. For this task White and his assistants proposed a companion institution—a Bank for Reconstruction and Development of the United and Associated Nations. Unlike the fund, which built an international institution on the foundation of prewar currency arrangements, the bank marked a distinct and ambitious departure from the prewar era when private market forces supplied global capital needs.[47]

In 1941 and 1942 Treasury experts could not divine the extent of postwar economic disruption, nor could they anticipate the breakdown of Soviet-American cooperation. But, based on the interwar experience, they did assume that private capital would be unavailable at a reasonable interest rate to arrest social and political decay and sustain prosperity. According to White, private capital "has suffered too many losses. It has been too severely discouraged by depreciating currencies, exchange controls and defaulting governments, to justify the hope that investors will lend large sums to a foreign country." He concluded, "Only a non-profit institution with enormous resources can afford to undertake the task of supplying adequate amounts of capital on the gigantic scale that will be necessary after the war."[48]

White did not view the international bank as a permanent replacement for private capital. Instead, after the combined operations of the two global agencies had restored confidence in currencies and established the stable conditions conducive to private capital movements, he expected private investments to revive, perhaps initially as direct investment in branch plants, mines, and factories. Eventually, as the climate improved, lenders would again channel funds to governments, municipalities, and corporations. Even then, however, the international bank would have a role: it would provide a yardstick for private lenders and interest-rate competition.[49]

Although Treasury drafts of the bank gave equal billing in the title to reconstruction and development, experts at first tended to emphasize the former objective. For instance, an April 1942 draft gave primacy to these goals: providing capital for economic reconstruction of the United Nations, facilitating a rapid and smooth transition from a wartime to a peacetime economy, supplying short-term capital for trade, and helping to strengthen monetary and credit structures of countries by redistributing the world gold supply. After these White listed other objectives, including elimination of global financial crises and reduction of the likelihood, intensity, and duration of world-wide economic depressions. Only then did the statement vaguely refer to development; the bank would "raise the productivity and hence the standard of living of the peoples of the member countries."[50]

Other objectives show that White and his aides conceived the institution as a multipurpose agency to treat a multitude of ills. It would promote "democratic institutions" throughout the world and ease the solution of many economic and political problems confronting a peace conference. The bank would also provide for financing and distributing essential relief items—such as food, clothing, and commodities—in war-devastated areas. It would help assure reasonable prices and access to scarce raw materials and promote stable commodity prices.[51]

Structurally the bank was to resemble the fund in membership, organization, and management. Only members of the fund would be eligible for membership in the bank. Altogether the participants would subscribe $10 billion in capital, with each contributing at least a sum equivalent to 2 percent of its annual national income. Thus, the United States would pay in at least $2 billion. A complicated formula would assign each member at least fifty votes—with additional votes for members with large subscriptions—but the heaviest contributors would have a controlling voice in decision making. However, no country would have more than 25 percent of the voting power.[52]

Like the fund, its twin would have a board of directors, composed of a representative from each member, which would administer activities. An executive committee or the bank's president would supervise daily operations. Important decisions, including loan approvals, purchases and sales of securities, and selection of officials, would require a two-thirds majority vote of the board of directors. White hoped that these necessary procedures would not produce cautious and conservative banking policy, because this would defeat the bank's purposes. He suggested that the managers be "men with varied experience who are more than bankers in their outlook and less than college professors in their decisions."[53]

Out of its $10 billion capital stock—at least 50 percent payable in advance, half in gold—the bank would make short- and long-term reconstruction and development loans to governments and political subdivisions. Loans, however, were contingent on a repayment guarantee from the borrowing country's government and on the unavailability of private loans at reasonable interest rates. To make certain that a loan would "serve directly or indirectly to permanently raise the standard of living of the borrowing country," White stipulated that the bank carefully study the loan application. This last restriction might be relaxed, however, if the loan was required to provide emergency relief to prevent social deterioration, avoid political disruption, or serve humanitarian purposes.[54]

Basically, White wanted the bank to provide cheap, long-term loans to deserving countries without restrictions on disbursements. In order to offer generous repayment provisions and low interest rates—not over 3 percent—White expected the bank would have to rely extensively on its own funds in the early years. Whenever possible, however, the bank should guarantee low-interest private loans. To enhance the prospects for repayment, and to improve the bank's credit rating, White emphasized that loans should be productive, generating, if possible, the means for repayment.[55]

Anxious to make provision for a future expansion of bank lending, White proposed that the bank have authority to issue "non-interest bearing currency notes," which would be "as good as gold." Here was a proposal for an international paper currency backed with gold. Briefly, the bank management could create, under specified conditions, an international paper money to supplement gold and national currencies as reserves and balancing items. As long as the global institution held a 50 percent gold reserve against paper notes, it could lend quantities to borrowing governments.[56]

This scheme had several advantages. Not only did it allow the bank to expand its lending capacity and add to world liquidity, but it established an international market for the United States' monetary gold. Provided the paper money inspired confidence, there was nothing to prevent the bank from printing more paper to purchase more gold, effectively transferring monetary gold from official holdings to the international agency. With approximately $30 billion of monetary gold in circulation, the bank might have created $60 billion of liquidity.[57]

White does not seem to have sensed the far-reaching consequences of this suggestion, because it was drafted hastily under wartime pressure. With modifications in the arrangements, or an amendment to the bank's charter, this might have become an automatic mechanism for credit creation, perhaps without the 50 percent gold requirement. It might also, like Special Drawing Rights in more recent times, have become an instrument for redistributing resources from the rich to the poor countries.

Neither White nor his aides had explored thoroughly all aspects of this proposal, but White, for one, saw the Bank for Reconstruction and Development as potentially more useful for member countries than the more conventional fund. He saw the bank as the beginning of a world central bank, which could perform essentially the same services for member nations that a national central bank offered member banks within a country. These services included accepting deposits, acting as a clearing house for funds and checks, and dealing in gold and securities. Viewed as a continuation of the trend toward centralization of banking in public hands, White's proposal was an extension of government regulation and organization to international finance. But government was not simply assuming a banking function; it was also moving beyond the usual boundaries of money and finance to take charge of relief, to stabilize commodities, and to assure access to raw materials. The Treasury draft did not emphasize these items, but, in suggesting that an international bank organize, regulate, and supervise production and marketing arrangements, White was taking a broad interpretation of international monetary and financial cooperation, one that sought to relate not just currencies and capital but also commodities and commerce.[58]

Far more than the Stabilization Fund, concerned with short-term currency imbalances and a code of monetary conduct, the Bank for Reconstruction and Development was an active instrument for reshaping the structure of international economic relations. As a lending agency it would have broad authority to finance trade and to lend for long-term development and reconstruction. And, with resources limited only by its ability to exchange paper currency for monetary gold, the bank could undertake an active role in supplying the liquidity needed to sustain a high level of world economic activity and to offset a depression. In short, Morgenthau's aides imagined this still-skeletal draft as a flexible global central bank capable of spearheading a concerted attack on economic distress and political instability.

Having fashioned a comprehensive program for interallied financial and monetary cooperation, the Treasury experts were naturally eager to present their proposals at a United Nations financial conference. If the Treasury delayed, White told Secretary Morgenthau on May 8, other agencies would prepare their own drafts, seize the initiative, and preempt Treasury interests. Morgenthau concurred, and a week later he carried a black binder with Harry White's "magnum opus" when he visited President Roosevelt.[59]

At first Roosevelt suggested that the Treasury turn over their program to Cordell Hull for consideration, but Morgenthau protested, telling the president that these suggestions "can only happen if you get behind" this program. Roosevelt acquiesced and agreed to read the binder of materials, including drafts of the fund and bank as well as a tentative agenda for a conference and a draft of a presidential invitation to other governments.[60]

A Treasury memorandum summarized the proposals, emphasizing that they would contribute to economic stability and enlist the support of peoples everywhere in the struggle against the Axis. "In the flush of success our enemies always dwelt upon their 'New Orders' for Europe and for Asia. There could be no more solid demonstration of our confidence that the tide is turning than the announcement of the formulation in concrete terms, and the preparation of specific instrumentalities for what really would be a New Deal in international economics."[61]

Immediate consideration of these mechanisms was necessary, the Treasury told Roosevelt, not only to dramatize and publicize postwar goals but also for an overriding practical reason. No one could forecast when the war might end, and, because it might take a year to convert working drafts into operating institutions, speed was necessary if the Allies were to be better prepared than at the close of World War I. If Roosevelt approved, Morgenthau proposed to invite other agencies to work with the Treasury in making preparations for an international conference in Washington.[62]

On May 16, Roosevelt agreed. Now the Treasury had a mandate to coordinate and direct government planning on postwar measures to stabilize currencies and increase international investments. The determined Morgenthau had demonstrated that he could move with greater speed and agility than Cordell Hull, and his agency had won an important clash.[63]

Thus, six months after the United States became a cobelligerent, this country had indicated its intention to create a new world economic order based on the principles of an efficient distribution of international labor, convertible currencies, and maximum utilization of human and physical resources. The Atlantic Charter and the Master Lend-Lease Agreement enunciated the substance of these principles and provided the parameters for technical craftsmen like Harry Dexter White. And White, unlike his counterparts in the phlegmatic State Department, rapidly conceived, with the aid of his economic staff, a comprehensive program for achieving those goals. Consciously benefiting from previous mistakes and from experiences with active governmental economic planning on the national level, the Treasury aides offered a new vertebrate international economic order with a code of rules and twin institutions. The fund, primarily concerned with currency stabilization, and the bank, possessing broad authority to create liquidity and engage in reconstruction-and-development lending as well as countercyclical activities, reflected a trend the depression had accelerated in many advanced countries. Enlightened economic planners, not self-regulating market forces, would oversee and manage the new system, subject to the limits established by the founding nations, in the interests of global peace, prosperity, and harmony. It was an economist's vision, but one that had not yet been exposed to public or foreign criticisms.

3

America and Britain: Divergent Approaches to a Common Goal

For nearly a year after Pearl Harbor, the United States and its new allies struggled bravely to blunt Axis offensives in Asia, the Middle East, and Eastern Europe. But one defeat followed another, and, as the danger mounted, the president warned Americans to prepare for the worst. "Enemy ships," he said, "could swoop in and shell New York; enemy planes could drop bombs on war plants in Detroit; enemy troops could attack Alaska." Despite the string of military setbacks and the threat of enemy attacks on North America, 86 percent of the people believed in May 1942 that the United States would eventually win the war. Even so, until summer, when naval victories in the Pacific broke the back of Japan's sea offensive, more citizens thought the country was losing the war than winning it.[1]

In these dire circumstances, President Roosevelt and his leading advisers were fully mobilizing military forces and stimulating war production. At a time when the smoke of battle shrouded outlines of the postwar world, top officials had little time, and less inclination, to consider the intricate problems of peacemaking. Moreover, until the military situation altered and the geographic outlines of the future world became visible, there was little reason for the president to devote precious moments to a consideration of peacetime relationships. Instead, middle-echelon specialists in the State and Treasury departments—among other agencies—could debate privately the various approaches and present their recommendations at the appropriate time.[2]

Secretary Morgenthau, once he had received President Roosevelt's approval to direct financial and investment preparations, lost no time establishing a forum of experts to deliberate and revamp the Treasury proposals, so that this phase of postwar planning would be ready for early inter-Allied negotiations. At his request officials from the Treasury, State, and Commerce departments, as well as the Board of Economic Warfare and the Federal Reserve Board of Governors, met on May 25, and the group agreed that Harry Dexter White should chair an interdepartmental committee to examine the Treasury blueprints.[3]

This technical committee, composed in Morgenthau's words of "people who do the work," met frequently during the next two years to frame the American proposals and to conduct discussions with other members of the United Nations. Among the twenty-four specialists were a number of prominent economists—including Harry White and Edward M. Bernstein from the Treasury; Leo Pasvolsky and John Parke Young from the State Department; and E. A. Goldenweiser and Alvin Hansen representing the Federal Reserve. In general the experts were economists or lawyers, not businessmen and bankers, and this was consistent with a pattern that emerged in the New Deal years. Roosevelt and Morgenthau remembered that bankers had been partially responsible for the banking crisis and for resisting the gold-purchase program. As a result, the New Deal had recruited a new pool of professional talent from the ranks of unemployed academic economists and reform-oriented graduate students.[4]

Harry White, though willing to consult experts from other agencies, continued to guide the discussions, and on occasions he and the Treasury acted independently without group approval. Because the specialists were, above all, spokesmen for different administrative interests and perspectives, disagreements over procedural questions —especially the timetable and forum for international discussions— soon erupted between representatives of State and Treasury.

While Hull's surrogates conceded the Treasury's primary responsibility for monetary proposals, they insisted that these harmonize tactically and conceptually with other administration programs being prepared under State Department jurisdiction. Basically, State Department aides argued that the United States should move cautiously and quietly until the military situation improved, and then in close collaboration with Great Britain. A hastily arranged financial conference, they claimed, might break down and thus jeopardize United Nations cooperation on other crucial postwar issues. Moreover, until the military situation clarified, it was superfluous to refine technical details that might not correspond to political realities. Finally, taking a position that was consistent with the Anglo-American commitment in the lend-lease arrangement, the State Department insisted that financial discussions should be confined to the British. The most articulate proponent of this great-power approach was Assistant Secretary Dean Acheson, often a proponent of cooperation with London. According to him, the English were nervous that Washington would arrange a large meeting, present a plan, and force London to accept it without so much as a frank, private discussion. The British, he added, had a pathetic feeling that Washington was going to write the ticket; they wanted, and felt entitled to, an opportunity to express their views.[5]

The Treasury had no intention of allowing the State Department, or the British, to dictate procedure. At the root of these objections, Morgenthau suspected, was a resentful Cordell Hull, boiling because Treasury had outmaneuvered him and gained presidential approval to frame the monetary and financial dimensions of postwar organization. Even so, Morgenthau was reluctant to provoke a direct confrontation; "I haven't got energy enough . . . to get into an interdepartmental fight."[6]

Instead, the dispute came to a head in a technical meeting July 10. There White presented a Treasury recommendation that the United States send letters to finance ministers of thirty-six nations inviting them to send qualified advisers to a technical meeting in Washington later in 1942. As preparation for this general session the United States would discuss general principles with governments having competent technical representatives in Washington—namely, Britain, Canada, and perhaps China. The Soviet Union did not have a financial expert in Washington. If the technical meetings revealed a basic consensus on both principles and procedures, the Treasury proposed issuing invitations to a formal monetary and financial conference.[7]

Hull's helpers, Assistant Secretary Adolf Berle and Leo Pasvolsky, objected. The whole plan was premature, they said, in view of unfavorable military conditions in Africa and Russia as well as the appearance of German submarines along the Atlantic coast. Under these circumstances a postwar conference would seem about as sensible to the average man as "building castles in Spain." Moreover, premature disclosure could bring on a bitter, perhaps partisan, debate over postwar goals as critics pandered to the general disquiet and accused the administration of fighting a war in order to "give the United States to the world afterwards." In light of these circumstances, they recommended proceeding cautiously until Washington developed a "carefully considered strategy" to enlist public support for world economic collaboration. As a substitute, Berle and Pasvolsky favored holding quiet bilateral talks with a few important allies. Not only would these sessions permit an exchange of technical ideas, but also reports of these meetings would undoubtedly leak to the press. And public reaction to the rumors would permit the government to determine if "the time was ripe for more formal negotiations."[8]

The two agencies did not resolve this important procedural difference until after more discussions in July and early August. Finally, they agreed on a format that would facilitate technical discussions but would reduce the prospects for a premature public debate. The government would notify various friendly governments that an American staff group was considering a monetary fund, a bank, and other international mechanisms. Then the technical committee would begin informal exploratory talks with representatives of Australia, Brazil, Britain, Canada, China, Mexico, and the Soviet Union. When these concluded, Morgenthau and other cabinet members could evaluate the results. If further action seemed advisable, they would seek President Roosevelt's approval for a preliminary conference of specialists to draft an annotated agenda and other documents necessary for a formal conference of ministers.[9]

This decision, opening the door to bilateral talks, marked a significant departure from Hull's policy of postponing international discussion of all matters relating to Article VII of the Master Lend-Lease Agreement. Although eager to fashion the economic platform for peace, Hull, who was after all a former congressman familiar with the legislative pitfalls of World War I preparations, assigned caution a higher priority than aggressive pursuit of economic principles. Of course, had Hull and his assistants completed specific postwar trade proposals and had they displayed similar leadership in monetary and investment matters, the secretary might have interpreted the past differently and urged greater haste to complete postwar preparations before the expected resurgence of domestic isolationism. But this is unlikely. Hull seemed genuinely convinced that the administration must prepare the public for the United States' global responsibilities, and he was certain that premature disclosure would only polarize the public, damage the Democratic party, and shatter prospects for international cooperation. As he said, "The greatest danger to the whole postwar planning, second only to the importance of winning the war . . . is the question of securing the support of the electorate for our postwar course." Unless, he added, "the most careful, sound and tactful course is pursued, . . . the government supporting any . . . plan and program will be completely swamped at the first election held after the last shot is fired."[10]

What apparently persuaded the secretary of state to relent was growing indication that if the United States hesitated others would seek unilateral solutions, including bilateral currency and restrictive trade agreements. Berle employed this argument to help melt Hull's resistance, and Ambassador Winant corroborated that American reluctance to open long-term lend-lease negotiations had strengthened British proponents of autarky and disheartened the supporters of multilateral cooperation. Thus, torn between the insistence of others that further delay might doom prospects for an open world economy and his own fears that haste could destroy the domestic consensus needed to effect that design, Hull wavered and agreed to preliminary talks on one segment of the postwar program—monetary and investment matters.[11]

Behind Britain's interest in bilateral discussions on the terms of future economic relationships lay a sense of urgency and a feeling of despair, not simply renewed devotion to liberal economic principles. Economists in London recognized that the pressures of war were rapidly, and perhaps permanently, transforming the economic basis of the Anglo-American relationship. Nothing illustrated these changing circumstances better than the fact that living standards were improving in the United States as the government appropriated billions of dollars for the military, while overriding military priorities brought belt-tightening in England. As the *Economist* indicated, American output increased 51 percent during the first three years of the European war, largely because the depressed American economy had been operating below full capacity. This increase enabled the United States to rearm and led to higher living standards and a sustained flow of new business investment. But Britain, hampered by blockades and bombardments, had increased output only 20 percent in four years, and it had accomplished this by slicing private consumption, reducing business investment, and liquidating overseas assets. Basically, the war had terminated the long American depression and established the basis for postwar growth and expansion, but in England the conflict was speeding Britain's decline as a vigorous competitor and as a healthy banker to the world by delaying the modernization of industrial facilities and forcing the sale of overseas assets.[12]

What this meant was that Britain would likely experience serious balance-of-payments difficulties in the years ahead. As a resource-poor and food-scarce nation Britain had traditionally relied on her competitive industrial exports and overseas earnings, from investments and services, to finance her trade deficit. As late as 1938, for instance, income from investments, shipping, and services paid for more than a third of food and material imports. But the war, by hastening the deterioration of manufacturing facilities, the sale of overseas investments, and the accumulation of a mounting sterling debt, posed difficult adjustment problems. In order merely to adapt to these new conditions, it appeared Britain would need protected export markets and as much as $2.5 billion annually in balance-of-payments assistance.[13]

In the opinion of British experts their country had two fundamental choices: restrictionism or expansionism. The former meant turning away from multilateral trade and payments, and relying instead on the resources of a closed commonwealth trading-and-currency system. This option, involving extensive reliance on trade barriers and currency controls, would resemble the policies Nazi Germany employed in the 1930's. While, on the one hand, it would effectively split the postwar world into rival commercial and monetary blocs, it would, on the other hand, help insulate Britain and her empire from low-cost foreign competition and from the deflationary effects of another American depression. In Britain an unlikely coalition of socialists and conservative imperialists favored this alternative—the socialists to achieve full employment and domestic reform, the imperialists to preserve traditional ties with the Commonwealth. But, although these interests were articulate and enjoyed some support in the cabinet, where Churchill and Beaverbrook attached considerable importance to preserving the empire, the rigid restrictionist view had little appeal to official economists.[14]

Unlike restrictionism, which contradicted the spirit if not the letter of the Atlantic Charter and the Master Lend-Lease Agreement, the second option—expansionism—depended on the generosity of the United States. For, if Britain was to embrace convertible currencies and multilateral trade, she would need outside aid. But, if this could be acquired within the context of a reform of international economic institutions, Britain would probably achieve the benefits of specialization as well as some protection against deflation and economic warfare. Most of all, it would allow Britain to take an active role in world economics consistent with principles her economists elaborated in the nineteenth century.[15]

No individual agonized more over the implications of this choice than John Maynard Keynes, adviser to the Treasury and author of the famous *General Theory of Employment, Interest, and Money.* Early in his career Keynes steadfastly supported the multilateral alternative, and he argued brilliantly that free trade was both a doctrine of economic advantage and a "principle of international morals." But interwar experience and his analytical work altered Keynes's thinking, and he increasingly wondered if the benefits of unrestricted capital and trade movements could be reconciled with the requirements of a stable, fully employed domestic economy. This pessimism appeared in June 1941 when, during lend-lease discussions, Keynes warned Hull's sensitive assistants that Britain might have to continue nationalistic controls. However, on the same trip he was so impressed with the modern Keynesian outlook of younger American economists that he thought it possible the two countries could devise an expansionary solution—one that would achieve the benefits of an open economy with the domestic safeguards against depression.[16]

Upon his return Keynes began to draft a proposal for the International Clearing Union that would, if adopted, achieve both economic objectives. In a version circulated within the British cabinet early in 1942 Keynes posed Britain's dilemma: either it would have to ask "particular favours or accommodations from the United States" or maintain trade-and-payments controls. He dismissed the latter course, saying that "bilateral agreements would put in great jeopardy not only the sterling area but the whole position of London as an international [financial] centre."[17]

A workable monetary system, Keynes thought, would be one that enabled Britain and other countries with insufficient reserves to take advantage of triangular trade and payments without resort to comprehensive currency controls, regular exchange variations, or domestic price and income adjustments to remove a balance-of-payments deficit. As a substitute for bilateral financial arrangements, which Keynes said "are likely to be influenced by extraneous, political reasons and put individual countries into a position of particular obligation towards others," he suggested the International Clearing Union. Briefly, this supranational institution would have authority to create and manage a new international currency for settling intercountry balances. On the basis of a formula that ignored existing gold or currency holdings, the union would distribute quantities of the new reserves to accounts of members. And, finally, so that the new balances would always be available for a variety of purposes, the British economist proposed a method for preventing leakage from the system and for recycling unutilized balances so that the fixed quantity of reserves would do more work.[18]

The new international currency, called bancor, would supplement, and gradually replace, gold and reserve currencies as the chief instruments for international settlements. Bancor, unlike the pool of national currencies and gold in White's stabilization fund, would exist only on the clearing union's books and would merely shift from one account to another within the union. In this respect, as Keynes mentioned, the proposal resembled a closed banking system in which credits were transferred internally but never withdrawn. Because the total quantity of bancor could not escape, Keynes emphasized that the "union *itself* can never be in difficulties." Altogether Keynes proposed to create $26 billion of the new bank money, a sum that could increase or decrease in the future at the discretion of members in order to provide enough world liquidity to sustain total demand. Initially, the union would allocate bancor to members according to their prewar position in world trade. This distribution of new financial assets would allow members—particularly, heavily indebted countries like Britain—to remove restrictions on all but capital movements, maintain stable exchange rates, and pursue stimulative domestic policies without fear of an external payments crisis.[19]

Critical of the prewar system that had depended on such exogenous factors as the availability of gold to supply increasing liquidity, Keynes essentially proposed to de-emphasize the auric metal. He recognized, however, that gold still possessed great psychological value, and that it still provided an uncontroversial standard of value; thus, he did not propose to replace gold immediately. Instead, he planned to employ gold to enhance, at least initially, the acceptability of bancor. The international bank money would be fixed (but not unalterably) in terms of gold. Actually, because members would state the value of their national currencies in terms of bancor, not gold, his new credit money would effectively replace gold as the *numéraire*, or benchmark, and standard of account in the new system. Moreover, to prevent occasional flights to the trusted monetary metal, which would damage the effectiveness of bancor, Keynes rejected two-way convertibility. That is, members of the clearing union could not automatically convert one reserve asset—such as gold, reserve currencies, or bancor—into another. The union would permit only one-way convertibility; a member could exchange gold for bancors, a provision intended to assure nations with large stockpiles of gold or deep-seated attachments to the monetary metal a stable market. Keynes also would allow the two founder states, Britain and the United States, sufficient power to alter the price of gold if they chose. He did not explicitly propose the de-monetization of gold, though this was the direction of his argument. "No object," said Keynes, "would be served by attempting further to peer into the future or to prophesy the ultimate policy of the founder States in this regard." More importantly immediately for the success of the clearing-union system was the provision that members could not exchange bancors, or national currencies, for gold at the clearing union. Keynes considered this requirement essential for avoiding monetary crises when members would desperately attempt to shift their assets from a fiat money to a commodity money.[20]

A distinctive feature of the clearing union was the way it placed pressure on both deficit and surplus countries to remove a payments imbalance. The Keynes plan recognized, as the White plan did not, that payments imbalances might result not only from faulty domestic policies in the deficit country but also from fluctuation in global demand or other external circumstances. To bring about equilibrium, Keynes proposed to tax both countries with excessive bancor credits and debits. Also, if a deficit accumulated above a certain level, the union's governing board could require that country either to devalue, impose capital controls, or surrender a portion of its gold and liquid reserves held outside the union. Similarly, the union could recommend, but not require, that nations with excessive credit balances adopt appropriate policies to restore payments equilibrium. A nation could take measures to inflate the home economy, appreciate its currency in terms of bancor, reduce tariffs and other import barriers, or expand international lending.[21]

Concerned with the critical problem of creating enough liquidity to place an expansionist pressure on world trade, Keynes devoted less attention to the related issue of exchange-rate alterations, and for a good reason. With the union recycling bancor, there would be less need for parity alterations if initial rates were properly selected. However, he clearly favored stable rates, chosen by members in agreement with the union. Although members might receive "special consideration" to adjust exchange values during the first five years of operation, countries could not later alter the value of their currency in terms of bancor without permission of the union's governing board.[22]

The future monetary order envisaged by Keynes would have an expansionary thrust that permitted stable, convertible currencies and encouraged a high level of trade, but it would not have free capital or trade flows. He accepted the widely held belief "that control of capital movements, both inward and outward, should be a permanent feature of the post-war system." In the future, he thought, no country could safely allow the flight of short-term funds. Long-term investment, which was not the immediate concern of the clearing union, could, Keynes said in a later draft, require a second complementary institution. On this issue Keynes and White held similar views: both doubted that private international lending would revive quickly in the postwar years.[23]

From Keynes's vantage point the troublesome question of trade barriers and preferential arrangements was distinctly secondary to the interrelated issues of expansion and convertibility. To please the American advocates of trade liberalization, Keynes provided that members agree to exclude certain import restrictions, barter arrangements, and export subsidies from future commercial treaties, but without affecting existing preferences. This approach, Keynes said, would at least "give some satisfaction to Mr. Cordell Hull over a wide field, since we should be accepting a non-discriminatory international system as the normal and desirable régime." If approved, of course, this solution also would help protect Britain and her Commonwealth preferential bloc from vigorous foreign competition in the difficult transition period.[24]

Keynes, like Harry White, favored a new form of functional internationalism that began with a supranational monetary institution and standards of international economic conduct as a better way to assure global prosperity and payments equilibrium than the ad hoc bilateral arrangements and informal guidelines that had characterized the prewar economy. The English economist in particular envisaged the union as the "pivot of the future economic government of the world." It might, he suggested, even finance a supranational police force and effect a financial blockade against peace-breaking countries. He also foresaw the clearing union working closely with other international boards to finance relief and rehabilitation programs, regulate the price of raw materials, and promote international investment and development. This type of functional activity, if coordinated by the union, could provide a "powerful means of combating the evils of the Trade Cycle, by exercising contractionist and expansionist influence on the system as a whole or on particular sections."[25]

Neither Keynes nor White intended for the superstructure of economic internationalism to interfere unduly with traditional trading and financial activities of businessmen and bankers. Keynes, for example, insisted that "the fabric of international banking organization, built up by long experience to satisfy practical needs, should be left as undisturbed as possible." As he explained, the clearing union would help central banks cope with the ultimate problems of settling and clearing currency balances, but it would not affect individual transactions, which the private market handled. Moreover, the English economist claimed that a clearing union would not significantly alter the network of financial ties that bound smaller American and Commonwealth countries to New York and London as international banking centers. At least Keynes did not intend for the clearing union to disrupt the sterling bloc or the dollar bloc.[26]

Far more than White, Keynes wanted the organization and future management of a global monetary organization to be supervised by the two great powers. The United States and Britain, Keynes suggested, could negotiate, as representatives of the American and Commonwealth nations, to work out important details, thus avoiding "the delays and confused counsels of an international conference." The two founding states, he proposed, should also permanently control the management and effective voting power as well as determine whether other countries qualified for membership. His intent here was to give countries with the greatest financial resources and experience a controlling interest; he did not intend to exclude nations —even former enemy states would eventually qualify for membership. On the question of Soviet participation Keynes seemed less eager than White. The British adviser frankly doubted that Moscow would want to be "a party to so capitalist-looking an institution," but if the Russians desired to join, the problem could receive "special consideration."[27]

The clearing union, Keynes recognized, could aid during the relief period, but it might also introduce complications. Until production had adjusted to peacetime conditions and industrial facilities had been replaced, the union might provide excessive liquidity. Thus, its implementation would depend on what other international assistance the United States intended—perhaps through a temporary extension of lend-lease to finance food and raw material purchases. Although Keynes saw the clearing union as a possible instrument of postwar assistance, he did not advance the proposal primarily as a device for overcoming Britain's transitional problems but for establishing a durable basis for an expansionary world economy.[28]

In drafts prepared for top British officials, Keynes bluntly analyzed how his clearing union would serve both world and British interests. It would provide a general framework for currency rehabilitation, satisfy the aspirations of Cordell Hull and Sumner Welles for trade liberalization, facilitate postwar relief and reconstruction, preserve peace, stabilize prices and the trade cycle, and encourage the creation of an "international T.V.A." (Tennessee Valley Authority). Britain would benefit in several ways: the clearing union would stimulate demand for her exports; it would permit Britain to achieve multilateral clearing and long-term equilibrium after the war without asking "particular favours or accommodations from the United States"; and it would allow her to devalue her currency without risking competitive depreciations or retaliation. Finally, Keynes added, attainment of a multilateral payments system was the solution most likely to preserve the sterling bloc and Britain's historic role as a world financial center. Brilliantly, John Maynard Keynes, the monetary magician from the British treasury, had conceived how to pull a camel through a needle's eye. His mechanism would, if adopted, allow a threadbare and gold-poor Britain to escape the weight of foreign debts and to recover a role of leadership in world finance.[29]

National advantage colored Keynes's draft as much as it did White's, but beneath hard assessments of self-interest there was already a consensus on basic principles, though not on technical details. Both economists understood that economic logic and practical experience dictated an attempt to create a durable, open world economy with maximum specialization among countries. But they also realized that new techniques of economic management—to a large extent the result of Keynes's pioneering contributions to economic theory— could strengthen an open system against the dangers of depression, prolonged exchange imbalances, and unilateral economic expedients. Implicit in their work was the confidence that international economic managers could, assuming nations subscribed to certain principles of good conduct, avoid the perils of an unregulated, uncoordinated open economy.

Before United Nations military commanders gained the upper hand and political leaders could visualize the outlines of the postwar world, British and American technicians had completed preliminary drafts of proposals that would fundamentally restructure the world economy in ways that an earlier generation of peacemakers had not even anticipated in the exuberance of victory. But, unless the specialists could reconcile difficult mechanical problems, which involved hard calculations of postwar national interests, these ideas, however magnanimous, enjoyed little prospect for adoption. Progress on the technical level depended in turn on the willingness of political leaders to define negotiating procedures and to accept the risk of public disclosure before the administration had consulted and shaped internal opinion.

Not until August 1942, when American economists received a copy of the clearing union and obtained initial British reaction to the White suggestions, could United States technicians identify differences and points of agreement. Sir Frederick Phillips, a British treasury official stationed in Washington, praised the American draft for offering solutions to a variety of vexing economic problems, including commodity-price fluctuations, blocked currencies, and trade barriers within a multilateral framework. But, Phillips told the Americans, the clearing union distributed more liquidity to countries with small gold holdings and it "went further in making possible the adjustments of the total volume of international currency to world needs." Also, he suggested that the British plan was more adaptable than the American to meet the threat of another world-wide depression. But, despite important mechanical differences, Phillips thought the two sides could reach agreement, and he urged early negotiations. Essentially, London was concerned, as Phillips indicated, about its postwar balance-of-payments problems, and it wanted Washington to provide a clearer signal of its intentions within the framework of a comprehensive, bilateral settlement. The discussions, Phillips emphasized, should include trade as well as financial considerations.[30]

London again extended a friendly hand, but Washington remained hesitant, inclined to postpone substantive discussions. A conjunction of personal suspicion, technical obstacles, and political caution appeared to justify further delay. For one thing, American experts needed time to study the clearing union, assess its implications, and determine how influential private voices would respond. Initially, some of the American experts, especially Adolf Berle, were skeptical of Keynes's motives. As Berle perceived it, the clearing union was essentially a "method by which American, and possibly other goods, could be made available to certain countries, notably Britain, on what was in fact though not in form a credit arrangement, terms of the credit being, of course, the degree of usefulness of this international currency." Until the technical and political implications of the overdraft system had been fully discussed, Berle and other state department aides wanted to avoid any impression that the two English-speaking countries were "making up a plan and then requiring everyone else to take it or leave it."[31]

Berle and Harry Dexter White questioned British motives—was the clearing union a clever device to tap American resources, or was it principally a sophisticated reform proposal that would benefit the United States and other nations? Their early reservations tended to confirm the British image of White and Berle as inveterate Anglophobes—individuals who thought Englishmen "diabolically astute in international finance" and determined to run "rings around anyone who would oppose their Machiavellian projects" to advance the British Empire. The active role of Berle and White may have done little to establish British confidence, but the two men did recognize, perhaps because of their deeply engrained suspicion of English proposals, the far-reaching ramifications of Keynes's clearing union. This came out, for instance, when White accompanied Morgenthau to Britain in October 1942 for talks on other matters. At that time White told Keynes that the United States could not accept the clearing union with its potentially large command of American resources. Keynes naturally defended his work and pointedly told White that his own plan for capital subscriptions was economically obsolete.[32]

Even in private technical conversations the advantages of the rival proposals could not be considered solely in economic terms. Mechanical perfection would be irrelevant if final drafts were unacceptable on political grounds to their countrymen. And, in both Britain and the United States there were vocal elements fearful of the other country's intentions. On his side, Keynes had to placate both socialists and imperialists who suspected that the chief American ambition was to open the British Empire and yoke the United Kingdom to a modernized gold standard that would prove incompatible with the yearning for imperial preference or sterling-bloc commitments and with the autonomy necessary to maintain a high level of employment. Similarly, White recognized that he would face virulent domestic opposition if he approved a proposal bearing the imprimatur of John Maynard Keynes. During the war Keynes was already regarded by conservative American businessmen and legislators as the most dangerous advocate of reckless economic experimentation and irresponsible deficit spending. For that reason, it was reasonable to assume that some critics would attack the clearing union as a foolhardy scheme to experiment with unsound Keynesian principles on a global scale.[33]

Harry White personally might have preferred to push forward with technical consultations, and even an international conference, but he recognized on the basis of preliminary exchanges and on the administration's assessment of probable domestic uproar that circumstances did not permit an early conference—certainly not until after the 1942 elections provided a clearer indication of the public mood. Although the stakes were high—reconstruction of a viable international economy—the Roosevelt administration, like the Nixon administration thirty years later, opted to postpone extensive, probably controversial, deliberation over fundamental global monetary reform until these issues could be considered without concern for emotional political reverberations.[34]

But, instead of laying to rest political anxieties, the congressional elections revived fears of a postwar resurgence of isolationist sentiment in the United States and Britain. On election day the Republicans gained 47 seats in the House of Representatives and 9 in the Senate, giving the opposition its largest minority in Congress since Franklin Roosevelt triumphed ten years before. Another indication of this trend, which political observers noted, was that only 5 of the 115 congressmen with isolationist records failed to win reelection. The pattern was not conclusive, but the *New Republic* expressed concern that in 1944 Republican governor Thomas Dewey of New York might win the presidency and become the second Warren Harding, delivering Americans from the clutches of the internationalist Democrats. *Time* also saw a "striking parallel" between 1942 and 1918, when the Republicans won control of the Senate and proceeded to block the League of Nations. Across the Atlantic the *Economist* commented somberly, "It is by no means certain that in the United States victory does not mean a return to Hardingism."[35]

Government officials are often adept at interpreting recent events to support their policy recommendations. Thus, had the 1942 elections seen a resurgence of internationalist support, some officials would have undoubtedly interpreted this trend as a public mandate for a vigorous initiative on postwar planning—perhaps to conclude future arrangements before the public mood shifted again. As it was, however, officials in the State Department and the Foreign Service emphasized that the strong isolationist vote emphasized the urgency of completing the postwar design before a tide of political reaction capsized the proposals for international cooperation in the 1944 presidential elections. According to Joseph Jones, a journalist who analyzed postwar trends in Hull's agency, conditions seemed more opportune for a positive domestic and foreign program than they might six months later.[36]

A similar message came from the U.S. embassy in London, where economist Ernest Penrose reported that British officials saw a parallel between conservative trends in Congress and the ill-fated League of Nations struggle a generation earlier. Unless Washington opened economic negotiations, thereby demonstrating its commitment to a liberal economic settlement, London might succumb to the pressure from restrictionists who advocated a unilateral solution for Britain's difficulties. The critical issue, at this stage, was progress on international monetary reform. If both countries devised a settlement that would ease Britain's postwar payments adjustments, Penrose said, "there is an excellent prospect that the British . . . will fully cooperate on lines acceptable to us in the solution of the other aspects of international economic relations, including the subject of preferences and discriminations." Hull's goal of nondiscriminatory trade, then, hinged on the progress of discussions on the monetary front. These calculations, together with improvements on the military side, apparently explain the State Department's decision, a week after the congressional elections, to initiate informal discussions with London on all topics covered in Article VII of the Master Lend-Lease Agreement.[37]

Private discussions had continued with British experts in Washington during the autumn political campaign, but the postelection decision to move forward on a broad range of technical issues gave new impetus to consideration of the controversial monetary plans. American specialists had not yet composed their views on currency stabilization, and some—particularly the Federal Reserve experts—considered the Treasury draft, which had already undergone several revisions, "quite immature from a technical standpoint. . . ." Yet Berle and White were eager to initiate discussions with foreign representatives, as the technical committee recommended before the elections. An important tactical consideration influenced this decision: American monetary experts feared that further delay might either discourage London or enable it to develop a ground swell of foreign support for the draft Keynes desired. Already, Berle knew, English technicians had discussed their clearing union with various dominion and exile governments. Two of them, South Africa and Canada, advised Washington that further delays would only impede the quest for a durable, open monetary system.[38]

At this stage of the expert discussions the American specialists concentrated on only one phase of Harry White's program—the stabilization fund. This emphasis was justifiable on several grounds. The specialists, who had other responsibilities besides long-term planning, could not easily refine both proposals simultaneously. Also, it was a question of priority. The Americans recognized that exchange stabilization was a precondition for sound international investments, not the reverse. Without stable currencies it would be difficult to revive a flow of long-term capital. Furthermore, White anticipated that, if he submitted both proposals in a package, Keynes might offer a compromise: Washington could accept the clearing union, and London would approve a version of the bank. This solution, whatever its technical advantages—and White was not privately unsympathetic to the clearing union—could pose grave political difficulties. Critics, suspicious of New Deal programs and hostile to anything bearing Keynes's name, would dismiss both schemes as blank checks on American resources. From the Treasury standpoint, the stabilization fund, which was after all merely a modest extension of the tripartite arrangements, was more palatable politically, if not economically.[39]

During the autumn and winter sessions, as Washington specialists and resident British officials evaluated the two currency proposals, attention turned to several crucial monetary questions. Would there be a new international currency? Would both surplus and deficit countries have some responsibility for restoring international equilibrium? On the question of an international currency Keynes was more innovative than the Americans, for he envisaged the creation of *bancor*. This expression, which was a hybrid of *bank* and *or*, a French word for *gold*, seemed to associate the new monetary system too closely to traditional banking practices, and White offered a substitute. He suggested his own bookkeeping unit, called *unitas*, which would be equal to $10 in gold and would bear at least popular association with the concept of United Nations unity. Actually, as White knew, unitas was not a substitute for bancor. The latter was an international currency transferrable within the clearing union for settling debts, while the former was merely an artificial unit in which members could express their currency values and in which the fund's accounts would be kept. At least in his stabilization fund, White had no intention of introducing a fiat global currency that could expand or contract at the discretion of members with a controlling vote.[40]

Of greater importance at that time was the issue of whether an international currency agency should discipline both countries with favorable and unfavorable balance-of-payments positions or merely nations with persistent deficits. As a probable surplus country in the postwar years, the United States took a position that it would abandon a quarter century later when America's persistent deficit compelled financial authorities to reconsider the adjustment question. Basically,

White insisted, as he would throughout the Bretton Woods discussions, on a version of the social rule: deficit countries were living beyond their means and should be penalized for their profligacy. Under his plan deficit countries would eventually have to either deflate their domestic economies or devalue their currencies according to rules that would avert competitive devaluations. But the British, representing a probable deficit country, argued vigorously that imbalances were not solely the responsibility of the deficit country. In the Keynes plan they proposed that countries accumulating bancor credits also face international pressure. Essentially, Keynes proposed not to glorify creditors, but to tax them in the interests of restoring international equilibrium.[41]

In seeking to establish the principle of parallel responsibility, the British were attempting to place international pressure on the United States. For in London, as in other countries, there was a compelling fear that the United States dollar might become scarce in the postwar years as Washington vainly refused to redistribute its monetary reserves through a payments deficit, or as another American depression cut imports and transferred the recession outward to other trading countries. White was reluctant, partly for political reasons, to accept Keynes's symmetry, but the Americans were eager to allay London's concern. Thus, the Treasury experts suggested a scarce-currency clause, one that would countenance discrimination against the dollar. If a general shortage of any currency developed, the fund might declare that money (probably the dollar) scarce and permit other members to discriminate against the exports of the scarce-currency country. Evidently, the American technicians thought that possible resort to the scarce-currency provision would encourage the United States to take corrective action before a dollar shortage emerged, perhaps by inflating the domestic economy, removing tariffs, or expanding foreign lending.[42]

At first the British experts, eager to collect support for Keynes's elegant draft, did not grasp the implications of this concession, but as it eventually became apparent that Washington would not accept the clearing union the English treated the provision as an acceptable consolation prize. Economist Roy F. Harrod, Keynes's associate and future biographer, hailed it as a remarkable feat. Now, if the United States followed high-tariff policies, as it had in the 1920's, trading partners might "discriminate against the purchase of American goods . . .

and . . . maintain their own full employment in the presence of an American depression." For the "first time," Harrod wrote later, the Americans had indicated "they would come and accept their full share of responsibility when there was a fundamental disequilibrium of trade. . . . I felt an exhilaration such as only comes once or twice in a lifetime."[43]

The Americans, although eager to reconcile the rival proposals for monetary cooperation, had no intention of negotiating a preliminary Anglo-American understanding as London wished. Instead, determined to seek a broader basis for the future monetary order, Washington transmitted, in February and March 1943, copies of a revised version of the stabilization plan—one including a "scarce-currency" provision and a clause allowing the fund to purchase blocked currencies—to Britain, the Soviet Union, China, and thirty-four smaller countries. In addition, Secretary Morgenthau sent an invitation to the finance ministers of these governments to send representatives to Washington for discussions of international monetary cooperation along these or related lines.[44]

London had already begun its consultations with other governments, and inevitably the subject of these conversations leaked to the press. And, when members of the British Parliament requested a complete explanation, Churchill's government proposed that the two English-speaking allies jointly release their documents. Washington demurred. Suspecting that the British might have "leaked" their clearing union in order to smoke out the American draft, White and his aides prepared instructions that Chancellor of the Exchequer Sir Kingsley Wood not mention the American version. Wood might, however, simply say that "other governments were likewise working on the problem of monetary stabilization with a view to appropriate action."[45]

Hints in the English press that Washington might have a companion monetary program elicited inquiries from congressmen, forcing Morgenthau and Roosevelt to consider disclosure of the White program. In particular, powerful Michigan Republican Arthur Vandenberg demanded to know if the Treasury contemplated any "commitments . . . involving a radical devaluation of the American dollar," a step that Vandenberg thought beneficial to Britain. Because Morgenthau needed the Michigan senator's support on other legislative matters, he decided, with President Roosevelt's approval, to inform congressional leaders and issue a press release. Roosevelt consented from necessity, not conviction. "These things," he told Morgenthau, "are too early. We haven't begun to win the war." And he insisted that the Treasury stress that these currency discussions were "purely exploratory" and "in no way a binding matter."[46]

Before Morgenthau and his British counterpart could prepare a joint press release, Paul Einzig, a prominent London financial columnist, obtained and published a version of the American proposal. This news story, arriving as it did just before Morgenthau informed congressional leaders, sparked a round of angry charges from suspicious conservatives who saw in the administration's secrecy another New Deal plot to scatter the nation's wealth to the four corners of the earth. Before the outbursts translated into debate or hostile resolutions, Morgenthau promised House Speaker Sam Rayburn that the administration would consult Congress "before we make up our minds." The episode, coming shortly after Washington released its proposals to other governments, convinced Morgenthau that "we just can't take all these countries into our confidence." Now the global monetary experts had a second problem; not only did they face difficult discussions with allies, but they also had to guide public debate on the obscure monetary issues. In the future phases of the monetary negotiations the issue of public acceptability would have a more transcendent role.[47]

A year had elapsed since President Roosevelt authorized Henry Morgenthau and his experts to direct monetary planning. In retrospect, much time was lost haggling over procedural, jurisdictional, and mechanical questions, and some of this lost time undoubtedly restricted the quantity of achievements the planners could attain before the war ended in 1945. But this experience, together with a similar round of monetary preparations in the early 1970's, indicates that at least in the early stages of monetary diplomacy there are frequent delays until drafts have been refined and compared and elite opinion prepared.

Even so, in a succession of individual agreements from the Atlantic Charter to the Master Lend-Lease Agreement to the exchange of currency plans, both Britain and the United States had indicated a common inclination to work together for a world with expanding trade and easily convertible currencies. Although not of paramount concern to the negotiators, this postwar world would be one predominantly organized by private, not government, interests. The two sides did not consider the market economy a barrier to postwar cooperation with socialist economies, though undoubtedly it would present some problems, nor did they regard differences over national influence or economic mechanisms an insurmountable obstacle to postwar co-operation. The mechanics of the currency program as well as its acceptability to smaller countries and domestic constituencies posed the difficult issues for future consideration.

Consultation and Consensus

"Victory in this war is the first and greatest goal before us. Victory in the peace is the next." These sentences in President Roosevelt's state-of-the-union message cogently expressed the central objectives of American foreign policy early in 1943 as the military tide began to turn decisively against the determined Axis coalition. But, as Roosevelt and his top advisers knew, progress toward these dual goals required comprehensive planning and continuous inter-Allied consultation.[1]

Concerned with the immediate problems of coordinating United Nations military initiatives and preserving great-power unity against centrifugal pressures, the president continued to function as commander-in-chief and his own secretary of state. Cordell Hull remained in the background as Roosevelt met on three occasions with Winston Churchill at Casablanca, Washington, and Quebec. The chief executive also talked over common problems with the British prime minister and Chinese leader Gen. Chiang Kai-shek and in November held his first tripartite summit with Churchill and Joseph Stalin in Teheran.

Roosevelt himself proceeded cautiously on postwar political and economic arrangements. While he regularly gave lip service to the principle of international cooperation, he carefully spoke in noncontroversial generalities and avoided specific commitments. This vagueness reflected both instinctive political caution and a determination to avoid previous peacemaking errors. "After the first World War," Roosevelt told the press, "we tried to achieve a formula for permanent peace, based on a magnificent idealism. We failed."[2]

As pressure gradually mounted from internationalist groups and congressional activists for a more concrete discussion of postwar plans, Roosevelt gradually relented and authorized global meetings on such noncontroversial, functional matters as food and agriculture, and relief and rehabilitation. These moves would blunt criticism that the administration was neglecting postwar problems and would allow Washington to gauge the extent of public support for more comprehensive arrangements, such as a peacekeeping organization and monetary institutions.

The administration's policy of postponement harnessed second-echelon figures like Harry Dexter White, who would have preferred an accelerated timetable, but it gave the specialists valuable time, which might otherwise have been unavailable, to consult with three important groups. First, it enabled policymakers to measure and evaluate public response to published versions of the Keynes and White proposals. Second, the delay enabled far-reaching consultations with smaller countries, which helped to clear up confusion and to avoid unnecessary friction. And, finally, it enabled further inter-agency discussions in an effort to harmonize the American position for critical negotiations with Lord Keynes and British technicians. During 1943 these activities proceeded simultaneously, and each influenced the technical development of the international monetary proposals.

Publication of the rival monetary proposals, popularly known as the Keynes and the White plans, sparked a vigorous public debate in the spring and summer of 1943. But, unlike controversy over a new League of Nations, this debate was restricted principally to an educated elite of economists and businessmen familiar with the complexities of international finance and the options available to decision makers. Also, the economic debate was far more than a dispute over the relative merits of internationalism or isolationism, for on this plane that distinction had little relevance to the resolution of practical problems. Autarky, the economic counterpart of isolationism, appeared to augur a return to the truncated international economy in which rival nationalisms had once before damaged the world's economic health and peace. League of Nations experts repeatedly pointed out that autarky distorted optimal commercial patterns and produced an inefficient allocation of global resources. Politically, it encouraged bilateral deals that, in turn, often endangered the economic and political independence of weaker countries and intensified international frictions. Despite these warnings, autarky did have some residual attraction among British intellectuals and continental authorities where controls had traditional appeal, seemed attractive ideologically, or promised to protect domestic employment from foreign export competition or the effects of another depression.[3]

Interdependence, the opposite of autarky, had wide appeal in the United States, the British government, and the League of Nations. Both international trade doctrine and interwar experience confirmed the advantages of this course. The case for multilateral trade rested, the experts knew, on its potential contribution to the full and efficient allocation of world resources. As League of Nations expert Folke Hilgerdt told the American Economic Association, the argument for multilateralism hinged not on the "necessity of multilateral trade for any particular country," but on the general need for world equilibrium. In an open-trading regime, with nondiscriminatory trade and convertible currencies, nations normally experienced a trade deficit with some countries and a trade surplus with others. The United States, for instance, in 1928 balanced heavy imports from tropical areas with sales to industrial Europe. Britain, however, offset her North Atlantic deficit with a current-account surplus on tropical trade. A multilateral solution, then, contributed to world efficiency, and it also reduced "tensions of the kind that are instrumental in bringing about war."[4]

Because bankers often criticized the specific mechanisms that Keynes and White proposed to structure an open world, liberal journals sometimes denounced them as "monetary isolationists." But the phrase was inexact and inappropriate, for international bankers hardly favored autarky. Like White and Keynes, they wanted a peaceful, multilateral world. Self-interest, as well as sentiment and economic logic, dictated this preference. Commercial bankers, for instance, prospered from currency transactions and from short-term trade financing, while investment bankers wanted stable currency values and relatively unencumbered trade to facilitate the placement and amortization of loans. As Edward Brown, chairman of Chicago's First National Bank, told Congress in 1945, "The more there is, why, the more money we make." To the bankers self-interest and national interest corresponded, and both militated in favor of an open world economy. As the American Bankers Association declared in a 1943 resolution, "Our own progress and well-being, and that of the world, require our active participation with other countries in dealing with post-war problems."[5]

In the United States the monetary debate centered not on the relative advantages of autarky or interdependence but on the relative advantages of specific modes of international cooperation. Keynesians, and others sympathetic to government management, generally favored a highly structured world economy with intergovernmental mechanisms and rules regulating currencies, investments, and trade, among other items. Traditionalists, however, generally favored a return to some version of the invertebrate nineteenth-century world with limited government interference and the predominance of automatic market forces. Both the managed and laissez faire models permitted multilateral trade and convertible currencies, but the two regimes each had strengths and weaknesses that affected their suitability for postwar circumstances.

Basically, Keynesians feared the international consequences of a postwar depression, and they thought the published version of the White plan was too narrowly constructed and too limited in scope to cope with that contingency. Privately, Harry White may have shared this assessment, for his unpublished 1942 plan for an international bank held out the possibility that his mechanism might engage in countercyclical lending to reduce the intensity of economic depressions. Keynesians like Alvin Hansen argued that, although modern economics with its emphasis on maintaining adequate aggregate demand could prevent another collapse, it was doubtful the American public would countenance such stimulative techniques except in wartime. Accordingly, an American depression would have the same paralyzing consequences as the 1929 collapse, bringing a serious dollar shortage and forcing other countries to erect autarkic trade-and-currency controls.[6]

In the face of a major depression Hansen knew that the stabilization fund would be unable to maintain currency convertibility and stable exchange rates. The treasury fund, he said, would fail "just as the restoration of the International Gold Standard following the last war failed." A larger fund, perhaps with $12 billion in currencies, would provide temporary relief, obtaining time for more fundamental adjustments to take place, but it was insufficient unless accompanied by parallel mechanisms to maintain full employment in developed countries and to provide long-term development loans. Pessimistic that the United States would use macroeconomic policy to correct a depression, Hansen wanted to create international agencies that would automatically funnel surplus savings from economically mature countries to others needing outside assistance for reconstruction and industrial diversification.[7]

Multilateral lending, the essence of Hansen's prescription, was not a self-serving way to stimulate American employment and bolster the capitalistic system, as Marxists would argue, though it would have that effect. Instead, he saw it as a device to structure the international economy, creating mechanisms to assure global full employment as well as the efficient utilization of economic resources. Perhaps because Hansen himself participated in the American technical deliberations, he did not embrace the Keynes plan; but his suggestion, intended to cope in a Keynesian way with unemployment on a world scale, was based on a similar perception of future economic events. What he and other exponents of the new economics saw was the inherent interdependence of global prosperity, efficiency, and peace. A durable open world, the Keynesians thought, must be managed and structured.[8]

To liberal editorial writers who found Keynesian logic compelling, the British plan had more appeal than the American draft. The *New Republic* and the *Nation* both applauded Keynes for according full employment higher priority than stable exchange rates. *New Republic* writer George Soule dismissed White's proposal as "legalistic, pedestrian, and unimaginative." Even *Time* and *Fortune*, the principal vehicles for Henry Luce's viewpoint, said that the clearing union held more promise than the stabilization fund for coping with acute problems of stabilizing currencies, averting depressions, and promoting investments. Keynes, said *Time*, had merely extended "internationally the practice of domestic banking system as exemplified by the U.S. Federal Reserve System." And *Life* editorial writer Russell Davenport, another Luce employee, privately told skeptical Republican congressmen that the American plan—the creation of Morgenthau's "self-styled experts"—was hopeless, while the British plan was at least workable.[9]

If Keynesians preferred the British plan, traditionalists liked neither recommendation. Both enhanced the powers of government and circumscribed the operations of the marketplace. Both, asserted the *Commercial and Financial Chronicle*, are "utterly revolutionary"; they rest on the assumption that "government is possessed of wisdom not given to ordinary citizens." The *New York Times*, not yet sympathetic to Keynesian economics, criticized Keynes and White for assuming "the world can be saved only by increased governmental management of economic affairs, by increased government power." In place of comprehensive planning and more alphabetical administrative agencies, the *Times* offered an uncomplicated panacea—reviving the international gold standard and requiring governments to follow domestic policies likely to inspire business confidence and attract private investment. *Newsweek*, also hostile to extensive government involvement, identified Hansen as the link between Keynesian theories of deficit finance—essentially, "borrowing public funds to spend your way to prosperity"—and White's scheme to apply these theories globally. The Keynes program, it asserted, merely provided for an "expansion of the doctrinaire democracy" that Alvin Hansen conceived for the National Resources Planning Board, an agency then under fire from congressional conservatives.[10]

Bankers and orthodox economists had similar reactions. Criticisms from these sources reflected more than a doctrinaire commitment to laissez faire and hostility to the latest economic theories. They also marked a renewal of the friction that characterized relations between the New Deal and Wall Street during the 1930's. Bankers, many of whom were Republicans, had not forgotten that Roosevelt vigorously attacked the "malefactors of great wealth" and the "privileged princes" to consolidate his political majority and then employed his legislative majority to regulate and reform the financial community— separating commercial from investment banking, invalidating gold-payments clauses in private contracts, and devaluing the dollar. To some bankers the Keynes and White proposals confirmed dark suspicions that "radical" New Dealers were preparing another assault on the financial community, so that Roosevelt and his bureaucratic managers could distribute American resources throughout the world. Harry C. Carr, president of the First National Bank of Philadelphia, offered a typical comment: Both schemes seemed "to be based upon the same idealistic, but totally impractical collectivism that has characterized so much of the New Deal thinking of the last twelve years."

Others saw the proposals as a thinly veiled design to transfer monetary sovereignty to a new "super-government" that would then lend funds in competition with private sources. The Economic Policy Commission of the American Bankers Association concluded, after studying the recommendations, that "excessive government lending will drive out the private enterprise which is the best hope for continuing progress."[11]

What concerned the bankers as much as the prospect of government-subsidized competition in lending was the possibility that excessive lending would ignite inflationary forces, thus undermining domestic and international stability. The traditionalists, unlike the Keynesians who talked of stagnation and depression, worried about the corrosive effect of inflation. And, if the Keynesians worried about a repetition of the 1930's, the bankers foresaw a repeat of the post–World War I boom-and-bust scenario. Then an export boom, fostered by government lending, overstimulated the home economy, causing real-estate speculation, overextension of farm production, and industrial overexpansion. The cumulative process ended in a sharp depression that compelled borrowers to default and banks to close. From this perspective a prudent approach to economic internationalism required, not extensive government planning and countercyclical lending, but a greater respect for the recuperative powers of the market. If governments simply balanced domestic budgets, lowered tariffs, and maintained stable currency values, the world would recover from the distortions of World War II without bureaucratic management and supranational institutions.[12]

In approaching monetary reform the traditionalists offered two general prescriptions—a return to the gold standard or a key-currency approach to monetary stabilization. The first appealed to proverbial "gold bugs" like Benjamin Anderson, a onetime Chase National Bank official, who thought a return to an automatically adjusting gold standard should proceed as it had after World War I with stabilization loans and restrictive domestic policies. However sound this advice was, it seemed more nostalgic than practical to government decision makers. The impetus of international monetary efforts in the 1930's had been to manage gold, not to accord it greater autonomy. More important, an automatic gold standard raised the bogey of depression and unemployment to citizens in the United Kingdom who thought this approach had an inherent deflationary bias.[13]

Consultation and Consensus

John H. Williams, an economist who served simultaneously as vice-president of the New York Federal Reserve Bank and as dean of the Harvard Graduate School of Public Administration, offered a more practical alternative—the key-currency approach. Basically, this was the position of experienced currency experts who wanted to build on the foundation of great-power cooperation achieved in the Tripartite Agreement in order to stabilize the currencies of major countries. While Keynes and White tacitly rejected a great-power initiative when they proposed a general stabilization of all currencies, Williams considered universal solutions too ambitious for postwar conditions. Unlike the official suggestions, the key-currency solution could proceed in piecemeal fashion without creation of an international board. While Williams did not endorse a formal mechanism, such as a fund or clearing union, he favored extensive informal collaboration among governments to synchronize domestic policies in key-currency countries, especially the United Kingdom and the United States.[14]

Williams did not consider himself a Keynesian, but as an intelligent and practical economist he recognized that international monetary stability depended fundamentally on the internal stability of the world's most powerful nations. As he said, "From this experience of the interwar period I come back always to the conclusion that the problem of international monetary stability is primarily that of maintaining a state of proper economic health in the leading countries." Since the interwar experience also suggested that smaller countries primarily depended on the economic health of larger nations, Williams saw no harm in permitting these countries to vary their currencies. "It might help them somewhat, without too seriously affecting the larger countries." From this standpoint, then, the crucial aspect of postwar currency stabilization was the economic health of dominant nations. In its emphasis on great powers the Williams solution represented a fundamental alternative. While the Keynes and White schemes resembled the universalistic League of Nations route to collective security, the key-currency proposal represented the economic counterpart of Walter Lippmann's great-power approach to world political organization.[15]

Since the key-currency solution emanated from the New York Federal Reserve Bank hierarchy, it was probably doomed from inception—the administration was as suspicious of Wall Street as the banking community was of Washington. Nevertheless, Williams and the

Federal Reserve Bank vainly urged the Board of Governors to sponsor the proposal in a bureaucratic battle with the Treasury for President Roosevelt's ear. They argued, in part, that adoption of either the Keynes or the White solution would simply encourage other governments to postpone agreements on "more difficult and even more important international problems," namely, tariff reduction, protection of international investments, and commodity price regulation. Also, in an international agency with a majority of its members debtors, pressure might grow for less stringent restrictions on the use of quotas.[16]

For these and other reasons, the Federal Reserve Bank favored dividing the stabilization problem "down into its parts" and proceeding cautiously and selectively. As a beginning, Britain and the United States should coordinate domestic policies to assure stable prices, incomes, and employment, and after internal harmonization they could then establish a stable rate of exchange between the two currencies that financed most of world trade. At that point the informal Anglo-American monetary alliance could consider the currency problems of peripheral countries. They might offer rehabilitation and stabilization credits to countries agreeing to relax discriminatory trade and currency controls. In this fashion Britain and America could exercise leadership and influence to help the world through a troubled transition period into the sunlight of an open economic order with convertible currencies and nondiscriminatory trade barriers. And, with equilibrium restored, the dominant financial powers might sponsor some form of global stabilization fund to cope with periodic payments disequilibria. Despite the logic of Williams's appeal, his plan was incongruent with the general United Nations framework then being elaborated in Washington. The Federal Reserve Board of Governors, eager to guard its own prerogatives from the Treasury, displayed little interest in challenging Morgenthau with an option carrying the imprimatur of the experienced, but temporarily discredited, banking community.[17]

Broadly stated, the American debate over global financial cooperation focused on two points: the philosophical issue of government planning versus a self-operating system, and the practical question of seeking economic interdependence through a universalistic or selective approach. Almost without exception the contestants rejected autarky and favored a multilateral system based on convertible currencies and a gold *numéraire*. There was surprisingly little discussion in academic or official circles of creating a new international currency, of utilizing floating exchange rates to restore equilibrium among major currencies, or of maintaining price stability in the world's dominant economy. Instead, a legacy of controls, fluctuating currencies, and unemployment disposed the Keynesians and the traditionalists to debate the most appropriate ways of avoiding a recurrence of interwar problems.

Meanwhile, American and foreign monetary specialists were holding bilateral consultations to exchange views on the monetary drafts, assess other aspects of postwar economic cooperation, and determine the implications of further progress. This necessary procedure, although tedious and repetitive, allowed twenty governments (the Soviet Union chose not to participate at this time) to take part in the monetary drafting at a stage when each could influence the eventual outcome. For the most part, foreign technicians also shared the underlying commitment to an open monetary system, and, as a result, most of the discussions concentrated on ways to reconcile the competing British and American drafts and on additional instruments to speed the reconstruction or development of smaller nations.[18]

Like Britain and the United States, Canada had talented technicians, and they resourcefully offered a compromise monetary program that Canada hoped would bridge the Anglo-American differences. Briefly, the Canadians assumed Washington would not accept Keynes's overdraft system, so they suggested the International Exchange Union, similar to the fund, with an $8 billion currency pool, which would afford deficit nations more "breathing space" to remove disequilibria. The representatives from Ottawa thought a larger pool and a provision allowing devaluations up to 5 percent, with the exchange union's approval, would provide added flexibility without jeopardizing the operations of a fixed-exchange rate system.[19]

What the Canadian technicians sought to avoid was either an economic collision between Britain and the United States or a great-power key-currency solution. Both of these would expose smaller countries to outside political pressures, said Louis Rasminsky, the managing director of Canada's foreign-exchange board, and leave the northern dominion in a difficult economic position between the sterling and dollar blocs. A general multilateral payments system was the only solution consistent with Canada's desire for political independence and economic prosperity.[20]

Australia, concerned that the White plan would prove inadequate to shelter smaller nations from another international depression, favored the clearing union. When Harry White explained that he could not join proposals for currency stabilization and full employment because of probable political repercussions, Australian negotiators James Brigden and H. C. Coombs responded, ". . . we, like you, have our political problems, and above all, we have problems peculiar to an independent economy."[21]

In talks with representatives of the British Empire, the American experts shared a common bond. All understood traditional international trade doctrines, approved in principle the goal of multilateral world economy, and recognized the importance of international cooperation on currencies, trade, and investments. Their disagreements were not doctrinal disputes but differences growing out of the dissimilar economic and political circumstances facing their homelands.

But experts from continental European countries, which suffered extensive war damage, displayed some sympathy for bilateral controls and regional arrangements as intermediate steps to full and general convertibility. In fact, Belgium and Luxembourg approved a bilateral clearing agreement in September 1943. France also favored this procedure. "It appears inevitable," wrote Hervé Alphand of the French National Committee to Harry Dexter White, "that certain measures for control of production, international trade, and rates of exchange should follow for a short time at least until after the cessation of hostilities in Continental Europe."[22]

To representatives of Gen. Chiang Kai-shek's beleaguered government the economic merits of the currency proposals were less important than the political implications. After a lengthy debate the Chinese decided to support the American position, principally because the United States had resources to rehabilitate her oriental ally while Britain was, Chiang's advisers thought, a potential competitor. The Chinese Nationalists, conscious of long-term economic needs, told Washington they wanted more than a stabilization fund. They also favored an international agency that could supply reconstruction assistance and long-term development capital.[23]

Similarly, Latin Americans were less interested in currency stability than in outside development assistance, as well as commodity stabilization. Chilean and Mexican technicians criticized Keynes and White for assuming that currency stabilization was a precondition for commodity price stabilization, export expansion, and domestic stability, rather than the reverse. Exchange stability, said several, hinged on the ability of Latin American nations to expand, or maintain, their export earnings. Because primary-product exporting nations were subject to market fluctuations beyond their control, Hermann Max, a German-born economist with the Bank of Chile, asserted that these nations could not participate for long in either scheme without parallel programs to stabilize commodity prices and increase exports. Víctor L. Urquidi, a prominent Mexican economist, concurred. From his perspective even the broad-gauged clearing union was inadequate for coping with the variety of economic problems facing the postwar world. Unless the great powers created other mechanisms to help revive capital movements and to assure expansionary domestic economies, Urquidi and Max anticipated that Latin American governments would need to rely on exchange controls, tariffs, and exchange-rate variations to insulate their home markets from destabilizing outside pressures.[24]

Another major Latin American power was, however, more critical of the Keynes proposal as an inflationary device for distributing purchasing power to the war-damaged European economies. Brazilians shrewdly perceived that bancor might, by increasing the demand for products in a supply-short world, erode the purchasing power of their accumulated dollar balances. But the White plan also seemed incompatible with Brazil's long-term interests. According to economist Octavio Gouvea de Bulhoes, it placed the burden of payments adjustment on deficit countries, not symmetrically on surplus and deficit countries. Like Keynes, the Brazilian expert favored a provision that would also penalize prosperous, surplus countries, perhaps in a way that would redistribute international reserves to the deficit countries for development and diversification projects.[25]

The technical talks, lasting through the spring and summer of 1943, did not bring an agreed statement, nor was that intended. But they did permit necessary debate and, perhaps most important, reminded the American experts that the smaller countries saw currency stabilization as but one portion of the international economic mosaic. Without parallel institutions to assist in development and reconstruction, it seemed doubtful that primary-producing countries could participate effectively in arrangements to stabilize currencies and remove artificial exchange barriers. As Adolf Berle noted, "Practically every Government in talking to us had indicated that their attitude toward monetary stabilization was contingent in some degree on the long-term credit situation." Unless Washington sponsored other programs to stimulate long-term capital transfers, the uncertainties of an unstructured open world economy might induce smaller countries to shun interdependence for autarky.[26]

While Harry White and members of the technical committee examined the problems of currency stabilization with foreign representatives, American specialists refined the Treasury proposal. Based on the comments of outside evaluators and the criticisms of those within the administration—particularly the Federal Reserve Board—the burning issue was how the United States could contribute to global economic equilibrium without adopting a plan that would accentuate domestic inflationary pressures in the postwar period.[27]

For Federal Reserve economists E. A. Goldenweiser and Walter Gardner the critical problem was how to satisfy the world's need for American dollars without dangerously expanding U.S. domestic money supply and reserve holdings. Both the clearing union and the stabilization fund, they said, dealt inadequately with two aspects of this problem—the desirable quantity and distribution of international reserves and the future of gold in the new monetary system. In proposing to create $30 billion of international money to supplement approximately $11 billion of monetary gold, which was distributed unevenly among nations, there was a real danger that all $41 billion of international purchasing power might flow into the United States, increasing banking reserves and fueling an inflationary postwar boom. In a second "golden avalanche," the United States might obtain all of the world's monetary gold. Then, the Federal Reserve economists argued, other nations, having depleted their reserves, might demonetize the auric metal as a medium of international payments, leaving the United States with billions of dollars in gold. If, on the one hand, Keynes's proposal seemed certain to multiply "foreign drafts upon American productive power," White's remedy, on the other hand, appeared insufficient. It would, they argued, create only $2.5 billion of additional liquidity—an inadequate supplement to foreign gold holdings—and thus encourage many nations to retain "direct controls that handicap international trade and investment."[28]

As a solution to this dilemma, the Federal Reserve specialists offered a proposal that would increase international reserves without at the same time endangering domestic stability in the principal industrial countries. Briefly, they urged a $15 billion pool of currencies—substantially larger than White's $5 billion fund—to which both Britain and the United States would subscribe $2 billion. To prevent demand from concentrating on a single currency, like the dollar, this plan would automatically increase the voting strength of a surplus country in the fund's management whenever other countries drew the strong currency. Conversely, a deficit nation would lose votes in the global currency agency. And, to restore international equilibrium, the fund might require deficit members to undertake currency devaluation or to control capital movements. In the interests of global balance, the agency might recommend, but not require, that deficit and surplus countries modify their internal policies.[29]

Fearful that gold movements might again disrupt monetary relations, the Federal Reserve experts recommended a set of controls. Fund members would agree to purchase (sell) gold only from (to) the fund. The international body would purchase all the gold offered, but no member would have to buy gold in excess of its quota. Unlike the initial Treasury plan, this suggestion seemed certain to protect the United States from large, unwanted gold imports while it assured members a larger pool of currencies with which to cushion their payments adjustments. Unless members voted at some future time to increase quotas or to amend the articles of agreement so as to provide for a new reserve unit, the Federal Reserve suggestion linked the expansion of international liquidity to gold production. At that time production of monetary gold was expected to rise about $1 billion annually, enough to satisfy needs. Retrospectively, while this recommendation may have understated postwar requirements for additional reserves, it did at least check disruptive gold movements.[30]

For the most part the differences among the proposals were discussed in private drafting sessions, but the issue burst out in a bitter exchange between White and the Federal Reserve experts during a three-day conference with specialists from nineteen countries, held in June 1943. On that occasion the Federal Reserve, much to the displeasure of White, presented its proposal to regulate gold. Foreign specialists were critical. For them, said Goldenweiser, "Gold is still a great deal of fetish. . . . what they want to do is to contribute as little as possible of real value, which to them means gold, and get as large a drawing power as we are willing to stand for." When Alvin Hansen openly questioned the wisdom of an American commitment to accept all gold mined in the world, White lost his patience. Such theoretical ideas sound good at an economic convention, he retorted, but that group does not determine government policy. To allay fears that Washington might do as Hansen proposed—restrict its gold purchases —White vigorously reaffirmed the Treasury's longstanding promise to buy and sell gold at $35 per ounce. From White's standpoint this commitment to interconvertibility was imperative if others were to have confidence in the postwar system. Frustrated and unimpressed with this argument, Goldenweiser commented in his notebook, "White does not seem to realize that the Treasury of the United States will not necessarily always mean Morgenthau and Harry White and . . . their successors may take a different line." Later events proved Goldenweiser right, but for different reasons. To stem a gold drain, not a gold influx, Secretary John Connally and expert Paul Volcker opted to suspend the gold convertibility pledge in August 1971.[31]

Based on the comments elicited in this series of consultations, White and his interdepartmental technical committee revised the stabilization fund, introducing several modifications to meet some of the criticisms. Revisions called for increasing aggregate quotas from $5 billion to $8 billion and for requiring that members contribute 50 percent of their quotas in gold. Moreover, in order to ease the difficult task of selecting appropriate exchange rates, members would be permitted to alter their exchange parities as much as 10 percent during the first three years of the fund's operation without the approval of other members. Finally, to satisfy those who feared the fund would be dominated by the United States, the new draft proposed to reduce American voting strength, although this country would retain sufficient influence to block any alteration in the gold value of unitas.[32]

These major changes did not satisfy everyone. The gold provisions continued to disturb both Federal Reserve and British specialists— but for different reasons. Federal Reserve experts wanted the larger gold contributions, but they complained that quantities of foreign gold could still flow into the United States, complicating the task of domestic monetary management. British experts, however, saw larger gold quotas as a concession to the New York banking community, and they suspected that the fund would emerge as little more than a varnished version of the gold-standard adjustment system. One British financial writer told Ernest Penrose, the embassy economist in London, that "the revised White Plan went so far to meet the views of bankers that it would be better to have no plan than anything like it."[33]

Previously the Treasury had avoided public relations to create elite support for its proposals. Although in White's opinion many press accounts ranged from "facetious to outright hostility," he considered it senseless to explain and defend a draft that "we ourselves would want to back away from." But, now, with preliminary technical soundings complete, White and his aides made several efforts to assure the banking community, in particular, that the stabilization plans would not interfere with private financing of trade or with foreign-exchange transactions. On the contrary, the fund would aid private bankers, because countries with temporarily adverse payments could draw on the fund without having to devalue or employ exchange controls—steps that would reduce the volume of world trade. More concrete and cogent defenses of the Treasury handiwork, however, had to await the conclusion of bilateral negotiations with Britain, and perhaps the Soviet Union.[34]

The long-postponed Anglo-American monetary negotiations began in September 1943, after the specialists had reached an informal understanding on a currency compromise. That agreement, based on an exchange of letters between Harry White and Lord Keynes, established the framework for direct bargaining on aspects of the monetary settlement.

Anticipating these crucial deliberations, White had informed his British counterpart in June that the United States must attach four preconditions to its participation in a currency organization. First, the United Kingdom must agree not to alter its exchange rate prior to the beginning of fund operations. Second, the currency agency must function on a contributory, not an overdraft, principle as was envisaged in White's proposal, but not in Keynes's plan. Next, the total American financial commitment must not exceed $2 or $3 billion. And, finally, the United States must retain a veto over any change in the gold value of the new currency unit. These provisions, White asserted, were the minimum consistent with his country's national interests and acceptable to Congress.[35]

Keynes, naturally enough, would have preferred that the Americans adopt his clearing union as the basis for negotiations, but he prudently abandoned the struggle and accepted the substance of White's principles on August 10 for they were, after all, compatible with Britain's long-term interest in a multilateral world economy. Keynes also stipulated Britain's minimum terms for adhering to the fund. Briefly, the fund "must not buy or sell currencies, but only transfer unitas in its books," a condition apparently intended to assure that the global agency would not intervene actively in national exchange markets. Total quotas, he added, should approximate $10 billion—and of these "initial subscriptions must include a small proportion of gold" and the remainder in negotiable securities. Finally, in what was a clear indication that Britain intended to retain sovereignty over its exchange rate, Keynes stipulated that fund members "must not be deprived of reasonable facility to alter their exchange rates if they thought this necessary."[36]

The importance of this exchange cannot be overestimated. In effect, Britain agreed to abandon the clearing union so that the two countries could move forward together in quest of a more structured international monetary order. The compromise brought an important change in the mood and tone of bilateral discussions. As Keynes's associate Lionel Robbins later recalled, "Once we had recognized the political unacceptability of the unlimited liability of the creditor, the rest was a compromise between essentially friendly negotiators."[37]

Underlying political factors contributed to this compromise, for by the summer of 1943 both London and Washington were eager to conclude postwar monetary arrangements. On the American side, for instance, officials thought increasingly of the need to conclude technical talks, summon an international conference, and obtain congressional approval before the 1944 presidential election introduced unpredictable political controversy. Likewise, Churchill's government, long anxious to reach a comprehensive understanding on monetary and transitional issues, welcomed this opportunity for accelerating the pace. Along Whitehall there was growing concern that delays would only endanger the prospects for a comprehensive accord and doom the chance for erecting a liberal economic order. On both sides of the Atlantic, officials noted with alarm that exile governments, chaffing at great-power inaction, had begun to draw up their own postwar currency plans—bilateral currency arrangements, such as the Belgium-Luxembourg-Netherlands accord announced in September 1943.[38]

For more than three weeks in late September and October the spotlight centered on the direct negotiations between John Maynard Keynes and Harry Dexter White, two vain and intelligent monetary specialists, and their subordinates. The two principals made a startling contrast. Keynes, the cerebral representative of the British treasury, possessed all of the charm, self-assurance, and even vaingloriousness of England's aristocracy. But in Washington he encountered his American antithesis, Harry Dexter White, a pragmatic and abrasive bureaucrat with seemingly inexhaustible energy and persistence. Socially and psychologically the two had little in common except their outlook on economic issues and their deep dedication to monetary internationalism. These intellectual bonds were not enough to prevent occasional personal references from disturbing the serious deliberations. In one exchange White impulsively addressed the titled Keynes as "your Royal Highness," and then watched with glee the Englishman's ill-disguised irritation. On other occasions, rude remarks brought temper tantrums, and either Keynes or White stalked from the room, leaving subordinates to soothe the ruffled egos and redirect discussions.[39]

Even with stormy interludes, a "vital elixir" of professional respect transcended the discussions and promoted technical solutions to technical problems. More than anything, this understanding emerged because the two men, despite personal differences, could respect the technical competence of both delegations. Accordingly, each side could occasionally step away from national prejudices and positions in order to approach problems with academic detachment. Here Keynes excelled. Several times he disturbed officials in London when he departed from instructions, usually because he considered the British position inferior or inadequate on some technical issue. Out of the Anglo-American economic seminar emerged a clearer understanding of what was feasible given each country's national interests and political constituencies.[40]

Both sides recognized that the currency agency must concentrate on maintaining stable, convertible currencies and not serve as a vehicle for reconstruction assistance. Other problems would require other institutions. The American officials now frankly saw the fund as "only one of the instrumentalities which may be needed in the field of international economic cooperation." They favored other mechanisms to provide long-term reconstruction and development loans, to provide relief and rehabilitation assistance, and to support commodity prices. Likewise, Keynes and his aides accepted the premise that economic internationalism must occur on a functional, piecemeal basis, so that no single agency was burdened with multiple, perhaps conflicting, responsibilities. Accordingly, they decided not to burden the fund with blocked sterling balances; instead Britain would negotiate a separate settlement with creditors.[41]

The talks concluded with a "draft directive or statement of general principles," designed to guide British and American officials in subsequent drafting sessions. Among the understandings, the two countries agreed that total fund quotas would not exceed $10 billion, with Washington contributing $3 billion and London about $1.3 billion. Also, any member might impose exchange restrictions on transactions in a currency declared scarce, and it might withdraw without penalty. Briefly, the fund would be enlarged and modified to protect an individual member's sovereignty against outside influences.[42]

Most important, the Washington discussions confirmed the technical understanding between White and Keynes—namely, the future currency organization would resemble the stabilization fund with its limited command on each member's resources and not Keynes's clearing union with its unlimited liability. Agreement on this basic issue shifted the monetary talks to technical items, including the fund's authority and the rights and obligations of individual members. Among the most important questions still unresolved were whether to have stable or adjustable exchange rates, an international currency, and limited or unrestricted access to the fund's pool of currencies and gold. Considerations of these complex topics continued from the autumn of 1943 to the spring of 1944 before the two countries reached a tentative compromise.

On the critical adjustment issue Keynes became insistent that, if the fund was not to have a closed system of liquidity, it should at least tolerate occasional exchange-rate variations. Otherwise a deficit country might have no choice but to remove an imbalance by internal price and income adjustments or by violation of its commitments to exchange-rate stability. Realizing that the British public felt strongly that their country should never again deflate the home economy to restore balance-of-payments equilibrium, the Cambridge economist suggested a procedure for orderly exchange-rate variations. The articles of agreement, he argued, should allow members to alter their parities freely, provided total adjustments did not exceed 10 percent in each ten-year period. White responded that, although provision for a single 10 percent change would make the agreement more elastic and durable, Congress would never accept a formula for renewable exchange-rate adjustments. When White refused to yield, fearful that more concessions would jeopardize approval of the fund and only convince skeptics that the fund was an ineffective instrument for securing orderly exchange rates, Keynes chose to drop the issue, at least temporarily.[43]

Keynes had abandoned bancor and the clearing union, but he still hoped to reshape the stabilization fund in its image. Unitas, the Englishman argued, should not be merely a standard of account; it should also be an international medium of exchange subject to international control. The Americans suspected that his principal motive for monetizing unitas was to provide Britain, and other nations, additional resources for the purchase of American goods. As much as the Americans wanted to relieve Britain's transitional difficulties, they recognized that this formula was potentially inflationary and vulnerable to congressional criticism as a type of concealed lend-lease.

Eventually, after further consideration, London agreed to remove all references to unitas—either as an international medium of exchange or unit of account. The British reluctantly abandoned this item only after reminding the American financial negotiators that the United Kingdom could not join the fund until "it saw how the difficulties of the transitional period were to be met." In essence, Keynes and his colleagues were saying that, if Britain was to become a partner in the stabilization enterprise, the United States must provide transitional payments assistance through the fund mechanism or from separate bilateral agreements.[44]

Would a member have an automatic right to borrow from the fund, or would it borrow at the fund's discretion? Throughout the bilateral negotiations this issue troubled the experts, and it was not ultimately settled until after the fund began operations in 1947. Throughout the postwar planning exercise, Keynes argued consistently that members had a right to draw stipulated sums from the world agency. He included this principle in his clearing union, and late in 1943 he insisted that members must have a similar automatic access to their fund quotas if the pool was to enjoy general confidence. After Keynes and White agreed to a $10 billion pool, which was substantially smaller than the original clearing union, the British became even more insistent that the fund not act "too grandmotherly" in scrutinizing each transaction. Obviously, the British wanted to hold open the possibility of employing their drawing rights for acute transitional needs. Debate continued on this point, but finally the British experts accepted the argument that, at least in the transition period, drawings must be restricted. Otherwise, the fund might become "waterlogged . . . by having to meet abnormal short-term needs with resources which would be inadequate."[45]

The British visit in September 1943 also provided the first opportunity for a thorough bilateral discussion of a mechanism parallel to the fund to revive international capital movements. This item, though an integral part of White's early preparations, was pigeonholed while technicians concentrated on currency stabilization. But the international monetary experts knew that currencies and investments were halves of the same walnut, and, in the months after talks with smaller countries, White and his aides reconsidered the international bank.

The basic rationale for an international investment institution appeared in a version of the bank proposal completed in September 1943. Outside capital—either government or private—was essential to help war-devastated countries rehabilitate and attain a constantly improved standard of living. "Without adequate supplies of capital available recovery in Europe and Asia will be slow and sporadic; civil discontent and international bitterness would in time assume disturbing proportions." Not only was outside capital essential for rehabilitation, but it was also considered vital to future political stability and friendly international collaboration. It is, the draft said, "a decisive factor in preventing civil wars, unending heavy expenditures on armaments, and subsequent clash of foreign policies." The Treasury asserted that "to spend hundreds of billions of dollars to conduct war, and then balk at investing a few billions to help assure prosperity and rising standards of living would be a strange manifestation of wise policy." Moreover, an international bank was defensible in economic terms both for the United States and for the international community as a whole. "Foreign trade everywhere would be increased; the real cost of producing the goods the world consumes would be lowered, and the standard of living of peoples everywhere would be raised."[46]

Advocates of an international investment program were not worried about finding profitable outlets for private investment. Instead, the government specialists doubted that private sources would invest sufficient long-term capital to meet global needs. Thinking that the pre–World War II investment losses would discourage future private ventures—especially, portfolio financing—the experts anticipated that governments might have to supply the bulk of the capital needed for reconstruction and development purposes. The situation was so serious and vital to postwar stability that Harry White and Adolf Berle flirted with the idea of negotiating an international agreement to create a consortium of government lending agencies. This consortium would not require congressional approval and thus could be formed even if the legislative branch seemed unreceptive to a permanent international bank.[47]

Initially, however, the experts were determined to formulate a proposal that Congress would approve. It must conform to four general principles, the U.S. specialists decided. First, a bank must represent genuine international cooperation and provide for shared responsibilities. Second, other members must subscribe more than a nominal amount of capital. Third, as with the fund, voting power in the bank should be proportional to a member's financial contribution. Finally, the new bank should supplement, but not replace, private financial institutions. To overcome expected political resistance at home, the specialists recommended that the bank not compete with private investments at reasonable rates of interest but, instead, stimulate the overseas flow of private capital through investment guarantees and risk sharing.[48]

The Treasury bank proposal, discussed with the British, scarcely resembled the bold and imaginative bank for reconstruction and development that White envisaged in the spring of 1942. Conscious now of the widespread concern that foreign demand might exceed American resources and of Congress's sensitivity to proposals that appeared to sacrifice sovereignty over monetary matters, White deleted reference to the bank issuing its own notes. In addition, the technicians sheared sentences about the bank financing an international commodity corporation or providing short-term credit for financing trade. These last alterations came after Will Clayton, a powerful official in the Reconstruction Finance Corporation and a prominent Texas cotton factor, asserted that the items were not politically feasible.[49]

Unlike the Americans, Keynes and his advisers had not devoted much attention to international investments, and at first he manifested little interest in the topic. His principal concern, naturally enough, was how Britain would overcome her transitional economic problems, not how she would finance global investments. As an economist Keynes was doubtful, too, that capital-exporting nations ever recovered savings invested abroad without extending new loans to facilitate the transfer, and thus he approached the topic with a professional pessimism.[50]

Commenting on the American draft, Keynes criticized it as too restrictive and unimaginative. It restricted the recipient's use of borrowed funds and obliged the bank to extend only loans with prospects for repayment. As a consequence of these stringent requirements, Keynes thought the bank "would not make many loans." Furthermore, he questioned the old criterion, incorporated in the draft, that each loan must generate foreign exchange for its own amortization. Development loans, he said, should not depend on the borrower's capacity to service the debt from an export surplus. In addition, he recommended that a bank have authority to invest in equities as well as fixed payment bonds.[51]

White, at least for argument's sake, could not agree. If a bank followed Keynes's generous lending policies, he said, creditors would gain—aside from cheaper imports that grow out of improved production abroad—only the "satisfaction that accompanies what we call WPA expenditures." For political reasons, if not for economic reasons, the bank must provide practical benefits to the recipients and to American business. The bank's loans, he repeated, must "represent the safest kind of investment and . . . help our exporters and importers." Anything less, White insisted, would jeopardize congressional approval.[52]

Throughout the preliminary staff work Morgenthau and his aides were anxious to avoid the impression of an Anglo-American special relationship—precisely what the British sought to achieve. The monetary planners recognized that smaller countries in the Commonwealth and Latin America had a legitimate interest in consultations, but they sought to include the Soviet Union in the preparations with all of the respect accorded a great power and an ally in the war against Germany. In part, this concern for Russia was a conscious effort to avoid another mistake in World War I planning, but, as Morgenthau and his aides soon discovered, Washington was more interested in the Soviet Union than the Soviet Union was in monetary planning. On several occasions the secretary invited Moscow to send technical experts and to offer their suggestions, but none arrived in 1943. Only after Secretary of State Cordell Hull personally requested Soviet participation during the Moscow foreign ministers' meeting in October 1943, did the Soviets show interest.[53]

During this period Washington had little indication, even from articles in the Soviet press, what Stalin's aides might desire or accept. Not until December 1943, when the American embassy sent an article on postwar monetary cooperation written by Eugene Varga— a Russian economist nearly as important in his country as Keynes was in Britain—did the Treasury have concrete clues. The Soviet Union, Varga asserted, had no particular interest in currency stabilization because its systems of state controls guaranteed exchange-rate stability. He acknowledged that the Soviets would benefit from a system in which trade could be conducted on the basis of "gold currency of fixed value" and hinted that his government might approach negotiations with other objectives in mind. Moscow, he said, was interested in "undertakings and measures capable of hastening rehabilitation of the Soviet economy."[54]

White and the technicians learned more precisely what the Russians wanted when economists arrived in January 1944. They desired a role for gold that would provide an assured market for Soviet gold production and outside help with reconstructing the Soviet economy. After examining the stabilization fund draft, the Soviets suggested a few modifications that would further benefit their homeland. Occupied countries should contribute less gold to the fund. Moreover, newly mined gold should be excluded from computations of a member's gold reserve, and the ruble exchange rate should be exempted from fund regulations because this rate bore no relation to Soviet competitiveness.[55]

Long hopeful that economics would bind the Soviet Union to the West and a peaceful world community, White thought none of these points—except possibly newly mined gold—were insuperable, and after the first sessions he voiced cautious optimism that Russia would participate in a conference and eventually join the world agencies.

Recognizing that Russia, with its state-controlled foreign trade, needed the fund less than the fund, for political reasons, needed Russia, White hoped that a generous reconstruction loan would induce Moscow to cooperate in this and other postwar enterprises. His proposal for a $5 billion credit was based on repayment over thirty years from the sales of raw materials. This suggestion, which was consistent with White's longstanding desire to involve Russia in postwar planning, offered the Russians hard currency for purchases of capital equipment needed to accelerate postwar rehabilitation and industrialization. The United States would benefit from imports of raw materials, but, as White stressed, the principal objective was to "provide a sound basis for continued collaboration between the two governments in the postwar period."[56]

As a result of extended consultations between governmental specialists, members of the United Nations had moved toward a new consensus on monetary cooperation. Once formal arrangements had been negotiated in a plenary conference and subjected to the ratification procedures of nation participants, there would be, at the least, an international stabilization fund with about $10 billion in gold and national currencies to cushion adjustments in a fixed-exchange rate system. Gold, convertible in dollars at an established price, would provide the benchmark of the new system, but major currencies would also provide some of the reserves. In addition, the fund would be the centerpiece of a set of rules and obligations that governed exchange-rate adjustments and the use of exchange restrictions. Still under discussion were such important questions as whether a member would retain the right, and under what conditions, to adjust its parity; how the fund would function both in terms of national representation and in terms of providing assistance to members; and whether the fund would begin operations soon after its creation or only after the world recovered from wartime disruption.

Furthermore, technicians were in general accord that this currency-stabilization organization could not function successfully without parallel international agencies—especially a bank for reconstruction and development. In this area, although the U.S. Treasury had a proposal, there had been only limited preparation. But, in view of political circumstances in the United States, the only major country that could invest abroad extensively in the postwar years, it was certain that the bank would not create its own international purchasing power but rather work hand in glove with existing financial institutions. Even so, the private financial community was at first suspicious and skeptical. The bankers were less certain than the youthful Keynesian economists that the private sector could not meet postwar needs, and they viewed with concern the creation of an international agency that might pursue political dictates rather than marketplace logic.

Technical problems remained after the specialist talks, but these were not insurmountable. The chief obstacles were political, because top political leaders soon had to formally ratify the experts' decisions.

5

Prelude to Bretton Woods

The prospect that World War II might conclude before leaders of the victorious United Nations fashioned an institutional framework for a new world order troubled many Americans in 1944. If leaders of the coalition could not translate their mutual ideals into concrete mechanisms for permanent cooperation at the apogee of wartime collaboration, there were dangers that the postwar period would witness a resurgence of the nationalism that produced the century's greatest conflict.

Anxiety about postwar relationships was not unwarranted. Despite such general pledges as the Atlantic Charter, the United Nations Declaration, and the Moscow Declaration, the outlines of future world organization remained largely on the drafting boards of postwar planners. Both the Hot Springs Food and Agricultural Conference and the United Nations Relief and Rehabilitation Administration (UNRRA) foreshadowed lines of collaboration on specific issues, but neither dealt with the basic long-term problems of global political and economic organization. Against this background of deliberate postponement, some officials foresaw grave difficulties if the European war concluded before the autumn presidential elections.[1]

Ambassador John G. Winant reported from his London listening post that these, and other, considerations were jeopardizing the chances for permanent Anglo-American economic cooperation. British Cabinet officials, increasingly divided on postwar issues and exhausted physically and emotionally from the long conflict, anticipated, somewhat fatalistically, a revival of American isolationism. Republican conservatives, they thought, would win the November elections, reject international commitments, and oppose macroeconomic measures to assure full employment. In this climate of opinion more and more labor and business leaders were pressuring the British government to postpone international economic commitments. According to Winant, Lord Keynes also observed this trend and as a result desired to expedite, not postpone, the negotiations.[2]

If Britain seemed less disposed to seek a multilateral solution for its economic problems, American sentiment ran more strongly than ever in support of collective action. Polls showed overwhelming public backing for an international peacekeeping system. This ground swell apparently emboldened congressional advocates of parallel economic obligations, and, on March 7, three Democratic senators—Elbert Thomas of Utah, Harley Kilgore of West Virginia, and Harry Truman of Missouri—introduced a resolution requesting President Roosevelt to summon a United Nations international economic conference. Observing that, in passing the Fulbright and Connally resolutions, Congress had already expressed support for a global security organization, the three senators now urged the legislative branch to make a similar commitment to economic internationalism. "The United States cannot . . . shirk leadership in postwar economic collaboration. . . . Our own industrial accomplishments have nominated us," they said, "as the nation that must assume a position to guide others in the pathway of peaceful production. And our national needs and economic welfare dictate that we apply ourselves to this work at once."[3]

While loyal Democrats clambered aboard the internationalist bandwagon, Republicans increasingly tended to draw a fine distinction between postwar political collaboration and Roosevelt's monetary plans. The former enjoyed too much support for effective opposition; the latter did not. In the Senate, for instance, Robert Taft quickened his attack on "international financial panaceas" designed to place "American dollars into foreign hands." And, in the other assembly, Illinois Representative Charles S. Dewey, eager to force debate on a Republican alternative to Treasury schemes, pressed for hearings on his plan for the Central Reconstruction Fund.[4]

Essentially this proposal, once labeled the Bank for International Cooperation, called for appropriating $500 million for use in joint account with foreign governments to promote reconstruction, re-habilitation, and currency stabilization. This plan had several advantages, Dewey said. First, it did not establish a permanent world agency, and, second, it kept management in American hands. Dewey also claimed that the Central Reconstruction Fund would achieve the same objectives as Morgenthau's fund and bank. Moreover, when its resources became depleted, Dewey expected that private international bankers would provide supplementary assistance, as they had after World War I. Briefly, Dewey's proposal would provide outside assistance for internal stabilization without extending government involvement over international finance. Dewey, a former assistant secretary of the treasury under Andrew Mellon, knew that this idea was acceptable to his friends in the New York financial community.[5]

Dewey conceded that political considerations influenced his action. Like administration officials, he feared that the war might end before the United States and its allies had completed preparations for the postwar period. Optimistic that Republicans would sweep the autumn elections and that a more conservative Congress would block the "almost visionary" schemes devised in Roosevelt's Treasury and in Britain, Dewey resolved to gain support for a "palatable" substitute before the war concluded.[6]

Prospects for an early victory in Europe, signs of apathy in Britain, and a desire to complete arrangements before the autumn political contests all spurred the United States' monetary planners in early 1944. Further postponement, they recognized, might jeopardize all prospects for a decent and durable postwar world. As Emilio Collado informed Secretary Hull, unless the government acted promptly, introducing its program and emphasizing publicly the mutual dependence of economic and political programs, the initiative might pass "from the administration to Mr. Dewey."[7]

The prospect of Dewey—a distant cousin of Republican presidential candidate Thomas E. Dewey—gaining the upper hand did more to energize the partisan Morgenthau than information that the two proposals were actually contradictory, not complementary. White and other aides, alarmed by the narrow objectives of Dewey's proposal, patiently explained to Morgenthau that Dewey favored national action while the Treasury envisaged permanent international cooperation. Morgenthau, who never really understood the details of Dewey's monetary proposals, preferred to think of the plan as the administration program with a Republican label, and the secretary resolved to keep the "Republicans from stealing the show." Thus, as he admitted several weeks later, ". . . from all standpoints, we felt it was good for the world, good for the nation, and good for the Democratic Party, for us to move."[8]

Persuaded by his aides that the international negotiations must conclude before the Republican Convention, Morgenthau asked the president, on April 3, to approve an accelerated timetable. First, the great powers—the United States, Britain, and the Soviet Union—would issue a joint statement, as they had done on other postwar topics. This declaration would represent the views of technical experts, not necessarily their governments. Then, Morgenthau would issue invitations to a formal monetary conference and appear before the appropriate congressional committees to explain Roosevelt's program. The president approved.[9]

Throughout the long monetary preparations, Harry White and his technicians took the initiative, generated proposals, and handled bilateral consultations; but now Morgenthau himself took an active part in completing the final arrangements. Eager to settle matters before the summer political conventions, Morgenthau zealously turned to the immediate task of obtaining British and Soviet support for the joint statement. When London failed to respond quickly to a cable proposing an immediate agreement, Morgenthau's aides suggested that Churchill's government was trying to obtain a better deal from the State Department, which had recently raised some technical questions about the bank. Morgenthau preferred to believe that international bankers were the villains. "It is the same group in London that it is here, that is fighting this thing. It is a question of whether the Government should control these things or a special country club of business and the Federal Reserve."[10]

Exasperated with the delay, which prevented the administration from counteracting Dewey's bill, Morgenthau finally decided to inform London that he was going to present the American program to Congress whether Britain agreed or not. Two days later, on April 15, Redvers Opie, financial advisor to the British Embassy in Washington, told White that his government simply wanted a technical clarification to avoid future misunderstandings. Basically, London thought the fund, designed for stabilization under more normal conditions, could not function satisfactorily unless there were a companion organization for long-term investments and some provision for making short-term reconstruction loans to war-damaged countries. Also, London recognized that after the war the fund would begin its operations gradually, supervising exchange-rate adjustments and offering consultative assistance before allowing members to draw on their quotas. Finally, Britain warned the Treasury that, unless Washington devised an arrangement for easing Britain's balance-of-payments adjustments during the postwar transitional period, the United Kingdom would be unable to accept the obligations of fund membership.[11]

This statement indicated to Morgenthau that the two English-speaking powers were near agreement—though they had not drafted an acceptable public statement. Now Morgenthau boldly cabled Moscow, informing the Russians that the British had agreed to a joint statement. Stalin's government had not replied when Morgenthau left for Congress on Friday, April 21, to inform legislators that technical experts had composed a set of principles for an international monetary fund. The Soviet response arrived in the middle of Morgenthau's testimony. Foreign minister V. M. Molotov said Moscow would support the Treasury project, even though Russian technical experts had serious objections, "if it is necessary to the Government of the United States of America to have the voice of the U.S.S.R. to secure due effect in the external world." The Soviet position revealed little enthusiasm for monetary cooperation, but the undaunted Morgenthau later boasted to President Roosevelt that it was highly significant the Russians wanted to "be associated with us in the eyes of the world."[12]

On April 21, a carefully phrased joint statement was released in Washington, London, and several other capitals. It was not a finished draft but a statement of principles, representing a consensus of experts from participating nations that the "most practical method of assuring international monetary co-operation is through the establishment of an International Monetary Fund." Briefly, the experts recommended a stabilization fund with about $8 billion in gold and local currencies—ultimately to reach $10 billion for the whole world. As a condition of membership each country would establish a par value for its national currency in terms of gold, but a country might alter its parity by 10 percent after consulting the fund, and by a larger amount if the fund gave prior approval. The plan included the so-called scarce-currency provision, and it permitted members to maintain restrictions on capital movements but not on payments for current international transactions. The statement also acknowledged that the forthcoming transition period would be one of "change and adjustment," and as a consequence members might temporarily maintain exchange restrictions employed during the war.[13]

As presented now, the fund was to be a permanent institution for monetary consultation whose resources would give confidence and time to members for the correction of payments maladjustments "without resorting to measures destructive of national or international prosperity." It would not function as a relief or capital-investment agency but only as an instrument for stabilizing currencies and promoting multilateral payments on current account transactions. These rules and procedures, experts thought, would avoid competitive depreciations or restrictive exchange regulations that hampered mutually beneficial international trade in the past.[14]

Because the joint statement conformed closely to the American position, London elected to record openly its own reservations. The document "in no way commits the Governments concerned." Moreover, a member "need not assume the full obligations of membership until satisfactory arrangements are at its disposal to facilitate the settlement of its balance of payments difficulties arising out of the war." Once again Churchill's government signaled Washington that British support for the new monetary order hinged on the availability of assistance to make sterling convertible. The British also announced, in what was evidently an attempt to assuage some internal criticism, that the rules would not "interfere with the traditional ties and other arrangements between the members of the sterling area and London."[15]

Unlike a foreign government, the Federal Reserve System could not afford the luxury of public dissent, even if phrased in diplomatic terms. Chairman Marriner Eccles complained privately that the Treasury draft still made no provision for preventing gold from entering the United States, nor did it provide the Federal Reserve with new tools to control or counteract a gold inflow. Though Eccles agreed not to express public criticism, he initially declined to endorse the joint statement. He relented, however, after aides warned that noncooperation would only serve to diminish the Federal Reserve Board's role in financial matters and strengthen the New York banking interests

who had "opposed every reform in banking and finance for a generation."[16]

Having triumphed in the first phase of his preconference diplomacy, Morgenthau now turned his attention to the monetary conclave. As Morgenthau told his aides—including Harry White, Edward
Bernstein, and counsel Ansel Luxford—he was anxious for Roosevelt's
sake that the conference succeed. The secretary could "always go
back and raise apples," but Roosevelt needed "a record of success for
his first conference. If it is a failure, it is a black mark against him."[17]

Assessing prospects, Harry White forecast that Britain and smaller
countries would approve the plans but that Russia might resist until
other participants exempted her newly mined gold from quota computations. Because such an exception must apply equally to other
gold-producing countries, thus increasing the amount of foreign
monetary gold available for purchases of American products, White
doubted that the issue was negotiable. If either Britain or Russia declined to participate, White opposed holding a conference. If the
Soviet Union alone declined, White favored postponing a plenary
session "not because they are important economically, but because
it starts off on the wrong foot. You already have an obstacle to begin
with, and this thing has got to click on all cylinders or it will sour."
The others—Luxford and Bernstein—agreed. It was better "not to
have a conference than to show up the United Nations as divided."[18]

For Morgenthau the forthcoming conference was not merely a test
of support for monetary cooperation but also a test of Soviet and
British willingness to collaborate with the United States in postwar
enterprises. Essentially, Moscow had to decide whether "to play ball
with the rest of the world on external matters, which she has never
done before." Similarly, Britain must choose whether to "play with
the United Nations, or . . . the Dominions." "Both of these countries
have to make up their minds, and . . . I am not going to take anything
less than a yes or no from them."[19]

But events demonstrated that neither the Soviet Union nor Great
Britain desired to make the monetary conference the irreversible
test of postwar relationships. On May 2 the Soviets agreed to send a
delegation, but, perhaps significantly, this representation would not
include the commissar of finance. After Morgenthau and Cordell Hull
warned the British that their failure to participate would jeopardize
other dimensions of postwar cooperation and have an "unfortunate

impact" on the international cooperation movement in the United States, London requested more time to consult her dominions and hold a parliamentary debate.[20]

A bitter debate in the House of Commons on May 10 revealed the reasons for Britain's vacillation. A strong undercurrent of anti-Americanism surfaced as critics, generally unfamiliar with the technical problems of monetary collaboration, assailed the published joint statement. Membership in the fund, they charged, would link sterling too closely to gold, place the burden of payments adjustment on debtor countries, and compel Britain to remove trade-and-payments restrictions designed to protect the sterling bloc and imperial preference. Some also claimed that the fund agreements inhibited Britain from utilizing trade and exchange controls to shelter the home market from a postwar American depression. Nevertheless, after the fury subsided, the House of Commons agreed without a division to support the government, and Sir John Anderson, the chancellor of the exchequer, promptly notified Morgenthau that Britain would attend. But, the chancellor added, his country was "not at this stage ready that our representatives should be authorized to commit the Government to acceptance of a scheme." Also, no British minister could attend the conclave; ostensibly the war situation required continuous work at home.[21]

Morgenthau, the buoyant optimist, gained less than he desired. Neither of the United States' major allies would give cabinet-level status to the monetary conference, and both asserted that participation in no way foreclosed their option to reject eventual membership in the global institutions.[22]

Assured that at least the conference would not collapse—though its results might not satisfy Britain, Russia, or Congress—the Treasury secretary turned his attention to other details, including choice of a convention site and selection of delegates. He approved a State Department recommendation that delegations meet in the luxurious Mount Washington Hotel, a resort located at Bretton Woods in New Hampshire's rugged White Mountains. This location was selected primarily because Lord Keynes, who had a heart condition, preferred a cool place, and because the government needed a large hotel in the East with adequate convention facilities. The Mount Washington satisfied both requirements.

Later the secretary laughed at reports he chose Bretton Woods so that a coterie of Jewish bankers—including himself—who allegedly owned the hotel could benefit from priorities on linen and plumbing. Walter Sullivan, an aide, jokingly told Morgenthau that when he was asked if the secretary owned a 25 percent interest in the hotel he had replied negatively. Morgenthau owned fifty percent, and he, Sullivan, held the other fifty!

President Roosevelt and Morgenthau, conscious that Woodrow Wilson had ignored Congress and damaged his prospects to win approval for the League of Nations, determined to select delegates who represented diverse executive, legislative, and public constituencies but who would still back the administration's proposals. Since it was billed as a financial conference, Morgenthau would lead the delegation. Roosevelt quipped: "Here's where you get a medal, Henry." The president selected Fred Vinson, from the Office of Economic Stabilization, to serve as Morgenthau's deputy. A former Kentucky congressman, Vinson had the confidence of powerful friends on Capitol Hill; his presence would allay suspicions and preserve a healthy liaison with legislators. Other delegates were chosen from executive agencies with foreign economic interests: Dean Acheson, State; Marriner Eccles, the Board of Governors; Leo T. Crowley, Foreign Economic Administration; and, naturally enough, Harry Dexter White. After further consultation Roosevelt appointed a woman, Mabel Newcomer, a Vassar economics professor; and a Chicago banker, Edward Eagle (Ned) Brown.[23]

In choosing Brown, a commercial banker who served as president of the Federal Reserve Board's advisory council, Roosevelt and Morgenthau deliberately circumvented the influential New York banking community. Although the State Department had recommended W. Randolph Burgess, an influential official in the American Bankers Association and president of the National City Bank, Morgenthau vetoed that suggestion on the grounds that a Wall Street representative might sabotage the administration program. Brown, on the other hand, was intelligent, independent, and cooperative. His presence would reassure open-minded bankers and strengthen the program's appeal to the traditionally isolationist Midwest.[24]

Choice of congressional delegates raised vexing political problems, for while the administration desired bipartisan backing it was unanxious to boost individual Republicans in an election year. Senator Robert Wagner of New York and Representative Brent Spence of Kentucky, chairmen respectively of the banking and currency committees, were natural selections since their committees would likely scrutinize any legislation. And, after further consideration, the White House agreed to take a chance on Jesse Wolcott, the ranking Republican on the House banking committee.[25]

Choice of a Senate Republican, however, proved more troublesome. At first Roosevelt sought to avoid isolationist Charles Tobey, ranking Republican on Wagner's committee, because he was running for renomination and this recognition would undoubtedly aid his campaign in the bitter New Hampshire primary. Morgenthau approached two other senators, John Danaher of Connecticut and Arthur Vandenberg of Michigan, but neither would permit personal ambition to undercut their New Hampshire colleague. Instead, the Senate Republicans voted on June 9 to back Tobey. Faced now with an incipient partisan struggle, Wagner urged Roosevelt and Morgenthau to reconsider. Reluctantly, on June 14, the president capitulated, but he confided to aide James Byrnes: "If this were not an election year, I would go ahead and offer the place to the best available Republican and let them make an issue out of it. I feel that I am spineless and almost weak-minded in yielding up the right of it, but I hereby do so for the sake of some wrong-headed thought of avoiding a party fight. I agree to the appointment of Tobey even though I still think he is a moron and will do us no good."[26]

As later events demonstrated, Roosevelt had underestimated Tobey's gratitude. No sooner had Morgenthau officially tendered the invitation than the onetime isolationist said: "I think it's a great constructive idea. I'm with you a hundred percent." At the conference administration aides arranged maximum publicity for Tobey and even persuaded Lord Keynes to visit Tobey's hometown to meet local dignitaries "who had never seen, much less met, an English lord." Not surprisingly, the publicity helped Tobey win renomination and reelection, and he emerged in the Senate as an enthusiastic supporter of international cooperation.[27]

In addition to the delegates, the president appointed a number of legal and economic advisers to provide technical support for the delegation and the conference. This list included specialists from the Treasury, State Department, Federal Reserve, and other government agencies with an interest in monetary matters. Conspicuous among the technicians were a number of controversial New Deal figures—

including Ben Cohen, Mordecai Ezekiel, Isador Lubin, and Alvin Hansen—whom conservatives and international bankers regarded with suspicion. The government had not included Benjamin Anderson, Randolph Burgess, Charles Dewey, or John Williams, who were critical of the accords; instead, it chose a cast of advisers who shared the administration's desire to extend government influence over international finance and would loyally back the joint statement.[28]

Meanwhile, Morgenthau's subordinates attempted, unsuccessfully, to conciliate the bankers. But in one of several meetings Harry White indelicately and perhaps inadvertently said that banks needed stricter public supervision, like railroads and big corporations, and for this purpose the government intended to transfer the nation's monetary capital from New York to Washington. A Treasury spokesman later denied these press accounts, but the episode temporarily illuminated the broader context in which the monetary reform proposals were being considered and the difficulty of bridging basic philosophical differences. For Morgenthau and White did think the government should impose federal control over international finance, just as the New Deal had earlier expanded government regulation of domestic banking and currency. Years later Morgenthau vigorously defended his position. The big bankers were "selfish." "Franklin and I," he reflected, "moved the money capital from London and Wall Street to Washington, and they hated us for it, and I'm proud of it. . . . The important issue was who governs, and the New Deal made the government govern American banking and monetary affairs."[29]

Memories of combat between the government and the financial community, a subsidiary theme in New Deal political history, continued to impair mutual confidence and trust vital for harmonious public discussion. For example, Lord Keynes's comment to the House of Lords that the joint statement was actually the "exact opposite of the gold standard" produced unexpected reverberations. Gold would serve as the common denominator, Keynes stated, but this did not mean that the internal value of sterling must conform rigidly to its gold value. On the contrary, the exchange value might vary to comport with whatever internal value resulted from Britain's domestic policies. Unlike the traditional gold standard, the new system would superordinate a member's monetary autonomy.[30]

Later, Randolph Burgess, who was more familiar with the technical proposals than most financiers, told Morgenthau that Keynes's speech had strengthened resistance in the American banking community, where many still did not understand the implications. The bankers, Burgess said, "are distrustful of any program for giving away American gold; they are distrustful of all spending programs, especially when sponsored by Lord Keynes who is thought of as the advocate of the government spending theories which you yourself have so vigorously opposed." And, Burgess might have added, but did not, the bankers were suspicious of any plan emerging from the Treasury that involved structural reforms.[31]

In his self-appointed role as an intermediary, Burgess tried to relay Wall Street's concerns. What the financial community feared most of all was that the fund would accentuate inflationary tendencies. Unrestricted drawings on the fund's pool of currencies would contribute to price increases, and promises of supplementary reserves would psychologically encourage other nations to deplete their stockpiles of foreign exchange. Inflation, he reminded the Treasury, had disrupted economic reconstruction after World War I; "we do not want to do the same thing again." In view of this danger Burgess recommended that the monetary conference establish machinery to facilitate regular monetary consultations and postpone plans for a currency pool. Later, as specific problems emerged, nations could negotiate bilateral credit arrangements. Although he recognized that Britain would need a $2 billion credit, Burgess opposed a prompt and comprehensive stabilization program because other countries had adequate reserves. Further attempts to push the fund, he warned, would create a "political football," and the "danger . . . is that we might repeat the tragedy of Woodrow Wilson with the treaty."[32]

A similar recommendation to postpone the fund came from the New York Federal Reserve Bank. In an assessment passed to the board of governors, the bank argued that the fund was not designed to cope with acute transitional adjustment problems. Moreover, the joint statement did not "meet the test of American self-interest." Instead of requiring debtors to adjust internal prices and incomes—the traditional way to restore payments equilibrium—the proposal permitted deficit nations to discriminate, under provisions of the scarce-currency clause, against American commerce whenever a dollar shortage developed, thus placing "the onus of international adjustment on this country alone." Critical of the joint statement and opposed to an extension of government influence in international finance, the New York bank conceded that the compromise statement did at least seem to improve earlier drafts. The proposal recognized that the fund should concentrate on the distant task of maintaining stable, convertible currencies in a balanced world economy, leaving immediate postwar problems—relief, reconstruction, and blocked currencies—to separate negotiations. Moreover, since the fund would now tolerate exchange controls and allow some exchange-rate variations during the difficult transitional period, it would not apparently impede reconstruction efforts.[33]

But the board of governors, more in touch with the internationalist mood of Washington and more sensitive to Keynesian-type analysis, disagreed. The fund had technical deficiencies, but approval of the monetary arrangements was an important test of America's willingness to collaborate in rebuilding the world order. Consultant Alvin Hansen, who was instrumental in shaping the Federal Reserve position on this issue, asserted that, if Bretton Woods failed, there was little hope for supplementary economic agreements on investments, commodities, and commercial policy. And, without a network of international ties, parallel political agreements designed to assure future peace would certainly fail. "Having become internationalist on political lines," Hansen claimed, "there is the gravest danger that the United States shall remain isolationist on economic lines." Unless the United States provided the leadership and demonstrated its commitment to permanent international arrangements, "nationalistic policies tending toward economic isolation are almost certain to prevail. Economic nationalism and isolationism, rival economic blocks, and international friction will likely be intensified."[34]

While the administration could count on the support of all executive agencies—including the quasi-independent Federal Reserve Board—it could not prevent the bankers from enlisting congressional Republicans. Twenty-one Republicans—including Charles Dewey and Clare Boothe Luce—declared in a letter to the *New York Times* that they had not found a single Republican who favored Morgenthau's blueprint. They urged Congress to establish an American Reconstruction Fund, under supervision of an American board of directors, to provide credit to those countries that took necessary steps to stabilize their domestic currencies. As this letter indicated, Dewey's unilateral approach to stabilization had continuing appeal to Roosevelt's opponents, who hoped that the autumn elections would permit a Republican majority to write a new postwar economic program.[35]

Other resistance developed in the Senate. A bipartisan coalition of twenty-six senators, all from western silver states, warned President Roosevelt on June 21 that the new monetary system should make some provision for silver. Fearful that the silver bloc, which had demonstrated its strength in the 1930's, might extract additional government subsidies for the precious metal, the Treasury replied that silver was already as good as gold. Under provisions of the Silver Purchase Act the government was obliged to buy domestic silver, and this policy carried an implicit obligation to support the world market price as well. Thus, since the Treasury had agreed to buy all foreign silver offered, another country might easily convert silver to dollars, and dollars to gold.[36]

This logic did not satisfy the silver industry, eager to obtain an international commitment that would assure the permanent interconvertibility of silver and national currencies at a fixed price. Accordingly, it solicited the diplomatic support of Latin American nations, who produced three-fourths of the world's silver supply. The Mexican government was receptive. Mexico quickly mobilized Peru and Bolivia, both large silver producers, and announced that it would work closely with North American silver interests, silver-using countries like India and China, and others to secure recognition for silver as a monetary metal. Despite fanfare at home, the Mexicans privately indicated they would be satisfied with a vague endorsement. And Morgenthau's aides, eager to avoid a bruising battle over a peripheral issue, hinted that the United States would support an innocuous resolution encouraging interested nations to give further study to the monetary uses of silver.[37]

Now only technical issues stood in the path of a successful conference. After President Roosevelt formally invited forty-four countries to participate in a conference beginning July 1 at Bretton Woods, Treasury experts arranged another preparatory session to assess outstanding issues, prepare an agenda, and draft articles of agreement for both an international monetary fund and an international bank. Morgenthau himself had doubts about this procedure, for it seemed to shift actual decision making from political officials to technical specialists. As he complained to White on the telephone, this was "leaving me completely high and dry . . . and then you expect us to come up there and sign on the dotted line, and it won't work. It just won't."[38]

The secretary reluctantly acquiesced, and White, after consulting with representatives of Britain, China, and the Soviet Union, invited representatives of twelve other governments to join the four principal powers in a preconference drafting session at the Claridge Hotel in Atlantic City, late in June. The others were Australia, Belgium, Brazil, Canada, Chile, Cuba, Czechoslovakia, the French National Committee of Liberation, India, Mexico, the Netherlands, and the Philippines. These final discussions, however, did not prove as successful as White had hoped, because security arrangements for the D-Day invasion of Europe interrupted Atlantic shipping and delayed the arrival of British and European-exile government officials on the *Queen Mary*.[39]

Eventually Keynes and his surrogates, including distinguished economists Lionel Robbins and Dennis Robertson, arrived. They brought several proposed modifications in the joint statement that the Britishers said were designed to satisfy criticisms raised in the recent parliamentary debate. The adjustment issue bothered the average Englishman, said Keynes, because he remembered 1931 when the government, bowing to outside pressures, had postponed domestic recovery in order to honor gold obligations and to satisfy international bankers. To conciliate critics, who persisted in interpreting the joint statement as a return to the gold standard, Keynes wanted three clarifications. The articles of agreement must indicate that each fund member retained "ultimate freedom" over its exchange rate. Furthermore, there must be no hint that a nation's domestic economic policies might be "dictated from outside—e.g., by a group of bankers sitting on the Board of Stabilization Fund." Finally, since officials anticipated that Britain might need more than three years to complete transitional adjustments and accept the obligations of convertibility, Keynes insisted that each member retain the right to determine when it could honor membership obligations requiring the dismantlement of currency restrictions. Briefly, Keynes wanted specific language to assure each nation monetary autonomy.[40]

White responded in a predictable way: "We should not budge one bit." Although he was personally sympathetic, domestic pressures restricted the American bargaining position, too. If he consented to these changes, critics would claim the fund was incapable of achieving its principal objective—stable exchange rates. In devising and presenting the American plan, the United States government had consistently taken the position that the proposal would avert a repetition of currency instability. "The cardinal point in the Fund," White asserted, "is stability of exchange rates. . . . Therefore anything that would suggest to the public that this is *not* the main aim would undermine all faith in the Fund."[41]

While insisting on exchange stability, the American delegation did not intend exchange rigidity. In previous discussions the American delegation had accepted a modification allowing members to alter exchange values as much as 10 percent without fund approval. This concession, while not apparently satisfying the British public or parliament, posed difficulties for the Americans, White added. "We have subjected ourselves to increasing criticism on the ground that we are legitimizing instability. If we go one step beyond this we will bring down the whole structure like a house of cards. People will say that this is just a credit scheme, and not a device to bring about stability." The United States Treasury did not expect support from extremists who "wanted us to have freedom to do as we please with the dollar rate," White said in reference to criticisms from New York bankers, but it did need the aid of business groups fearful of depreciating and fluctuating currencies. Thus, on this issue, the conflicting needs of public opinion in Britain and the United States left the negotiators at an impasse.[42]

If the two principal powers could only agree to postpone their disagreements for additional discussion and drafting, the Atlantic City sessions at least allowed them to identify the festering issues, to consider alternative solutions, and to examine, in total, approximately seventy amendments to the fund, most of them noncontroversial. On the bank, however, Keynes and White found their positions more compatible. In earlier conversations in Washington, Keynes had displayed little interest in the international investment question, arguing, as he did in October 1943, that creditor nations seldom benefited from overseas capital exports. Thinking then of Britain as a potential creditor, he knew that with little surplus capital England had no overriding interest in the investment question, and, indeed, her subscription to the bank might add strain to the postwar sterling.

In Atlantic City, Keynes reversed his position and agreed to support the formation of a world bank. He acted independently without London's formal approval, because in his transatlantic talks with exile-government officials—especially those from Norway, Czecho-slovakia, Belgium, and Poland—Keynes became convinced that the smaller countries needed additional reconstruction assistance. Bank lending, he now thought, might provide a useful financial bridge be-tween aid from UNRRA and short-term stabilization drawings from the fund. Also, though Britain wanted and expected a bilateral credit, or postwar lend-lease, from the United States, the Cambridge econ-omist may have seen the bank as a potential vehicle for crucial transitional assistance.[43]

Five working days on the seashore did not permit the deadline-conscious monetary experts to resolve all disputes, for many required top-level political decisions. Nor did it allow the specialists to com-plete necessary drafting—particularly the bank's charter. Yet, the At-lantic City discussions did serve an important purpose: they enabled the technicians to meet as a group and explore various options out-side the glare of publicity that always surrounds formal international conferences.

White's final task before Bretton Woods was to prepare the large American delegation for the negotiations. This presented more than the usual difficulties, for a number of the delegates—including the congressional representatives—were no more familiar with the fund and bank proposals than was the average citizen. Except as a courtesy, it was not necessary for the Treasury to educate the American dele-gates in all the technical nuances, for President Roosevelt had already carefully circumscribed the delegation's authority. At Morgenthau's request, he stipulated that fund modifications "not fundamentally al-ter the principles set forth in the joint statement" and that bank de-liberations be governed by the principles agreed upon by the Ameri-can technical committee. Moreover, the president reminded the delegation, which did not include any prominent opponents of the proposals, that they had the "responsibility for demonstrating to the world that international post-war cooperation is possible." In short, the American representatives were encouraged to follow the lead of their economics teacher, Harry Dexter White, and his principal, Henry Morgenthau.[44]

During his extensive briefings White skillfully related the economic blueprints to the larger problems of restoring a stable and prosperous world and to the underlying symmetry of American and foreign interests. The world needed a set of rules, White said, to prevent nations from arbitrarily altering currency rates without regard for the interests of other countries. Unless there were international guidelines and assistance to facilitate currency stabilization, he saw little prospect for enduring peace and economic rehabilitation. If other countries were unable to obtain outside aid, there would be continuing instability and anarchy leading to another round of competitive depreciations, such as the world experienced in the 1930's. And economic chaos would have grave political implications. As White said, "People are not going to stand for prolonged unemployment in Europe. They will kick over the traces for Communism, or some other 'ism.'" For this reason critics who favored postponing the fund, in order to reduce the risk of loss, were not "being conservative," but were "gambling with the political stability of Europe and the world."[45]

At a time when global peace and prosperity hinged on successful international economic collaboration, White regarded many criticisms of his fund "absurd and unrealistic." In particular, he dismissed the Williams proposal, that Britain and the United States first establish a dollar-sterling exchange rate, as a "naive" suggestion. It was true, he said, that a key-currency solution was important, but it was inadequate because, historically, currency trouble spread from the smaller countries. "As each country gets into trouble and begins to depreciate its exchange, it catches on to not the next country, geographically, but the country closest to her from the point of view of competition. . . . more and more it spreads like ripples and the first thing you know the large countries like France, the Netherlands, and the United Kingdom are affected." Unlike his more comprehensive approach to stabilization, the key-currency approach had a serious disadvantage: it would create major trading blocs, "which would do more to threaten world economic peace than even chaos in the currencies."[46]

Sensitive to charges that fund contributions might be lost, White reviewed provisions to safeguard holdings and protect the American contribution. For one thing, he said the fund could not become depleted or lose its gold value. If France, for instance, purchased dollars from the fund's pool of currency, it would supply an equal amount of francs; then, as her balance-of-payments situation ameliorated, France would repurchase its currency. Meanwhile another member might purchase francs, and this transaction, part of a continuing process, would reduce the fund's holdings of French currency and increase its holdings of some other currency. If France, or any other member, devalued, it was obligated to make up the difference, so that the total pool of currency had a constant gold value. In the event that a general shortage of dollars, or some other currency, developed, the fund could employ its $2 billion of gold to purchase the scarce currency. If this type of transaction depleted the fund's gold holdings, it might negotiate a loan from, for instance, the Federal Reserve System. However, if American authorities refused the loan, fund members could simply terminate their purchases of dollar items and redirect their imports to other suppliers. Assuming that the United States continued to import, world dollar holdings would climb again, permitting members to repurchase their currencies from the international monetary fund. This recycling mechanism demonstrated, White claimed, that "anyone who says that you are throwing money down a rat hole, or exchanging good money for a lot of cheap currencies . . . just doesn't understand."[47]

At least in discussions with noneconomists, White was reluctant to concede any arguments to his nondelegate opponents. But in briefing the American delegates White had tacitly admitted that, at least in the volatile transition period following the war, his fund could not continue to function unless the United States stood ready to replenish its dollar holdings—thus creating a potentially inflationary demand for American resources—or unless the United States was prepared to tolerate an embargo on exports while continuing to purchase foreign goods. As the critics said, the fund was designed for a balanced world economy, not the distorted postwar period when the United States would be the principal supplier of reconstruction items and international liquidity. White could not concede this anomaly unless he were to jettison the ideal of a closely structured international economy for the more practical, but less binding, obligations of the key-currency approach.

White chose to escape the dollar-shortage dilemma differently. In briefings he admitted that the fund could not restore world equilibrium without parallel arrangements for relief and reconstruction assistance. Unless the United States supplied dollars through an international investment bank or bilateral arrangements, "there would be terrific pressure on the Stabilization Fund," as other countries clamored to obtain short-term reconstruction assistance from their fund quotas. White did not expect the fund to supply reconstruction needs, but he rejected the argument that if the fund was not a reconstruction agency it should suspend all operations until war-disrupted members recovered political and economic stability. Provided there were proper controls governing access to the fund's pool of currencies, he thought the international agency could still assist members to achieve "political stability and economic promise" after they declared new exchange rates. White did not elaborate, but apparently he gave priority to establishing a new currency alignment, under fund auspices, and would tolerate controls—both exchange restrictions and limitations on access to the fund's pool—until circumstances gradually permitted the fund to achieve its potential and members to fulfill their obligations.[48]

While it was difficult to anticipate precisely how the fund would function, if at all, immediately after the war, White saw the institution and its code of monetary conduct as the framework for a multilateral trade-and-payments regime, which most international economists considered compatible with the long-term interests of all nations. Unlike other participants at Bretton Woods, he reminded the delegates that only the United States could supply the leadership to achieve this goal, for it alone had the gold and production to satisfy postwar requirements. Unlike Britain with a weakened monetary position, the United States, White said, had enough gold at Fort Knox to "dominate . . . the financial world, because we have the where-with-all to buy any currency we want."[49]

White recognized that his country had the financial power to reshape the world monetary system in the American image, but he had no intention of flaunting this strength in a way that would jeopardize or offend the legitimate interests of other countries. Such a blatant use of American financial muscle could only damage international confidence and cooperation on other political and economic matters; most of all, it might drive others to the desperate expedient of autarky. Accordingly, he cautioned the delegation not to "think of this Fund merely as [the] United States against the rest of the world." In short, the long-term evolution of international trade depended on the willingness and ability of many nations to import, accept gold in payments, make overseas investments, and relax artificial barriers. Over the long run, then, the fund would serve the general interest of all nations not only by providing a cushion—a revolving pool of currencies—to ease temporary payments maladjustments but also, and perhaps more importantly, by establishing a legal framework for continued monetary cooperation.[50]

Despite this overarching community of interest, White understood and advised the American delegation that they must be prepared to make concessions so that Great Britain and the Soviet Union, in particular, would have no hesitation about becoming partners in this novel experiment. With domestic opponents determined to block any arrangement that seemed to restore the prewar gold standard, White pointed out that the British delegates "can't be pushed too far or they will break off because they will have difficulty in Parliament." Similarly, because the fund offered little direct benefit to a nation with state trading, the Americans must adopt a flexible attitude in their deliberations with the Russians. As White emphasized, following Roosevelt's own basic position, Soviet participation was essential for world monetary order and for global political cooperation: "You can't have a cannon on board ship that isn't tied down because that one can do a lot of harm if they are not in."[51]

A number of intricate technical issues would dominate discussions at Bretton Woods, and, to inform the delegates of these and the American negotiating positions, White and his experts circulated several background memoranda. Allocation of quotas in the fund, the most controversial issue on the agenda, raised not only the difficult matter of determining each member's drawing rights and hence its influence over fund policies, but also the delicate question of accommodating actual influence to national prestige. China, France, and India were likely to demand large quotas. China, nominally a member of the four major allies but actually a much smaller influence in global economic affairs, wanted the fourth-largest quota, while both France and India desired the next largest. The American experts, anticipating this disagreement as well as other requests from some Commonwealth and Latin American governments for larger contributions, had devised a formula for assigning quotas. It took into account such objective criteria as gold holdings, fluctuations in foreign trade, and the importance of foreign trade to national income. All these adjustments, the Treasury indicated, would have to take place without increasing aggregate quotas above $8.5 billion. There were several other limitations. The American allotment must under no circumstances exceed

$2.75 billion. Britain might have $1.3 billion, but the United States must retain a quota larger than all members of the British Empire combined. Finally, Russia and China must have the third- and fourth-largest quotas, leaving the remainder for apportionment among other participants, as long as the Latin American governments secured fair treatment.[52]

A second problem concerned gold contributions. Though others had accepted Washington's condition that a proportion of each nation's quota be paid in gold, several countries, pleading special circumstances, desired to reduce these initial payments so as to have more gold reserves available for use immediately after the war. Russia and France, in particular, argued that because of disproportionately heavy war damage they should be allowed a 50 percent reduction. In this case if, as American technicians suspected, the Soviet Union had between $1.25 and $1.5 billion in monetary gold, Moscow would save at least $62.5 million. This amount was less significant than the principle involved. For, if the Soviet Union and France obtained special conditions, the American technicians anticipated that the British would also insist on a similar reduction, arguing that physical destruction was less damaging to a country's economic position than loss of foreign exchange and liquidation of international investment. And, if in the interests of equity a number of countries were allowed smaller gold contributions, the fund would have substantially less gold to sell for scarce currencies, thus jeopardizing the fund's operations during periods of acute payments disequilibrium.[53]

American specialists also anticipated a sharp debate with the Soviets over several technical matters. For one thing, Moscow insisted that the articles of agreement not infringe on its right to alter its exchange rate without fund approval. From the Soviet standpoint, since the ruble's value had no bearing on Russia's international transactions, it would not harm the fund for the Soviet Union to be exempted from the general requirements. White and his aides recognized that the argument had merit, but they feared an exception might provoke confusion in the United States and invite other countries to argue for a similar waiver. For these reasons it was decided to respond that, if the Russian rate has no effect on international monetary matters, "it may be presumed that the Fund will take the view that no harm is done in permitting a change in the ruble rate." On a different matter, White expected the Soviets to insist, irrespective of quota allocations, that the four great powers—America, Britain, the Soviet Union, and China—each retain at least 10 percent of aggregate voting power, since these countries had world responsibilities. White, however, did not think the Soviets would fight for this principle. After all, the Soviet Union warranted 10 percent of the votes on the basis of her projected quota, and it seemed unlikely that the experts from Moscow would hold out simply to give Chinese Nationalists more influence.[54]

Smaller countries might also seek to exert more influence over the fund's voting structure and management. Mexico, Australia, and Belgium, the Treasury memorandum indicated, had already insisted that no member have more than 20 or 25 percent of aggregate votes. The Mexicans simply desired to enhance the position of smaller countries, but the Australians, and possibly the Belgians, also favored this modification in order to remove the American veto over fund policy. White, however, had no intention of yielding; any concession would only complicate the inevitable congressional debate. In addition, White believed that members with the greatest interest in currency stabilization should have proportionately greater influence in determining policy. The United States, he said, must hold sufficient votes to ensure that "quotas cannot be changed in a manner detrimental to our interests and that no amendment to the Fund proposal can be enacted without our approval." To properly protect American interests, the Treasury calculated that this country must hold at least 20 percent of the votes—and under no circumstance could the United States accept a smaller percentage of total votes than the entire British Empire. As a corollary applicable to the consideration of certain requests to borrow from the fund, the Treasury said that both it and Canada wanted a flexible voting formula that would enhance the voting power of countries with surplus payments positions and reduce the influence of governments with deficits. Such a modification would further ensure that deficit members did not determine fund policy. Though Keynes favored this change, White anticipated vigorous objections from Australia and other smaller countries who were already fearful of great-power dominance.[55]

Another item that appeared in earlier technical discussions promised to emerge in the plenary discussions at Bretton Woods—the proposal for sanctions on surplus, not merely deficit, countries. Australia, Britain, and Canada all favored penalizing nations that permitted a surplus to continue uncorrected. Apparently anticipating a prolonged dollar shortage as the United States continued to earn more from exports, investments, and other sources than it spent on imports, aid, and other transfers, these countries proposed a reverse interest rate for excessive foreign exchange balances. Such a penalty, they thought, would induce the United States to reduce import barriers, increase foreign investments, or provide more relief and reconstruction assistance. Here the Americans proposed to stand firm. To help cope with the dollar shortage the Americans had already approved the scarce-currency clause, and White again argued that anything so novel as a reverse interest rate would only arouse more opposition in Congress.[56]

Finally, the American experts warned delegates that Anglo-American differences over two fundamental matters—exchange-rate flexibility and access to fund resources—would likely surface again at Bretton Woods. Unable to gain approval of Keynes's expansionary clearing union, the British continued to lobby for a general agreement establishing a procedure for periodic revisions of exchange rates. Here the arguments remained essentially the same. London wanted a flexible arrangement that would satisfy influential British citizens who were preoccupied with the lesson of 1925. While Keynes and his followers wanted to place the burden of adjustment on exchange rates, not on domestic economies, White feared that periodic realignments would renew currency instability and disrupt trade and investments. The two countries, caught between the British fear of unemployment and the American desire for exchange stability, somehow had to determine just how much exchange-rate flexibility was consistent with the requirements of a strong global monetary system.[57]

Should fund members have automatic access to the international agency's resources, or should the fund's executive committee consider each transaction? Proponents of the first course—namely, Britain and her two smaller allies, Greece and the Netherlands—took the position that drawings were a right, and as a result the fund's manager should have operational authority to make most decisions. Washington, still eager to limit the American liability, favored keeping this authority in the hands of the executive committee. To settle the issue, at least temporarily, the Treasury specialists hoped to introduce language assuring each member a right to borrow up to 25 percent of its quota within each twelve-month period, provided these drawings were used in accordance with fund objectives. This careful phrasing would, the Treasury lawyers thought, permit the fund to scrutinize and disallow purchase, and it would at least show potential members that the United States was not disposed to emphasize the point. Although White and his aides did not say so explicitly, they apparently intended to defer the issue for discussion until after the fund had been created.[58]

Partly because the experts had devoted less attention to details of the international bank than to the fund and had not yet issued a joint statement of principles, the delegates needed a thorough briefing on this project's rationale as well as on the issues of disagreement with other governments. This second financial agency, White said, would help meet the widespread need for reconstruction capital, a problem that he now regarded as "more serious than . . . monetary problems." Unless other countries obtained between $1.5 and $2 billion annually in long-term foreign investment capital to hasten domestic reconstruction-and-development employment opportunities in industry, White foresaw dire consequences. There would be "a depression, political instability and a low level of foreign trade, which will threaten everything that we are fighting for in this war." Unemployment and social unrest would spread, he thought, from war-devastated nations to other members of the international community, including the United States. "There is nothing," White emphasized to the American delegation, "that will serve to drive these countries into some kind of 'ism'—communism or something else—faster than having inadequate capital." Interestingly, though the bank was to be called a bank for reconstruction and development, White chose to stress its potential contribution to reconstruction, not long-term development assistance. To some extent, political conditions justified this choice of arguments. As the magnitude of postwar disruption became visible a consensus gradually emerged, among both Keynesian planners and orthodox economists, that some type of immediate assistance was essential to supplement the activities of the United Nations Relief and Rehabilitation Administration. An argument stressing the desirability of permanent transfers of capital from the rich to the poor countries would invite a searching debate on the merits of international investment mechanisms at a time when disruption, not development, posed the greatest challenge to global peace and stability. Except in the most general terms, neither White nor his assistants had given much attention to the long-term implications of an international bank.[59]

In briefing the delegates, White indicated that there were three methods of transferring capital to needy countries. First, private investors might make some loans—perhaps to Britain, Holland, and France—with superior credit ratings. But, even with the fund helping to reduce the risk of exchange-rate fluctuations or controls, White saw little prospect that private investors would supply adequate quantities of capital to central Europe, China, and enemy nations. Possibly the United States might engage in bilateral lending to satisfy these needs, under the direction of either the Export-Import Bank or the Reconstruction Finance Corporation, but White disliked this second option. "To attempt to get the United States to make even part of the loans that are necessary all over the world is to make a sucker out of our taxpayers. It would mean that our taxpayers have to bear the entire risk of loans of that character." Instead, the Treasury expert stressed the advantages of a third approach, a United Nations bank that would share the risks among all members in proportion to subscribers.[60]

The international bank that White described to delegates bore little resemblance to the multipurpose institution American experts proposed in 1942. That first international bank would have accepted deposits, issued its own currency, financed international trade, and supported commodity prices, among other tasks. The latest draft was hardly a bank in the conventional sense, with the right to accept deposits and create money, but a fund for guaranteeing foreign investments. Its members would subscribe about 20 percent of a $10 billion total capitalization—approximately one-third coming from the United States. The bank might make directly long-term loans from paid-in subscriptions, provided recipients agreed to spend the funds in the country supplying the currency. The remainder of total subscriptions, available at the bank's request, would guarantee productive loans made through private underwriting companies, White said. Because the aggregate sum would insure any loans against losses resulting from a default, he expressed confidence that the bank would encourage a revival of private capital movements.[61]

Although the fund appeared more controversial than the bank, White expected some sharp disagreements about the bank proposal to emerge during the Bretton Woods deliberations. For one thing, a number of countries, including China and Czechoslovakia, thought that the bank should make gold loans for reconstruction of national monetary systems. These governments thought gold loans would help restore public confidence in domestic banking systems. White had once favored gold loans, but now he thought the bank should confine itself to productive loans. If a member needed foreign exchange reserves, it could easily draw on the fund; and if it desired additional gold reserves, it could negotiate directly with private bankers, who had traditionally provided stabilization loans.[62]

Other opposition might come from Britain and the Soviet Union, who, not expecting to export capital after the war, desired to reduce their subscription to the bank. The American experts intended to resist this modification. If a war-ravaged country, like the Soviet Union or perhaps Britain, had no resources available for foreign investment, the bank would not lend its subscription. But, to strengthen the multilateral guarantee against defaults, the Americans insisted that all members should stand ready to contribute funds up to the amount of their subscriptions. If some members reduced their subscriptions, the bank would guarantee fewer loans and, as a consequence, would make a smaller contribution to promoting the global economic stability beneficial to all countries. White also discussed some of the more technical issues, including the controversial ratio between guarantees and total capitalization, but in the preliminary briefings he indicated that the American delegates should anticipate greater controversy over the fund, not the international bank.[63]

With preliminary preparations complete and an agenda prepared, the Americans were ready for Bretton Woods. The international conference would involve intricate negotiations on complex technical issues, but the broad outlines of the postwar monetary institutions were settled. Morgenthau and White had set the stage for what they expected to be a successful conference—one that would bring international approval for the first global experiment with permanent economic organizations.

Five days at Atlantic City did not give sufficient time for resolving all disputes or even for drafting all the differences, especially on the international bank. But the working technical sessions, White said later, permitted important exploratory talks. "There was no attempt," he claimed, "to iron out any differences, no attempt to get any agreement." Thus, though White might have desired to conclude all the business at Atlantic City, the circumstances of war delayed the arrival of European delegates and frustrated that design.[64]

6

Bretton Woods

Henry Morgenthau, John Maynard Keynes, and seven hundred other delegates and monetary experts from more than forty nations boarded two special trains in Washington and Atlantic City on June 30 for the all-night trip to Bretton Woods in northern New Hampshire. Here in a quiet alpine setting, remote from wartime turmoil, the financial diplomats and technicians would work for three exhausting weeks to conclude over two years of negotiations on some of the most complex issues ever considered by governments in an international forum. And, unlike their predecessors who convened in London eleven years earlier, the Bretton Woods delegates would exhibit a spirit of unity and international altruism conducive to success. As a result, the unprecedented achievements would immortalize the conference as a landmark in global economic history.[1]

Like Hot Springs, Virginia, site of the first important postwar conference in 1943 on food and agricultural problems, Bretton Woods was little more than an isolated resort for vacationing socialites. In 1772 King George III awarded this mountainous tract to Sir Thomas Wentworth and several other English noblemen, and the name Bretton Woods represented Wentworth's contribution to the future. His ancestral home, near Bretton, England, was called Bretton Hall. The locale gained prominence as a vacation retreat in 1902 when the large Mount Washington Hotel opened. During the summer months, when heat and humidity stifled life in Boston, New York, and Philadelphia, many prominent families adjourned to Bretton Woods, or nearby towns.[2]

Closed for two years during the war, the recently reopened Mount Washington lacked many of the conveniences desired for a business or diplomatic conference. Insufficient office space, inadequate accommodations, rusty plumbing, and an inexperienced staff were supplemented by Boy Scout messengers and military personnel. Even so, the Spanish Renaissance-style stone-and-frame hotel had lavish recreational facilities and magnificent scenery. The hotel, shaped like a capital Y, had two octagonal towers five stories high, and these contained many of the 485 rooms. The resort complex also had a spacious ballroom seating seven hundred persons, elegant shops, an indoor swimming pool, a stock ticker, and a post office. Situated on an elevated plateau overlooking an eighteen-hole golf course, the Mount Washington was surrounded by some thirty thousand acres of the White Mountain National Forest. Pines, hemlocks, and birches concealed the noisy Ammonoosuc River, plunging eastward toward the Atlantic Ocean.[3]

From the hotel's curving terrace, delegates had a striking panorama of the rugged presidential range and nearby Mount Washington, the highest peak in New England. Steep glaciated ravines rose out of the green woodland near the hotel and climbed upward beyond the timberline to windswept alpine gardens beneath the mountain's rocky and forbidding summit. A famous cog railway carried thousands of summer visitors from a base camp near Bretton Woods to the summit of Mount Washington each summer. When the usually heavy morning fog lifted, monetary experts could see the unusual railway climbing and twisting along the Ammonoosuc Ravine toward the distant Tip-Top House. The view bore a resemblance to the Alps, and appropriately enough natives of New Hampshire often referred to this area as the Switzerland of North America.

Morgenthau did not allow this inviting recreational setting to distract delegates from their deliberations. At an inaugural session held a few hours after arrival, he read President Roosevelt's welcoming message, which was drafted in the Treasury. Talks at Bretton Woods would have far-reaching political and economic implications, Roosevelt said. Previously, international conferences had dealt with military policy or emergency measures—such as relief or food distribution—but this would be the "first time to talk over proposals for an enduring program of future economic cooperation and peaceful progress." As such, the conference would "test our capacity to cooperate in peace as we have in war." "The spirit" of the discussions would "set a pattern for future friendly consultations among nations in their common interest." The president acknowledged that the fund and bank constituted only one phase of the arrangements needed to "ensure an orderly, harmonious world," but they were a vital phase requiring successful international cooperation. "Only through a dynamic and a soundly expanding world economy can the living standards of individual nations be advanced to levels which will permit a full realization of our hopes for the future."[4]

A few minutes later the delegates, complying with a custom that a host nation preside, elected Henry Morgenthau president of the Bretton Woods Conference. In his acceptance speech, prepared earlier and timed to assure maximum publicity in the Sunday newspapers, the U.S. Treasury secretary stressed the importance of successfully completing a permanent institutional framework to cope with international economic problems. The problems of international exchange and investment, he reminded delegates, were "beyond the capacity of any one country, or of any two or three countries." These were, he continued, multilateral problems requiring multilateral cooperation. "If we are forehanded enough to plan ahead . . . and to plan together," foreign exchange disruption could be prevented, the collapse of monetary systems avoided, and a sound currency for the balanced growth of international trade provided. In building a stable and durable monetary order as well as in coping with the wartime destruction, countries, Morgenthau emphasized, needed to plan. The negotiations ahead would require wisdom, statesmanship, and good will, but he reminded the delegates that they had a responsibility to construct "a dynamic world economy in which the people of every nation will be able to realize their potentialities in peace."[5]

On Monday, after a nominating committee presented its recommendations based on a draft prepared in the United States Treasury weeks earlier, delegates organized three working groups, or commissions, to consider the fund, the bank, and other means of financial cooperation. These commissions, comprising the formal conference structure, would hold private discussions in which each nation had a single vote. The conference structure, while nominally democratic—it gave each participant equal voting power—could not alter global political and economic realities: others might combine to vote against the United States position, but no plan for currency stabilization and reconstruction assistance would work without United States support. Delegates to the conference were authorized only to recommend the results of their deliberations to their respective governments; they could not commit their nations to a postwar economic plan.[6]

Secretary Morgenthau had hoped to make Bretton Woods a conference of finance ministers, whose presence would give added weight to the final recommendations. But, in fact, while fifteen governments —including Belgium, Brazil, Canada, China, and the French Committee of National Liberation—did send their finance ministers, war conditions or political concerns prevented the vast majority from following suit. Lord Keynes chaired the British delegation; M. S. Stepanov, the deputy people's commissar of foreign trade, led the Soviet group; and senior diplomats or central bank governors chaired most of the remaining delegations. Tiny Guatemala, however, chose to send only Manuel Noriega Morales, "a post-graduate student in economic sciences" at Harvard University.[7]

In reality, Bretton Woods was an advanced technical conference where actual power again rested in the hands of the economic specialists who staffed each delegation and the conference technical staff, who translated and interpreted the intricate questions of procedure into practicable language. Along with the economic draftsmen, lawyers took a critical part in the deliberations and negotiations. The specialists prevailed except on several sensitive political issues, which the technicians referred to senior cabinet officials for final approval.

John Maynard Keynes and Harry Dexter White, the two economists whose collaboration had produced the joint statement of principles on the fund and had paved the way for final consideration of the international bank, dominated the Bretton Woods Conference as they had preliminary meetings. Conscious of American concern that his presence could jeopardize later discussion of the recommendations in the United States, Keynes agreed not to address the conference at its opening session. Also, he consented to supervise the commission on the international bank, though his own preparations had been directed more to the problem of currencies than to long-term international investments. In this capacity Keynes's brilliant powers of analysis and exposition, as well as his reputation as the generation's most creative economist, helped overcome the doubts of smaller countries, alleviate conflict, and promote the final compromise. Despite his many strengths, Keynes was not the most efficient chairman, but his brilliance and fairness overcame occasional resentments. Even under the most adverse circumstances—Keynes experienced a mild heart attack after one evening session and had to guard his strength carefully throughout the conference—he was, as an American technician stated, the "General blazing the way" for international monetary cooperation.[8]

Harry Dexter White lacked the professional eminence of Lord Keynes, but throughout the conference he impressed foreign delegates with his fairness, inexhaustible energy, and leadership. White managed to function effectively at Bretton Woods on no more than five hours' sleep and as a result accomplished "something that gives him the right to a great deal of recognition." White, like Keynes, depended on a staff of technical advisers, among whom Edward Bernstein was the driving intellect. As a technician, Bernstein had no equal, and he repeatedly impressed delegates and reporters with his encyclopedic knowledge of the intricate provisions. As another American expert said praisingly, Bernstein was "really an amazing thinking and talking machine. You could push a button and the stuff would pour out with perfect clarity. He worked 27 or 28 hours a day without showing signs of strain."[9]

Many delegates from the smaller countries, especially Canada, also contributed forcefully and incisively to the technical deliberations, but not all of them displayed equal enthusiasm for work. Except when their national interests were at stake, as in the allocation of quotas, some looked for outside diversions. Twenty registered for dancing lessons with Mignon MacLean, a blonde diplomat from the Arthur Murray studios. A group of Chinese officials went mountain climbing in the nearby national forest and surprised a trigger-happy hermit who mistook them for Japanese bent on subverting the conference. The shaken Orientals escaped, but not without a temporary loss of dignity on the mountain trail. Others partial to more sedentary activities retired to one of the hotel bars or to movie theaters to watch the latest Hollywood productions. One popular showing was Cecil B. DeMille's *Story of Dr. Wassell*, a film starring Gary Cooper as the famed Dr. Wassell—a real-life Arkansas physician who won a Navy Cross for evacuating wounded Americans from Java.[10]

After completing preliminary formalities and approving a nominating committee's recommendations, delegates turned first to the wide-ly discussed, but still controversial, fund. At the insistence of the United States, Harry Dexter White chaired these deliberations, al-though much of the work occurred in smaller committees that con-centrated on aspects of the fund's charter. The committees examined and revised such specialized matters as the fund's purposes, policies, and quotas; its operations—including transactions with the world body, par values, and apportionment of scarce currencies; the fund's organization and management; and its form and status—involving a member's obligations, amendment, and later interpretations. Only fragmentary or general minutes of these sometimes heated delibera-tions remain, and most of the compromises are so specialized that they need not be discussed here.[11]

For the most part, however, the American delegates successfully withstood challenges on basic issues that might have introduced greater exchange-rate flexibility, relaxed the conditions governing use of the fund's resources, or reduced the American influence over or-ganization and management. Although sensitive to congressional opinion, the American delegates were not unsympathetic or irrespon-sive to the needs and interests of other participants. Available records show that the votes involved a shifting coalition—occasionally bring-ing Britain and the United States together to resist a proposal from India, or alternatively joining the United States and Latin America against another coalition. Naturally, since the conference draft was largely the handiwork of American and British technicians, these spe-cialists often found themselves in the position of defending or ex-plaining the implications of a specific phrase or clause. At first the American technicians encountered the confusion of representatives of the smaller countries, who were either unfamiliar with the proposal or hostile to some provisions, so the Americans distributed compre-hensive guides to the concerned delegates. Most of all, they empha-sized repeatedly that the fund was "not conceived in the narrow spirit of protecting the financial interests of traders and their backers but in the spirit of far-sighted concern about the general well-being."[12]

While the specialists meeting in committees were able to remove some ambiguities or contradictions, and to insert others when differ-ences prevented compromise, the most important decisions on the fund—as well as on the future of great-power cooperation—took place in private bilateral meetings, particularly those held between the United States and the Soviet Union, and between the United States and Britain. The Soviet problem overshadowed, at least in political significance, the technical deliberations, and at one point threatened to disrupt the conference.

Long sympathetic to the Soviet Union, which had been excluded from postwar conversations during World War I, Morgenthau and White were persuaded that future world peace depended on their success at persuading the Soviets to cooperate in constructing the postwar order. Stalin, it was true, had endorsed the concept of collective security during the Moscow foreign ministers' meeting in October 1943, but Bretton Woods, the first conference on permanent postwar institutions, was the initial test of Soviet intention to fulfill that pledge.[13]

Much to the disappointment of the American delegates, the Soviets were reluctant, or hesitant, to interpret their participation as a portent of cooperation on economic, political, and security matters. Moscow, for instance, failed to send a prestigious delegation that might at least have included the finance minister or Eugene Varga, a noted economist. Moreover, unlike other delegates at the opening plenary session —including the representatives from China, Czechoslovakia, Cuba, Brazil, and Canada—the Soviet speaker M. S. Stepanov did not identify the establishment of international financial institutions with world prosperity or peace. He gave no indication that the Soviet Union regarded the conference's work as essential to Soviet or world interests.[14]

In private sessions Soviet representatives candidly admitted that their country with its state-controlled economy had little need for international arrangements to stabilize exchange rates, eliminate payments restrictions, or fashion a multilateral trading system, although they did concede that convertible currencies were desirable. As Stepanov said, "All the problems facing Soviet Russia can't be solved through the International Monetary Fund." Even though the arrangements were designed for a world of market economies, not state-controlled economies, the Soviets did see two possible gains from participation in the fund—reconstruction assistance and recognition that their country was in fact a great power. Thus, if membership in the fund brought aid and prestige without involving heavy contribution or exposing the Soviet Union to the edicts of an international agency, the Soviets seemed inclined to approve the results.[15]

In briefing the United States delegation White had indicated that the fund needed Russia perhaps more than Russia needed the fund, and the Soviet experts seemed to sense that this mood strengthened their bargaining position. As is characteristic of Soviet negotiators, they proved skillful, tenacious, tireless, and unyielding. Whenever news arrived of another military victory on the eastern front, where the Red Army was hurling back Hitler's armies, Soviet officials presented another demand. But negotiating with the Russians proved doubly difficult because the Soviets had difficulty translating English and because they had to consult Moscow on even minor modifications in their position. Often as not, they simply repeated arguments in the course of a bargaining session rather than take a position not authorized in Moscow. E. A. Goldenweiser, the Federal Reserve monetary expert, was sympathetic to their plight: "I could not help feeling that they were struggling between the firing squad on the one hand and the English language on the other."[16]

The most troublesome issue was the appropriate size of Russia's contribution to the fund, for this sum established both her borrowing rights and her voting power. The matter had come up first in bilateral technical talks early in 1944. On the basis of a formula prepared in 1943, the Treasury technicians concluded that a quota of $763 million would satisfy Soviet monetary needs. However, during the course of his March 1944 conversations with Soviet specialists, White suggested a more generous quota. The Soviet Union, he said on one occasion, could reasonably expect 10 percent of total quotas and only slightly less in total votes. A day later, apparently forgetting or rephrasing this concession, White promised that Washington would support a one-third increase in the Soviet subscription when the monetary conference convened. Considered separately, each concession pointed to a quota of about $1 billion. The Russians, however, interpreted these statements at Bretton Woods to mean that their government would obtain a quota slightly lower than Great Britain's projected $1,270 million contribution. Informed of the disagreement, American delegates were at first reluctant to grant a $1,200 million quota because this would require either renegotiating all contributions or increasing the total sum beyond the publicly announced $8.5 billion ceiling, or $10 billion when enemy countries were admitted to full membership. Eager to assuage Soviet grievances, Morgenthau's group decided to "associate itself with the Soviet delegation in efforts to obtain an increase in the quota for the USSR at this conference."[17]

At this point Morgenthau returned to Washington, leaving matters in the hands of Fred Vinson and the technicians. Seeking guidance from the full delegation on how much he should offer the Soviets, Vinson convened a meeting on July 5 to discuss the appropriate tactic. Vinson found that the Treasury technicians inclined to lay aside their formulas and give the Russians a generous offer so as to prepare the way for Soviet-American collaboration on other postwar issues. Harry White conceded that the Russians probably wanted a large quota so they could use their drawing rights as a concealed loan, but he believed Moscow could, and would, repurchase her borrowings within four to seven years, thus not jeopardizing the fund's future operations. Indeed, if creditworthiness were the sole issue, White had no objection to a $2 billion quota. Other Treasury officials, though reluctant to be "out-horse-traded," favored a generous offer, perhaps $1,200 million. As Ansel Luxford said, apparently thinking of a future struggle to win congressional approval, "to sell this thing to the country, you have got to have Russia in the Fund." This, he added, was "much more important than the rest of the quotas put together." Federal Reserve Chairman Marriner Eccles agreed that it would be disastrous for future international cooperation if the conference collapsed because the American delegates were prepared to concede British demands but were unwilling to approve a Soviet quota of more than $1 billion.[18]

The line of argument taken by White, Eccles, and other Treasury aides did not appeal to banker Ned Brown. The "position of the USSR with the world . . . is a question for the State Department and not this Delegation to settle." Dean Acheson agreed.[19]

Nevertheless, after more debate White, Luxford, and Goldenweiser persuaded the delegation to offer the Soviets $1.2 billion, provided they withdrew other claims. Justifying this decision, White said it seemed "childish" to argue about $200 million when the United States was already shipping the Soviet Union $5 billion annually in lend-lease assistance and was considering long-term bilateral credits. Even if Stepanov and his surrogates were only bargaining, White opposed prolonging discussions, stalling the conference, and risking adverse publicity. "I say the whole Monetary Conference must be peanuts if you are willing to abandon a project because you are not willing to let Russia buy an additional hundred million dollars' worth of goods on credit." Morgenthau, who was anxious to avoid a confrontation with the Russians that might generate unfavorable publicity on the eve of the Democratic Convention, concurred by telephone. "They're doing such a magnificent job in the war," the Treasury secretary said, "that I've got a weak spot for them."[20]

The matter did not end with a quick settlement. The American delegates presented their proposal: Russia could accept either a $1.2 billion quota and relinquish other claims or a $900 million quota and a 25 percent reduction in her gold subscription. But, as Dean Acheson had anticipated, Stepanov insisted on having both the larger quota and the smaller gold contribution. When Morgenthau returned to Bretton Woods several days later, he personally took up the issue. "I am quite shocked," he told Stepanov, "that you people should say to us, 'We want one billion, two hundred million *and* the twenty-five percent.' That," Morgenthau asserted, "isn't the spirit which my Government has approached this problem with; it isn't the spirit expressed by Mr. Molotov to me; and it isn't the spirit of your Minister of Finance, where he said we would do this thing side by side, which means like partners." If the Treasury acceded to the Soviet position, Congress would certainly defeat the entire proposal.[21]

The Soviet government, Stepanov replied, did not want a "decisive position in the Fund," and it certainly did not expect the fund to solve Russia's postwar reconstruction problems. Sensing that the reconstruction problem was the clue to a compromise, Morgenthau promptly suggested that, if the Russian government would accept his offer, "I am ready any time . . . to take up the next question, which seems to me the question of how Russia is going to get manufactured goods in this country." Here the Treasury secretary was alluding to a plan already under consideration in the Treasury—a proposal for a long-term multibillion dollar loan to ease postwar adjustments. As an incentive to Soviet collaboration he was suggesting not merely larger short-term drawing rights in the fund—which White considered a concealed loan—but another bilateral credit.[22]

As the two sides negotiated, word of the snag leaked to journalists who were permitted to attend the conference and the plenary sessions. In a sensational and somewhat distorted account of the friction for the *New York Journal-American*, Samuel Crowther claimed that the "inner squad of New Dealers, none of whom are delegates but who are running the show, hold that unless Russia be appeased in every respect she will take Slavic Europe and a large part of Asia into her hands after the war."[23] Ultimately, with the concurrence of Moscow and President Roosevelt, the Soviet delegates took the $1.2 billion quota and a provision exempting newly mined gold from fund requirements for a few years. Technicians, meeting under the auspices of Commission I, rejected the Soviet request for smaller gold contributions for war-damaged countries, but they did approve another provision allowing members to change "the par value of its currency without the concurrence of the Fund if the change does not affect the international transactions of members of the Fund." In weighing these delicate issues, the specialists, especially the American and British experts, sought to reconcile the Soviet Union's desire for independence with the requirements of a monetary compact that would assure stable currencies and allay the fears of those who would assert that the compromises had destroyed the fund's effectiveness. The final language was necessarily ambiguous, but in balance the Soviets had won most of their points—especially a larger quota and a waiver for newly mined gold. They would, however, have to provide some economic information to the fund, which might, though the experts did not think so, be considered an unwarranted impingement of Soviet privacy.[24]

The Soviet quota controversy delayed final consideration of other quotas, but after it was settled Fred Vinson worked diligently to readjust other allocations so that the total sum would remain at $8.8 billion, the figure previously released to the public. This was not easy because, in boosting the Russian allotment, Vinson had to cut the quotas of the United States, the Union of South Africa, the Netherlands, and China. For the Chinese, acutely conscious of national honor and insistent that they retain a quota commensurate with their political status as a senior partner in the wartime alliance, the shift led to a larger contribution to the bank, contrary to the general pattern. Among the Latin Americans, in particular, status was also a crucial consideration. With Argentina excluded from the talks because of its Axis sympathies, Mexico and Brazil obtained the largest quotas in this region, but Cuba, Colombia, and Chile all vied for the third ranking. Private negotiations eventually produced a compromise—each would have a $50 million quota. Other nations, including France and India, were less than pleased with the final outcome, but it did show that nations could arrange such delicate issues through political compromise, not a technical formula.[25]

The small and medium-sized powers were not the only ones concerned about questions of prestige. That sensitive issue divided the British and Americans, too. Throughout the long chain of monetary conversations, Keynes and his colleagues had, at critical moments, deferred to the Americans on the size, shape, and functions of the stabilization fund, though the concessions were not unreciprocated. Now, at Bretton Woods, Keynes, more sensitive than ever to the criticisms of his domestic constituency, sought to secure at least a semblance of parity for Britain in the postwar economic structure. He argued that at least one of the institutions, perhaps the fund, should have its headquarters in London. If both were placed in the United States, he said, it would only confirm the opinion of opponents who alleged that the United States intended to dominate postwar finance. On this item, as on others that seemed likely to spark controversy in Congress, the American delegation refused to yield. Recalling that twenty-five years earlier another Democratic administration had given insufficient weight to congressional opinion, Morgenthau insisted that this time we "shouldn't make the same mistake Woodrow Wilson made."[26]

When Keynes continued to press his position, the Americans bluntly reminded him that Washington had enough support to place the agencies wherever it liked. Realizing that he could acquiesce, withdraw from the conference, or register a public protest, Keynes evaluated his options. Recognizing that in a floor fight Britain would probably be outvoted by the United States and its smaller clients, such as Costa Rica and Nicaragua, the choice was to concede or to leave the conference. He soon rejected the latter alternative because it would shatter two years of work on a multilateral trade-and-payments system as well as imperil Anglo-American cooperation on other urgent matters. Reluctantly, Keynes agreed to support a motion that the country with the largest quota—namely, the United States— should provide headquarters for both institutions. He did, however, reserve Britain's right to raise the issue again in the context of future intergovernmental discussions.[27]

Two other delicate matters of national sovereignty came up in the bilateral talks. The first, which had appeared frequently in Anglo-

American technical conversations, concerned the right of a fund member to unilaterally change the value of its currency without approval of the international body. The arguments were familiar, but, at Bretton Woods, Britain, and especially Australia, insisted that no country should have to submit proposed changes in its par value to the fund for approval. Finally, after more lengthy deliberations in public and private, a majority of the participants approved a provision, similar to the joint statement, allowing members to alter their exchange values by an additional 10 percent if the fund approved this request within seventy-two hours. To allay fears that the fund might block further adjustments and compel a member to defend an overvalued exchange rate, the final agreement stated that an unauthorized change would make a member ineligible for fund resources but it would not ipso facto violate the articles of agreement. Though not fully satisfactory to the participants, this concession added a little elastic for which some members would be grateful in later years.[28]

Should an international agency have the authority to report publicly on a member's domestic policies? British and American experts, as well as the Soviet delegates, had reservations about the political implications of this provision. From Morgenthau's perspective it was another provision that Congress might construe as an unwarranted and dangerous infringement of United States sovereignty. As a result, the two English-speaking powers drafted a clause allowing the fund to report publicly on national economic conditions tending to produce a "serious disequilibrium" in international payments only if members holding two-thirds of the total votes approved. To reassure the Soviet Union, they prepared another clause forbidding the fund to "publish a report involving changes in the fundamental structure of the economic organization of members." These clauses, the delegates thought, would allay internal apprehensions without seriously encumbering the monetary organization's performance.[29]

The success of this first experiment with an international stabilization agency would depend heavily on its management and its approach to monetary problems. At Bretton Woods the difficulty was not just to specify procedures for electing executive directors (each of the five members with quotas would select a director, and at least seven more would be elected, with the smaller American nations having two directors) but to determine their duties. Broadly speaking, Keynes favored defining a set of rules and giving a single managing director responsibility for administering those rules. With the director's authority closely circumscribed by the articles of agreement, each member would presumably have, and exercise freely, its right to draw on the fund up to established limits. The directors themselves would meet infrequently, as they were also to have monetary responsibilities in each of the representative governments. If Keynes was more laissez faire than the Americans—establish rules and allow members to act with minimal interference—White and the Americans seemed more paternalistic. While leaving such basic decisions as the authority to alter the price of gold, suspend a member, or liquidate the fund in the hands of the governors, who met annually, White proposed that the inner executive committee—the executive directors, not the managing director—would have considerable discretionary authority to determine whether a member could utilize its quota, or perhaps even exceed its quota. The issue was not finally resolved until later, but the delegates did approve a compromise requiring the directors to "function in continuous session." Moreover, the executive directors, according to the articles of agreement, would have the important authority to interpret disputes over interpretations, with final appeal to the board of governors. In coping with this critical issue, as in dealing with other important but then insoluble issues, the conference preferred ambiguity to unpleasant decisions.[30]

Preoccupied with the difficulties of creating an effective payments system, the great powers—the United States, Britain, and the Soviet Union—displayed less interest in altering the articles of agreement to satisfy the desires of less-developed nations. At Bretton Woods the most articulate, and persistent, advocate of what was later called the "third world" was India. That delegation, without the support of a major industrial country, urged a more explicit acknowledgment of the fund's responsibility for promoting the development of "economically backward countries." In conference debate Sir Shanmukham Chetty explained that, historically, "international organizations have tended to approach all problems from the point of view of the advanced countries of the West. We want to insure that the new organization . . . will avoid this narrow outlook and give due consideration to the economic problems of countries like India." His proposal was rejected, partly because it appeared to alter the fund in a manner that exceeded available resources and because it seemed to impinge on responsibilities of the international bank. But it also appeared to invite the fund to assume the blocked sterling credits of India and other Commonwealth members—an issue that intersected with the complicated, and in the estimation of major powers, more urgent problem of helping an economically weakened Britain achieve currency convertibility.[31]

During the Bretton Woods sessions the American specialists apparently did not foresee, or appreciate, the extent of Britain's postwar payments difficulties. It was critical, White recognized, to find a permanent solution for wartime sterling debts, then estimated at $7 billion; but, because London preferred to negotiate directly with her creditors, rather than to load this debt on the fund, the Americans sided with Britain—the issue of war indebtedness must be settled by the countries concerned. Keynes has an "incipient revolution on his hands," Morgenthau told American representatives, "and . . . we will let the British Empire fight it out without making us a cat's paw." On two other aspects of the British payments problem the Americans professed optimism that the fund and bank would provide indirect assistance. White said that Britain would need to expand its exports rapidly after the war to purchase essential imports and that during the transition period Britain might require supplementary assistance to help finance her import surplus. On the former problem White anticipated that, as a result of the fund and bank stimulating world trade, British exports would soon generate sufficient foreign exchange earnings to meet import requirements. In the transitional period ahead, he saw no reason why Britain with its excellent credit rating would be unable to borrow at reasonable interest rates from private lenders. Perhaps because references to an Anglo-American loan would call into question the practicability of the international mechanisms, White avoided any specific discussion of long-term credits, and he expressed confidence that Britain would not, as her officials said, use the fund as a "grab bag." Thus, discussions continued on mechanisms for currency stabilization in a balanced world economy without any concrete analysis of how individual countries, especially Britain, would assume these future obligations.[32]

In general the articles of agreement that emerged from over two weeks of deliberation resembled, with only minor alterations, the essential framework proposed in the Anglo-American joint statement. More hands and minds had contributed to drafting the fund's birth certificate, and as a consequence the participants could all claim some credit for the successful delivery. In fact, though, the new arrival was the offspring of an Anglo-American monetary marriage of convenience, and to astute observers the American genes seemed, and were, dominant. In its purposes, operations, and structure the fund bore the unmistakable mark of Harry Dexter White and his Treasury colleagues.

The founding fathers had taken a bold stride forward in approving a code of monetary conduct and in creating an international agency to advise and assist members in achieving stable and convertible currencies, but one large question remained: When and in what form would the fund commence operations? The articles of agreement were necessarily ambiguous on this point. The agreement would take effect not earlier than May 1, 1945, after governments with 65 percent of the total quotas had signed the agreement. If sufficient members had not approved by December 31, 1945, the instruments would probably never take effect: the United States was obliged to return all subscriptions unless the agreement had come into force. After the proper signatures and the initial designation of exchange par values, the fund would determine when it could begin exchange transactions, "but in no event until after major hostilities in Europe have ceased."[33]

Among the American delegates there was no consensus on the most likely date. Ned Brown, for instance, believed, like other bankers, that the fund should not properly begin until after both theaters of the war ended and until a "country has gotten at least a minimum of economic stability." Otherwise, destitute members would likely employ their quotas for relief, not for currency stabilization, and the fund would not work as it was designed. Harry White disagreed. He thought the fund could open its doors within a year of Bretton Woods —perhaps before the Asian war concluded. Most of all, he disputed the assumption that the fund should delay exchange operations until a minimum of stability was restored. Instead, he asserted that fund resources could be employed to stabilize world economic conditions, "preventing revolutions" that might endanger world "peace and prosperity." War disruption, he argued, was analogous to cyclical swings resulting from harvest failures or great conflagrations, which also produced balance-of-payments problems; thus the fund should make its resources available to members for three-to-seven-year periods. If, as Brown anticipated, the fund ran short of dollars during the transition period, White suggested that it might borrow from the

Federal Reserve System. Currency convertibility and nondiscrimination, he recognized, were long-term goals, but White thought the fund could promote these objectives best by taking an active role in easing transitional adjustments. He was, however, thinking of selective, not general assistance to the potentially prosperous European countries—not immediate and uncontrolled transactions with all potential borrowers. Essentially, Morgenthau's top monetary assistant believed that the fund's executive directors, responsive as they were to the weighted voting of members, could be entrusted with considerable discretionary authority. Brown, however, innately cautious, as bankers often are, feared that four-fifths of the members—those needing additional reserves or exchange—would draw heavily on the fund for immediate requirements and would thus weaken the fund as a mechanism for stabilization in more normal circumstances.[34]

As a series of compromises were being fashioned in Commission I and in bilateral negotiations to launch the fund, separate discussions on other forms of economic cooperation took place in the "third" commission under the direction of Mexican Finance Minister Eduardo Suárez. Although peripheral to the central task, these sessions took up a number of independent, but controversial, matters that delegates considered important—either to remove remaining vestiges of Axis influence in global economic affairs or to guide future multilateral discussions on other modes of economic cooperation.[35]

One of the most controversial items was the future of the Bank for International Settlements (BIS), an agency created to facilitate the transfer of German reparations from World War I. The bank, headquartered in Basle, Switzerland, also served in the interwar period as a forum for central bank cooperation, bringing together at monthly meetings European central bankers and representatives of several large private American banks who owned stock in the institution. But, before and during World War II, critics said, the bank had collaborated with the Nazis, allowing Germany to obtain Czech gold holdings. Now, at Bretton Woods, the Norwegian delegation proposed that the conference recommend liquidation of the BIS.[36]

For Morgenthau and other United States delegates the Norwegian initiative posed an unexpected dilemma. Before the conference he had not given a "second thought" to the BIS, Morgenthau said, but the issue raised difficult legal and moral issues. For one thing, as Dean Acheson and Lord Keynes pointed out, the conference had no authority to recommend dissolution of another international agency. Against this legal position were other considerations more important to Morgenthau and his aides. The BIS had apparently collaborated with Nazi Germany on several occasions, and, although later evidence would rebut such accusations, the Americans could not easily vote against the Norwegian resolution, they thought, without fostering misunderstanding. Morgenthau and White also feared that inaction would strengthen the BIS and revive the influence of private bankers after the war. Leon Fraser of New York's First National Bank had already suggested that the Basle-based institution, not Morgenthau's monetary agencies, should supervise postwar stabilization lending. Thus, the Treasury secretary wanted to support the Norwegian position "as a matter of international propaganda" and as a way to undercut private banking power.[37]

Any belief that he and other delegates had to avoid a vote for legal reasons vanished when liberal columnists trumpeted the Norwegian position. I. F. Stone, a frequent supporter of Treasury policies, accused the international bankers of plotting to salvage the "Nazi-dominated Bank for International Settlements" so as to "establish a bilateral Anglo-American financial pact under which Wall Street and the City would be able to dictate international monetary policy and block social and economic reform through their control of foreign lending." This conspiracy, Stone asserted, had the support of prominent Republicans like John Foster Dulles, foreign policy adviser to presidential nominee Thomas E. Dewey.[38]

With pressure from liberals at home and with the BIS issue a potential embarrassment to President Roosevelt during the forthcoming Democratic Convention, Morgenthau obeyed his own instincts and the delegation unanimously voted to support the Norwegian effort. State Department representative Dean Acheson doubted the propriety of this stand, which encroached on other foreign policy issues, but his boss Cordell Hull deferred to Morgenthau. Despite some resistance from Keynes and J. W. Beyen (leader of the Dutch delegation and himself a former president of the BIS), who wanted a less binding resolution, the conference approved a strongly worded resolution calling for liquidation of the Bank for International Settlements at the "earliest possible moment." After the war, when Morgenthau's successors sought to implement this resolution, the Europeans preferred to postpone the execution, and eventually the BIS gained a new lease administering recovery funds.[39]

The third commission also debated international action to discourage neutral nations from allowing enemy countries to transfer or conceal assets outside the reach of the probable victors. When the conference met, there were already reports that Germany had begun to transfer its assets abroad to find "safe haven." If it was successful, a number of the Allies feared that another generation of Nazis would employ the hidden resources to subsidize another quest for world domination. Before delegates met at Bretton Woods, the United States had already begun to discuss the "safe haven" problem with neutrals, and, with encouragement from the French and Polish delegations, the three countries successfully sponsored a resolution calling on neutral nations to take appropriate measures that would prevent the disposition of looted assets and the concealment of enemy assets. Although the British opposed, saying that this question had little bearing on topics that the conference was summoned to consider, the resolution gained widespread approval.[40]

On other matters, Suárez and his commission recommended action proposed by smaller countries. As a sop to silver-bloc interests, especially Mexico and Peru, interested nations were advised to give further study to the use of silver as a monetary metal. Also, they approved a resolution, advanced with the backing of Peru, Chile, Brazil, Bolivia, and Cuba, recommending that participating governments seek agreement on measures to reduce obstacles to world trade, to encourage an orderly marketing of staple commodities, to deal with problems arising from the cessation of war production, and to harmonize national policies for maintaining high levels of employment and rising standards of living.[41]

Much to the disappointment of Australia, however, the commission rejected its proposal that participant governments "accept concurrently an international agreement" pledging to "maintain high levels of employment in their respective countries." An international commitment to expansionary domestic policies, the Australians insisted, was necessary to persuade ordinary people to accept the monetary agreements and to ensure that fluctuations in aggregate demand would not again disrupt the international economy and bring another round of currency depreciations and tariff abnormalities. The proposal failed not because the economic planners were unsympathetic to the goal but because they considered an explicit statement politically impracticable.[42]

In voting on these issues, as well as on other proposals before the conference, Washington usually had the support of Latin American delegates. Luis Machado of Cuba and Antonio Espinosa de los Monteros of Mexico, organizers of the Latin bloc, worked hand in glove with Morgenthau's assistants. In return the United States representatives assured the Latins that they would have the right to choose two executive directors for both the fund and the bank, giving Latin America additional influence in the management. As Ansel Luxford confided to Morgenthau, Machado agreed: "We would get a vote on any issue we wanted to, and get the support of the whole group if we would just let them know in advance, because they are so happy about having two positions cinched on the Directorate." Throughout the conference other foreign delegates watched the solid Western Hemisphere coalition with amazement. But Washington was not the only one with client supporters, though the United States did have more than other countries. Britain could count on the backing of the Netherlands and Greece, as well as her Commonwealth allies, on most issues.[43]

Not until July 11, when Commission I had completed the most difficult aspects of its work on the fund's charter, did Bretton Woods delegates concentrate their intellectual energies on the bank for reconstruction and development. To discuss sections of the document prepared at Atlantic City, which contained British and American suggestions as well as alternative provisions, Lord Keynes, chairman of Commission II, announced the formation of four technical committees. They would consider such subjects as purposes, policies, and capital; operations; organization and management; and form and status.

At a preliminary organizational meeting Keynes discussed briefly the origins, objectives, and functions of the proposed bank, so that representatives from smaller nations who had given this dimension of world economic cooperation less attention would have some background for formal negotiations. According to Keynes, the bank scheme owed its origins "primarily to the initiative and ability of the United States Treasury," in its larger context. The bank was designed to "make loans to the countries of the world which have suffered from the devastation of war, to enable them to restore their shattered economies and replace the instruments of production which have been lost or destroyed." This institution would complement the United Nations Relief and Rehabilitation Administration, limited to immediate relief and reconstruction assistance, and would fill a serious gap in postwar proposals for lasting international cooperation. While, as Keynes emphasized, reconstruction lending would be the bank's main task in its "early days," the investment agency would gradually devote its attention to "developing the resources and productive capacity of the world, with special attention to the less developed countries."[44]

Concerned about the implications of a postwar world without adequate mechanisms for international investment and reconstruction assistance, Keynes threw himself into committee work, as much as his physical condition would permit, and pressed weary delegates to compromise differences. His noble intentions notwithstanding, the British economist soon found other delegates less able to sustain his own frenetic pace. In commission meetings, for instance, Keynes would call out a provision hurriedly, and then before others, sitting in chairs without desks, could locate the appropriate section, the Englishman declared, "I hear no objections, and it is adopted." After some grumbling that Keynes was the "world's greatest economist and its worst chairman," Morgenthau persuaded the Cambridge economist to pursue a more deliberate, less arduous discussion.[45]

While Keynes's group approved sections of the bank's birth certificate before the document was submitted to the entire conference, much of the actual drafting and critical decisions took place in subcommittee sessions or in informal meetings involving economists, lawyers, and delegation leaders. In particular, Professor James Angell, a Columbia University economist serving with the Foreign Economic Administration, and Emilio Collado, a State Department economist, took charge of late-evening work on the bank's charter.

There was so much to do and so little time that for a while it seemed the conference would adjourn as scheduled on Wednesday, July 19, without completing the bank proposal. However, Keynes and Morgenthau, with the approval of others on the steering committee, decided to extend the sessions several days. When the hotel manager protested that this would disrupt vacation plans of paying guests— some of whom were charged $96 per day for room and board in contrast to the monetary delegates, who were assessed $11 daily—

Morgenthau exploded, threatening to seize the hotel. David Stoneman, president of the Bretton Woods Company, realizing that military policemen were prepared to carry him out of his hotel as they had Sewell Avery from his office at Montgomery Ward a few weeks earlier, yielded to the appeals of Fred Vinson. The government promised to help disappointed guests make other plans for accommodations.[46]

Among major issues discussed in hectic meetings of Commission II was the politically sensitive question of whether the bank should give equal emphasis to reconstruction and development, or give one priority over the other. All participants—including Moscow's Marxist economists—agreed that the new institution should facilitate long-term private capital flows; political ideology and polemics had no place in the pragmatic Bretton Woods deliberations. Essentially, countries suffering most from the war, including Russia, Czechoslovakia, and several other European nations, insisted that the bank give immediate priority to reconstructing and restoring economies destroyed in the global conflict. But, less-developed countries outside the war zones, such as India, Mexico, and Venezuela, argued vigorously that economic development should have at least equal emphasis so as to establish the precedent for a long-term world commitment to economic development. Eventually, delegates settled on an ambiguous, but diplomatic, compromise. The bank's executive directors should give "equitable consideration to projects for development and projects for reconstruction alike." This solution postponed an ultimate decision and enhanced the bank's own discretionary authority to shape its objectives and programs.[47]

If lending objectives were of principal concern to potential borrowers, lending capacity interested nations most likely to export capital. Under terms of the articles of agreement already drafted in preliminary meetings, the bank was to be more of a loan-guaranteeing agency than a lending institution. The bank could lend only 20 percent of its $10 billion authorized capitalization directly to members or their representatives—and as a consequence the charter required this percentage paid in advance. Of this 20 percent, 2 percent was payable in gold or dollars and the remaining 18 percent in national currencies. Effectively, since the American dollar was expected to be the only convertible currency, the bank would have only the American paid-in subscription plus the other 2 percent from remaining members to use for direct lending. But in guaranteeing loans the new bank could draw on its entire $10 billion capitalization—paid-in and on-call—to back private loans. Only if there were heavy defaults and a borrowing country declined to compensate the international agency for losses on loans to its residents would the bank actually need to draw on the remaining 80 percent from the guarantee fund.[48]

Since only United States dollars were expected to be convertible during the bank's first years of operations, some delegates wondered whether the global finance agency could effectively contribute to reconstruction and development while holding the confidence of private investors, who must supply the bulk of capital for bank-approved projects. To allay concern and assure the financial community that this new institution was managed with due regard for creditor interests, Dutch delegates urged a conservative ratio of loan guarantees to total capitalization—never more than 75 percent of unpaid subscriptions. But some eager borrowers, especially Poland, responded that such a low ratio would inhibit lending operations and delay recovery, and thus they favored 300 percent.[49]

Among American delegates, there was initially a wide range of opinion, as there was among national delegations generally. Ned Brown and Warren Pearson, who represented the Export-Import Bank, urged that the ratio not be over 100 percent; while at the other extreme Harry White and Edward Bernstein spoke for a more liberal limit—perhaps 200 percent. Basically the conservatives argued that caution and prudence were absolutely essential to build confidence in this first experiment with an international bank. As Dean Acheson said, "the most important thing" is to "assure that the Bank can function at all, and in order to function at all it must be sure to build up confidence—people must believe that its guarantee is good, that it is conservatively run." Moreover, a lower ratio would more likely encourage a steady expansion of bank lending, for, by inspiring investor confidence, it would ease the task of securing additional capital to finance reconstruction and development projects.[50]

Harry White disagreed. A 100 percent limit was "reactionary," not conservative, and unnecessary. Low interest rates, flexible repayment provisions, and a long-term emphasis on productive lending would reduce danger of defaults, he thought, and make a conservative lending ratio unnecessary. Also, since any decision to modify the initial ratio at a later date would require approval of all member governments, it seemed more reasonable to endow the bank at birth with authority commensurate with its heavy reconstruction and development responsibilities.[51]

With American delegates White used another argument to support his plea for a higher lending ratio. Initially, he said, American technicians calculated the world would need capital exports of between $15 and $20 billion in the postwar decade. Since the higher figures seemed "enormous," the technicians decided to recommend a $10 billion subscription-and-loan ratio of between 150 and 200 percent, which would allow the bank to guarantee necessary private investment. As he told skeptical congressman Wolcott, "We are not in this thing for charity. We feel that the more loans that can be made, providing they are sound loans, the better for the world and the better for us. It means more trade, more productivity. It means less unemployment." In arguing this line White was not saying loans were indispensable to full employment at home; rather he was only relating U.S. international and domestic economic objectives, showing delegates how foreign lending reinforced a full-employment program at home.[52]

As much as he wanted a higher lending ratio, White recognized that it would increase congressional opposition. If three or four bankers nodded their heads sagely in front of a congressional committee and said the bank was risky, then "the best plan in the world isn't worth the paper it is put on if it isn't going to be passed." Thus, with the advice of congressmen on the delegation, the American representatives recommended, and foreign delegates accepted, a proposal that the bank's outstanding guarantees and loans should not exceed 100 percent of unimpaired subscribed capital, reserves, or surplus. As it turned out, what determined the bank's lending capacity in its first years of operations was not the ratio of loan guarantees to total capitalization but the ratio of loans to paid-in subscriptions of convertible currencies and the unpaid proportion of the American subscription. Briefly, the bank's strength was proportional to the size of U.S. contribution, not aggregate subscriptions.[53]

The bank charter, which emerged from late-night drafting sessions and committee discussions, was deliberately ambiguous on some controversial points and understandably conservative on procedural matters; yet it was surprisingly flexible in allowing bank officials and member governments to shape the institution's future role. Not only must officers and executive directors settle the vexing question of how to ration resources between development and reconstruction projects, but they must also devise a lending philosophy, criteria for selecting and analyzing projects, and procedures for supervising procurement and utilizing disbursements. The articles of agreement provided only general guidelines. They did not, for instance, indicate priorities for agricultural, industrial, or infrastructure lending. Subject to only a few restrictions, the bank could guarantee, participate in, or make loans to any member, or any political subdivision, business, industrial, or agricultural enterprise within a member. However, the recipient of a loan must fully guarantee repayment of principal and interest—effectively, the debtors would unilaterally guarantee repayment of their borrowings. Also, in assessing a loan application the world bank must determine that under "prevailing market conditions" a prospective borrower was unable to obtain the credit elsewhere under conditions reasonable for the borrower. In addition, the international bank must appoint a competent committee to study each proposal, and this loan committee must recommend the project. "In making or guaranteeing a loan the Bank shall pay due regard to the prospects that the borrower will be in position to meet its obligation under the loan; and the Bank shall act prudently in the interest both of the borrowing member and also of the guaranteeing members." Finally, the articles of agreement required that "loans made or guaranteed by the Bank, except in special circumstances, shall be for the purpose of specified projects of reconstruction or development." This last restriction was sufficiently vague to allow the interpretation that the bank could determine when circumstances warranted broader lending programs.[54]

In essence, the bank's lending criteria approved at Bretton Woods reflected the stringent lending standards that Harry White and his advisers had inserted in their original proposal to satisfy cautious bankers and to avoid a repetition of the ill-considered loans that left a bitter memory to debtors and creditors alike in the prewar period. Briefly, the bank would focus on self-liquidating productive loans for specific projects, not for broad programs. And its management would carefully investigate proposals and supervise disbursements to ensure that proceeds were actually used for specified purposes. Furthermore, the international lending agency would normally provide only foreign exchange, not local currency components of a loan. Important as these formal regulations were in shaping a cautious approach to international lending, they left considerable discretionary authority to bank managers. Officials of the bank must determine whether other loans were available at reasonable interest rates in whatever time span they selected. Administrators also had latitude to determine what was a productive loan and what was a project. Did the latter, for instance, involve merely a power station or a country's entire energy system; did it mean an engine, an entire railroad system, or perhaps a complete transportation grid? Effectively, then, Bretton Woods postponed a number of key policy decisions and transferred a broad range of authority to officials in the new institution.

Moreover, while the final agreements stated that the "Bank and its officers shall not interfere in the political affairs of any member; nor shall they be influenced in their decisions by the political character of the member or members concerned," what constituted political interference would depend in the last analysis on how the bank interpreted its activities. The provision stated that "only economic considerations shall be relevant to their decisions," but the delegates apparently did not consider whether this precluded the bank from insisting on certain conditions to increase the prospects for repayment or productive use. Were measures to balance government budgets, control inflation, pay private external debts, or regulate government ownership legitimate or unwarranted interferences with a nation's political system?[55]

Organizationally, the bank was a mirror image of the fund. A country, in fact, could not join the bank unless it was a member of the fund. Both bodies would have a supreme authority, called governors, and a smaller group of executive directors who would supervise the general operations of the bank's president and administrators. Members with the five largest subscriptions would each elect an executive director, and he would cast a weighted number of votes. It was unclear from the articles of agreement whether the executive directors or the president and management would consider individual loan applications. All of these and other delicate matters would evolve from decisions made by the governors at their first meeting and from experience in the first years of operation. The agreement would remain open for formal signature until December 31, 1945, for Bretton Woods participants. At an inaugural meeting of the board of governors, which could not come until May 1945 at the earliest, members would select executive directors. Sometime later "the Bank shall notify members when it is ready to commence operations."[56]

Paralleling these discussions on essentially technical matters were political negotiations on each member's subscription to the $10 billion bank. Basically, many smaller delegations, conscious that their subscriptions had no direct bearing on their access to long-term loans, wanted to make a smaller financial commitment to the bank than to the fund. As they recognized, a larger fund quota enlarged a member's drawing rights, but a larger bank subscription only increased a country's potential liabilities—it would lose more proportionately if there were heavy defaults. Keynes, in his opening address to Commission II, had indicated what most delegates knew already: after the war only the United States and a few other countries would have an investible surplus for international lending. Thus, at least in the near future, the collective guarantee resulting from subscriptions would primarily protect American investments. The problem for smaller countries was how to reduce their subscriptions without either jeopardizing creation of the bank or offending the United States, which, through its executive director, might have considerable influence over borrowing.[57]

The most difficult negotiations on this point took place with the Soviets, who, having obtained a $1.2 billion quota in the fund, desired a bank subscription of not more than $900 million. The Russians were adamant until one hour before the final plenary session on July 22. Then suddenly and dramatically they accepted a $1.2 billion subscription. This unexpected *volte-face* boosted actual subscriptions to $9.1 billion—below the $10 billion maximum—and electrified delegates. A few minutes later the jubilant Morgenthau interpreted the Soviet decision as further "indication of the true spirit of international cooperation demonstrated throughout this Conference."[58]

For the impressionable Morgenthau this evidence of Soviet intentions was at least as important as the conference's substantive accomplishments. Moscow's decision to cooperate appeared to vindicate the Treasury's conciliatory diplomacy throughout the conference. Several days later, still gloating over the turn of events, the secretary told his aides that Dean Acheson had criticized the Treasury for being "too generous" to the Russians. But Morgenthau claimed that the European situation had influenced his decision to mollify Moscow. The Russians, he noted, would soon enter Berlin and then perhaps consider a separate peace with Germany. ". . . the Russians are going to be sitting in Berlin and they will say, 'Listen, the last conference, what did you do, you hit us on the nose and you kicked us in the shins.'" The United States was vulnerable to a separate peace, and "these dumb-clucks in the State Department can't see that." Morgenthau proudly told President Roosevelt that, after the Russians approved the larger subscription, even the skeptical Acheson had hailed this move as a "great diplomatic victory for the United States and . . . a matter of great political significance." The president, Morgenthau suggested, might want to hail this voluntary action as further evidence that the Soviet Union desired to "collaborate wholeheartedly with the United States in a program for the maintenance of world peace and prosperity."[59]

The bank's articles of agreement contained some hastily drafted provisions and some hedged with ambiguous compromises, but most delegates agreed that the final product was the best that could be achieved, given the limited time and divergent national attitudes. Summarizing the achievements of Commission II, Belgian delegate George Theunis praised the bank as an "entire new venture. So novel was it, that no adequate name could be found for it." In so far as the accords covered capital subscriptions, loans, guarantees, and bond issues, the new agency seemed properly titled. Yet it was not a conventional bank; it would accept no deposits, make no short-term loans, and operate on a nonprofit basis. "It was accidentally born with the name Bank," he said, "and the Bank it remains, mainly because no satisfactory name could be found in the dictionary for this unprecedented institution."[60]

American officials also interpreted the international bank as a "great improvement" over prewar practices in international lending. With the bank functioning, private underwriters would no longer charge borrowers extortionate rates of interest, pocket commissions, and then sell high-risk bonds to unsuspecting small investors. Henceforth, private loans would compete with loans made or guaranteed by the bank; the new agency would act as a yardstick on international lending. The effect, Morgenthau asserted at the final plenary session, "would be to provide capital for those who need it at lower interest rates than in the past and to drive only the usurious money lenders from the temple of international finance." The reforms would help revive the flow of international capital, necessary if nations were to rehabilitate and develop their economies. Without the bank, technician E. A. Goldenweiser thought, this "investment would probably never get under way after the shock that it has suffered by the experience in the twenties and thirties and the War."[61]

Not all delegates shared Morgenthau's unbounded enthusiasm, for in the course of the lengthy deliberations some suggestions had naturally enough been rejected, and some disagreements had been suppressed in oblique language. The Latin Americans, for instance, had loyally supported the United States on crucial points, but some of the delegates had hoped that the conference would also take positive action on other aspects of global economic cooperation—especially tariff reduction, commodity price stabilization, and antidepression programs. The Canadians, and some of the American technicians, agreed that the conference had settled only a portion of the immediate problems. As the delegate from Ottawa said, "No such monetary and investment organizations, however perfect in form, can be expected to long survive the economic distortions of high tariffs, restrictive trading arrangements or enormous fluctuations in food and raw material prices such as marked the years between the wars."[62]

In order to avoid any last-minute cracks in conference solidarity, which might invite adverse political comment, delegates agreed to sign the articles of agreement *ad referendum*, thus avoiding any explicit recommendation to home governments. As Lord Keynes said, "We merely submit it for what it is worth to the attention of Governments and legislators concerned." Australia, disappointed that others had not manifested sufficient concern in the negotiations for arrangements to assure global full employment, instructed its delegate L. G. Melville to sign only for purposes of certification. Other formal reservations, it was agreed, would be appended to the minutes of the appropriate commission and not attached to the Final Act.[63]

Several delegations did register reservations that way. France and India, both dissatisfied with their fund quotas, which they thought did not correspond to their postwar position in world politics, entered their objections. The Soviets also added several technical reservations and clarifications, but these sentences seemed to identify friendly differences and not designate fundamental disagreements.[64]

The closing plenary session convened at 9:45 P.M. on July 22. When Lord Keynes rose to move acceptance of the Final Act, delegates gave him a standing ovation. It was a tribute not just to a fellow delegate and an eminent economist but also to one who, despite physical infirmities, had supplied vision, intelligence, and eloquence of a kind seldom seen at technical conferences. In his address Keynes observed that previous international conferences had a poor record. The successes at Bretton Woods he politely, and correctly, attributed to the "indomitable will and energy" of Harry Dexter White and, ironically, to the lawyers who have "turned our jargon into prose and our prose into poetry." But, Keynes added, "I wish they had not covered so large a part of our birth certificate with such very detailed provisions for our burial service, hymns, and lessons, and all." When he concluded, the delegates rose again and serenaded, "For He's a Jolly Good Fellow."[65]

Two minutes after the delegates voted to accept the Final Act, Morgenthau declared in his farewell address—carried live over national radio—that the Bretton Woods Conference "has successfully completed the task before it." Delegates had openly faced their differences and reached an agreement, which was a "sign that the people of the earth are learning how to join hands and work in unity." But he cautioned the delegates: "We are at a crossroads, and we must go one way or the other. The Conference has erected a signpost—a signpost pointing down a highway broad enough for all men to walk in step and side by side. If they will set out together, there is nothing on earth that need stop them."[66]

As soon as Morgenthau gaveled the session to a close, delegates crowded into the downstairs reception rooms to celebrate their accomplishments and the apparent determination of the United Nations coalition and its associates to cooperate in peacemaking as they had in war. Bretton Woods was over. This first conference on permanent international organization had succeeded.[67]

Selling the "Magnificent Blueprint"

"We have to go out from here as missionaries, inspired by zeal and faith," Lord Keynes exhorted the Bretton Woods delegates. "We have sold all this to ourselves. But the world at large still needs to be persuaded."[1]

As others celebrated the technical accomplishments, Keynes was already thinking about the remaining obstacles, especially how to obtain formal approval from governments for this first experiment with economic internationalism. This political problem was in some respects the most difficult barrier of all, for it touched such sensitive issues as national prestige, sovereignty, and interest. And, unless delegates could convey their own infectious enthusiasm for the Bretton Woods institutions to apprehensive legislators and skeptical interest groups, short-sighted opponents might destroy two years of technical discussion and negotiation and doom the postwar generation to a cycle of economic and political conflict. Keynes himself hoped that the critics would find the plans "so much better than they expected, that the very criticism and skepticism which we have suffered will turn things in our favor." "How much better," he suggested, "that our projects should *begin* in disillusion than that they should *end* in it!"[2]

As Keynes knew, the decisive contest for Bretton Woods would take place in the U.S. Congress. The articles of agreement provided that neither the fund nor the bank could begin operations until members with 65 percent of the quotas or subscriptions had given their formal approval. Since the United States would have about 28 percent of the votes, as well as the currency reserves and industrial resources required to rehabilitate other countries, Bretton Woods could not function practically without American participation. The attitude of Congress, then, would determine, as it had in the League of Nations battle twenty-five years earlier, whether the United States intended to assume international obligations commensurate with its real power. A defeat would shatter the Bretton Woods dream, disrupt economic relationships, and poison the climate for other forms of international cooperation. Accordingly, until the United States made its choice, Britain and other countries planned to suspend judgment.[3]

Delegates had good reasons for doubting America's resolve and for proceeding cautiously. Before and during the conclave, private bankers, prominent newspapers, and influential Republicans had all loudly voiced their opposition to Morgenthau's proposals. Bankers Winthrop Aldrich and Thomas Lamont, for instance, told Australian delegates the "Conference would fail any way because it would never get the approval of Congress." Editorials in the New York Times, the Wall Street Journal, and the Chicago Tribune condemned government management and international alphabetical organizations. The Wall Street Journal warned that Congress would probably reject any monetary plan based on the Anglo-American Joint Statement, and it advised foreign delegates to give careful attention to the "constructive" suggestions of international bankers who favored fixed exchange rates, balanced budgets, lower tariffs, and unrestricted capital movements.[4]

More disturbing to Morgenthau and other American delegates, however, were the efforts of a few "saboteurs," carrying press credentials, to penetrate the conference and pigeonhole wavering foreign delegates who might be swayed by New York Times criticisms. It was, Morgenthau joked, another case of the chicken and the egg—"which comes first the New York Times editorials or the saboteurs?" He was also embarrassed by the antics of one silver lobbyist who roamed the corridors and even interrupted one of Morgenthau's press conferences.[5]

While Ned Brown, Charles Tobey, and Jesse Wolcott—those most sensitive to outside criticisms—patiently tried to reassure other delegations that the United States would cooperate in constructing the postwar economic order, Senator Robert Taft dropped a verbal bomb-shell in Washington. Congress, the Ohio Republican asserted, would not approve any plan that placed "American money in a fund to be dispensed by an international board in which we have only a minority voice." Taft's comment brought swift rebuttals from delegates and even from some periodicals, like the *Magazine of Wall Street*, *Fortune*, and *Time*, but it indicated another source of potent opposition when the proposals reached Congress. A loose coalition of isolationists, Republicans, bankers, and laissez faire conservatives could be expected to battle resourcefully and relentlessly, and neither the administration nor foreign governments knew the strength of this opposition.[6]

After the conference E. A. Goldenweiser conveyed his own anxieties to Federal Reserve officials. Other governments cooperated at Bretton Woods, he said, because "the United States was leading. . . . they all need the United States so much that to follow its leadership is a natural inclination." Recalling the Versailles debate, Goldenweiser expressed his own hope that "our Congress will find it impossible to turn these agreements down because . . . our leadership in the world will be jeopardized. I think the world cannot be prosperous now without American leadership."[7]

Morgenthau had successfully directed the preparations from the beginning, and now he resolved to push Bretton Woods past congressional opposition. Soon after the conference, he directed Edward Bernstein and Ansel Luxford to devote themselves exclusively to the task of obtaining needed votes. Also, he ordered aides to devise an elaborate public and congressional relations campaign.[8]

After evaluating the political situation, Luxford, who handled Treasury congressional contacts, concluded that it was necessary to take the Bretton Woods program directly to the public. As he told Morgenthau, an Office of War Information survey conducted during the conference indicated widespread public apathy and disinterest "because there is no comprehension of the issues involved." Among the minority of citizens who ventured opinions, this study found a "clearly defined apprehension that the United States will be a 'sucker' nation, playing 'Santa Claus' to the world and 'outsmarted' by others, especially by England." According to those surveyed, Bretton Woods needed "more simple, more direct, more educational, more compelling" publicity.[9]

Selling the "Magnificent Blueprint"

As Luxford realized, widespread apathy and ignorance had a short-term advantage for the Treasury. It discouraged either political party from conducting the 1944 presidential campaign on Bretton Woods. Thus, there would be a political moratorium on this issue until early 1945 when the new congress assembled and considered the fate of the international monetary organization. This delay gave Morgenthau and his aides several critical months in which to "capitalize on this situation" and organize a comprehensive educational campaign.

To sell Bretton Woods, Morgenthau's assistants enlisted the talents of Randolph Feltus, a New York public relations man, and devised one of the most elaborate and sophisticated campaigns ever conducted by a government agency in support of legislation. The first phase involved a broad-gauged educational program to "penetrate the public consciousness on a national scale" so as to "stimulate public interest, crystallize public opinion, and make that opinion vocal." Specifically, it aimed to enlist the support of all elite groups and individuals who might influence congressional deliberations, particularly the World Peace Foundation, the Council on Foreign Relations, the Foreign Policy Association, the United Nations Association, the League of Women Voters, and others. Then these organizations, who had "ostensibly . . . responded to the education phase," would begin "aggressive 'selling' of the idea."[10]

In carrying Bretton Woods to the public, Treasury planners recognized that they must successfully explain in "simple, everyday terminology, understandable to the man on the street," how the program contributed to world cooperation and benefited the United States economically. Since businessmen were "not as vitally concerned with the welfare of the world as . . . with their own personal immediate future," the Treasury thought, it was essential to interpret Bretton Woods as a "good business deal for the United States." A direct approach, emphasizing self-interest, would avoid the stigma of nebulous government theorizing and enhance the appeal of a program that had other more important justifications.[11]

Morgenthau, it was decided, would take a prominent role, addressing elite audiences, such as the Detroit Economic Club, which "included all of the important industrialists in the Detroit area." On the appointed occasion Morgenthau proved that he, too, could be persuasive. He told the Detroit businessmen that Bretton Woods would assure foreign markets for a million automobile sales per year. Later, in Minneapolis, he again associated the financial proposals with local business interests. Stable exchange rates would expand foreign demand for American wheat. Similarly, he told farmers in the Red River Valley that discriminatory exchange rates squeezed agricultural income as much as if a farmer caught his hand in a threshing machine. Then, in St. Louis, Morgenthau forecast that Bretton Woods would enable the world to absorb "half our cotton, one-third of our tobacco, and nearly one-fifth of our production of wheat, rice, lard and similar crops."[12]

Other Treasury personnel also turned salesmen during the winter of 1945. Bernstein and Luxford, for instance, frequently spoke to banking and trade groups, presenting arguments calibrated to the sophistication and economic concerns of their listeners. Bernstein reminded delegates to the National Foreign Trade Convention and the Bankers Association for Foreign Trade that the fund would prevent blocked currency and exchange instability such as had disrupted commerce and payments before World War II. "The Fund," he said, "would assure businessmen that they would have an opportunity to engage in international trade on a fair competitive basis; that the proceeds of their exports would not be blocked; and that they would receive payment for their exports in their own currency or in gold." The New York Board of Trade heard Luxford claim that this country must sell 12 to 15 percent of its manufactured and agricultural products abroad after the war. Bretton Woods would help, and as a shipping center New York would benefit.[13]

To reach other audiences, the Treasury organized informational luncheons for reporters and columnists; prepared radio scripts, pamphlets, and articles; and even subsidized short moving pictures. In each of these approaches the public relations and technical experts avoided intricate, and generally confusing, discussions of currency parities and balance-of-payments mechanisms; instead, they stressed the far more comprehensible need for world security and expanding trade. Feltus helped journalist Frank Gervasi prepare an "enthusiastically favorable" article for the mass circulation *Collier's* that dramatized these twin themes. The article, entitled "Bretton Woods or World War III," claimed that "the stability of the political house that's built in Europe will depend on the solidity of its economic foundations." "Nobody," Gervasi wrote, "paid enough attention to the foundations after the first World War and in the general gerrymandering, a pompous Italian peasant and a sadistic Austrian paperhanger built the dungeons of Fascism and Nazism."[14]

For maximum impact on a more sophisticated audience interested in international affairs, Treasury staffers ghosted an article for *Foreign Affairs* that would appear under Secretary Morgenthau's signature. Hearing this, the secretary warned his phrasemakers not to "use three dollar words I don't understand myself. It is most embarrassing." The piece would be dignified and effective, Harry White responded, and it would contain no words worth more than "one dollar ninety-eight."[15]

Many who attended the conference as delegates, technicians, or visitors, displayed their enthusiasm for Bretton Woods by preparing accounts suitable for technical, regional, internationalist, and business audiences. Readers of the *Southern Banker*, for instance, discovered a sympathetic piece bearing the signature of Erle Cocke, a Fulton, Georgia, banker who had witnessed the New Hampshire deliberations. Rebutting charges of New York bankers and news critics, Cocke assured readers that the American delegates were not "wild-eyed visionaries and enthusiasts seeking for crack-brained solutions of the world's ills." Actually they were "hard-headed realists and businessmen seeking to pave the way for international monetary and economic cooperation on the tried and tested principles of American economic success." Approval of the Bretton Woods institutions would, he forecast, boost export sales of southern cotton, tobacco, and peanuts.[16]

Since the technical implications of Bretton Woods were comprehensible only to specialists, the Treasury informally mobilized the support of leading economists. Harvard Professor Seymour Harris, himself a Treasury consultant, organized the Economists Committee on the Bretton Woods Program, which polled the membership of the American Economic Association (AEA) and reported that 90 percent of the economists polled as well as sixteen of eighteen former presidents of the AEA supported Bretton Woods. That indicated, Harris's group claimed, a remarkable degree of unanimity among scholars of all political persuasions.[17]

International economists generally approved efforts to create an open world in which trade and capital could promote the most efficient allocation of resources, but this did not imply unqualified support for the Bretton Woods arrangements. Jacob Viner, probably the nation's most distinguished international economist after the death of Frank Taussig, had several reservations about the fund. It appeared to give more sanction to exchange-rate variations as a "normal procedure for relieving pressure on international balances" than was common in the past or desirable in the future. Also, the fund seemed too tolerant of exchange controls on capital account, and it seemed to grant "completely automatic access to what are essentially intermediate-term credits." Moreover, both the fund and the bank lacked adequate resources to facilitate Britain's safe adjustment to a multilateral world. Recognizing that some of these shortcomings could be remedied later, Viner praised the accords as an "American blueprint for the postwar economic world." He concluded that the "magnificent blueprint," with its provisions for world institutions to help stabilize currencies, assist capital flows, and promote high levels of economic activity, represented a marked improvement over prewar expedients. Economic implications aside, Viner feared, like many of his colleagues, that Congress might reject Washington's grand design as it had Woodrow Wilson's League of Nations. "If it is to be rejected, to be torn into shreds," he implored, "at least let it not be by American hands."[18]

Economist Henry Simons, one of Viner's colleagues at the University of Chicago, had a different perspective on monetary planning. Although government officials and private bankers battled verbally over how to secure convertibility and a durable pattern of stable exchange rates, Simons dismissed this controversy as less important than how to maintain a stable commodity value for the dollar. To this Chicago economist, what nations actually sought when they established currency convertibility as a paramount international monetary objective was to protect the value of their own reserve assets in terms of goods and services. Since the maintenance of a convertible currency would compel a government to pursue domestic policies intended to achieve price stability, the quest for convertibility seemed an indirect, and somewhat circumspect, device for attaining a laudable objective—safeguarding the real purchasing power of international money.

Nevertheless, because governments were sensitive to political pressures, they might evade or abandon their commitments to internal price stability if policies supporting currency convertibility were incompatible with domestic prosperity and high employment. For this reason Simons considered the Bretton Woods approach to stable money risky and undesirable. In place of a multilateral pledge to convertibility, he wanted the United States to provide economic leadership commensurate with its dominant position in the global economy. Washington should declare its intention to maintain a stable price level at home, thus avoiding recurrent aberrations of inflation and deflation. Such a pledge to a world fearful that another American depression would again disrupt international economics seemed, to Simons, necessary for establishment of a smoothly functioning international monetary system and a durable pattern of stable exchange rates. Like some other monetary economists, Viner's colleague blamed prewar currency disruption on America's failure to pursue a monetary policy that maintained internal price stability and prevented a contraction of money supply, prices, and employment; he did not blame America's chronic balance-of-payments surplus and the global dollar shortage, as some Keynesians did.

Returning to the orthodox gold standard did not excite Simons as it did Benjamin Anderson and some other conservative economists. The Chicago academician believed this panacea would only confuse the real relationship between the dollar and gold. Because America holds over half of all monetary gold, he argued, "the value of gold is thus merely a fact of the American gold price and of the commodity value of gold—i.e., of our fiscal policy." Nevertheless, Simons conceded that it might be expedient politically to hitch gold to the dollar. But, "to think of hitching the dollar to gold is almost not to think at all. One does not hitch a train to a caboose."[19]

Assuming American leaders understood and accepted the implications of a pledge to maintain stable prices, Simons knew that monetary and fiscal tools were available to effect the policy. When deflation threatened, the Treasury and Federal Reserve banks had only to engage in open-market operations, converting consols into currency. Conversely, to halt inflationary pressures, monetary agencies could issue new consols and absorb currency. Unlike many youthful Keynesians who favored adjusting federal expenditures to sustain a compensatory fiscal policy, Simons proposed to adjust government revenues through changes in personal income tax exemptions. And, with an unrelenting commitment to price stability in the United

States, Simons expected that it would be easy for smaller trading nations to remove occasional payments deficits with internal wage and price-level adjustments or small exchange-rate alterations.

A generation later, when inflation gnawed away foundations of the Bretton Woods system, Simons's critique seemed refreshingly prescient. But in 1945, after a cycle of depression and wartime disruption punctured confidence in laissez faire solutions and enhanced confidence in government planning and deficit spending, Keynesian policymakers paid little attention to Simons. Partly because the Chicago economist failed to argue his position vigorously, persistently, and lucidly, opponents of the Bretton Woods agreements lacked a creditable alternative. Instead, the loose coalition of opponents, which included such unlikely bedfellows as the isolationist *Chicago Tribune* and Wall Street bankers, relied on emotion-laden and shopworn arguments. To an apathetic public and an uncomprehending Congress these points often seemed anachronistic and self-serving.

At one extreme were opponents of the *Chicago Tribune* variety, who were monetary and political chauvinists. Col. Robert McCormick, and his anonymous editorial writers, castigated New Deal dreamers, Great Britain, collective security, free trade, and Bretton Woods with the help of Illinois Congresswoman Jessie Sumner. A cartoon captioned "Shady Deals" revealed the *Tribune*'s position. In the shadows of two groves of trees—one identified as Bretton Woods and the other as Dumbarton Oaks—lurked thugs with blackjacks, knives, and bombs preparing to blow up America, cut her throat, and steal her money.[20]

Visceral unilateralism, depicted favorably in the *Chicago Tribune* and the Hearst papers, revived memories of the League of Nations struggle and its consequences. Undoubtedly, it helped to discredit more constructive options, such as Chicago Congressman Charles Dewey's approach. Dewey was not a McCormick favorite, but like the *Chicago Tribune* he hoped to obstruct, and subsequently defeat, Roosevelt's monetary programs. Adoption of Bretton Woods, he cautioned in a radio address to constituents, would compel "mothers and wives . . . to increase your family budgets a little more to help provide the cash through extra taxes or buy a few more government bonds." In contrast to Morgenthau's idealistic international altruism, he suggested his own "intelligently selfish" reconstruction program that would use Export-Import Bank lending for agricultural and industrial export sales. Dewey saw his initiative as a substitute for Bretton Woods, but actually the two plans were complementary. The Export-Import Bank could fill the gap between lend-lease and the inauguration of fund and bank operations.[21]

More telling criticism of Bretton Woods came from individuals familiar with currency conditions—the international bankers. While it is true that the bankers were battling, at least in their own estimation, to shield their special interest area from more extensive government supervision, they were not generally hostile to global political cooperation, nor were they insensitive to global needs. If self-interest shaped their view of national interest, the same charge could be applied to the Treasury proposal: it strengthened the hand of bureaucracy and broadened the mandate for administrative intervention. Politics, far more than economics, handicapped the banking critics, for they were identified with money power and with short-sighted resistance to all New Deal programs. And, since the bankers were often prominent Republicans, it was easy for the administration and informed citizens to dismiss specific criticisms as partisan attacks.[22]

Winthrop Aldrich, chairman of the Chase National Bank, contributed to this confusion when he delivered a searing indictment of the Bretton Woods accords on September 15, 1944. At the request of the Republican National Committee, he addressed the Executives' Club of Chicago and charged that "currency manipulation will not solve the basic economic problems of a war-ridden world."[23]

Like many other international bankers, Aldrich considered the fund a gimmick for avoiding necessary internal cost-and-price adjustments to remove a payments deficit. His ideal was an automatic, self-regulating system anchored to gold, not a managed-credit system like the fund. Since, he said, members could automatically purchase foreign currencies up to 200 percent of that country's quota over a period of years without reference to internal budgetary conditions or to prospects for repayment, it was likely that the fund would find its supply of dollars depleted. At that point either the scarce-currency clause might come into play, allowing debtor countries to discriminate against American exports, or the United States might sell more dollars to the fund. Either way the United States, a surplus country, would be penalized for the benefit of deficit members. If, as Aldrich suspected, Washington opted to provide more dollars, exports would boom, distorting domestic prices, encouraging overproduction, and inviting a seemingly inevitable postboom bust. In short, the scenario was a replay of the post–World War I experience.

The Chase official also worried that the fund would become a "mechanism for instability rather than for stability." The fund seemed to encourage exchange-rate alterations, and these liberal provisions seemed to invite a repetition of the currency restrictions and competitive depreciations that characterized monetary experience in the 1930's.[24]

Far more serious than these technical defects, Aldrich thought, was misplaced concern with currencies and lending; discriminatory trade barriers and other impediments first had to be removed or reduced if nations were to repay their international obligations. Of greater urgency than a monetary conference, he indicated, was a world trade conference to devise a commercial code for removing discriminatory trade barriers.

Essentially, Aldrich favored a key-currency approach to postwar currency stabilization. If Britain agreed to dismantle her preferential system and join in forming an open trading system, America would provide a grant-in-aid large enough to stabilize the sterling-dollar currency rate. Other nations, needing stabilization or reconstruction and development loans, might better negotiate with the Export-Import Bank. Here Aldrich's and Dewey's recommendations joined: both would depend on unilateral, and temporary, American lending for currency stabilization and reconstruction.

Had the world not experienced a great depression with extensive joblessness and currency anarchy, the Aldrich-Dewey appeal for a traditional, ad hoc approach to stabilization might have won acceptance. But conditions had changed and so had public opinion. Across the Atlantic, Aldrich's message translated as a return to the gold standard and unemployment. Commented London's *Economist*, "The restoration of a true gold standard—and, perhaps, of 10 million unemployed—fits admirably into this setting of domestic soundness."[25] And, in the United States administration, supporters eager to compile political debating points turned Aldrich's statement to partisan advantage. Pennsylvania Democrat Joseph Guffey took the Senate floor to assail the international bankers, "Mr. Dewey's political mentors," of irresponsible economic isolationism. Republican campaign strategists, appalled also that Aldrich had endorsed a British loan and lower tariffs in Chicago, where these were unpopular, decided to remove Bretton Woods from the campaign portfolio. Presidential nominee Thomas E. Dewey and his running mate Governor John W. Bricker would concentrate their fire on other, less abstruse New Deal targets.[26]

Technicians in Washington interpreted Aldrich's attack as more than campaign rhetoric; it indicated that the banking community was still determined to push a key-currency approach instead of the universalistic Bretton Woods program. In a memorandum circulated at the specialist level, E. A. Goldenweiser disputed Aldrich's suggestion that tariff reductions be negotiated before currency stabilization. Vested interests, the Federal Reserve expert thought, could block tariff revisions; but the less-controversial Bretton Woods agreements could, by removing currency instability, improve the political prospects for successful negotiations on commercial policy. The New York bankers' postwar financial strategy was also deficient tactically, Goldenweiser concluded, because a key-currency approach was unacceptable to Great Britain and incompatible with the aspirations of the United Nations. At the nub of the disagreement, however, Goldenweiser saw the issue that had troubled relations between Washington and Wall Street since 1933: would the "great financial interests" or the government direct the United States' international monetary relations? Goldenweiser, like others in the administration, including Roosevelt and Morgenthau, believed that international bankers had mishandled reconstruction during the 1920's, and he did not propose to "entrust the postwar world to their management."[27]

Neither Washington nor foreign governments liked the key-currency solution, but bankers presented it as the centerpiece of a "logical compromise" to satisfy the banking community, gain additional support in Congress, and contribute to global financial rehabilitation. This compromise, bearing the support of Allan Sproul and John H. Williams, president and vice-president of the New York Federal Reserve Bank, called for the bank, not the fund, to take responsibility for all exchange-stabilization lending. If this were done, Sproul and Williams thought the fund could be "postponed," perhaps permanently, or at least until countries stabilized their domestic economies. Because Britain's war debts—estimated then at $12 billion in sterling debts—posed the greatest threat to financial reconstruction, Sproul and Williams favored a key-currency approach, involving a loan or grant to restore sterling convertibility. The suggestion, in fundamental respects, was little more than a yellow leaf from Benjamin Strong's notebook.[28]

But the New York Federal Reserve Bank no longer shaped international financial policy, as it did under Strong, and officials in the Treasury and the Federal Reserve Board of Governors attempted to persuade the New York bankers that the key-currency idea was unacceptable politically to foreign governments and the Roosevelt administration. If adopted over official objections, it would simply drive others toward an autarkic rather than a multilateral solution to their economic problems. As Goldenweiser stated, most countries would prefer to work out their own salvation by methods "which proved so disastrous" in the interwar period than to solicit temporary loans from the world bank.[29]

Both the bankers and the government sought to avoid an open political battle in Congress that could jeopardize international cooperation on other matters besides economic problems; thus, the two sides conducted private consultations. On January 4, 1945, for instance, Randolph Burgess, the new president of the American Bankers Association (ABA), and several other prominent bankers visited the Treasury to discuss matters with Morgenthau and his aides. An ABA committee, Burgess said, would soon recommend a compromise similar to the Sproul-Williams suggestion. The bank should be modified, but the fund, with its provision for automatic borrowing, should be postponed.[30]

Visibly irritated at the banking community's opposition, conservatism, and short-sightedness, Morgenthau observed that only recently during the war had bankers, by selling war bonds, finally repaired reputations damaged in the depression. But, if the bankers adhered to their narrow perspective on Bretton Woods, "they would put themselves in the position of sabotaging an international undertaking—the first attempt to bring order out of the postwar financial chaos, and one in which the leadership of the United States was at stake."[31]

Later, after Morgenthau and his aides left, Goldenweiser raised what he considered the fundamental issue: Was it in the bankers' interest to challenge the administration? As he saw it, the financiers could not afford to fight Washington, because a defeat for the monetary proposals would be both a major disservice to the nation and a public relations blunder for the bankers. "A defeat of the Bretton Woods proposals would mean a loss of leadership chances for the

United States and without American leadership chances of a reasonably good situation developing after the war would be greatly reduced." Goldenweiser did not say so, but a collision with the administration might provoke Roosevelt again to denounce the "economic royalists" and the "malefactors of great wealth."[32]

Burgess conceded that the Bretton Woods proposals were, for all their faults, better than nothing, but he and his friends determined to push for a more favorable compromise. On February 4, three banking groups—the American Bankers Association, the Association of Reserve City Bankers, and the Bankers Association for Foreign Trade—released a joint report, prepared under Burgess's direction. They recommended what was essentially the "logical compromise" favored in the New York Federal Reserve Bank.[33]

Briefly, Congress should reject the fund, provide the international bank with additional lending authority, and stabilize the dollar in a fixed relationship to the English pound. The bank could, in addition to its reconstruction and development lending, provide stabilization loans to members with inadequate reserves. This latter change was more significant than it might first seem. While members of the fund could apparently draw automatically on their quotas—up to certain limits—members of the bank could borrow only with the discretionary approval of the institution's management. Moreover, the United States could veto, if it wanted, all loans contemplated from the paid-in portion of members' subscriptions. To ensure that the bank adhered to prudent lending policies, the report recommended that the American governor and the executive director be "men of tested banking experience." Last, the bankers wanted Congress to create a cabinet-level committee to make policy decisions that would guide the actions of American representatives on the bank's board. Clearly, if Congress approved these modifications, the future of international cooperation would be even more in doubt. Other nations might demand their own changes in the Bretton Woods arrangements, which, at the very least, would delay the beginning of any monetary and financial program.[34]

Predictably, the ABA report was praised in the New York Times and Wall Street Journal and condemned in the Treasury and the liberal press. Morgenthau himself summoned a press conference to say that the ABA proposal would, if adopted, kill the Bretton Woods agreements and jeopardize international economic cooperation. He hoped that the bankers would see "just a little further than their own immediate business and realize that no instrument can be perfect."[35]

Samuel Grafton, one of Morgenthau's favorite columnists, charged that the bankers were more concerned with their balance sheets than with global peace and harmony. If the ABA had its way, he asserted, "profits on world stabilization would take precedence over stabilization itself." The New York Post, a liberal paper that customarily supported the New Deal, now claimed that the isolationist American Bankers Association had "launched a campaign to wreck the Bretton Woods Monetary Agreements." Monetary isolationism, the Post concluded, would no more effectively insulate the United States against a depression than political isolation kept it out of World War II.[36]

Morgenthau's followers, who interpreted the report as another round in the struggle between isolationism and internationalism, had oversimplified the conflict. Bankers, Ned Brown indicated privately, had technical objections, it was true, but fundamentally they distrusted Roosevelt, his New Deal assistants, and their postwar designs. The fact that Roosevelt would appoint the quixotic Henry Wallace secretary of commerce, now that he was no longer vice-president, made the financial community more apprehensive. Might not Roosevelt select some similar "crack-pot" to supervise international lending and monetary matters unless Congress stipulated that Roosevelt appoint only "men of tested banking experience."[37]

Thus, as Congress assembled to take up the Bretton Woods program, and other legislation, the administration anticipated a bitter struggle on postwar financial matters. The impending confrontation was not simply a contest between international commitments and unilateralism; it was a basic disagreement over approaches, institutions, and philosophy. The laissez faire tradition, self-interest, and experience persuaded the bankers that the British financial problem required priority over a general stabilization program. The administration, fearful that bankers were merely reviving old ways and again challenging public authority, insisted on a comprehensive United Nations approach. Special consideration of Britain's needs would have to wait until after the general framework of postwar collaboration was complete.

The preliminary skirmishes over Bretton Woods occurred as President Franklin Roosevelt faced a host of vexsome military, political, and economic issues. The chief executive was, despite the strains of nearly twelve years in the Oval Office, still determined to avoid the mistakes and obstacles that had frustrated and destroyed Woodrow Wilson's hopes for a better world. "This new year of 1945," Roosevelt said in a summary of his state-of-the-union message, broadcast on January 6, "can be the greatest year of achievement in human history. . . . We Americans of today, together with our Allies, are making history—and I hope it will be better history than ever has been made before."[38]

On the international scene the president expected 1945 to bring the "final ending of the Nazi-Fascist reign of terror in Europe." The Allies would also close in on the "malignant power of imperialistic Japan," but Roosevelt did not hint that the Pacific War would end in the year ahead. Also, he expected to see the "substantial beginning of the organization of world peace—for we all know what such an organization means in terms of security, and human rights, and religious freedom." To conclude the war and make a permanent peace, Roosevelt thought that he must preserve the great-power alliance, especially with Britain and the Soviet Union, against disintegrative forces—isolationism, nationalism, suspicion, ideological conflict, and political rivalry. "We need the continuing friendship of our Allies in this war," he emphasized in his radio message. "Indeed, that need is a matter of life and death. And we shall need that friendship in the peace."[39]

The rapid flow of events did not allow Roosevelt to concentrate on preparations for his critical summit meeting in the Crimea with Joseph Stalin and Winston Churchill. There were urgent domestic matters as well. While concluding the war, the United States must plan "to transform an all-out war economy into a full-employment peace economy whenever demobilization becomes possible." Outwardly optimistic about the prospects for nearly sixty million jobs in peacetime, the president was nevertheless making preparations to combat conversion problems and an economic slowdown. Public works projects, stronger social security and unemployment compensation, a national employment service, tax reform, and deficit spending would all be employed, if necessary, to stimulate the economy and create jobs.[40]

Domestic prosperity and successful international cooperation were related, and the president believed that active government must offer leadership to achieve both. "We have learned that just as the United States cannot afford to be isolationist in its political philosophy, neither can it stand the malignant effects of economic isolationism." For these broad reasons the administration attached considerable importance to gaining congressional approval for American participation in the International Monetary Fund and the International Bank.[41]

The White House elaborated its foreign economic plans and reiterated the interdependence of political and economic mechanisms for postwar collaboration in a presidential message released while Roosevelt was returning from Yalta. The Bretton Woods institutions were the "product of the best minds that 44 nations could muster," the president stated, and both the fund and the bank were required if nations were to move toward a "more united and cooperating world." The fund, which provides currency support, "spells the difference between a world caught again in the maelstrom of panic and economic warfare culminating in war—as in the 1930's—or a world in which the members strive for a better life through mutual trust, cooperation, and assistance." Its sister, the International Bank for Reconstruction and Development, would supply much of the postwar financial assistance necessary if war-torn nations were to undertake economic restoration without resort to discriminatory trade practices, competitive currency depreciations, and other forms of economic warfare "that would destroy all our good hopes." Along with the Bretton Woods institutions other arrangements were necessary to cope with postwar disruption and economic dislocations. The president indicated that he would soon submit legislation to establish a United Nations Food and Agriculture Organization, extend reciprocal trade, facilitate an international agreement on reduction of trade barriers, control cartels and the marketing of surplus commodities, revise the Export-Import Bank, and repeal the Johnson Act, which prohibited lending to nations in default on World War I debts. All these were important, the president concluded, because the world stood at a point "full of promise and of danger." It could "either move toward unity and widely shared prosperity or it will move apart into necessarily competing economic blocs."[42]

The interwar experience offered convincing evidence that effective international organization required both political and economic institutions, but the Roosevelt administration's decision to dramatize this interdependence in 1945 reflected a realistic assessment of domestic political currents. Until the 1944 presidential election results effectively interred fears that the voters and Congress would reject Roosevelt's leadership, as they had Woodrow Wilson's in 1918, it seemed that the United Nations might experience the same fate in Congress as the League of Nations had. But the election returned Roosevelt to office and preserved his majority in Congress. Moreover, the fact that public opinion polls showed more than 70 percent of the people approving a new League of Nations had compelled many of the prewar isolationists to back membership in the United Nations. Support for political collaboration, however, did not extend to international economic cooperation. Despite the publicity given the Bretton Woods meetings, only 23 percent of the public, as late as May 29, 1945, could even relate Bretton Woods to world affairs. Because the average citizen displayed so little interest in abstruse economic matters, it was quite possible that Roosevelt's Republican opponents and the international banking community would persuade Congress to reject Bretton Woods while it approved the United Nations. This prospect, together with memories of the Versailles battle and its consequences, encouraged Roosevelt's followers to stress, as Morgenthau did, that "political and economic security from aggression are indivisible."[43]

Memories and forebodings also affected the selection of legislative procedure. Cognizant of the perils that treaties often encountered in the Senate, where approval required a two-thirds majority, the Treasury decided, after consulting Secretary Hull, to have the Bretton Woods agreements written as multilateral executive agreements. Then, since Congress must authorize funds for the American quotas and since the administration pledged to consult Congress, the Treasury proposed an uncomplicated procedure. The White House would merely ask both branches of the legislature to approve, by majority vote, an enabling act authorizing the president to accept membership in the Bretton Woods institutions. This method had precedent. In 1934 Congress passed a resolution permitting President Roosevelt to accept membership in the International Labor Organization, a League of Nations affiliate.[44]

The legislative phase of the Bretton Woods struggle opened on Wednesday, March 7, when Congressman Brent Spence convened hearings. As is the custom when the legislature takes up major administration bills, a cabinet member, Henry Morgenthau, came as the first witness. Morgenthau, preferring to talk in broad principles while leaving specific details for other witnesses, stressed that the proposal, House Resolution 2211, was vital to world political and economic security. The two institutions were, he said, as "interdependent as the blades of scissors. One will not work very well without the other." Under questioning Morgenthau urged legislators to approve the accords before the United Nations conference opened in San Francisco on April 25. Favorable action on monetary matters would demonstrate to the world that the United States means business, and it would "strengthen the hand of the American delegation."[45]

Morgenthau, who referred difficult questions to Dean Acheson and Harry Dexter White, was a less effective spokesman than Fred Vinson, the former congressman and Bretton Woods delegate. Vinson, like the Treasury secretary, was often unfamiliar with technical matters, but his personal rapport with committee members made Vinson an effective witness. He assured congressmen, who were irritated by the Treasury experts or confused by complicated economic jargon and unfamiliar issues, that the administration had, throughout the conference, solicited and followed the advice of congressional delegates. Bretton Woods, he emphasized, was a nonpartisan effort in which Democrats and Republicans cooperated to "avoid the rocks upon which the League of Nations broke." Vinson succeeded so well in allaying fears that Texas Congressman Wright Patman exclaimed, "I do not think that the President could have selected a man who would have met with more approval on the Hill among Members of Congress, than yourself."[46]

Ordinarily, congressional hearings allow proponents and critics of a bill to educate legislators, express alternative opinions, and solicit modifications. The Bretton Woods deliberations served each of those purposes. On the one side, the Treasury mobilized an army of influential citizens and groups to echo Acheson, Harry Dexter White, Edward Eagle Brown, and Vinson, who defended the agreements. To give evidence of wide support, they invited spokesmen for the American Farm Bureau Federation, the Americans United for World Organization, the Congress of Industrial Organizations, Independent Bankers, National Grange, the League of Women Voters, and others. On the other side, opponents lined up a cast of prominent bankers, including Randolph Burgess, Leon Fraser—president of the First National Bank of New York—and financial expert Edwin Kemmerer. Also, Benjamin

Anderson, Allan Sproul, and John H. Williams testified or expressed written opinion. Billed as an epic confrontation between Washington and Wall Street, the debate essentially repeated most of the shop-worn arguments heard repeatedly in public.[47]

Until Senator Robert Taft and a small band of determined obstructionists challenged the propriety of an international bank to guarantee private lending in June, the fund was the center of controversy. Briefly stated, technical debate concentrated on two complicated, related issues. First, would the International Monetary Fund actually help remove dislocations and distortions during the postwar transitional period and speed progress toward the ideal of an open world with stable, convertible currencies? Second, would the fund mechanisms and rules promote an equitable and effective adjustment of the payments disequilibria that occasionally disturb a system that simultaneously seeks exchange-rate stability, convertibility, and independent national economic policies?

As suggested earlier, the bankers and Treasury planners actually disagreed more on procedures than on principles. Both Wall Street and Washington sought an orderly monetary regime that would contribute to an efficient use of world resources, global prosperity, and international harmony. Both agreed that the United States should, and could, exercise leadership to promote regular monetary consultation, an orderly pattern of exchange rates, and the removal of exchange restrictions on trade—and, if feasible, on capital movements. Neither side advocated flexible exchange rates; instead, countries should peg currencies to gold or gold-convertible currencies. And, at least in principle, both accepted the need for short-term credit facilities to cushion adjustments. Broadly stated, these recommendations emerged from prewar experiences; if World War II had not intervened, the principles would no doubt have appeared as major industrial countries extended and elaborated the Tripartite Agreement.[48]

Basically, the bankers argued, as they had before, that an international fund was unnecessary, premature, and unworkable in disordered postwar conditions. Randolph Burgess pointed out that most potential members did not need a multinational fund, for they already had adequate reserves. Neutrals and Latin American governments, for instance, would have nearly $20 billion. But the countries who did need outside assistance—Britain, France, and several other European countries—had requirements in excess of their fund drawing rights.

John Williams anticipated that Britain would have $15 billion in blocked sterling debts and a current-account deficit of between $1.2 and $2 billion annually during the difficult adjustment period ahead. But, because London could only draw $325 million annually from the fund for four years, approval of the currency fund would not give Britain the line-of-credit necessary to dismantle exchange controls and assume obligations of full membership in the open-world order. Thus, since it was obvious Britain would rely on controls for stabilization whether the fund was available or not, it followed logically that postponement of the fund would not prevent countries from stabilizing their currencies in this manner. As Williams analyzed the situation, approval of the fund might actually postpone the emergence of a multilateral world because it would discourage separate, bilateral initiatives to create the proper conditions for sterling convertibility. As he said, "The worst bargain we could make . . . would be to adopt promptly the Bretton Woods agreement *in toto* but be left with the discriminatory trade and exchange practices and without the bases for genuine cooperative efforts."[49]

If the practical monetary experts thought that Bretton Woods did too little for sterling, they recognized that it did too much for the Soviet ruble. Russia had a state-controlled currency and thus did not require a cushion of reserves to remove exchange restrictions; yet, delegates gave Moscow a $1.2 billion quota, which was essentially an intermediate-term reconstruction loan. The bankers were correct from an economic point of view, but the administration had always viewed Soviet participation in political terms. As a result, Ned Brown, the Chicago banker, had little alternative but to uphold the Treasury line. A $1.2 billion loan was "not too high a price to pay for her cooperation, even if we forget, which representatives of the United Nations at Bretton Woods did not, her tremendous losses in human lives and in property destroyed and the great part she has played and is playing in the war."[50]

Opponents revived other familiar criticisms: automatic access would exhaust the currency pool, impair the fund's effectiveness in the posttransitional period for which it was designed, and waste the American contribution while sparking inflation within the United States. As Senator Taft put it vividly, adoption of the fund was like "pouring dollars down a rat hole."[51]

White and his allies countered with assurances that the fund could not become depleted, because "there is no unqualified right to credits from the fund." Directors could halt currency transactions if they concluded that a country was acting contrary to the fund's purposes. Moreover, White assured Congress that, even with the "greatest expedition by our Congress and by the legislative branches of other countries," the agency would not become operable for a year or more. Thus, to rebut one criticism that drawings would drain the fund of usable currencies, the administration tacitly acknowledged the first objection—the fund would not be likely to play a major role as a short-term creditor in the transitional period. Despite its limitations, the government still thought that the fund would inspire confidence and encourage other nations to prepare for transition to a world of convertible currencies—not for a drift to permanent bilateralism and discrimination. And this was the strongest argument for the International Monetary Fund: it directed and committed members to a mutually desirable, if immediately unattainable, goal—a world of stable, convertible currencies.[52]

Under conditions more normal than were expected to prevail immediately after the war, bankers doubted that the fund's rules and procedures would promote an orderly and equitable adjustment of payments imbalances. Bretton Woods, they noted, submerged the concept of two-sided adjustment, such as prevailed under the textbook gold standard. Instead, the new accords placed too much emphasis on exchange depreciation by debtors and too much responsibility on creditor countries—namely, the United States in the foreseeable future—to correct a payments gap.

The gold standard, admitted Allan Sproul, erred in requiring excessive monetary and fiscal stringency from deficit countries, but Bretton Woods went to the other extreme. It imposed little pressure on debtors and encouraged them to think that after fund assistance was exhausted they had merely to announce a fundamental disequilibrium and, in consultation with the fund, select a new exchange parity. These exchange-rate adjustments would penalize a surplus nation for the economic mismanagement of a deficit country. As the opponents pointed out, the fund's rules appeared to reward profligacy. "A government may pursue the policy of an unbalanced budget, or a policy of raising its costs or hampering its export industries, and may devalue its currency indefinitely if that is the effect of its policies."[53]

As Harry White anticipated in negotiations with the British, the fund's foes argued that it legitimized currency instability. In sanctioning periodic exchange-rate alterations to maintain equilibrium, the International Monetary Fund (IMF) articles appeared to discourage currency stability, which government officials claimed was a principal advantage of the new regime. In retrospect, the bankers made an important point. They correctly anticipated that Bretton Woods would fail to promote orderly and equitable exchange-rate adjustments, but the bankers were mistaken in assuming that deficit parties—especially industrial countries—would rely more extensively on exchange depreciation than on domestic fiscal and monetary policy to restore equilibrium. As it turned out, the IMF agreements tended to discourage necessary parity changes, not the reverse.

Morgenthau's witnesses generally agreed that the fund could not pressure a member to deflate its home economy and that some exchange-rate adjustments were necessary. But establishing a procedure for orderly parity changes did not mean that the fund would, in practice, legitimize exchange instability. In fact, the opposite was true. In joining the fund, governments accepted a previously unacknowledged principle: Exchange variations were matters for international consultation, not unilateral action. Accordingly, "the stability offered by the fund will be far greater than the world has seen since 1914; and it will be far greater than we can possibly expect in the postwar world without international monetary cooperation."[54]

If the bankers thought the fund too lenient on deficit countries, they considered it too burdensome for surplus nations. Without taking into account the causes of a payments disequilibrium—had debtors simply lived beyond their means?—the scarce-currency clause permitted, when invoked, discrimination against a surplus country whose currency was unavailable in adequate supply. In accepting this provision, said the bankers, the Treasury assumed complete responsibility for any future dollar shortage, whatever its cause. And, when others invoked this provision to justify discrimination against American goods, this country must either acquiesce passively or expand lending and investments to correct the shortage. In short, the scarce-currency clause "puts this country in a position where it must either break the heart of the world and withdraw from the fund, or loan many more billions to foreign countries."[55]

Harry White sought to allay these criticisms with further assurances that it was "not highly probable" the clause would be invoked. The responsibility for correcting a payments maladjustment, he added, was "not a unilateral one." But here his interpretation was at variance with Lord Keynes's analysis, as Senator Taft bluntly noted. Keynes had told the House of Lords, "The Americans . . . have, of their own free will and honest purpose, offered us a far-reaching formula of protection against a recurrence of the main cause of deflation during the interwar years, namely, the draining of reserves out of the rest of the world."[56]

If both White and Keynes were correct—that is, the scarce-currency clause would not be utilized because the United States had tacitly assumed responsibility for removing a global dollar shortage—what did Washington have in mind? Policies to expand imports, provide foreign loans and investments, or maintain domestic full employment? White, who tended to underestimate postwar disruption, seems to have thought, as did some American Keynesians, that a domestic full-employment policy would prevent the postwar recession the scarce-currency clause was intended to counteract, if necessary.

But, before Congress concluded deliberations, the administration had conceived a multifaceted program to remove the dollar gap, then expected to approach $25 to $30 billion during the postwar decade. In June 1945, estimates were highly tentative, but they called for extensive official lending. The international bank would supply $9 billion, the Export-Import Bank $5–10 billion, and private sources another $10 billion as direct investment in foreign plants and facilities. The Export-Import Bank would serve as the principal short-term conduit until the international bank began lending in 1946. According to State Department analysts, the comprehensive program also depended on approval of a domestic full-employment program, which, in conjunction with a liberal trade policy, would expand world economic activity and trade. By the summer of 1945, then, the administration no longer looked exclusively to the Bretton Woods mechanisms to bridge the transitional period. The international bank would assume an important role in facilitating private capital flows and reconstruction lending, but, increasingly, the Bretton Woods package now seemed more appropriate as an intermediate-term framework for monetary cooperation than as a full solution to immediate difficulties. Nevertheless, while Washington had begun to accept the need for unilateral assistance, its basic policy contained ambiguities. Was it tactically feasible to press for swift implementation of the Bretton Woods accords? Did the administration have a plan for easing Britain's financial adjustments and for implementing a key-currency solution within the construct of the Bretton Woods arrangements?[57]

How Washington intended to underwrite Britain's move to convertibility remained purposely vague during the congressional hearings. Legislators knew, of course, that Keynes had hinted to the House of Lords that supplementary arrangements were contemplated. These, he said in May 1944, would be "another chapter of international cooperation, upon which we shall embark shortly if you do not discourage us unduly about this one." However, Treasury officials discouraged speculation about a future British loan. In June 1945, Harry White reportedly told legislators in executive session that the United Kingdom would definitely not need aid; sterling-bloc creditors were expected to forgive London's war debts. Keynes himself had encouraged this thinking. If White knew that others in the administration were already contemplating a long-term low-interest loan, he did not admit it. His denial was consistent with established policy —both the universal approach and tactical requirements dictated no talk of alternative arrangements. If the Treasury conceded in the midst of congressional hearings that Britain might actually need special help, this, it was believed, would confuse issues and seemingly confirm the bankers' arguments that the fund was, in fact, inadequate and thus might be safely postponed until more normal conditions existed. These were not the only reasons for White's position. Personally, he suspected that the scheming British were stronger than some Anglophiles asserted and worried that in assuming an obligation to rehabilitate Britain this country might actually jeopardize its own financial and political position in the postwar world.[58]

Here White found himself isolated from Morgenthau and other Treasury staff, including E. M. Bernstein and Ansel Luxford. The impressionable Treasury secretary visited Britain in August 1944, chatted candidly with Churchill, and returned home with news that England was broke. For the next year he endeavored to find some means for putting England "back on her feet." Initially, he and Roosevelt thought lend-lease would fill the breach, and at the Quebec Conference in September the president approved Churchill's request for $3 billion in nonmilitary aid during Phase II, the period between the defeat of Germany and that of Japan. But Germany did not fall as quickly as some expected, and as time elapsed Roosevelt, under pressure from Congress and the military, retreated from his pledge. Nevertheless, to the British the president's word was sufficient justification to think that the charming New York patrician would find a way—perhaps another "brain-wave," Keynes suggested—to ease London's financial adjustments.[59]

Publicly, the Roosevelt administration backed away from extended lend-lease in March, after Congress explicitly restricted that aid program to military purposes. While testifying on Bretton Woods, Dean Acheson found it necessary to pledge: "Nothing is being done, or will be done, in regard to any country under lend-lease for post-war purposes. That statement I wish to make categorically." He also denied knowledge of any proposals for postwar loans.[60]

Germany's defeat in May forced officials to consider British needs again, and suggestions for a long-term loan circulated. White, however, continued to oppose a key-currency approach, but his aides Bernstein and Luxford gradually adopted a different view. Fearing that Britain's precarious finances would jeopardize their grand design for a multilateral world, they inserted a hint of future moves in the Senate majority report on Bretton Woods. "Only after there is assurance that the fund and the bank will be available to encourage world trade and investment will it be possible to determine further steps needed to help with Britain's balance-of-payments problems." Meanwhile, Britain's friends in the State Department, including Assistant Secretary William L. Clayton, privately discussed a $2–3 billion loan extending over thirty years. Rapidly changing military and political circumstances compelled the Truman administration to adjust its plans, but, until Congress moved on Bretton Woods, the executive branch chose not to divulge these shifting assessments publicly.[61]

During the protracted hearings in both House and Senate, Treasury officials worked closely with Democratic congressional leaders and outside interest groups in order to enhance the prospects for passage. Feltus and the technicians supplied congressional backers and administration witnesses with ghosted speeches, questions, and testimony. Senators and representatives who preferred to write their own statements found the Treasury eager to provide outlines, arguments, and evidence, including statistics and appropriate quotations from Woodrow Wilson, Thomas Jefferson, and other statesmen whose wisdom bridged the centuries.[62]

No doubt Treasury assistance did facilitate discussion of the financial arrangements, which, after all, exceeded the technical competence of most politicians. At least once the tactic backfired, however, when a witness supplied with a prepared statement conceded that he did not understand what he was saying. Eager to show Congress that some bankers endorsed Bretton Woods, the Treasury had mobilized the Independent Bankers' Association, a small group claiming to represent two thousand country banks in forty states on Main Street, not Wall Street. With government assistance the small bankers prepared and issued a report praising Bretton Woods as a means for averting "another era of economic warfare with all of its tragic consequences to world peace." But, under persistent questioning, Ben DuBois, secretary of the Independent Bankers, conceded that, although he was "one of the 12 best economists" in Sauke Centre, Minnesota, he knew little about international finance. Yes, the Treasury helped prepare his testimony. Harry Dexter White, he admitted, might even have written the Independent Bankers' Report.[63]

The issues seemed irretrievably drawn and both sides seemed determined to yield nothing. But on March 20, as the bankers trudged to Capitol Hill to testify, the Committee for Economic Development (CED) released a Hegelian compromise intended to satisfy both the government and the bankers. Inspired by Beardsley Ruml, the cerebral treasurer of R. H. Macy & Company, and bearing the support of a number of moderate business leaders, this report proposed to strengthen the international bank so that it could make short-term stabilization loans in the transitional period, as well as long-term project loans for reconstruction and development. With the bank taking a more active role in the abnormal postwar period, the fund, designed primarily to cushion short-term fluctuations in an orderly world where international transactions tended to balance, would not have to assume the burden of financing unstable conditions. According to the CED analysis, if the bank engaged in stabilization lending, the fund would not misuse its resources and become frozen with unwanted currencies, as the bankers feared. In short, Ruml's committee agreed with the banking analysts that the fund was an inappropriate instrument for transitional assistance, but, unlike the ABA, the Committee for Economic Development accepted the Treasury argument that the fund could serve other useful and important purposes, such as international consultation.[64]

Ruml's report, suggesting as it did a compromise that would not seriously alter the Bretton Woods accords, pointed toward a workable solution. And, within forty-eight hours, both sides offered favorable comments. A spokesman for Morgenthau welcomed the CED suggestion as "constructive and clarifying." Randolph Burgess agreed that it was an "interesting suggestion . . . that might be accomplished without violating any of the arrangements reached at Bretton Woods."[65]

Privately, E. A. Goldenweiser found the episode extremely amusing. The CED alternative, arriving at a psychologically opportune moment, enabled the Treasury to make an inconsequential concession to its foes, "who fear they will lose the fight." That way the bankers could retreat gracefully, claiming victory. Politics aside, Goldenweiser thought the change unnecessary. At Bretton Woods, he said, delegates considered authorizing the bank to make stabilization loans, but, to avoid arousing the bankers, who traditionally made stabilization loans, the delegates had avoided an explicit statement. What the whole matter showed, Goldenweiser joked, was that government experts were more eager to protect private banking interests than those who wrote the CED report. Nevertheless, the formula offered a convenient fig leaf. "The C.E.D. made the egg stand on its end and the performance seems to have fascinated not only the authors of the report but the onlookers. If this helps build up a majority for the agreements—it will be to the good." Even so, it was "amusing to watch the C.E.D. with a Ruml grin dancing an elephantine polka to solemn music while assorted dignitaries clap their hands in unison."[66]

In public and private the ABA adopted a more conciliatory attitude after publication of the CED recommendations. On March 21, for instance, Burgess told the House Banking and Currency Committee that, although he favored postponement, bankers would tolerate the fund if no alternative existed other than total rejection of the Bretton Woods package. Burgess admitted that, if he were a member of Congress and if the bill failed to gain appropriate amendments, he would hold his nose, swallow a glass of orange juice, and take his medicine by voting for the legislation. The bankers still had serious reservations, but, as Burgess's testimony indicated, they would grudgingly suspend their resistance if this was the only way to construct a multilateral world economy.[67]

These indications of crumbling resistance came at a time when administration opponents apparently held enough votes to block Bretton Woods. On March 22, for instance, Spence told Morgenthau that a majority of the banking committee—including all Republicans and two Democrats—wanted to vote against the bill. Bretton Woods was not the only component of Roosevelt's foreign economic program facing heavy opposition. Previously lend-lease opponents had tacked on an amendment prohibiting the use of these funds for postwar relief, reconstruction, or rehabilitation. And congressmen displayed little enthusiasm for extending reciprocal trade, repealing the Johnson Act, or expanding the Export-Import Bank's lending authority to meet postwar needs. Moreover, sharp questioning indicated that Congress was in no mood to approve a postwar loan for the Soviet Union. All of these taken together confirmed the New York Post claim that, while officials in Washington worried over Stalin's attitude toward the United Nations and postwar cooperation, Congress itself had done nothing to demonstrate America's willingness to cooperate with the world.[68]

Undecided about how to assuage the opposition, Morgenthau consulted his aides. Should the Treasury explore the possibility of reaching an informal settlement with the bankers? Not at this time, argued Harry White. Burgess was a "rattlesnake," and, if the Treasury delayed, the weight of domestic opinion would eventually compel Burgess and his friends to approve the package on Treasury terms. Bernstein saw the situation differently. Burgess had made "a point for the record," but now he wanted to call off the fight so as to minimize unfavorable international repercussions. Accepting this argument, Morgenthau directed Assistant Secretary Daniel Bell to supervise informal discussions and report back.[69]

What Bell, Luxford, and Bernstein discovered was that the bankers were divided. Burgess wanted to work out a compromise that would satisfy his followers without requiring either amendment of the Bretton Woods agreements or postponement of the fund. And, in a meeting on April 2, he and the Treasury representatives tentatively agreed on a compromise that might include three basic changes in the enabling legislation. First, to meet criticisms that American policy in the fund and bank might be uncoordinated, Congress would stipulate that a single individual would represent the United States as executive director in both institutions. A second American would serve as governor of the fund and bank. Also, the bill would establish an interdepartmental committee, with the Treasury secretary as chairman, to formulate American policy toward the twin institutions. Burgess insisted that this group include the secretaries of Treasury and State, chairman of the Federal Reserve Board of Governors, the foreign economic administrator, and the president of the New York Federal Reserve Bank. Because Henry Wallace would be a "red flag" to bankers already distrustful of administration intentions, the secretary of commerce should not participate. Finally, the two sides agreed to include the essence of the CED recommendation—that the bank extend short-term stabilization loans.[70]

Burgess also wanted definite assurances that Washington would press other nations to establish the headquarters of both the fund and the bank in New York, where they "would not be under undue political influence," and that the government appoint Ned Brown as either the American governor or executive director. Morgenthau's assistants refused, however, to discuss possible appointments.[71]

This formula at first encountered resistance in New York and Washington. Officials at the powerful New York Federal Reserve Bank, including Sproul and Williams, considered Bretton Woods peripheral to the primary postwar economic problem—Britain's monetary weakness. Winthrop Aldrich, chairman of the Chase National Bank, also opposed the compromise, partly because he believed that Morgenthau was harassing his bank over foreign funds control regulations in reprisal for Aldrich's own opposition. Convinced that the bankers could win in Congress, Aldrich reluctantly concluded that the bankers had a responsibility to help the "Treasury . . . save its face," but not with a premature compromise.[72]

Despite the still unfavorable attitude of a majority of congressmen on the banking committee, Morgenthau was more confident now that the Treasury could win without Burgess's support, and he backed away from the compromise. He reasoned that supporters could push the bill through the House without amendments or reservations, but that Senate conservatives might present more formidable opposition. Thus, to minimize alterations in the Bretton Woods package, Morgenthau hoped to delay concessions until absolutely necessary. "If we've got to do any horse-trading," he said, "let's do it in the Senate." But, Dean Acheson, now chief congressional lobbyist for the State Department, recommended a more conciliatory approach. He anticipated that an influential bloc of isolationist Republicans, led by Congressman Joseph Martin of Massachusetts and Senator Robert Taft, would accept the United Nations, which had overwhelming public support, and vigorously oppose foreign economic commitments, including Bretton Woods and reciprocal trade. If this analysis were correct, then it seemed more prudent to offer a few concessions that would win over Jesse Wolcott and other moderate Republicans before opposition hardened along partisan lines. Nevertheless, Morgenthau opted to postpone a decision until he had thoroughly canvassed the issue with Spence and other Democratic leaders in Congress.[73]

As Morgenthau waited, the legislative outlook improved dramatically. First, the unexpected death of President Franklin Roosevelt in mid-April erased many of the partisan "antagonisms of 12 embattled years," as Senate reporter Allan Drury said. Congressional opponents, suspicious that Roosevelt and his global planners intended to scatter American resources to the far corners of the globe, had already slapped down Roosevelt's scheme to employ lend-lease for postwar reconstruction and demonstrated their strength on other issues, including the protracted Bretton Woods hearings. But the elevation of Truman brought to the White House one sensitive to congressional concerns, and, when the new president promptly urged Congress to implement Roosevelt's program, the prospects leaped upward.[74]

Second, as more time elapsed the Treasury's effective public relations campaign crystallized broad-based elite-group support for Bretton Woods. By late April more than a hundred organizations—including business, civic, labor, religious, educational, trade, and peace groups—were providing active support. The American Federation of Retailers mailed circulars to 1.8 million outlets, urging expressions to Congress in support of Bretton Woods. The Congress of Industrial Organizations (CIO) promised its members 5 million jobs from foreign trade if they helped persuade Congress. The League of Women Voters organized 5,000 discussion groups in 35 states and placed more than 100,000 pieces of literature in doctors' offices, beauty parlors, and other public places. One pamphlet, aimed at children, showed the United States surrounded by a high tariff wall. This country declined to exchange autos, eggbeaters, and rubber dolls for wool, cameras, and silk. As a result, other countries lacked jobs, their people became poorer and poorer, and their children thinner and thinner; soon "countries got madder and madder," and "everybody began rattling their GUNS." But, the tract continued, the Bretton Woods accords would make it possible for the world to live in peace. And, on the last page, children found a picture of their parents, relatives, and neighbors mailing letters to senators and congressmen in behalf of the Treasury program.[75]

Evidence does not show that the children's appeal tipped the scales, but public support did translate into pressure on Congress. By mid-May, for instance, the House Banking and Currency Committee —to say nothing about individual congressmen—had received 25,000 pieces of mail in favor of Bretton Woods and only 42 against. And, although a Gallup poll revealed that only 23 percent of one survey group could even relate Bretton Woods to world affairs, Congress understood the significance of interest-group opinion. Later, in the Senate, Robert Taft complained that Morgenthau had used tax dollars "in one of the most completely organized propaganda efforts which this country has ever seen. . . . That propaganda," he admitted, "has been successful in creating a large-scale public opinion which is now used by the proponents as evidence of the merit of the scheme."[76]

With the tide of public support shifting decisively in favor of international commitments, Wolcott approached the Treasury and offered to mediate. The bankers, he said on April 21, were now anxious to "save their faces" and would consent to "anything," and this compromise would gain widespread Republican support. Though Morgenthau disliked compromising with the bankers, he relented in early May and worked out several amendments with Congressman Spence that would satisfy the Republicans without requiring additional international negotiations. The most important changes included a provision that the United States representatives to the bank obtain an official interpretation "as to its authority to make or guarantee loans for programs of economic reconstruction and the reconstruction of monetary systems." In short, could the bank make short-term stabilization loans, and, if not, the American officials were directed to propose and support a prompt amendment in the articles of agreement. Similarly, the fund was to be asked for an "official interpretation" as to whether it could use its resources for more than current stabilization operations and as to whether the fund has the authority to "use its resources to provide facilities for relief or reconstruction or to meet a large or sustained outflow of capital on the part of any member." Again, if the answers were affirmative, the Americans were directed to propose and support amendments that would expressly negate these interpretations. Another modification would authorize the president to appoint, with the advice and consent of the Senate, a single governor for both the bank and the fund, as well as an executive director to serve on each body.[77]

Finally, to coordinate the activities of all government agencies involved in lending and monetary activities, as well as to coordinate policy in the bank and fund, the House committee proposed a National Advisory Council on International Monetary and Financial Problems. The secretary of the treasury would chair this group, which included the secretary of state, the chairman of the Federal Reserve Board of Governors, the secretary of commerce, and the chairman of the Export-Import Bank—but not an official of the New York Federal Reserve Bank. Broadly, these revisions corresponded closely to the recommendations offered by the CED and Randolph Burgess for the American Bankers Association. For the administration, this settlement ensured that the Treasury would have the dominant role in international monetary policy; the New York Federal Reserve Bank would not have a direct influence over the formulation of government policy. The bankers had not excluded Commerce Secretary Henry Wallace, but they and the CED effectively circumscribed the fund's postwar operations. Congress had stipulated that the fund's largest member should oppose short-term reconstruction lending that might block its resources and handicap operations in more normal circumstances.

The compromise, supported by Spence and Wolcott, encountered only symbolic opposition. On May 24, after Chairman Brent Spence introduced the alterations, which were acceptable to most Republicans, his Banking and Currency Committee voted twenty-three to three in favor of Bretton Woods. It was a remarkable turnaround. Six weeks earlier a majority had opposed; now only three World War II irreconcilables—Republicans Frederick Smith (Ohio), Jessie Sumner (Illinois), and Howard Buffet (Nebraska)—resisted. Harry White elatedly termed the outcome a "complete Treasury victory," and President Truman expressed his pleasure. In a telegram to Spence, the chief executive thanked the Banking and Currency Committee for providing bipartisan support for his international monetary program, and he singled out minority leader Wolcott for special praise. This example of bipartisan cooperation, Truman hoped, would "become the pattern for American participation in international economic and security cooperation."[78]

Now attention turned to the House floor, where Spence and Wolcott, in a further display of bipartisan unity, presented the committee's recommendation. Spence, an aging Kentucky representative with such poor vision that he read speeches with difficulty, insisted that he had never heard such unanimous praise "by all classes of the American people" for a single piece of legislation. "If the voice of the people is the voice of God," Spence continued, "we certainly have had irrefutable testimony in behalf of this legislation." When his turn came, Wolcott read letters of endorsement from Randolph Burgess and former Representative Charles Dewey to show that even the critics now favored Bretton Woods. Dewey, who was defeated in the 1944 congressional elections, conceded that if he were a member of the House he would now back the proposals. "Everyone," Wolcott concluded, "is in favor of the bill except those who would vote against the Ten Commandments as part of our national policy."[79]

Despite the bipartisan backing, a small group of midwestern isolationists resorted to verbal pyrotechnics in a last-ditch battle to embarrass the administration by delaying a vote until after the United Nations Conference adjourned in San Francisco. Congresswoman Jessie Sumner, whom Treasury officials considered the "mouthpiece of the *Chicago Tribune*," ranted that Bretton Woods was "the worst swindle in world history." It would force "the American people to pay tribute to foreign governments." And her colleague Howard Buffet charged that Bretton Woods was a mousetrap baited with American dollars that "certain selfish and greedy interests" had sold to the American people.[80]

But the leadership had the situation in hand. When the crucial vote came on Thursday, June 7, only eighteen Republicans voted negatively, and most of these had opposed draft extension, lend-lease, and reciprocal trade. Dean Acheson observed that the eighteen bitterenders "are almost a roster of absolute isolationists—all are within the daily circulation of the *Chicago Tribune*." Reporter Frank McNaughton credited the Democratic leadership—especially Truman, Sam Rayburn, and John McCormack—for achieving the bipartisan victory. These leaders, McNaughton wrote *Time* editors, "gave just where pressure had to be eased in order to win the most votes." But the Republicans also deserved credit for the unexpectedly large vote of approval. They realistically calculated that it was politically hazardous to oppose all internationalist measures, and, having gained important modifications to satisfy the bankers, they determined to concentrate their fire on reciprocal trade.[81]

Only the Senate now stood between Morgenthau and an American commitment to participate in global monetary organization. Elated at the House vote, Morgenthau and his aides did not underestimate the obstacles ahead. The administration had to overcome the determined resistance of Ohio's intelligent and persistent Republican Senator Robert A. Taft, who had announced his intention to fight in the Banking and Currency Committee and, if necessary, on the Senate floor. Against Taft, the administration could field no Democratic senator of comparable intelligence and persistence. Despite Republican warnings that the banking committee chairman, Robert Wagner, "isn't worth a damn," Morgenthau had no recourse but to work closely with the sometimes undependable New York senator.[82]

The Treasury soon discovered that publicity was the secret to Wagner's aid. To keep the New York Democrat from "dragging his heels," Morgenthau decided, as he related in farm idiom, to put a "little turpentine under his tail." Feltus supervised these arrangements. The public relations man encouraged some thirty organizations and prominent individuals to write Wagner their "faith in the sure and quick passage of Bretton Woods under his able leadership." Also, Feltus persuaded New York area radio commentators to publicize Wagner's new involvement in foreign affairs, and he arranged for several organizations to honor Wagner at cocktail parties and luncheons. The blaze of publicity conciliated Wagner, but not the fiercely partisan Taft.[83]

Long a conservative critic of New Deal–type economic planning and global intervention, the Ohio Republican saw the Bretton Woods proposals as a permanent experiment with government spending to promote prosperity on a global scale. The Bretton Woods bill would, he asserted in a minority report, involve "the expenditure of $5,925,-000,000 of the taxpayers' money with negligible benefit to the people of the United States."[84]

Ideologically and politically hostile to New Deal expedients, the Ohio senator had no intention of abandoning what seemed a hopeless fight against insurmountable obstacles. On this he differed with the pragmatic bankers. "They had barely started the fight," he wrote, "when they began to compromise and compromise for a few crumbs." Instead, Taft pushed forward, zealously studying facts and figures and asking witnesses pointed questions that revealed a keen mind—though Dean Acheson thought, an "utterly unscrupulous misinterpretation" of the accords and administration intentions.[85]

Unlike the bankers who accepted the bank and opposed the fund, Taft directed his attack at both institutions—particularly the bank. To William Howard Taft's son the bank seemed a far more serious departure from prevailing foreign and domestic economic policies than the fund, because it involved the government in a long-term program of public lending and guaranteeing private investments. Taft recognized that the bankers association approved the bank partly because "it is almost a subsidy to the business of investment bankers, and will also undoubtedly increase the business to be done by the larger banks." Like many midwestern conservatives Taft was critical of Wall Street economic power, but his objections to the bank went to the crux of the issue—was government lending in the interest of the United States and foreign countries? Like some economists—including Marxist critics of capitalistic exploitation—Taft assumed that foreign investments exacerbated international tensions and aroused anti-American sentiment in capital-receiving countries, where residents often perceived that foreign investors were exploiting natural resources and local labor. If Taft's view of private investments overlooked the mutual advantage for both recipients and donors, which international economists emphasized, he understood intuitively that capital was no substitute for local initiative in the development process. As he said: "No people can make over another people. Every nation must solve its own problems, and whatever we do can only be a supplement to its own efforts and to help it over its most severe barriers." A country, Taft added, "that comes to rely on gifts and loans from others is too likely to postpone the essential tough measures necessary for its own salvation."[86]

His objections to the fund resembled the American Bankers Association critique: it would fail to accomplish objectives of removing discriminatory barriers under present world conditions, and it would deal inadequately with British sterling. Like the bankers, he favored a key-currency solution that would help Great Britain to rehabilitate her trade-dependent economy and restore currency convertibility. The American dollar, he emphasized, was a weapon, and the United States should prudently use a loan to obtain trade concessions in the British Empire.[87]

Taft's parliamentary gymnastics and his biting queries dazzled Senate colleagues, discomforted witnesses, and amused reporters. Writer Allan Drury, enjoying the spectacle, described the antics as a "brilliant *tour de force* in economics by a brilliant man whose ability is thoroughly respected even by those of his colleagues who disagree with him most."[88]

But the Republican nationalist, and his small band of followers, could not sidetrack Bretton Woods in committee or on the Senate floor. They struggled determinedly but unsuccessfully against a tidal wave of internationalist sentiment and an unyielding administration. Senator Sheridan Downey's words probably reflected the general mood better than did Taft's tactics. "I do not imagine or claim," said the California legislator, "that one citizen out of a hundred in our world community possesses accurate or detailed knowledge of the provisions of the Bretton Woods proposal. . . . But to millions it has come, nevertheless, to represent a symbol of our sincerity, our determination, to make good on our promises and pledges of a better postwar world. A destruction or injury to that symbol would be a brutal blow to the morale and hope of the world."[89]

More than at many other moments of decision, memories of past mistakes disposed legislators to approve the international economic blueprint. A bitter struggle between the sick Woodrow Wilson and a Republican-controlled senate, led by Henry Cabot Lodge, torpedoed American membership in the League of Nations after World War I. But twenty years of conflict convinced many legislators that Wilson had been right and Congress wrong. As Pennsylvania Democrat Francis Myers indicated: "America had come a long way since Woodrow Wilson. His vision was not enough to convince us in those days. . . . Mr. President, I say, let us not be penny-pinchers for peace." And, first-term Senator J. William Fulbright, later an articulate critic of global involvement, echoed the same refrain in 1945. "We have tried self-sufficiency, and it has failed," the Arkansas senator said. "Let us try cooperation and participation. It can be no worse."[90]

With public attention riveted on the United Nations Charter and summit meetings at Potsdam, the White House urged Democratic leader Alben Barkley to force a vote on the Bretton Woods bill. Approval of this economic program, Truman said, would strengthen his position in meetings with British and Soviet leaders. And, on July 19, after defeating fifty-two to thirty-one a Taft-sponsored motion to postpone consideration, the Senate prepared for the final ballot. Barkley knew the battle was over. He chuckled to an inquiring reporter that Bob Taft certainly knew more about Bretton Woods than any one else, but "Bob can have the brains, I've got the votes." He was right. Several hours later the upper body approved, sixty-one to sixteen, a bill authorizing the president to accept membership in the International Monetary Fund and the International Bank for Reconstruction and Development. Congress needed more time to reconcile minor differences in the Senate and House bills, but the Bretton Woods battle was over. Morgenthau and Harry Dexter White had triumphed; they had sold Congress the "magnificent blueprint."[91]

Morgenthau's triumph, as important as it was in reversing the United States' long-term detachment from permanent international organizations and in signaling this country's determination to remodel the global economy along multilateral lines, was not sufficient to breathe life into the International Monetary Fund and the International Bank for Reconstruction and Development. Other nations, which together with the United States had 65 percent of the subscriptions to the twin institutions, also had to ratify the agreements no later than December 31, 1945. And, although American officials had encouraged Congress and the public to think that others would follow the American lead, the Treasury disclosed on November 14, 1945, nearly six weeks before the deadline, that only South Africa and Venezuela were ready to ratify the Bretton Woods accords. Many smaller powers dawdled, awaiting a clear indication of whether other great powers, particularly the United Kingdom, would opt for postwar monetary cooperation or turn inward to economic isolation.[92]

As policymakers in Washington recognized, the success of four years of monetary planning hinged in the end on decisions in London and Moscow. These two allies, along with Britain's economic clients Australia, India, and New Zealand, held more than enough votes to prevent the accords from being signed by countries with the requisite subscriptions. In the proposed fund the five would have $3.15 billion of quotas—or about 36 percent of the total. Eager to overcome any last-minute hesitation or resistance, the American policymakers understood that this country's economic resources linked membership in the Bretton Woods institutions with access to transitional aid that would cushion the difficult transitional adjustments and offer additional inducements to hesitant allies.[93]

Britain, once the world's dominant financial power and now a prospective partner in the Bretton Woods order, was the principal concern. The defeat of Germany and Japan necessitated the end of lend-lease, which had helped the United Kingdom to overspend its own income in prosecuting the war, and, as Clement Attlee's Labour government took over in July 1945, it faced a financial crisis of first magnitude—one that new Chancellor of the Exchequer Hugh Dalton later termed a "financial Dunkirk." Without assistance from the United States, the new government learned from John Maynard Keynes that it could hardly make sterling convertible, for Britain staggered under an estimated $12 billion in blocked-sterling debts and confronted the excruciating task of meeting short-term import requirements and expanding exports. Even with a scaling down of sterling debts, London would need $5–$6 billion to finance its payments deficit for the next three years. In such acute economic circumstances would London negotiate a credit that would enable it to collaborate with the United States in the Bretton Woods partnership, or would it abandon four years of planning for autarky?[94]

Keynes, who had invested so much in the Anglo-American effort at the expense of his personal health, knew that there was only one realistic option—multilateralism. On August 3, before Dalton had reassessed British options, the Cambridge economist told American officials that British technicians all favored sterling convertibility, but they feared that the new Labour government might be attracted to bilateralism. This would have serious consequences, Keynes said, and he personally wanted an interim aid program that would get rid of exchange restrictions immediately—not over five years, as the Bretton Woods agreements provided.[95]

In brief, Keynes was now sympathetic to the course long favored by John Williams and the New York bankers—a credit with strings requiring Britain to abandon swiftly its exchange controls on current transactions. And, on September 20, he suggested an informal solution. The United States would make available a $5 billion line-of-credit, and the United Kingdom would lift all exchange controls on current transactions on January 1, 1947. Thus, contrary to earlier accounts that saw an eager United States imposing convertibility on a reluctant Britain, Keynes and the British economists were urging the United States to take a strong stand, one that if successful would inhibit the new British government from embarking on an autarkic course. Under Keynes's scheme the United Kingdom would waive the Bretton Woods transitional period nearly four years before the agreements obligated sterling convertibility.[96]

But the British treasury advisers, confident as ever, underestimated the resistance at home to rapid convertibility. New instructions from London compelled Keynes to bargain on for more favorable terms, and, as tempers flared and exhaustion wore down the negotiators, it seemed for a while that talks would break down altogether. Ultimately, Britain accepted membership in the Bretton Woods institutions contingent on a $3.75 billion American loan, as well as a generous lend-lease settlement. This fifty-year line-of-credit, containing delayed-payments provisions, actually involved an interest rate of about 1.6 percent and was more favorable than the Export-Import Bank loans Washington provided France and other war-devastated countries. And, at American insistence, the British agreed to make sterling convertible on current account one year after the agreement took effect—or, as it turned out, by July 15, 1947.[97]

Were the Anglo-American financial arrangements sufficient to allow convertibility? Keynes himself had wanted at least $5 billion in return for accelerating the timetable, but the loan provided only $3.75 billion—a figure that represented a compromise between the U.S. Treasury, which favored $3.5 billion, and the State Department, which favored $4.0 billion. The loan was not as large as London desired, but, when taken together with a generous lend-lease settlement and a parallel $1.25 billion Canadian loan, it appeared adequate to satisfy the United Kingdom's minimum requirements. As Keynes told the House of Lords: "It is cut somewhat too fine, and does not allow a margin for unforeseen contingencies. Nevertheless the sum is substantial."[98]

Critics, including members of both the Labour and the Conservative parties, denounced the terms, but the convertibility concession was, as Sir Roy Harrod later indicated, merely the reaffirmation and application of the policy Britain had approved in signing Article VII of the Master Lend-Lease Agreement in 1942. At the time, the *Economist*, often spokesman for Britain's economic establishment, conceded that the convertibility string was a principle consistent "with the great tradition of sterling as a world currency" and one that "should not be regarded as part of the price reluctantly paid for financial assistance from the United States." Likewise the Truman administration, attacked for its overly generous terms, insisted that the British loan was a "special case," required because "no other country has the same crucial position in world trade as England." "The early realization of the full objectives of the Bretton Woods program," reported the National Advisory Council on International Monetary and Financial Problems, "requires an immediate solution to Britain's financial problem."[99]

Despite continuing friction with the Soviet Union over self-determination for Eastern Europe and occupation of enemy countries, Treasury planners remained hopeful until December 1945 that Moscow would formally approve the Bretton Woods accords. After all, Stalin's surrogates negotiated seriously and successfully at the 1944 international monetary conference, gaining a fund quota larger than their prewar position in international commerce warranted. Self-interest, as well as prestige in the postwar world, also seemed to justify Soviet involvement. As a partner in the monetary and financial institutions, Russia might draw on her fund quota for $1.2 billion in short-term assistance, gain a secure market for gold sales, and qualify for an International Bank reconstruction loan. During the conference Morgenthau and White yielded frequently to Soviet desires, and the Americans deliberately sweetened terms with the enticement of a bilateral postwar loan—thinking that American generosity would cement a wartime friendship, soften latent ideological differences, and enable the Soviet Union to take its great-power role in the new world order. All they requested, in return, was that Stalin's government accept the principles of functional international cooperation and limited economic interdependence in place of autarkic isolationism.[100]

Although Morgenthau interpreted Soviet actions at Bretton Woods as early evidence of Moscow's disposition to cooperate, his optimism was premature. Victory in the war against Germany still hinged on Soviet-American cooperation, and Stalin, like Roosevelt, preferred to keep his options open, avoiding irreversible long-term commitments as long as possible without antagonizing his ally. Convinced that the Russians would opt for accommodation with the West if the spirit of generosity continued, Morgenthau and his aides circulated proposals for a $10 billion low-interest loan, and they urged employing lend-lease for postwar reconstruction purposes. Enthusiastic as the Treasury was, it was not the only foreign affairs unit to think American economic aid might tip the scales and entice Moscow away from isolationism and expansionism. Ambassador Averell Harriman, and others in the State Department hierarchy, favored a tougher bargaining stance designed to use postwar aid as "one of our principal practical levers for influencing political action compatible with our principles." Roosevelt himself recognized that American economic power could be employed to influence Soviet conduct, and he delayed action on a Soviet aid proposal until after the February 1945 Crimea Conference.[101]

Domestic, as well as diplomatic, considerations dictated delay in early 1945. Not only were congressmen and citizens increasingly restive about the administration's apparent desire to reconstruct foreign nations with American resources, but the legislative branch prohibited any plan to use lend-lease for reconstruction purposes. Thus, until the administration developed and Congress approved a postwar financial program, including repeal of the Johnson Act (which forbade loans to nations in default on World War I debts, and expanded Export-Import Bank lending authority), neither Roosevelt nor Truman could conclude long-term assistance accords without defying the legislature. Moreover, by delaying aid discussions and protesting Soviet actions in violation of American interpretations of the Yalta agreements on Eastern Europe, Washington effectively signaled Moscow that political conduct and aid were intertwined. The United States would no longer provide unconditional aid as it had during the war, when the two were fighting a common enemy.[102]

In attaching strings to postwar reconstruction assistance and employing aid as a diplomatic weapon, the United States missed a golden opportunity to conciliate the Soviet Union with American generosity and thus establish a durable accommodation between the emerging superpowers, some historians claim. Whether unconditional aid would have allayed Soviet suspicions and sustained great-power cooperation is a point scholars may debate until Moscow opens its diplomatic archives and permits foreign scholars to assess freely Soviet perceptions. Nevertheless, on the basis of wartime haggling over lend-lease shipments, American diplomats doubted that Russia would bank foreign generosity. Despite these reservations and other delays resulting from a shift in negotiating tactics and congressional opposition to rehabilitation assistance, the United States did not withdraw the fundamental bargain it offered the Soviet Union at Bretton Woods. Indeed, after Congress expanded Export-Import Bank lending authority in July 1945, the Truman administration signaled its readiness to negotiate a $1 billion bilateral loan and perhaps extend other economic benefits to a cooperative Soviet Union.[103]

Basically, former State Department official Eugene Rostow correctly evaluated the situation when he wrote: "The problem had not changed. Nor had American policy." American policymakers wanted the Soviet leadership to choose between international cooperation and isolation, and they stood ready to entice Moscow away from autarky with reconstruction assistance, as they had the British government. But for Stalin the benefits were apparently not worth the costs. Interdependence and international cooperation would open Soviet society to Western influences, perhaps strengthening opposition to Stalinism, and such influences might prove incompatible with Russian security interests in Eastern Europe. These concerns dictated caution, and economic calculations reinforced this policy. For if the capitalist West entered a second depression, as some Soviet economists anticipated, Washington might gladly withdraw political strings and provide unconditional reconstruction assistance out of a self-serving need to boost employment. In that case Moscow could obtain outside help for reconstruction but avoid the perils of international commitments.[104]

Whatever the Soviet perception of events, V. M. Molotov, people's commissar for foreign affairs, indicated on December 31, 1945, that his government did "not find it possible at the present time" to sign the Bretton Woods agreements. Moscow, he said, wanted to "subject the questions touched upon in these drafts to further study in the light of those new conditions of the economic development of the world which are forming themselves in the postwar period."[105]

The Soviet leadership may have feared the obligations of membership in the monetary fund, requiring information on foreign-exchange balances, trade, national income, and balance of payments, but these do not seem to have been the critical issues, even though the Soviet government traditionally guarded this information. Rather, on the basis of recently concluded loan negotiations with the United Kingdom, Moscow could discern that Washington wanted its former allies to take an active role in the postwar international structure in return for economic help. And, for the suspicious men in Moscow, this raised the fundamental issue of autarky or interdependence. As Ambassador Walter Bedell Smith explained later, the Russians simply did "not wish to" join the Bretton Woods institutions. They "want to be able to act unilaterally as they have done in Balkans and will try to do in all areas where it is at all possible."[106]

While the Soviets vacillated and waited for another depression, the United States, Britain, and twenty-seven other nations moved to activate the Bretton Woods agreements. On December 27, with flash bulbs popping, ambassadors and ministers from participating countries gathered in the U.S. State Department's conference room, once the Navy library, to place their signatures on the agreements. Secretary of the Treasury Fred Vinson, who signed for the United States, issued a statement saying that "the history we are now writing is not another chapter in the almost endless chronicle of war and strife. Ours is a mission of peace . . . designed to establish the economic foundations of peace on the bedrock of genuine international coordination." But the four years of preparation for this occasion were, he added, only a "prologue. The birth of these two great international financial institutions is not an end in itself but only a means to the end of international peace and prosperity. Our task, therefore, has just commenced."[107]

For former Secretary Morgenthau and Harry Dexter White the occasion was a momentous one. The Bretton Woods institutions, Morgenthau said, were "another tree planted by the late President Roosevelt, which will grow throughout the years."[108]

Seventeen months after the historic conference at Bretton Woods, the first successful effort to prepare for the postwar era, the founding fathers had the satisfaction of seeing their handiwork translated into active mechanisms for currency stabilization and long-term reconstruction and development. Bretton Woods had conceived the first formal and permanent institutions for guiding international economic relationships. Despite the common vision of an interdependent global economy, impetus for these efforts, and parallel plans for tariff reduction and other forms of economic cooperation, the Americans had found that political necessity often dictated concessions with the logic of economic internationalism. But, in political tactics as well as long-range economics, the administration had demonstrated flexibility and resourcefulness in overcoming national anxieties, nationalism, and hesitance. Indeed, Morgenthau's successor, Fred Vinson, even adopted the bankers' key-currency approach to implement the Bretton Woods design. That Treasury efforts sometimes exceeded the bounds of legitimate executive conduct and that the institutions had technical imperfections, visible to a later generation, were not matters that concerned Morgenthau and White. They were convinced that the success of Bretton Woods would justify their deeds.

The Protracted Transition

Architects of the Bretton Woods system were men of practical affairs—finance ministers, government economists, politicians, and central bankers—not idealistic philosophers and poets. Yet, in their shared commitment to economic internationalism, the founding fathers were at heart visionaries and reformers intent on constructing a monetary regime that would avoid the errors and flaws that led to two global wars and a depression, shattered the political and economic fabric of international relationships, and left a serious financial dislocation. Their attitudes and actions reflected the prevailing liberal assumption that men of good will and intellect could overcome differences in order to conceive, establish, and manage an economic order beneficial to peoples and nations no matter what their political ideology or governmental form.

These economic internationalists assumed, for the most part, that with universal membership and adherence to a code of monetary conduct—prescribing fixed exchange rates, convertible currencies, and removal of restrictions on trade and payments—the Bretton Woods system would prove durable and adaptable. On the one hand, trade and capital movements, along with coordinated domestic policies, would promote a web of economic interdependence conducive to peace, progress, and stability. On the other hand, the fund and bank, these first experiments with functional international organization, would nurture the spirit of global cooperation, conciliate national differences, and cushion adjustments resulting from payments imbalances, wartime destruction, and economic backwardness.

But, in directing their vision to a distant star labeled international cooperation, and in seeking to persuade more skeptical countrymen that this distant light should guide policy, the economic architects erred. They overestimated the value of rules and institutions in a world upset by war and disturbed by resurgent nationalism. They underestimated the difficulty of making a smooth transition from a world weakened from depression, war damage, and inflation to the Bretton Woods ideal, resting on stable currency and prices as well as a general balance-of-payments equilibrium. They left a large planning gap between the removal of wartime controls and the inauguration of the new world order.[1]

These defects were not obvious to all. Until early 1947, when the Truman administration shifted course, planners thought other countries would make a relatively smooth and swift transition, lasting no longer than five years, from bilateralism to convertibility. During this adjustment period the new Bretton Woods institutions, supplemented with bilateral American lending, would facilitate the stabilization and policy adaptation.

If American officials badly underestimated the problems of implementing Bretton Woods, they did at least recognize the critical role that American power and influence had to play in this stage of the process. President Roosevelt and his aides had pointed the way; Presidents Truman and Eisenhower pledged to continue that program. Early in 1947, Truman told an American college audience, "We are the giant of the economic world. Whether we like it or not, the future pattern of economic relations depends on us. . . . We can lead the nations to economic peace," he promised, "or we can plunge them into economic war." Similarly, though the Republican party was more protectionist than the Democrats, Dwight Eisenhower proclaimed his support for nondiscrimination and currency convertibility. "The United States," he declared in his 1954 foreign economic message, "must take the initiative and, in doing so, make clear to the rest of the world that we expect them to follow our lead."[2]

What could the United States do to speed the transition from a world of controls to one of stable and transferrable currencies? Initially, the Truman advisers were inclined to rush preparations for effective international institutions. They hastened negotiation of the

International Trade Organization, which was to complement the monetary agencies and help fulfill Cordell Hull's desire for liberal, nondiscriminatory trading policies, but this program never gained congressional approval. The critical task on the monetary side, as Morgenthau's successors Fred Vinson and John R. Snyder understood, was to settle outstanding disputes over fund and bank policies and organization so that they could begin operation. As late as September 1946, Snyder exhorted foreign financiers and currency experts to "lose no time in speedily activating the fund and bank as effective instruments in a world sorely in need of their services."[3]

In moving forward Vinson and Snyder did not overlook the opportunity to extract political concessions that would ensure the United States a dominant influence, if that was in doubt. At Savannah, Georgia, in March 1946, Vinson gave John Maynard Keynes a blunt lesson in American politics. Among the issues up for consideration at these inaugural meetings of the fund and bank were the much-debated questions of where the two institutions would be located and whether the executive directors should be full- or part-time officials. Keynes still hoped that the fund and the bank could be technical organizations, free from national political pressures, and, accordingly, he wanted them situated in New York near the United Nations. Executive directors, he argued, should meet only occasionally to supervise the board policies of a trained professional staff. Keynes had expected Savannah to be a "pleasant party," and he was shocked when Vinson and his Treasury aides took a hard, nationalistic position. If the international agencies were subordinate to national policies, Vinson knew he could assuage congressional fears that New Deal–type liberals were surrendering American sovereignty to an international bureaucracy. Also, fearful that the global agencies might assimilate the Wall Street perspective if located in New York, Vinson announced to foreign delegates that the Truman administration wanted both agencies lodged in Washington. This smacked of great-power dominance, and Keynes voiced his disappointment. The fairy Carabosse would surely curse the new institutions, he said. "You two brats," he imagined her saying, "shall grow up politicians; your every thought and act shall have an *arrière pensée*; everything you determine shall not be for its own sake or on its own merits but because of something else."[4]

These disputes and other delays in recruiting a staff and formulating lending policy postponed the day when the international bank in-augurated operations. Nevertheless, Truman's assistants spoke san-guinely of the bank taking over as the "principal" reconstruction agency late in 1946, when it might lend and guarantee $7.5 billion of assistance. Most of this sum would come from capital raised in the New York financial market, and it would go for specific reconstruction projects, such as rebuilding factories, opening mines, and restoring railroads.[5]

Meanwhile the United States relied on bilateral lending—through the Export-Import Bank and a special authorization for Britain—to satisfy foreign needs and prepare the way for Bretton Woods. In 1945 Truman successfully urged Congress to increase the Export-Import Bank's lending authority to $3.5 billion, and a year later he requested another $1.5 billion. From one standpoint this lending program was a generous and humanitarian supplement to lend-lease assistance, which permitted foreign governments to augment their own resources and shortcut reconstruction at the expense of American citizens, who cheerfully tightened their own belts for the sake of promoting a more peaceful and healthy world. It is true that these government-subsidized exports cushioned some sectors of the American economy from abrupt reconversion, thus sustaining domestic employment, but this was not the whole story. In other areas, where supplies were short—such as foodstuffs—export sales contributed to scarcity and higher prices at home.[6]

Political and security considerations, not the fear of domestic de-pression, dictated this policy. Truman's helpers thought that bilateral lending could restore political and economic stability abroad and in that fashion accelerate the timetable for stable and convertible cur-rencies. In discussing lending criteria, State Department official Will Clayton emphasized that "attention should be given to economic stagnation and disruption abroad which, if allowed to continue, might well result in serious political and social disturbances in a foreign country." These disturbances, policymakers feared, might well pre-cipitate another round of political chaos and economic nationalism at a time when the world had a chance, under American leadership, to build a durable peace and a new prosperity.[7]

These concerns, as well as the natural desire to portray each loan as a good deal for the United States, led the American creditors to attach political strings. The $3.75 billion British loan bound the recipient to remove controls on current-account transactions by mid-1947 and committed her to accept U.S. proposals for an International Trade Organization. Likewise, a $650 million loan to France in May 1946 allowed Washington to simultaneously undercut the appeal of French Communists in the 1946 elections and to obtain French government support for multilateral trade.[8]

This piecemeal approach failed to speed up the Bretton Woods timetable because political strife and economic setbacks shattered optimistic assumptions about the prospects for continued great-power cooperation and prompt recovery. During 1947, continuing conflict with Moscow compelled American policymakers to reassess the advantages of universalism and sphere-of-influence policies. As painful as it was, the collapse of Soviet American cordiality was not a death-blow for multilateralism. Even Harry Dexter White, the fervent backer of Soviet participation in the monetary design, readily discounted the economic benefits of Soviet participation. Rather, Soviet involvement was important politically if countries were to establish a more structured world in which all nations had reciprocal obligations and responsibilities. Without Moscow's support, the United States gradually subordinated its long-range economic goals to the increasingly urgent task of erecting an economically viable and politically stable Western Europe as a counterbalance to Soviet influence. Stalin's decision to take a unilateral autarkic course and eschew the international organizations his negotiators helped to create shattered the dream of great-power harmony and universalism, but it did not destroy multilateralism as an attainable objective. Without the Soviet Union, the United States could easily have given leadership to a more restricted monetary order encompassing nations in Western Europe, the Western Hemisphere, and Asia who accounted for more than 90 percent of world trade in 1938, and this regime could provide its members the benefits of currency stability and convertibility as well as full and efficient utilization of productive resources.[9]

This version of the Bretton Woods world did not emerge in the 1940's, primarily because Western Europe failed to recuperate as rapidly as Harry Dexter White and other American planners anticipated. In 1946 and 1947 when Europe, including Britain, urgently needed to stabilize domestic prices and increase production so as to generate dollars from export sales in order to finance imports, strengthen currency reserves, and prepare for convertibility obligations, governments made uneven and inadequate progress. To some extent the performance gap developed from the general relaxation of tensions and the diffusion of civic and political energies to a welter of postponed tasks, including social reform and elections, but the war itself bore the major responsibility. Inflation distorted domestic and international price levels, and destruction reduced the quality of production available to recover world markets and meet internal demand. Statistics collected by the Organization for European Economic Co-operation show that its seventeen members had suffered heavily from the war. In 1947, their agricultural production was 83 percent of the 1938 volume, industrial production 88 percent of the prewar high, and exports only 59 percent.[10]

American leaders awakened to the economic and political consequences of Europe's distress in the spring of 1947, after an unusually severe winter brought crippling power and coal shortages and dramatically exposed the widespread misery and dislocation. Secretary of State George Marshall acted to prepare the American people for new responsibilities on April 28 when he said in a radio address that the "recovery of Europe has been far slower than had been expected. Disintegrating forces are becoming evident. The patient is sinking while the doctors deliberate." Soon his deputy, William L. Clayton, returned from Europe with the distressing conclusion that the United States had "grossly underestimated" the economic consequences of World War II. He estimated that the continent would need a large grant, averaging $6 to $7 billion over the next three years, to meet its import requirements, and much more assistance to restore convertible currencies. "Economic, social, and political disintegration will overwhelm Europe," he forecast.[11]

But, to Treasury economists who expected tangible progress in 1947 toward the realization of the Bretton Woods ideal, Britain's financial distress was a heavy blow. Despite $5 billion in aid from the United States and Canada, the United Kingdom's economy had not responded well, and this jeopardized the implicit objective of the Anglo-American loan—key-currency stabilization.

Understandably, Britain's Labour government blamed circumstances beyond its control for financial setbacks. These included coal and power shortages, soaring import prices (U.S. wholesale prices had, in fact, increased 40 percent since negotiation of the loan), the continent's slow recovery, and the persistent dollar shortage. But these were not the only explanations for Britain's payments deficit. Winston Churchill had a point when he charged that the Labour government had "frittered away" the American loan. For one thing, the Labour government was unwilling, or unable, to cancel accumulated sterling debts, for fear that this would speed the disintegration of an empire and the decline of London as a banking center. Accordingly, London allowed its Commonwealth creditors to draw on precious dollar reserves, and in 1947 these countries drew about $500 million from the dollar pool. Second, the Labour government, though aware of its external payments constraint, gave little priority to export promotion while it attempted simultaneously to expand capital spending and improve social services. The *Economist* calculated that half of the payments deficit was Britain's own making. "What is basically wrong with the British economy at the moment is that, as a nation, we are trying to consume much more than we produce."[12]

The fateful experiment with sterling convertibility began, as required, on July 15, 1947, but it was obvious to the British government that it could not maintain this policy long without exhausting remaining dollar reserves. Accordingly, the Labour government acted unilaterally in August, suspended convertibility, and scotched the first premature attempt to free the two currencies that financed the bulk of world trade. The inability of Britain to resume the responsibilities of a reserve currency was a severe shock for the Anglo-American effort to rehabilitate international finance along multilateral lines, but it did not force the two powers to discard convertibility as a long-term objective. In fact, Chancellor of the Exchequer Hugh Dalton assured Washington that the decision to reimpose currency controls was "purely emergency in character." London continued to believe that "as a long-run objective . . . convertibility is an indispensable element in British financial policy."[13]

The convergence of three factors—political disorder, European economic exhaustion, and depletion of the British loan—compelled the Truman administration to adjust its global priorities in 1947. Now an intensive program to rehabilitate and integrate Europe would take precedence over initiatives to reconstruct the world economy along multilateral lines. This policy shift marked only a change in tactics; it did not indicate any intention to abandon convertibility as an ultimate objective. As the National Advisory Council stated early in 1948, "The maintenance of exchange stability, the orderly adjustment of exchange rates, and the progressive removal of controls over current exchange operations are accepted objectives of United States international policy now, as they were in 1944."[14]

The regional aid program, popularly known as the Marshall Plan, was a comprehensive effort to "provide a cure rather than a mere palliative," as Secretary of State Marshall indicated. During the plan's five-year existence the United States financed the export of nearly 2 percent of its annual production on generous terms that avoided complicated repayment transfers. As Hugh Dalton commented later, "Marshall Aid was large in amount, smooth in operation, and practically without strings. Like Lend-Lease, it was an act of most imaginative generosity, coming only just in time to save its beneficiaries." While strings were minimal, Washington prudently requested assurances from recipients that they would take steps to balance domestic budgets and restore price stability so that these economies could eventually relax exchange barriers and make their currencies convertible, as the Bretton Woods agreements required.[15]

No doubt Marshall Plan recipients would gradually have recovered without heavy American assistance, but this second lend-lease program facilitated rapid recuperation and reduced the danger that prolonged economic and political chaos would topple democratic governments and bring to power radical groups eager to accommodate the Soviet Union. At least this was the American analysis. In 1954 a presidential task force concluded, "Friendly countries would have been forced to restrict their purchases of American goods and services to such a degree that economic and political chaos might well have ensued abroad." Fearful of that possibility and convinced that a recuperated Europe and Japan could become a partner in global economic relations, Washington willingly poured out more than $41 billion—including $31 billion in gifts—to speed the transfer of American resources in the eight years after World War II. Marshall Plan assistance alone appears to have paid for one-fourth of Europe's total imports between 1947 and 1950. Depending on adjustments for controls and local currency prices, American aid appears to have added between 5 and 10 percent to Europe's resources. This amount "played the crucial role . . . in financing essential import needs, accelerating investment and reconstruction, and permitting tolerable consumption levels."[16]

Economically, if not politically, the United States probably erred in not providing a larger portion of this assistance in the form of long-term loans. A generation later, loan repayments would have eased the burden of financing America's payments deficit and slowed the accumulation of dollar liabilities in European central banks and the Euro-currency market. In the climate of 1947, however, such a suggestion seemed the irrational folly of those too shortsighted to avoid the mistakes of reconstruction after World War I.[17]

The European Recovery Program, then, brought a reorientation of American priorities. In place of a quick push toward universalism and convertibility, the United States now counseled regionalism and gradualism. Accordingly, the Bretton Woods institutions, displaced as the principal vehicles for reconstruction, became institutional monuments to the zeal and idealism of a lost age. At the moment when Harry White and John Maynard Keynes anticipated the triumph of a new economic internationalism, the bank and fund lay dormant, awaiting the dawn of the Bretton Woods age.

President Truman and his aides initially expected the International Bank for Reconstruction and Development—popularly known as the World Bank—to assume "primary responsibility" for reconstruction lending. But the newly created bank lacked necessary authority, resources, experience, and prestige to carry out that heavy mandate, and it soon withdrew from reconstruction lending altogether and prepared to concentrate on development problems.[18]

One reason the new agency failed to satisfy its founders' expectations was that the Bretton Woods delegates devoted far more attention to creating the fund and specifying its operations than they did to establishing the sister institution. As a result, the bank's charter, largely neglected until late in the deliberations, left management considerable discretion over policies, practices, and priorities. The articles of agreement were so ambiguous, in fact, that early operations were marked by a persistent tug-of-war between the president and the executive directors to establish their respective spheres of authority. Aside from the unsettled issue of whether the new institution was to be president dominated or board ridden, management had broad authority to devise lending policies provided they conformed to certain broadly stated banking principles. Briefly, since the World Bank's objective was to facilitate and not compete with private investments, it must be satisfied that a prospective borrower could not obtain similar loans from private sources on reasonable terms. Except in special circumstances, the bank was bound to lend only the foreign-exchange costs of specific reconstruction-and-development projects. And, finally, bank loans were to be productive loans made after prudent consideration of repayment prospects. As it turned out, the bank president and his staff asserted authority to determine whether reasonable terms were available, whether there were good prospects for repayment, and whether to recommend a loan. Of course, less formal limitations existed in practice, depending on the power and personality of the president, as well as his determination to keep active directors from overinvolving themselves in the operational side of bank functions. Also, in the early years the bank was effectively restrained by the suspicion of outside bankers and by a perceived need to conciliate Wall Street before the International Bank undertook controversial projects, such as lending money to state-controlled enterprises.[19]

Obliged to exercise prudence and to evaluate repayment prospects carefully, the World Bank hardly seemed the appropriate vehicle for financing reconstruction of war-devastated areas needing low-interest, medium- and long-term aid and having serious internal dislocations that would discourage private investments. However, the Truman administration had repeatedly assured skeptical congressmen that the new agency was suited to this task, and, accordingly, Emilio Collado, first U.S. executive director, urged the bank to float its first bond issue and set caution aside, putting money to immediate use. However, bank president Eugene Meyer, an American financier and publisher, wished to move cautiously and prudently, and, when pressure to relax stringent lending requirements and undertake long-term, general-purpose reconstruction loans became overwhelming, the frustrated officer resigned abruptly in December 1946. Nevertheless, in the absence of bilateral aid mechanisms the World Bank was the only stopgap available, and at American insistence the agency did lend $497 million to France, the Netherlands, Luxembourg, and Denmark during the first phase of operations from May to August 1947.[20]

This initial experiment with general-purpose, or program lending, although favored by some economists alarmed about the balance-of-payments implications of European distress, seriously depleted the bank's paid-in subscriptions, damaged investor confidence, and forced a major adjustment in bank leadership and policies. From the beginning this financial agency lacked adequate sums of lendable funds and the prestige in banking circles required to borrow more. Bretton Woods had authorized a capital stock of $10 billion, but when the institution opened for business in 1947 it had only $8 billion in subscriptions—Russia and several other countries failed to join. As required, members paid only 20 percent of total subscriptions, or about $1.6 billion, but only the United States authorized the bank to use all of its paid-in proportion. Consequently, the 1947 reconstruction loans virtually exhausted the World Bank's lending capacity. By itself the French loan involved a commitment of more than one-third of loanable funds.[21]

How could the bank replenish its resources? In theory, it could either guarantee private investments or borrow directly from the banking community. But, while the founding fathers envisaged an active role for the bank as an international guarantor, the Bretton Woods agency never guaranteed either a foreign loan of a private investor or a public offering of a foreign government. Suspicion of guarantees, legal complications, and a general belief that direct borrowing and relending were cheaper to the ultimate borrower and more satisfactory to creditors shaped this decision. At first, however, the bank had difficulty even marketing its own bonds. For one thing, Federal Reserve banks and some states restricted the sale of bank bonds in the American market, and the banking community had an understandable lack of confidence about the offerings of an unproven international institution.[22]

It took time to remove legal barriers and dispel doubts. Wall Street, recalling how Henry Morgenthau claimed his World Bank would drive the "usurious money lenders from the temple of international finance," exhibited natural suspicion. It waited for clear evidence that the agency's multinational managers would adhere to sound banking principles, and early developments justified its caution. General-purpose lending for Europe, no matter how justified on other criteria, confirmed suspicions that the Truman administration intended to dominate the new organization and use its resources for politically defined purposes. Other hints of political intervention surrounded the abrupt resignation of Eugene Meyer in late 1946, and as a consequence President Truman had difficulty finding a qualified replacement. As much as anything else, the protracted search for a second bank president reflected the deep-seated anxiety in financial circles that Washington intended to treat the banking agency as a political arm of the American government rather than an independent financial agency, presumably sensitive to creditor interests.[23]

When John McCloy, a tough-minded Wall Street lawyer, finally accepted an invitation to take the bank presidency it was "at its lowest ebb, its reputation considerably tarnished, its accomplishments nil, and its problems mounting because of the worsening economic situation in Western Europe." McCloy's appointment was a turning point. Not only did the new executive resolve to strengthen the bank's image and secure investor confidence, but he also demanded, and obtained, from the executive directors a free hand to run the bank. McCloy, at that time, established the precedent of a strong-armed president. Also, McCloy promptly filled high positions in the World Bank with experienced private investment bankers, and his friend Eugene Black, formerly a vice-president of the Chase National Bank and eventually McCloy's own successor, replaced assertive New Deal economist Emilio Collado as executive director from the United States. This transfer of power from Roosevelt-type administrators to professional bankers mirrored the fundamental shift of power within the Truman administration, and it presaged important policy departures at the bank.[24]

As soon as the Marshall Plan took charge of European reconstruction, McCloy halted general-purpose lending and redirected bank efforts to the coordinate task—developmental lending. Perhaps McCloy himself overemphasized the bank's real concern with development problems in public statements, but his claim that the "development phase . . . is under way" at least identified the new policy direction. This shift also represented the president's pragmatic assessment that the bank "cannot and should not be expected to provide the answer to all or even a major part of the world's financial ills."[25]

Preoccupied with practical problems of establishing confidence for bond sales in the dollar market, as well as with safeguarding remaining resources and committing funds to sound projects, McCloy rejected pressures from some hopeful borrowers to interpret the charter liberally. Some members wanted the institution to subsidize buffer stocks, make anticyclical full-employment loans, and initiate a "soft-lending" policy, involving lower interest rates and easier repayment terms. However, the bank president determined that the proper mission was the less-ambitious task of providing "foreign financing required to carry-out long-term projects which will increase agricultural and industrial output of its member nations." Essentially, economic development at this stage meant providing foreign-exchange costs of infrastructure projects, while encouraging private capital to undertake larger industrialization tasks.[26]

Before the Marshall Plan preempted reconstruction lending, the World Bank temporarily behaved like a rich and generous uncle; under McCloy it swiftly advanced a different image—a cautious Aunt Sally, scrupulously applying stringent banking criteria to each loan application. In considering development projects, bank officials began asking if a prospective borrower had an overall development plan. Did it also have managers, skilled workers, and adequate local capital to complete the project? Were economic instability and unsettled political conditions likely to jeopardize the project and endanger repayment? Did prospective borrowers have a proper investment climate conducive to private lending? And when the bank had reservations, it did not hesitate to impose tough conditions and apply leverage to secure compliance. It might require a borrowing country to take measures designed to restore price stability in its domestic economy. Or, it might require a government to make payment on defaulted bonds as a price for the approval of a long-term development loan, as it did in making its first development loan, to Chile, in 1948.[27]

Critics complained that the World Bank was merely a bill collector for Wall Street, but, from the bank's perspective, conservative lending practices and occasional pressure on a questionable borrower contributed to that nation's economic development and served its long-term national interest, though not necessarily the self-interest of incumbent politicians. Ironically, in insisting on sound and prudent projects the new international agency quickly discovered it had more money than qualified borrowers, quite the reverse of circumstances in 1946 when loan requests greatly exceeded resources.[28]

Embarking on an uncharted mission of development lending at a time when only the dollar market could finance long-term projects, the World Bank devised a development philosophy and a pattern of activity suited to its position as a dollar bank. Thinking private capital would develop export products, such as tin, rubber, or petroleum; and reluctant to finance government-owned industries, which might scare private investors; and concerned about the measurable payoff of social overhead projects, like sanitation, education, and health facilities, the bank concentrated on high-visibility "economic overhead" projects—including electric power, railroads, highways, and communications. In meeting the foreign-exchange costs of infrastructure projects and offering technical assistance to plan these loans, bank economists argued that they were creating necessary preconditions for general economic development.

While loans varied in length—from two-year credits to Finland and Yugoslavia to thirty-year reconstruction loans for France—most heavy-equipment loans for power installations and transportation were for twenty to twenty-five years. Each borrower paid the same rate, though interest charges did vary according to the fluctuating cost of borrowing money on the private market. In removing creditworthiness as a factor in lending, the bank seemed to discriminate against nations with proven credit ratings. The bank agreed these countries could, in fact, borrow less expensively on a private market and encouraged them to do so in order that the bank could aid other countries. On all loans the bank charged borrowers 1 percent more than it cost the bank to borrow, so as to cover administrative expenses and accumulate a reserve against losses. In the late 1940's, when interest rates were relatively low by standards of the early 1970's, the bank charged, including special commission, between 4.25 and 4.50 percent for long-term loans and between 3.50 and 3.75 percent for short-term agricultural credit. Significantly, the rates less-developed countries had to pay were considerably lower than the average 6.59 percent yield on foreign bonds floated in the United States market during the 1920's.[29]

Cautious and prudent in its lending, the World Bank did not become a major source of international capital during its first eight years. By December 31, 1953, it had made only $1.750 billion in loan commitments, including the $497 million to Europe for reconstruction. Of the remainder, Western Hemisphere countries received $427 million; Europe, $257 million; Australia, $150 million; Africa, $201 million; and Asia and the Middle East, a total of $218 million. Disbursements naturally ran behind loan commitments, and, of the $1.23 billion actually released, the largest amount ($1.1 billion) was in dollars, the currency in short supply. World Bank loans did not simply finance American export sales; indeed, $255 million, or about

23 percent, was spent outside the United States. Compared to the American government, which transferred $41.3 billion to other countries in the same postwar period, the World Bank was definitely a secondary source of funds. Yet, at a time when private direct investments increased slowly (from $8.85 billion in 1946 to $13.55 billion in 1953)—most were in petroleum located in Latin America and the Middle East—the World Bank's contribution was proportionately greater than it was in the late 1960's, when private direct and portfolio investment again became important factors in development. By 1969, for instance, multilateral loans and credits (including the World Bank) accounted for only 12 percent of total loans and grants, while private sources supplied 30 percent. Governments provided the remainder.[30]

"The world has experienced an economic earthquake, whose rumbling began long before the war," World Bank President John McCloy told the third annual meeting in September 1948. That earthquake, together with the inevitable difficulties of launching a new enterprise, frustrated and handicapped the bank during its early years, but, with the gradual stabilization of economic conditions and the revival of investor confidence, it emerged in a strong position to undertake an expanding role as a public lender to emerging nations.[31]

Parents of the International Monetary Fund imagined that it would take an active part in creating and supporting a new multilateral currency system. Accordingly, the fund's broad mandate called for promoting international monetary cooperation, facilitating the expansion and balanced growth of world trade, promoting exchange stability and avoiding competitive exchange depreciations, and, among other objectives, establishing a multilateral system of payments. These were ambitious aims, perhaps unattainable ones, given the fund's limited resources and its restricted authority even in the most favorable international circumstances. But the founding fathers did not have a clear view of the future in July 1944; instead, since the world was still in flames and the amount of destruction unknown, the planners approached the future with their eyes fixed to a rearview mirror. In this respect, admitted one of Harry White's assistants afterward, the experts were like generals who "tend to plan for the campaigns already fought." This preoccupation with the past explains why the Bretton Woods delegates gave special emphasis to such goals as stable exchanges, avoidance of competitive depreciations, and removal of restrictions on current account transactions. And their blindness to the future helps to explain how the experts underestimated the difficulty of legislating stable and convertible currencies in an unbalanced world and why, as a result, the fund, like the bank, fell short of its founders' expectations.[32]

Initially, at American insistence, the newly organized fund concentrated on establishing an orderly pattern of par values, since a pattern of reference points was a prerequisite for stable exchange rates. And, on December 18, 1946, after communicating with members, the currency agency announced par values for thirty-two members. This was a major attainment because for the first time countries jointly announced a pattern of exchange rates. But in practical terms this achievement was less significant than it first seemed. Recognizing that monetary affairs were too disturbed to permit the selection of durable equilibrium rates, the fund had simply accepted whatever par values individual countries proposed. Tactically, this solution had two overriding advantages. First, it avoided charges of an international monetary dictatorship at a time when nations were sensitive about the sovereign right to determine their own currency rates. Second, it allowed many members to select overvalued currencies for the difficult transition period, so that they could increase the purchasing power of their export earnings and currency reserves.[33]

In 1946 few governments were ready to defend their new exchange rates in a free market. Except for the United States and four smaller dollar bloc countries—El Salvador, Guatemala, Mexico, and Panama —the others planned to rely temporarily on exchange controls and other restrictions. That way, they could regulate international transactions and gradually accumulate the quantity of reserves needed to maintain current-account convertibility in the future.

Effectively, the American dollar emerged from World War II as the only currency freely convertible, for Washington indicated it would continue the prewar Treasury policy of buying and selling gold at $35 per ounce, the price established after devaluation in 1934. In unilaterally promising to redeem its currency for gold, the United States accepted an obligation not specifically required under the fund's articles of agreement. Any member of the fund could discharge its responsibility by simply maintaining the value of its currency in terms of other national monies. Washington elected to support the dollar in this way so that gold would continue to serve as an international standard of account and as an instrument for settling balances. But the value of gold depended on the dollar, not the reverse. The United States accepted no permanent obligation to buy and sell gold, and at any time the Treasury might have elected to buy and sell sterling or some other reserve currency.[34]

Having determined par values, the fund could legally activate its currency-support operations. First, however, the agency had to resolve the issue that divided British and American negotiators throughout the monetary deliberations. Simply stated, could members with declared par values automatically draw on their quotas, as the British wanted, or could the fund restrict access in order to safeguard its holdings and prevent drawings from being used for reconstruction, as distinguished from short-term stabilization, purposes?

The matter was technical and complex, but its resolution would determine the fund's position in the new monetary order. Ultimately, members had little choice but to accept the American view that unrestricted access would exhaust the fund's pool of currencies and endanger its usefulness as a mechanism for cushioning temporary payments imbalances in a healthy world monetary system. The fund's executive directors effectively accepted the U.S. view in 1946 when they ruled, as Congress requested, that the agency was not empowered to finance long-term reconstruction. Acceptance of this principle implied that the fund would scrutinize all exchange transactions to see that they corresponded to the fund's currency stabilization objective. Accordingly, the fund declared in its first annual report that the "essential test of the propriety of use of the Fund's resources is . . . whether the prospective balance of payments position of the country concerned . . . will be such that its use of the Fund's resources will be of relatively short duration."[35]

Actually, the executive directors did, with American concurrence, permit some members with serious payments disequilibria to draw approximately $600 million in 1947 and 1948, but these were exceptions not tolerated after the European Recovery Program began operations. In fact, when the United States requested that the fund suspend transactions with Marshall Plan recipients, it complied. The 1947 annual report explained that the monetary agency was "intended as part of the permanent machinery of international monetary relations rather than as an emergency device to meet the special needs of the postwar years." Thus, a year after it first opened for business, the International Monetary Fund, like its financial twin, stopped almost all lending. Instead, as the Marshall Plan rehabilitated Europe and created the world the fund was designed to serve, the currency agency sat patiently on the sidelines, guarding its resources.[36]

Unable to supply the volume of assistance required to maintain the new network of exchange rates without the use of controls, the fund, as well as the United States, grew increasingly tolerant of the exchange restrictions and bilateral clearing agreements it was supposed to eliminate. Seven years after the war, the fund conceded that payments were not in balance and that exchange restrictions were the "order of the day."[37]

Nor did the scarce-currency clause in the fund's birth certificate prove an effective instrument for coping with the acute dollar shortage that effectively immobilized the fund during the reconstruction period. Members of the fund did not invoke Article VII, because it had been designed to treat a different disease with a similar symptom. White and Keynes anticipated that the provision would take effect if a major depression in the United States contracted world trade and investments and left dollars in short supply. But the post–World War II imbalance was the consequence of a war-related imbalance between European import requirements and productive resources, a situation quite different from a U.S. depression. Moreover, the United States recognized that Europe's dollar gap posed a formidable threat to global economic equilibrium and political stability, and, as a result, Washington did assume some responsibility for alleviating the imbalance. The European Recovery Program, and other assistance efforts, financed an export surplus, which transferred scarce capital goods and raw materials to Europe. Also, Washington acquiesced to trade-and-currency restrictions against American goods. In effect, members of the fund achieved the same effect with restrictions that were legal during the transitional period (Article XIV). For these, and other legal reasons, the International Monetary Fund did not invoke the much touted Article VII.[38]

Finally, during its formative years the fund made little progress toward stable, convertible currencies. Commenting on these early failures, the fund's official historian concluded, "The observer is bound to be impressed chiefly by what was not achieved." Outside critics showed less sympathy, and some argued that the "paper organization" should be dissolved or merged with the World Bank, a prescription that tacitly, at least, vindicated the views international bankers advanced during the Bretton Woods hearings.[39]

During the European Recovery Program period, the fund, it is true, often did little more than send out technical missions, collect statistics, and train financial experts from underdeveloped countries. Yet, in a less visible manner, the new institution was making an incremental contribution to the slow evolution of monetary cooperation. It recruited and trained a competent technical staff, who were insulated from the pressures and interests of national governments, and it developed an institutional outlook. Under its first managing director, Camille Gutt, a former Belgian finance minister respected for his commitment to sound and stable money, the fund increasingly took a strong stand against inflation. Basically, though its charter said nothing about inflation, the fund's experts recognized and alerted nations to the fact that internal inflation would undermine a system based on stable exchange rates and convertible currencies. As unpleasant as this message became to the Latin American structuralists, who essentially accepted inflation as the price of economic growth, Gutt's tough-minded approach pleased the once-suspicious American business and banking community. *Fortune*, for instance, portrayed Gutt as a "kind of financial Johnny Appleseed spreading the seed of fiscal common sense."[40]

What concerned monetary planners in the United States, Canada, and the International Monetary Fund as the regional rehabilitation approach took hold was the possibility that this expedient might become a permanent substitute for a general return to convertibility. Although most of the European countries accepted the Bretton Woods principles, there were reasons to fear this commitment might evaporate if Europe was not quickly reintegrated into the larger global economy. Overvalued currencies posed the immediate problem. Unrealistically high exchange rates had enabled the war-torn countries to obtain imports less expensively, but they had also discouraged these countries from competing on world markets. Their exports were overpriced. It seemed to American experts that, if Europe was to rejoin the Bretton Woods world, the recuperating countries must soon devalue their currencies and boost exports. And, since Britain still financed 40 percent of world trade, the road to Bretton Woods appeared to run through London.[41]

In preparing for the necessary currency realignment, the fund took an active role. At the urging of United States and Canadian representatives, who were in general agreement on the need for a more realistic parity structure, the fund consulted with individual members. British officials generally opposed a devaluation in the spring and summer of 1949. Arguments varied, but basically opponents contended that devaluation would increase Britain's food bill more than it added to export receipts.

Events showed that the United Kingdom could not afford the luxury of supporting an overvalued pound. Anticipating the much-discussed devaluation, speculators withdrew funds from Britain, and domestic businessmen stepped up import purchases. As a result, the drain on sterling reserves reached critical proportions by September 1949. To restore confidence the Labour government decided on a major devaluation and, after only *pro forma* consultation with the International Monetary Fund, announced a 30.5 percent cut in sterling. The pound would drop from $4.03 to $2.80.[42]

London's unilateral action had widespread consequences. It violated the spirit of the Bretton Woods agreements and revealed how ineffective the fund was as an instrument of monetary cooperation. As Robert Triffin commented, "Anxious to avoid an open flouting of the Fund's rules, the Board could do no more than approve wholesale" the devaluation requests. In addition, London's giant devaluation upset the admittedly inappropriate network of exchange values and brought a wave of competitive depreciations from thirty-one other countries who together accounted for two-thirds of world trade. Overeager to uphold their prewar values, partly for prestige and partly for the economic advantages of cheaper imports, the European countries postponed too long and then devalued too much.[43]

The sweeping 1949 monetary realignment revived discussion of a second push toward convertibility before Marshall Plan assistance ended in 1952. As a step in this direction, the United States took an active part in negotiations leading to the creation of the European

Payments Union (EPU) in 1950 and even contributed a $350 million capital fund. Its founders expected the EPU to promote multilateral clearing among European currencies and to support a progressive liberalization of controls on trade and payments. In fact, the EPU did serve as a "half-way house on the road from bilateralism to a full multilateral system," and after only three months' operation its members had already taken major strides. They removed 60 percent of existing quantitative restrictions on intra-European trade and adopted the principle of nondiscrimination.[44]

From the British viewpoint, however, the EPU seemed both a benefit and a liability. On the one hand, it offered London abundant credit to support the pound. But, on the other hand, the arrangement did not allow members to accumulate sterling reserves, and for this reason it contradicted the British objective of restoring sterling to its preeminent position in financing trade. Consequently, when Winston Churchill returned to power in 1951, the Conservatives solicited American aid for a second key-currency approach to convertibility. Recognizing that sterling was still too weak to hold a par value, the British proposed to ignore IMF rules and permit their currency to float in response to market conditions. The idea had some appeal in Washington, but opposition from the fund and continental countries, together with congressional criticism of additional loans, prompted the Eisenhower administration to reject either a "dash" for convertibility or an experiment with letting sterling "find its own level." Until Britain's reserves increased so that sterling could withstand market pressures, the influential Randall Commission recommended a gradual approach to general convertibility under the auspices of the European Payments Union. President Eisenhower concurred.[45]

Gradualism and its domestic counterpart, noninflationary growth, slowly restored European trade, production, and monetary reserves, as the Bank for International Settlements and the International Monetary Fund anticipated. During the 1950's, production in Britain and the six continental countries (Belgium, France, Germany, Italy, Luxembourg, and the Netherlands) who formed the European Economic Community in 1957 increased from $112 billion to $262 billion. Trade soared both among EPU members and with the outside world, indicating the competitiveness of European exports. The six, for instance, gradually increased their share of exports to the outside world from 10.5 percent to 15 percent of world trade. The future Common Market countries also increased their holdings of reserves—dollars, gold, and IMF positions—from $3 billion in 1950 (6.1 percent of world reserves) to $15.9 billion (26.3 percent of global reserves) a decade later. Though Britain's relative share of world reserves and trade actually declined, the 1950's witnessed a remarkable European recovery, which, together with the disappearance of the dollar shortage and the absence of a major depression, created conditions for a second assault on international monetary barriers.[46]

The long-delayed "dash" for convertibility began on December 27, 1958, when fourteen European countries—including Britain, France, Germany, and Italy—agreed to disband the EPU and permit nonresident currency convertibility. This was another measured stride toward free convertibility for current-account transactions. Simultaneously, Gen. Charles De Gaulle announced a 17.5 percent devaluation of the French franc as his country and its five Common Market partners prepared to launch their new experiment with regional economic integration in January 1959.[47]

In relaxing controls, the European countries knew that the International Monetary Fund would soon have $14 billion in quotas—representing a 50 percent increase for most countries, as well as some special adjustments for Canada, Germany, and Japan. These additional funds would provide an extra cushion against unanticipated pressures on convertible currencies.[48]

The announcement of limited convertibility coincided with the revitalization of the Bretton Woods institutions, particularly the fund. From the inauguration of the European Recovery Program to the outbreak of war in the Middle East late in 1956, the IMF had done little except conduct studies and guard its hoard of gold and national currencies. Administratively, however, the fund's directors approved a set of operating procedures governing drawings. Among these were virtually automatic access to a member's gold subscription, or gold tranchée; required repayment of drawings within three to five years, instead of a longer period as envisaged at Bretton Woods; and a higher schedule of charges on outstanding drawings. Essentially, while making it easier for a member to draw on portions of its quota, the fund was tightening repayment provisions so that the pool of currencies could do more work and members would have greater incentive to correct a payments imbalance promptly. Also, the fund took a more passive attitude toward exchange-rate alterations, especially among less-developed countries, and it acquiesced to floating rates and multiple exchange-rate practices.[49]

The fund again resumed active lending in 1956 during the Suez Crisis. Britain, under pressure to obtain additional dollars to pay for oil imports from the Western Hemisphere, negotiated a $738 million standby credit. This line-of-credit helped the United Kingdom to avoid exhausting its reserves and resorting to drastic bilateral controls that might have destroyed prospects for removing European currency restrictions. In two years, ending in April 1958, the fund loaned $1,780 million to Britain, France, India, Japan, and several other countries. This amount was more than the fund provided in its first ten years.[50]

The seven days in December and January 1958–1959 when Europe adopted limited convertibility and launched the Common Market, and when fund executive directors approved a 50 percent increase in quotas, marked an important turning point in post–World War II monetary relations. Occurring at a time of despair, when many bewildered Americans believed their country was losing the space and economic-growth races to its cold-war rival, these economic events signaled the close of a protracted postwar transitional period and the beginning of a new era of progress along converging tracks toward regional economic integration within a multilateral world economy. The monetary system envisaged at Bretton Woods, based on stable and convertible currencies and cooperation through international mechanisms, had become a reality. Characteristically buoyant, *Time* effused, "When the history of the 20th century is written, last week is likely to prove one of its watersheds." Western Europe "took its biggest step toward unity since the death of Charlemagne 1,145 years ago." Even Per Jacobsson, cautious Swedish managing director of the fund, exuded optimism: "The last days of 1958 provided the most spectacular move that has occurred in the monetary sphere since the end of the war."[51]

Efforts to aid less-developed nations also passed an important milestone during the winter of 1958–1959. The rise of Fidel Castro to power in Cuba gave new urgency to bilateral assistance programs for promoting self-sustaining economic growth in poor nations. As

Soviet-American competition sharpened and extended to the so-called Third World, the International Bank steadily expanded its own development assistance program. Lending commitments rose from the $350 million level in 1950 to over $700 million in 1958. And, as bilateral aid programs expanded and proliferated, and as borrowing nations pressed for the creation of other regional lending institutions like the Inter-American Development Bank, the experienced World Bank struggled to shed its image as a conservative financial institution and to establish a new role as principal coordinator of the international aid effort.[52]

At the bank's helm during this turbulent period was Eugene Black, a persuasive Shakespeare-reading southerner who followed John McCloy. Like his predecessor, Black concentrated initially on establishing a market for the bank's bonds, building its reputation for probity, and sustaining a high standard of performance in high-yielding, low-risk infrastructure loans. But in 1959 he persuaded governors to endorse a 100 percent increase in bank subscriptions, increasing the total to $21 billion without adding to paid-in capital. This change removed serious legal and psychological obstacles to an accelerated lending program, because in doubling the American subscription—previously the practical limit on borrowing—it ensured that the bank would have little difficulty financing a more active program of project lending. Able to borrow more, as a result, and free to draw on European capital markets, with the relaxation of currency controls, the bank gradually turned to new sources of funds, marketing its bonds in Western Europe. Though more costly than comparable borrowing in New York, this procedure speeded the transformation of the Bretton Woods agency from a dollar bank, dependent on American capital, to a truly international bank, capable of borrowing and lending a variety of national currencies.[53]

Convinced the principal barrier to greater flows of development capital was not the lack of money but "the lack of well-prepared and well-planned projects ready for immediate execution," Black and his assistants resisted calls in the United Nations for "soft loans," carrying negligible interest rates and having easy repayment terms. Thus, as the bank concentrated on doing what it did best, other development theorists formulated a capital-oriented theory of growth. Broadly stated, in this conception outside assistance performed a vital function in supplementing domestic savings so as to assure the high rate of investment required to achieve a target growth of per capita national product. Busy with their macroeconomic models, the capital theorists scorned the bank's cautious and narrow orientation to infrastructure projects, and they appealed, instead, for flexible development institutions to supply "soft loans" and grants.[54]

This outside criticism, as well as growing recognition that many borrowing nations might soon be unable to service high-interest loans, encouraged Black to reverse his position and place the International Bank squarely behind American plans for the new International Development Association (IDA). It would be a soft-loan affiliate of the bank, equipped to take greater risks and offer easier terms to the poorest nations unable to qualify for ordinary loans. This institution, established in 1960, began with $1 billion in subscriptions from affluent countries and a mandate to make fifty-year concessionary credits, carrying only a nominal service charge. Designed to assist the poorest nations—those with per capita incomes below $300—the IDA at first allocated 60 percent of its funds to India and Pakistan. Like its parent, the International Bank, the IDA used its funds to finance power and transportation projects, but it gradually adopted a more liberal approach suited to conditions in backward areas. It sponsored a wider variety of projects, including education and agriculture, made about 25 percent of its credit commitments to broad development programs, and even began to assist state-owned enterprises. Because IDA funds came from the legislatures of its affluent members, not the private capital markets, it could afford to support projects that satisfied development but not banking criteria.[55]

If the International Development Association filled one gap in the Bretton Woods arrangements, the absence of a soft-lending agency, the International Finance Corporation (IFC) satisfied another need. The Bretton Woods agreements called for the International Bank to encourage private enterprise, but the accords did not allow the bank to sponsor projects lacking host-government guarantees. This defect was partially removed in 1956 with establishment of the IFC, designed to lend public funds to private enterprise in developing countries without requiring formal guarantees. But the IFC began life with several handicaps. It had only $100 million in authorized capital and no authority to make equity investments, a constraint later removed.

The Protracted Transition

Creation of these two affiliates, the IDA and the IFC, added new dimensions to the International Bank and effectively made the so-called World Bank Group a community of diversified development agencies.[56]

Sixteen years after their creation, the Bretton Woods institutions had come of age. The global monetary system resembled the world imagined at Bretton Woods, and the International Bank, the nucleus of several development-oriented institutions, had the resources, experience, and incentive to take a leading role in the global war on poverty.

9

"Death of Bretton Woods"

Twice in the last century the world has experienced the benefits of a cohesive, smoothly functioning international monetary regime, and on both occasions the durability of these systems has depended on the strength of a preponderant nation. Before World War I, for instance, the gold standard functioned as it did largely because Great Britain, the dominant commercial and financial power, enforced Pax Britannica. London managed the gold standard, defined the informal rules and obligations, and controlled access to the world's most important capital market. In this invertebrate international economy, which linked the destinies of nation-states around the globe, British naval power reinforced that country's political and economic influence. But World War I, the emergence of the United States, and the 1931 financial collapse slowly destroyed Britain's dominant role and ushered in an era of economic nationalism.[1]

During World II the Roosevelt administration laid the foundations for another global monetary system—the Bretton Woods regime. The emergence of Pax Americana, like the evolution of Pax Britannica, reflected underlying economic, strategic, and political realities. As the country with over 50 percent of world industrial production and two-thirds of monetary gold, only the United States had the economic and financial resources required to assert effective postwar leadership and to make its currency the sheet anchor for other national monies. It is hardly coincidental that the period of dollar dominance corresponded to U.S. political and military preponderance and to the exhaustion of old rivals in Europe and Japan. Although this country soon lost the atomic monopoly it enjoyed at the conclusion of World War II, heavy military expenditures and a technology lead enabled the United States to maintain strategic supremacy until late in the 1960's. The prestige of the dollar, strategic supremacy, and a sense of noblesse oblige, which supported global involvement, all encouraged the United States to underwrite and sponsor the emergence of a stable and prosperous world system.

But, in the longer span of history, Pax Americana proved as transitory as Pax Britannica. American generosity and openness enabled other industrial nations to buy, borrow, or purloin the secrets of modern technology and shortcut their own recovery. And American policymakers, preoccupied with Soviet intentions, encouraged the once-fragmented European state system to gradually integrate economically and politically, thus creating from the ashes of Europe a new rival or partner in global politics.

Essentially, then, as the United States advanced its design for an open economic and financial order, it was encouraging the very diffusion and redistribution of economic and financial power that would compel modifications in the Bretton Woods design. Economic statistics document the gradual transformation of the post–World War II system. In 1950, for instance, the United States accounted for 39.3 percent of world gross national product and Britain contributed another 5 percent. Twenty years later the United States produced 30.2 percent and Britain only 3.6 percent. And, by 1970, the European community and Japan accounted for 21 percent, far more than 12.6 percent in 1950.

Since gross national product comparisons exaggerate the strength of a country with an overvalued currency and understate the production of others with undervalued monies, the redistribution of monetary reserves provides a more realistic, and more dramatic, indication of the underlying economic readjustments. In 1950, the United States held 49.8 percent of all monetary gold, reserve currencies, and IMF reserves. Britain had 7.1 percent. Twenty years later the dollar and pound remained important transaction currencies, but United States reserves were only 15.7 percent of the world total, and Britain's were 3.1 percent. However, Japan and Europe, including France, Italy, and Germany, had increased their proportion of total reserves from

7.3 to 37.7 percent. Ironically, the countries defeated in World War II, including France, had large and growing quantities of international purchasing power, while the United States, leader of the United Nations coalition against the Axis, had a thin purse and accumulating debts. In fact, the ratio of American reserves to liabilities in possession of foreign governments had declined from 1.63 in 1960 to 0.59 in 1970.[2]

During the 1960's three cumulative trends continued to alter the environment in which the Bretton Woods regime functioned. First, there was a diffusion and expansion of world economic power, marked by the recovery of Europe and the relative decline of the United States and Britain. Second, world trade and capital movements continued to expand, and, finally, an unprecedented degree of monetary and economic integration occurred. This last trend reflected deliberate governmental efforts to create common markets and preferential trading blocs, but it also represented an integration brought about by nongovernmental sources.

An impressive redistribution of economic power took place slowly and inexorably as governments continued to rely on tools of economic management to maintain high levels of employment and to promote economic growth. This redistribution, together with the relaxation of trade and exchange controls and the momentum of economic recovery, produced striking deviations in national growth rates. Real gross national product climbed 187 percent in Japan, 59 percent in Germany, 48 percent in the United States, and only 30 percent in Britain. The value of world trade jumped from $130 billion to $310 billion in 1970, and much of this reflected the soaring exports of Germany and Japan. Exports of manufactured products rose 400 percent in Japan, 200 percent in Germany, 110 percent in the United States, and 91 percent in Britain. As the figures suggest, Germany, Japan, and other Common Market countries were increasing their share of world exports at the expense of the United States and Great Britain.[3]

Statistical comparisons between centrally planned and free-market economies are necessarily hazardous, but it is clear that the phenomenal growth of Western trade and production had far-reaching implications for the Soviet Union and its satellites. Premier Nikita Khrushchev had boasted that his country would bury the United States economically, but during the 1960's Soviet economic growth lost speed. Moscow's economic managers successfully increased the Soviet Union's share of world production from 15.5 to 16.5 percent and overtook the United States in steel production, but they did not succeed in narrowing the vast income gap or in significantly improving consumer living standards.[4]

To some extent the redistribution of economic power failed to spread proportionate benefits to newly independent or other underdeveloped countries. Declining raw materials prices as well as limited participation in trade of manufactured products further reduced the less-developed nations' share of world trade from 33 percent in 1950 to 19 percent in 1970. Actually, the poorer countries as a unit grew more rapidly (5.6 percent) than developed nations (4.7 percent) from 1960 to 1971, but the per-capita income gap failed to narrow as higher population growth erased gains from faster economic growth.

Meanwhile, soaring trade and capital flows continued to integrate major non-Communist nations. Increasingly, they exported larger proportions of production and imported greater shares of items consumed. In 1950, for instance, the United States sold only 9.1 percent of production abroad, but twenty years later that figure was 12.8 percent. For West Germany comparable figures were 17.3 and 37 percent; for Britain, 42.8 and 47.9 percent; and for Japan, 18.3 and 30.1 percent. Greater economic interdependence meant that government had to weigh more heavily the external repercussions of policy decisions taken to boost employment, control inflation, stimulate growth, or remove a payments deficit or surplus.[5]

Similarly, long- and short-term capital movements brought a degree of monetary integration unparalleled in world history and unanticipated at Bretton Woods. A number of factors encouraged this process, including higher European growth rates, political stability, and progress toward European economic integration. These external, as well as domestic, considerations, encouraged American-based corporations to expand abroad. Direct investment more than doubled in the 1960's—from $32 billion to $78 billion. The flow to Europe nearly quadrupled and aroused concern about the American "takeover" of foreign corporations.[6]

For the stability of the Bretton Woods system, monetary integration had disturbing implications. Continuing dollar deficits placed a surfeit of dollars in Europe—in central bank accounts and private holdings— and these helped to create the Euro-currency market, consisting of bank deposits denominated in foreign currencies, frequently dollars. The increased disposition of European governments to invest excess dollar reserves in the Euro-currency market, as well as American controls on outward dollar movements, strengthened and expanded this new volatile pool of currencies beyond the control of national monetary authorities. Among the results of monetary integration were lower interest-rate differentials among major money markets. Accordingly, a change in interest rates, taken to stimulate or restrain one economy, could precipitate an outflow or inflow of short-term capital. This in turn, as events after 1967 demonstrated repeatedly, could unsettle currency markets and arouse concern among speculators, multinational corporations, and central bankers about the prospects for currency depreciations or appreciations. Briefly, monetary integration reduced the latitude of national economic managers to cope with domestic problems, for in an open world a change in the British discount rate or an increase in the American budget deficit could trigger disruptive capital movements and ultimately thwart one country's efforts to hold down inflation or reduce unemployment.

Fundamental alterations in the international economic environment raised questions about the suitability of Bretton Woods. Were its triple objectives—freely convertible currencies, stable exchange rates, and independent national economic policies—compatible goals or an irreconcilable trinity in the institutional and structural climate of the 1960's? If the goals were theoretically compatible, were disruptions the product of inherent defects in the Bretton Woods rules and mechanisms, which sought to attain those objectives, or did the difficulties stem from the unwillingness of members to adhere to existing rules and obligations?[7]

Diagnosis posed one set of questions; prescription presented another. Given the problem, should nations seek to restore order with greater exchange-rate flexibility, more trade or capital restrictions, or perhaps some version of supranational institutional integration? Choice of a solution depended on economic and political calculations. Which option seemed most compatible with the widest variety of economic objectives—efficiency and specialization, growth, full employment, price stability, and income distribution? From the American and foreign perspectives, which solution best harmonized with existing and future political and military relationships? If, for instance, the United States was expected to assume extensive security obligations, then how much compensation (and in what form) should other allies supply? Finally, was the proposed solution congruent with existing domestic political attitudes and interests?

Until the late 1950's members of the International Monetary Fund had little reason to consider these interrelated issues, for the fundamental problems had not emerged. Bilateralism and exchange controls inhibited capital movements and allowed policymakers on both sides of the Atlantic greater latitude over domestic policies. In this situation, Europeans, recognizing that they would soon have to remove transitional controls and adopt current-account convertibility, worried, as they had since World War II, more about a dollar shortage than a dollar glut. Old attitudes adjusted slowly to new circumstances. Pre–World War II memories, together with a dip in dollar imports during the 1949 recession, provided enough evidence, and myth, to make credible the old deflationary bogey—"when the United States catches cold, Europe catches pneumonia." Fearful of a chronic dollar shortage, a worry that economists analyzed at considerable length in scholarly treatises rolling from university presses, policymakers generally viewed with approval a dollar deficit that began in 1950. This deficit redistributed the United States' reserves and strengthened the monetary position of its allies and, indirectly, the entire Western bloc against the pressures of Soviet military, economic, and ideological power. The dollar deficit that most policymakers discussed in the early 1950's was not the loss of American reserves from excessive expenditures but the reverse. It was the gap between what other countries could purchase from their export earnings and sales to the United States and the volume of goods and services they wanted to buy.[8]

A turning point came in 1958–1959. Now a chronic dollar weakness, not a persistent dollar shortage, began to alarm policymakers in Europe and the United States. The problem was a sharp deterioration in the United States' basic balance, perhaps the best measure of a nation's overall payments position because it considered trade and service transactions, private remittances, government transfers, and long-term capital movements, but not volatile short-term capital flows. The basic deficit averaged $1.6 billion between 1950 and 1956 but widened to $3.8 billion in 1958 and 1959. The difficulty, as economists noted, was that the United States no longer earned enough on trade surplus to offset heavy expenditures for military equipment, foreign aid, and private investment—expenditures that the administration encouraged in order to strengthen the free world against the Communist challenge. The merchandise trade surplus, which averaged $2.6 billion between 1950 and 1956, dropped to $2.3 in 1958 and 1959. Meanwhile, purchases of military equipment from foreign suppliers climbed steadily from $576 million in 1950 to $3 billion in 1958 and 1959. Government nonmilitary loans and grants continued to generate a deficit averaging $2.5 billion in the decade of the 1950's. Also, the flow of long-term private capital increased from a $900 million deficit in the early 1950's to $2.1 billion in the two critical years. Shortly after taking office in 1961, President John F. Kennedy summarized the payments problem succinctly. "The surplus of our exports over our imports, while substantial," he said, "has not been large enough to cover our expenditures for United States military establishments abroad, for capital invested abroad by private American businesses, and for government economic assistance and loan programs."[9]

Many explanations for the shrinking trade surplus circulated. Some economists stressed the deleterious impact of rising export prices; others emphasized a growing preference for imported goods, a delayed effect from the 1949 European devaluations, or more vigorous import competition from German and Japanese manufacturers.[10]

For the next twelve years the dollar glut would prove the most vexing international monetary issue. And it was a problem the founding fathers had not foreseen. Preoccupied with how to avoid a postwar dollar shortage, they had inserted a scarce-currency clause, but the Bretton Woods designers neglected to prepare defenses against its reciprocal—a chronic surplus of dollars. This second dollar problem had three interconnected technical aspects. First, how should a dollar deficit be removed without sacrificing stable exchange rates, currency convertibility, or national economic autonomy? Should the United States or its creditors assume the adjustment burden? Second, was it possible to remove the dollar deficit without shutting off the supply of reserves that nations needed to finance expanding trade and to protect against unpredictable hot-capital movements? Finally, in a world with relatively uninhibited capital movements was it possible to avoid a confidence crisis, such as had disrupted the gold-exchange standard in 1931 when sterling, the dominant currency, also showed weakness?[11]

The United States' deficit underscored the shortcomings of the Bretton Woods approach to equilibrium. Ideally, members were expected to correct payments imbalances before a persistent drain exhausted reserves and borrowing capacity, compelling the deficit party to employ such illegitimate expedients as currency floats or controls. But the articles of agreement imposed no symmetrical obligation or pressure on surplus countries—except the somewhat vague scarce-currency clause—to help remove a disequilibrium. Presumably, an imbalance resulted from mismanagement in the deficit country, not from the mercantilisticlike efforts of its trading partners to accumulate reserves. Assuming that a debtor adhered to the rules, it had to remove an imbalance with restrictive monetary and fiscal policies or with controls on capital flows. If these failed, it might resort to the ultimate weapon—devaluation to remove a "fundamental disequilibrium." Except for an initial 10 percent devaluation, this approach required IMF approval. Presumably, devaluation would, by cheapening the weak currency, correct the deficit, not exacerbate the difficulty, such as might occur if exports did not expand sufficiently to finance more expensive imports.[12]

In practice, these procedures often proved cumbersome and ineffective. As experience showed, reductions in government spending to restore external balance sometimes contradicted domestic economic objectives—full employment or social services—and aroused public opposition. Likewise, restrictive monetary policy often had a perverse effect. Higher interest rates attracted inflows of foreign capital, and this in turn increased domestic money supply and fueled inflation. Also, to secure the needed balance-of-payments improvement, restrictive monetary and fiscal policies often took longer and required more deflation than the Bretton Woods delegates anticipated or than policymakers in the deficit country could apply without unacceptable political repercussions.[13]

Even so, some countries could employ internal policy to correct a disequilibrium more successfully than the United States. Fearful that an American recession might depress world trade and spread to other members of the world community, the founding fathers tacitly excluded deflationary policies from the American economic arsenal. Others might invoke the scarce-currency provision to offset the external repercussions of an American recession, but Washington must move cautiously. Actually, this provision was less of an encumbrance than were its undesirable political effects. President Eisenhower, for instance, successfully employed a budget surplus in fiscal 1960 to strengthen the balance of payments. It temporarily achieved the desired result, but Vice-President Richard Nixon blamed fiscal restraint for the rising joblessness that seemingly cost him the 1960 presidential election. A decade later President Richard Nixon ruled out monetary and fiscal policy to remove the United States' deepening deficit. As his international economic advisers observed afterward: "It would have been unreasonable to have demanded that the United States pursue a more restrictive growth and employment policy for balance-of-payments reasons. The domestic economic and political costs were already high, and the international results uncertain. No country could be expected to pay such a price simply to improve its balance of payments."[14]

As it turned out, governments avoided periodic parity alterations, and the system that experts had devised to assure exchange stability tended to encourage exchange-rate rigidity. One difficulty was that international rules established no criteria for determining when a parity change was appropriate. Since Bretton Woods discouraged periodic adjustments to correct anything but a "fundamental disequilibrium," an ambiguous phrase that certainly covered a persistent loss of reserves but less clearly short-term difficulties, major industrial countries sought to avoid parity changes as long as possible. Between September 1949 and 1965, for instance, France was the only important country to devalue; Germany and the Netherlands the only major ones to revalue. Canada, confronted with a heavy inflow of United States investments, chose to float its dollar, in technical violation of the IMF rules, between 1950 and 1962. A second factor militated against timely depreciations of major currencies. In orthodox banking circles devaluation signaled domestic mismanagement, and popularly elected governments generally sought to avoid confessions of economic error.[15]

Less-developed countries had fewer inhibitions and less access to outside assistance. Accordingly, from the end of 1948 to mid-1965, fifty countries allowed their currencies to depreciate more than 30 percent. Israel, Yugoslavia, Uruguay, Paraguay, Argentina, Chile, Brazil, Bolivia, Indonesia, and Korea all devalued more than 90 percent. This record, combined with the steady erosion of domestic purchasing power from internal inflation, prompted conservative currency expert Franz Pick to assert, "There have been nearly 1000 full or partial devaluations of currencies since the end of World War II, or about 37 such government bankruptcies every year."[16]

All these arguments against devaluation, and more, applied to the American dollar, for it was not simply the national currency of a major industrial power. In the evolving Bretton Woods system the dollar, as the only currency redeemable in gold, was the *numéraire*, or benchmark, for the entire par value system. Also, the dollar was the most widely held reserve asset and the leading vehicle currency in which nations financed world trade. If the United States tried unilaterally to devalue its currency in terms of gold—that is, to increase the price of gold—the process might prove disruptive. Since only Congress could change the price of the dollar, extended deliberations would take place while speculators scoured for gold, or so it was argued. Moreover, revaluation of gold would undermine the dollar's credibility as an asset as good if not better than gold and would benefit nations like South Africa, the Soviet Union, and France, who mined or held large proportions of their currency reserves in the yellow metal. Other nations, such as Germany and Japan, who held reserves in dollars at American urging, would lose by the amount of the devaluation.[17]

Unilateral devaluation, viewed as an increase in gold prices, would not necessarily remove an American payments deficit. Foreign governments, who supported the existing par value system with intervention in currency markets while the United States remained passive, could counteract American action. In short, devaluation of the dollar would require extended negotiations if it were not, policymakers thought, to engender competitive depreciations disrupting the entire network of exchange rates and endangering orderly trade and capital movements. Moreover, since the United States was an economic giant, accounting in 1970 for 14 percent of world exports, dollar devaluation might upset existing trade patterns. The competitiveness of American goods would improve, logically, in all markets—including countries with which the United States had a trade surplus as well as a deficit.[18]

Consequently, effective devaluation might have the same result as selective revaluation of other currencies against the dollar. That is, it would disturb existing cross rates. For instance, if Britain followed the dollar down—to protect the home market from a flood of American imports—but France did not, then British goods as well as American products would become more competitive in France. Similarly, French perfume would become less marketable in Britain and the United States. Conceivably, dollar devaluation would launch a wave of competitive depreciations, as sterling's fall in 1931 did, that would ultimately restore the old exchange-rate pattern. Also, dollar devaluation would have unpredictable military and political consequences. A cheaper dollar would probably discourage American capital exports and attract foreign investments into the United States, but it would increase the cost of foreign aid and overseas defense expenditures. Such constraints could reduce American influence on the world scene and bring a reduction of world commitments. Dollar devaluation, then, would not only undercut American prestige but might also hasten the disintegration of the American empire that had maintained free-world security.

Solutions for the dollar deficit inevitably raised a related issue— liquidity. Under the Bretton Woods system of fixed parities, monetary authorities needed liquid assets, such as gold or dollars, so as to intervene in foreign exchange markets whenever necessary to keep spot rates within 1 percent of the par value. In practice, so as to avoid the problem of inconsistent cross rates that would develop if every nation intervened, the United States adopted a passive role and simply stood ready to convert dollars and gold freely at the fixed price of $35 per ounce. As economists recognized, in a world with N currencies there are N-minus-one exchange rates that can be independently determined, and the United States satisfied its obligation by maintaining the link between gold and the dollar.[19]

The United States' unilateral pledge to allow gold redemption encouraged other governments to economize on the use of gold and to hold large portions of their reserves in dollars. As long as Washington supported the 1934 gold price, others could be certain that the auric metal would not appreciate, and, since gold holdings required security, a preference for that asset could prove a costly, and unnecessary, indulgence. Without materially enhancing risk—the United States after all placed its prestige behind the gold-redemption pledge —foreign authorities could hold dollars and earn interest.

In theory this gold-exchange standard had important advantages, including flexibility and elasticity, but experience in the interwar period showed one overriding disadvantage—fragility. If the dominant currency were weak and other monetary centers showed strength from cumulative surpluses, the system might prove crisis prone when governments and corporations shifted their assets. This difficulty appeared again in the late 1950's. For one thing, the supply of monetary gold did not rise to satisfy the need for increasing reserves to finance expanding trade. Instead, while Washington artificially held gold to its 1934 price, inflation doubled the value of other commodities between 1938 and 1948; consequently, gold production failed to keep pace with the demand for additional liquidity. For instance, between 1949 and 1958 world trade grew at a compound annual rate of 5.8 percent; gold reserves increased only 1.6 percent annually. Accordingly, government relied more heavily on credit reserves—largely dollars—and these holdings increased 9.3 percent annually.[20]

The U.S. balance-of-payments deficit, then, gave the world additional reserves to finance the expansion of world trade and to accumulate the cushion required if nations were to fulfill their Bretton Woods obligations—namely, maintaining current-account convertibility and fixed exchange rates. Between 1949 and the autumn of 1960, foreign gold and dollar holdings increased $27 billion. Of this, $21 billion derived from the United States' own gold losses and short-term liabilities (about $15 billion). During this redistribution and expansion of reserves, gold actually declined as a percentage of total monetary holdings, but this did not arouse much concern. After all, the United States pledged to redeem dollar liabilities on demand, and its word seemed as good as gold. In 1955, for example, the United States held nearly 57 percent of all monetary gold, and this stockpile was more than enough to honor that commitment.[21]

A Yale economics professor, Robert Triffin, upset the complacent attitude of monetary officials in 1959 when he warned that the United States' chronic deficit threatened to destroy the gold-exchange standard, not to increase its strength. This modern-day Cassandra, born in Belgium and a former employee of the Federal Reserve and the International Monetary Fund, diagnosed the dollar dilemma for members of the Joint Economic Committee of Congress. On the one hand, he said, if the United States managed to terminate its deficit, the world monetary system would experience an acute liquidity shortage. Dollars, after all, provided approximately two-thirds of the world's expanding monetary reserves. On the other hand, if the United States sought to postpone balance-of-payments equilibrium, the deficit would continue with catastrophic consequences. The quantity of dollar liabilities in foreign holdings would expand, further reducing the ratio between gold and credit money and leaving the system as vulnerable to a run on gold as the pre-World War II gold-exchange standard was in 1931. Then, the crisis led "to the devaluation of the pound sterling, to the collapse of the international gold exchange standard, and to the consequent aggravation of the world depression." Short-term palliatives designed to shore up the delicate system that relied on national currencies and gold for international reserves could contradict domestic policy objectives. If the United States, for example, tried to reduce interest rates to stimulate domestic growth and employment, this stimulus might weaken foreign confidence in the dollar and imperil the Bretton Woods arrangements.[22]

The Achilles heel, Triffin correctly perceived, was the dependence on national currencies to supplement gold for growing liquidity. A gold-exchange standard, Triffin's analysis of history seemed to demonstrate, could function successfully only as long as other countries retained confidence that they could, in fact, redeem dollar liabilities for gold at $35 per ounce. In the mid-1950's, as Europe and Japan replenished their reserves and revived trade, there was little cause for alarm. In 1953, for instance, total dollar balances in the possession of foreign government and international agencies amounted to only 57 percent of U.S. gold reserves. By 1958, however, that ratio was 86 percent, and future deficits would eventually place more dollars in foreign hands than the United States had gold for redemption.[23]

That occurred in 1960. Before the year ended, the United States' short-term liabilities exceeded $21 billion, and, as a result of steady dollar redemptions, the available monetary gold stock had fallen to $17.5 billion. Though symptomatic of the long-term erosion of U.S. monetary strength, this situation was not intolerable. A large percentage of the dollar liabilities were in private hands. Washington still held two-fifths of the Western world's gold stock, and this sum amounted to more than one and one-half times foreign official dollar holdings. Nevertheless, the Eisenhower administration could not honor its pledge in an emergency. Under existing law, $11.5 billion of the American gold stock was a reserve against Federal Reserve currency and deposits and was therefore unavailable for international settlements. Thus, without fully realizing the implications, the international trading community had gradually moved from a gold-exchange standard, allowing governments to redeem dollars freely, to a dollar standard whose strength rested on foreign confidence in the dollar. No longer could the United States honor its long-standing gold-conversion promise if all creditor nations attempted simultaneously to shift their reserves into gold. In that situation the U.S. Treasury would have little recourse but to slam the gold window.[24]

Triffin's dire forecast gained widespread attention late in 1960 when, during the presidential election, gold prices soared in London, temporarily rising to $40 per ounce. This flurry indicated the depth of concern about the dollar and the suspicion among speculators that John F. Kennedy might, if he won the November election, devalue the dollar as Franklin Roosevelt had done shortly after his election a generation earlier. Washington stemmed this speculative fever with sales from Treasury gold hoards, but the episode helped convince Kennedy that the balance of payments was one of the two (Cuba was the other) most dangerous, demanding, and intractable problems facing his administration. In retrospect, the 1960 gold surge marked a watershed in the evolution of the Bretton Woods system. As the Bank for International Settlements later stated, "The attention of the world had been drawn to the growing shortage of new gold and to the associated threat to the convertibility of the dollar into gold at the existing parity." Even when gold prices returned to normal in 1961, "the former absolute confidence in the dollar was never again restored."[25]

French President Charles De Gaulle perceived the political implications of the dollar standard more clearly than other leaders, and he decided to act. In a famous press conference in February 1965, De Gaulle attacked the special privilege others had accorded the dollar in declining to convert U.S. liabilities. The United States, he warned, "pays . . ., at least partially, with dollars which it alone can issue, instead of paying entirely with gold, which has a real value, which must be earned to be possessed, and which cannot be transferred to others without risks and sacrifices." And, to chip away at dollar dominance, De Gaulle did not hesitate to convert monthly dollar balances for American gold, just as he did not hesitate to loosen France's ties to the North Atlantic Treaty Organization.[26]

De Gaulle's nationalistic brinkmanship underscored the fatal flaw in the gold-exchange standard. If smaller powers could not discipline the dollar, by drawing down American gold reserves, without endangering the open world monetary system, then others had little recourse but to accept the consequences of an inconvertible dollar.

In that circumstance Washington might indefinitely spend billions of dollars overseas on military and political commitments, which, while protecting the West, also served to consolidate and strengthen American dominance. Also, American tourists, students, businessmen, and other travelers could journey around the world in increasing numbers, buying goods and services with overvalued, inconvertible dollars. And American corporations could invest abroad, creating new industrial empires that drew foreign nations tightly into an integrated, but American-dominated, economic community.[27]

But, dollar hegemony conferred benefits, as well as disadvantages, and these deterred other European governments from following De Gaulle's lead. First, as long as the Soviet Union posed a credible threat to Western Europe, the dollar standard enabled the United States to carry a disproportionately heavy military burden along with a major role in promoting the economic development of newly independent and disadvantaged nations. Military and politically, a move to dethrone the dollar—the financial equivalent of a nuclear exchange—would force other governments in the North Atlantic region to renegotiate their security and political alliances and undertake a costly, and perhaps politically controversial, build-up of independent or coordinated military defenses. The European nations, in short, were too weak to stand alone and too divided to stand together against both the United States and the Soviet bloc. Second, the surplus countries confronted the issue of whether greater monetary independence, à la De Gaulle, was compatible with expanding trade and economic growth. While Bretton Woods enthroned the dollar and gave the king privileges denied the commoners, it had at least expanded world production, trade, and a high level of employment. A move to curb American monetary dominance might well disrupt world commercial relations, precipitate a global depression, and encourage another round of dysfunctional political and economic nationalism. Behind the door at all times was the fear that the United States might slam the gold window and simply let the dollar float.[28]

Continuation of the dollar-exchange system, whatever its strengths and liabilities, depended on more than the acquiescence of foreign governments. It also rested on their coordinated ability to defend the existing system against an unwanted crisis, one provoked by disruptive capital movements. With integrated money markets and free convertibility of national currencies, money could move swiftly from one banking center to another in response to interest-rate differentials or speculative rumors. And a sudden inflow or exodus of hot capital would pose painful dilemmas for monetary authorities without a negotiated alternative to Bretton Woods. A hemorrhage of dollars, for instance, either would force foreign central banks to buy up all the dollars offered with local currency, thus preserving existing exchange rates at the cost of increasing reserves and swelling the domestic money supply, or would force other governments to erect obstacles. Floating currencies or controls would contradict the objectives of maintaining an open economic order with capital mobility, stable currencies, and interconvertibility.[29]

The dangers of an uncontrollable monetary crisis invited creative recommendations for coping with the related problems of international adjustment, liquidity expansion, and confidence. Academic economists, typically bold and reform minded, advanced a variety of fundamental reforms during the 1960's. In one category were recommendations for an automatic adjustment mechanism that reduced official management and permitted market forces to restore equilibrium. Briefly, deflationists like General De Gaulle's adviser, economist Jacques Rueff, and Michael Heilperin proposed to escape the Triffin dilemma by leading the world back to an automatic gold standard, accompanied if necessary by an increase in the gold price. To the charge that restoring the gold standard was like repealing the twentieth century, Heilperin responded, "The twentieth century, with its record of wars, tyrannies, and depressions, might be well worth repealing."[30]

The dangers of the gold-exchange standard led University of Chicago economist Milton Friedman, and others, in a different direction— toward floating exchange rates. A free currency, like free markets, he argued, would reduce government management and price fixing. It would "solve the balance of payments problem once and for all. No deficit could possibly arise to require high government officials to plead with foreign countries and central banks for assistance, or to require an American President to behave like a harried country banker trying to restore confidence in his bank." As Friedman pointed out, floating rates solved both the adjustment and liquidity problems, and he anticipated that this approach could function without disrupting trade and payments—a view that most bankers and government officials did not share in the early 1960's.[31]

Most thinking concentrated on ways to increase global liquidity as the United States removed its payments deficit. Triffin, convinced that it was absurd for an international monetary system to depend on the strength of national currencies, offered a plan resembling John Maynard Keynes's proposed clearing union, which would strengthen the International Monetary Fund and authorize it to act as an international central bank. This radically remodeled fund would create international reserves to satisfy the growing need for liquidity, though Triffin inserted several restrictions to limit its reserve-creating powers in the short run. But the basic objection to the Triffin solution among policymakers was the reluctance of nation-states to cede extraordinary powers to intervene in national money markets to a supranational authority. As President Kennedy's international financial expert Robert V. Roosa said, "The money created by a superbank would be the most high-powered ever generated by a man-made institution, yet it would have no supporting supergovernment to make good on its debts or claims."[32]

The visionary Triffin wanted to abolish the gold-exchange standard and substitute a superbank, but more conventional opinion discussed ways to strengthen the existing system and create more liquidity. Harry White's one-time aide Edward Bernstein, more recently research director of the International Monetary Fund, proposed several reforms to better integrate the working balances of members and access to fund resources. Later, he wanted to use national currencies as backing for a new fund-sponsored Composite Reserve Unit (CRU).[33]

As technicians and economists considered long-range reform, the Kennedy administration concluded that sweeping revisions were premature. Instead, it set out to strengthen the dollar on the grounds that an improvement in the American balance would create the proper climate for more sweeping discussions. Facing not only a persistent dollar drain but also lagging internal growth and unacceptably high levels of joblessness, Kennedy ruled out either deflation or devaluation. Kennedy had promised not to devalue during the 1960 campaign. In February 1961 he reaffirmed this pledge and announced a series of ad hoc measures intended to stimulate exports and slash the dollar outflow. Among these moves was a reduction in the duty-free allowance for returning American tourists and an order that the Defense Department procure domestic military items unless they were more than 50 percent as costly as foreign production. Later, in

1963, Kennedy requested an interest-equalization tax to discourage foreign borrowing in the United States, and he issued wage-price guidelines to limit inflation. Kennedy and his successor, Lyndon Johnson, employed a variety of ingenious selective incentives and restrictions to secure the same effect, including export expansion drives, limitations on bank lending and private capital movements, and even the use of special notes and bonds, denominated in foreign currencies, to entice dollar holders not to request gold. At times these expedients contradicted the United States' longstanding commitment to liberalization of trade and payments, but the administrations saw them as necessary to shore up a dangerously weakened dollar.[34]

Temporarily, policies adopted in the Eisenhower, Kennedy, and Johnson years did relieve pressure on the dollar and reduce foreign anxieties. In the early 1960's, while the European economy boomed, the United States had some excess capacity and relatively stable prices. Foreign crop failures boosted American agricultural exports. As a result, the critical basic balance improved from a $4.3 billion deficit in 1959 and remained below a $2 billion deficit until 1967.[35]

After 1964, however, the basic deficit began to widen again, and this adverse trend reflected not only the pressure of domestic inflation on American trade but also increased foreign military expenditures and a continuing outflow of long-term investment capital. Higher prices, resulting from a taut home economy, reduced the competitiveness of American exports, and consumers increasingly expanded their purchases of foreign automobiles, electrical appliances, and other items. Domestic inflation, coupled with the undervalued currencies of major competitors like Germany and Japan, gradually eroded the trade surplus until it vanished in 1971, for the first time since 1873, and a $2.7 billion trade deficit occurred. A parallel trend, increasing military expenditures, added about $7 billion in red ink annually to American accounts between 1966 and 1970. Long-term capital movements, now restrained by government regulations, averaged a $1 billion net deficit between 1966 and 1970, although investment income, generated from these and earlier capital exports, added about $4.5 billion annually to receipts.[36]

The cumulative dollar outflow, present in every year but 1967 (when the Middle East conflict brought temporary relief), slowly strengthened foreign dollar holdings and, conversely, reduced U.S. gold stock and reserve position. In ten years, from the end of 1960, dollar liabilities nearly doubled, from $11.9 billion to $20.6 billion. Simultaneously, Washington's gold holdings dropped from $17.8 billion to $10.7 billion in early 1971. The published data showed Treasury ministers and international bankers that the dollar glut was weakening the United States' international position and destroying confidence in the dollar-exchange standard. Unless the long-term trend was promptly reversed, it appeared the United States would continue to consume more than it produced and spend more than it earned. For Europe, eager to create a new identity and establish a more equitable North Atlantic partnership, this relationship became increasingly intolerable. Perhaps General De Gaulle had been correct all along.[37]

Macroeconomic tuning and stopgap controls failed to arrest the underlying deterioration in the United States' basic balance, but these measures did purchase about five years of time. That moratorium allowed major financial nations to strengthen networks of monetary cooperation, mobilize additional reserves for extinguishing a currency flare-up, and discuss calmly possible modifications in the Bretton Woods arrangements.

Initially, President Kennedy's economic aides concentrated on two general objectives—erecting more defenses for the dollar and pound sterling, and satisfying global needs for expanding liquidity. With White House encouragement the New York Federal Reserve Bank established an intricate network of currency swap arrangements among central banks, including the Bank for International Settlements. These bilateral facilities, like the lines of cooperation that had developed among central banks in the 1920's, removed financial rescues from the scrutiny of international assemblies and parliaments and enabled the secretive central bankers to mobilize as much as $11 billion to support a weak currency against reserve losses.[38]

Washington also labored to strengthen multilateral defenses. Since studies showed that the International Monetary Fund had inadequate resources to meet additional reserve needs and to cope with payments pressures growing out of hot-capital movements, the United States supported increases in IMF quotas—to $28.5 billion in 1971— effectively doubling that agency's quotas in a decade. Also, ten leading industrial countries formed the Group of Ten in 1962 and agreed to provide another $6 billion in supplementary credit to the fund. With the approval of prospective donors the fund could then activate these General Arrangements to Borrow (GAB) to strengthen the monetary system. In fact, these credit lines did enable the United Kingdom to borrow about $1 billion in additional currencies to avoid devaluation in 1964 and 1965. These moves to supplement fund resources reflected the harsh fact that "the Fund has never had sufficient usable resources from other countries to aid both the pound and the dollar at the same time."[39]

In the early 1960's no aspect of international monetary reform received more thoughtful study and discussion than liquidity. As Robert Triffin indicated in 1959, either the United States would halt the buildup of dollar liabilities, thus cutting off the principal source of additional reserves, or confidence in the dollar would deteriorate, undermining the system and leaving the world without any reserve asset but gold, which was not available in sufficient supply. "On this reading of the problem," the U.S. Treasury concluded in 1968, "world reserves are bound to be either short in quantity or shaky in quality."[40]

As confidence in the dollar ebbed in 1968 and pressure mounted on limited gold supplies, major countries made an important decision to deemphasize the auric metal. They abandoned all efforts to keep official and private gold transactions at $35 per ounce, effectively adopting a two-tier gold system. Supply and demand would dictate prices in the private market, but authorities pledged to use the 1934 price in official settlements. Also, they agreed not to sell monetary gold on the free market, and, privately, they reportedly decided not to redeem dollar balances for American gold provided Washington took steps to fight inflation.[41]

To supplement gold and dollars as reserve assets, the Group of Ten developed plans for a new unit, and, after extensive and protracted negotiations, fund members agreed in September 1968 to amend the articles of agreement and establish Special Drawing Rights (SDRs). This reserve asset would be defined in gold, but would not be convertible, and would exist only on the books of the International Monetary Fund. Unlike the quantity of monetary gold—which was after all dependent on such fortuitous factors as progress in gold mining, private demand, or dollars, which came from U.S. deficit— SDRs could expand as governments desired. Ironically, the first distribution of SDRs took place in 1970 as a worsening dollar deficit erased the liquidity shortage that the new asset was designed to remove. The resulting oversupply of liquidity would discourage IMF members from approving a new schedule for SDRs allocations in 1972.[42]

Basically, this series of monetary reforms improved the fabric of intergovernmental financial cooperation, enhanced the IMF's prestige as the SDRs "traffic director," and took important steps to supplant gold and dollars as reserves. But political differences prevented parallel achievements to strengthen the exchange-rate adjustment system and to reduce the inherent vulnerability of a multiple-reserve asset system in a world with integrated money markets and independent national economies. As experts in many countries realized, a monetary regime that permitted its most powerful member, the United States, to finance deficits indefinitely with its own liabilities and inhibited that country from unilateral devaluation was crisis prone. In neglecting parallel reforms to promote prompt adjustments and to buoy confidence while they created SDRs, members of the International Monetary Fund had filled the bathtub without repairing the leaks.[43]

A series of short tremors often precedes a major earthquake. A similar phenomenon occurred in international finance between 1967 and 1971, and these monetary tremors gradually destroyed confidence, weakened currency defenses, and shattered the pattern of exchange rates established in 1949. Moreover, the net effect of these currency depreciations was to remove the dollar's last layer of protection and to cut the competitiveness of American exports. The International Monetary Fund acknowledged in April 1971 that the overweight dollar actually appreciated 4.7 percent since 1959.[44]

This round of economic disturbances, striking one major currency after another, resembled in its intensity the competitive depreciation cycle of the 1930's, and it followed a familiar pattern. A serious payments disequilibrium first emerged between one country with a large deficit and at least one nation with a large surplus. Officials sought to correct the imbalance with monetary restraint and capital controls. These remedies failed, often because the deficit country had unemployment and unutilized productive facilities and because the surplus countries, already experiencing inflation, preferred to accumulate more reserves than to tolerate rapid inflation. When massive, overwhelming short-term capital movements threatened to deplete the deficit nation's reserves and exhaust its borrowings, as well as to swell the surplus country's reserves to unacceptable levels, authorities moved reluctantly and belatedly to alter exchange rates. These long-delayed adjustments thus involved major alterations in currency values.[45]

Sterling collapsed first. Although Britain's 1949 devaluation brought temporary improvement, the pound began to weaken in the 1950's. Reluctant to devalue again, because the London banking community feared this would strip sterling of its reserve and transactions role, a succession of British governments—Conservative and Labour—attempted to live off borrowed reserves as they tried to tune up the sluggish domestic economy. Heavy borrowing and emergency restrictions enabled Prime Minister Harold Wilson to avoid devaluation in 1964; but, in 1967, after inadequate growth, another Middle East conflict, and mounting unemployment, the final act in sterling's decline opened. The trade balance deteriorated, and speculative outflows eroded reserves and strained the patience of creditors. Even an 8 percent discount rate, the highest since World War I, failed to restore confidence in the pound. Accordingly, Wilson devalued sterling 14.3 percent in November. It was a heavy blow to British prestige and to the efforts of central bankers to protect a major currency against speculative pressures. As the Bank for International Settlements commented later: "Heavy borrowing from abroad delayed the second devaluation; it could not prevent it. The basic situation had been too much weakened and confidence worn too thin by years of indecisive action."[46]

The fall of sterling also marked the failure of American efforts to prop up Britain as an international banker and as global policeman in order to reduce the strain on this country's resources. In the aftermath of London's decision, Treasury secretary Henry Fowler acknowledged that "devaluation of the pound puts the dollar in the front line in the defence of the world monetary system." And, for the next forty-two months, Washington felt the strain of that sole responsibility. Speculation against the dollar upset international currency markets and forced the United States, along with its European partners, to close the London gold market in March 1968. This crisis, widely interpreted as an indication of declining confidence in President Lyndon Johnson's economic policies, may have contributed to his decision not to seek reelection in 1968. In 1969 disruptive capital flows whipsawed the French franc and brought an 11.1 percent devaluation along with a 9.3 percent revaluation of the German mark. The following spring a heavy inflow of dollars compelled Canada to abandon its par value obligations and refloat the dollar. These events underlined the fundamental weakness of the American dollar and the international monetary system.[47]

A temporary improvement in the United States' basic balance in 1969 postponed monetary collapse and revived hopes in Washington that the dollar might escape the ultimate humiliation. Macroeconomic restraint, begun under President Johnson and continued by President Nixon, attracted short-term funds to the United States and gradually improved the trade balance, but not enough to exhibit long-term strength. As the new administration shifted to an easier monetary policy late in 1970, more than $6.5 billion flowed outward in search of higher interest rates. The basic balance deficit, not these short-term flows, caused the greatest concern, for the movement of interest-sensitive funds would reverse when the structure of interest rates altered. But the continuing deterioration in the basic balance, measuring trade and long-term capital, among other items, indicated fundamental weakness. As the United States economy picked up momentum, the deficit seemed certain to widen.[48]

Early in 1971, as the giant American economy awakened from its managed slumber during the two preceding years, Washington contemplated a new balance-of-payments policy. For over a decade, despite continuing deficits, the United States had sought to protect the dollar's special position with token redemption of foreign dollar holdings, political pressure, capital controls, and a mixture of monetary and fiscal restraint, with only limited success. Now proponents of change favored a passive approach, which was accurately termed "benign neglect." Advocates of this alternative recognized that the dollar was effectively inconvertible into other reserve assets, except in small amounts, and that this country could not devalue unilaterally. Unable either to maintain the gold-exchange standard or to modify the system without endangering orderly trade and payments, this country should abandon efforts to stem the dollar outflow and instead simply manage the domestic economy to avoid the extremes of serious inflation or depression. While the United States neglected its balance of payments, other governments could, if they desired, revalue, float, inflate, or impose controls to keep from absorbing additional dollars. Effectively, then, the United States should abandon convertibility, enthrone the dollar standard, and permit other governments freedom of action.[49]

Proponents of passivity—especially the Council of Economic Advisers—emphasized these advantages. First, it would remove the payments constraint on economic policy and allow the government to adopt appropriate macroeconomic strategies for coping with domestic unemployment, inflation, and growth. Second, "benign neglect" would either pressure Europe and Japan to acquiesce to the implications of dollar dominance—including the inflationary spillover from an overheated American economy—or induce others to speed up monetary reform negotiations, which would gradually reduce the dollar's position in a new world monetary regime. Economist Thomas Willett told the congressional Joint Economic Committee that this strategy was a device for "shocking the rest of the world" into a second Bretton Woods Conference.[50]

As appealing as the slogan "benign neglect" was to some academics and policymakers on this side of the Atlantic, it was hardly a short-term panacea for the overburdened dollar. For one thing, it assumed other governments had the economic and political latitude to appreciate in a haphazard pattern against the dollar. But a nation fanatically committed to neomercantilism, like Japan, might frustrate adjustment by continuing to maintain its export surplus and to accumulate dollars in its central bank. Meanwhile, less competitive American exports would suffer, a rising tide of imports would strengthen protectionist sentiment in Congress, and the United States would find it more burdensome to pay interest on expanding dollar liabilities. And, while the United States might service this debt with long-term investment earnings, fears that Americans were using an overvalued, inconvertible currency to buy up foreign property might induce other governments to restrict or expropriate this country's overseas holdings. Most of all, "benign neglect" underestimated the political bitterness and economic instability that might result from frequent interest-sensitive capital movements between monetary centers. European opposition to a passive approach surfaced in the concluding sentence of the Bank for International Settlement's annual report: "The continuous piling-up of official short-term debt by the United States and the contention that other currencies rather than the dollar have the main responsibility for the adjustment process can hardly be the last words on the subject."[51]

Despite the dangers and dissatisfaction, the passive approach enjoyed a limited success in May 1971, when waves of dollar selling compelled the Bundesbank to absorb $2 billion in two days, adding to the $3 billion Germany purchased in April. Unwilling to continue supporting the dollar, Germany closed the exchange market and soon allowed its mark to float upward 8 percent, as Canada had done in 1970. Austria, the Netherlands, and Switzerland also appreciated their currencies, while Belgium erected new controls.[52]

After these independent actions by strong currency countries, only one money remained seriously undervalued—the Japanese yen. Although Japan had a $1.2 billion trade surplus with the United States in 1970 ($3.2 billion in 1971) and $4.8 billion in reserves (these increased to $12.5 billion in August 1971), exporters, shipbuilders, and import competitors opposed any yen revaluation. And Prime Minister Eisaku Sato flatly rejected American suggestions that Japan should contribute to a new monetary alignment. Washington, then involved in the delicate process of opening a diplomatic dialogue with China and in negotiating the return of Okinawa, as well as in obtaining a "voluntary" restriction on Japanese textile exports, apparently considered but postponed further pressure—including discriminatory duties on Japanese imports.[53]

As the impasse continued, pressure mounted on the Nixon administration to abandon its "passive" strategy in favor of unilateral activism, or "unbenign neglect." With money markets already jittery from the spring turbulence, Washington released trade statistics showing a widening deficit, and these confirmed suspicions at home and abroad that the dollar was seriously overvalued. Another run on the dollar developed in early August after Congressman Henry Reuss, who chaired a Joint Economic Committee subgroup, released a report recommending a general currency realignment and suggesting that the Nixon administration formally suspend convertibility. This, recalled the Bank for International Settlements, "sounded like a tip straight from the horse's mouth," and during the next week $3.7 billion flowed into Europe to hedge against a possible devaluation. European governments, in turn, pressed Washington to convert more dollars into reserve assets. "By August," reported the Council of Economic Advisers, "the private and public pressures to convert the dollar into other assets—foreign currencies and ultimately reserve assets or their equivalent—became overwhelming."[54]

Meanwhile, the Treasury reassessed the balance-of-payments position, and on the basis of new forecasts reached a disturbing conclusion. During the last half of 1971, these studies indicated, the basic balance would reach a record deficit. In 1972 the trade deficit might approach $5 billion. And, without a sharp improvement in trade, interest payments to foreigners would rise almost as rapidly as investment income, meaning that the United States could not hope to live off its investment earnings, as Britain did in the nineteenth century. Furthermore, long-term capital flows and government grants would probably continue to drain away about $6 billion annually, unless the administration imposed drastic new controls and reduced its support for foreign aid and military commitments. Understandably, the Treasury favored another option—"drastic action" to generate a current-account surplus large enough to cover private capital flows, foreign aid, and military expenditures.[55]

Domestic, economic, and political calculations reinforced, and perhaps supported, urgent measures. In August 1971 evidence accumulated that, while prices were moving upward faster than anticipated, economic growth would be inadequate to achieve the president's 4.5 percent jobless target in mid-1972. Also, a restive labor movement and sympathetic congressmen were pressing for quotas that might reverse the United States' long commitment to trade liberalization and invite retaliation against American exports abroad.[56]

Unexpectedly, then, the Nixon administration found itself in the political and economic dilemma that Cassandras anticipated a decade earlier. Domestic slack, joblessness, and an imminent election militated against restrictive monetary and fiscal policies to correct a payments disequilibrium in the classic fashion. Moreover, policymakers correctly understood that this alternative—underwriting the country's international responsibilities—would impose an exorbitant price on the American people in lost jobs, income, and internal disruption. But to ignore the balance of payments, as proponents of a passive approach suggested, would be equally unacceptable. Currency chaos, controls, and diplomatic friction would probably damage business confidence at home and rupture the already frail monetary system.

President Nixon moved dramatically to solve his economic dilemma on Sunday, August 15. Appearing on national television, after conferring with his advisers at Camp David in the Maryland mountains, Nixon announced "bold action" to "create more and better jobs; . . . stop the rise in the cost of living; . . . protect the dollar from the attacks of international money speculators." His New Economic Policy included a wage-price freeze, suspension of dollar convertibility into gold and other reserve assets, and a temporary 10 percent import surcharge. The last measure, he added, would end when "unfair treatment is ended." In blunt, chauvinistic language Nixon notified U.S. trading partners that the time had come to negotiate a new monetary order. Others should bear "their fair share of the burden of defending freedom around the world" and agree to exchange-rate changes that would enable "major nations to compete as equals." "There is no longer any need for the United States to compete with one hand tied behind her back," the president stated.[57]

The international aspects of the New Economic Policy pleased some Europeans no more than "benign neglect." Previously, central bankers complained that coexistence with the mammoth American economy was like a man being in a rowboat with an elephant. Whenever the elephant shifted position, Europeans feared the boat would be swamped. Nixon's sudden activism they now compared to a jet pilot who hears a knock in his engine and decides to tinker with the motor while flying at 20,000 feet, rather than landing at a nearby field where mechanics of all nationalities are waiting to look at the plane. Most criticism was directed at the surcharge, which seemed a classic example of financial brinkmanship or recidivistic nationalism.[58]

The critics had a point. For, in abruptly slamming the gold window and in brandishing a big stick, the surcharge, Nixon and his flamboyant Treasury secretary John Connally were substituting shock therapy for the patient diplomatic negotiations that characterized the evolution of global monetary cooperation for twenty-five years. And, in linking monetary reform to concessions on trade and defense burden sharing, they were complicating the negotiating process and enhancing the possibility that brinkmanship would destroy the open world economy that it was intended to strengthen and reform. Also, in ig-noring International Monetary Fund obligations to maintain fixed parities and in violating other global agreements prohibiting sur-charges, the world's most powerful country was unilaterally shattering the rules it had helped to construct and, accordingly, exhibiting a wanton disregard for established procedures, even if they were out-moded. Certainly other less important industrial nations had violated these principles when expediency dictated—Canada and Germany, for instance, resorted to floating exchange rates, and Japan delayed the removal of trade-and-currency restrictions. But the sins of others did not justify a declaration of economic warfare, nor did abrupt action contribute to the spirit of mutual understanding and coopera-tion required to overcome inequities and devise more flexible guide-lines.[59]

In view of these ramifications, why did the administration select "unbenign neglect" to force the reforms that patient diplomacy and secret negotiations might have achieved without the glare of publicity and fears of economic disruption? Several factors undoubtedly con-tributed to this decision. First, the waves of speculative selling had created a crisis atmosphere that required emergency surgery. Second, the Nixon statement served to dramatize the administration view that the time had passed for palliatives and stopgap measures. Instead, the crisis offered an unexpected opportunity to achieve fundamental reforms that would be less acceptable to all powers in more tranquil times. And, finally, there was a sense of frustration and an inclination to experiment, since whatever emerged could hardly be more crisis prone than existing arrangements. Treasury Undersecretary Paul Volcker summarized these calculations in November 1971.

It has become all too clear that the international economic system was subject to increasing strains and recurrent crises and that fundamental reforms, not makeshift repairs, were necessary. It had become even clearer that the U.S. balance of payments deficits were no longer sustainable. These deficits were not sustainable financially in light of the cumulative strains on our reserve position and the strong speculative forces they engendered. They were not sustainable economically in light of the distortions which they forced on trade and investment patterns. And they were not sus-tainable politically in light of the encouragement they offered to protectionist pressures in the United States and the restiveness they caused abroad about the need of other countries to absorb large and continuing outflows of dollars.[60]

Officials' statements understandably neglected the extent to which politics affected President Nixon's decision. Convinced that joblessness had cost him victory in 1960, the president needed time to rekindle the home economy and cut unemployment so as to neutralize the economic issue before voters went to the polls in November 1972. With time running out, it seemed that only a sudden break with existing policies and obligations would allow the administration to meet its pressing political timetable. Even with the added stimulus, as it turned out, the government managed to push the unemployment rate beneath the 5.5 level on the eve of the presidential elections.

Nixon's 10 percent surcharge, critics said, was unnecessarily provocative, imprudent, and unneeded. It antagonized the Europeans, who had a trade deficit with the United States; irritated Latin Americans and other less-developed countries, who interpreted it as an unwarranted impediment to their expansion of semiprocessed exports; and angered the Canadians, who argued that their floating dollar would reverse the trade deficit. Undoubtedly, the surcharge was a club to force the United States' Atlantic trading partners to negotiate a range of outstanding issues, but it was principally aimed at mercantilistic Japan. In briefing reporters, Secretary Connally and his advisers made it unmistakably clear that the surcharge was imposed primarily to bring a revaluation of the Japanese yen. If Japan resisted, as it did briefly after President Nixon closed the gold window, other countries could not easily revalue against the dollar without giving Japanese exporters a competitive advantage in third-country markets. Had Japan heeded earlier invitations to relax import controls and revalue the yen, it is unlikely that the Nixon administration would have employed the shock therapy that some Japanese described as a "reverse Pearl Harbor."[61]

President Nixon's statement was widely interpreted as a death sentence for Bretton Woods. This was true in a narrow sense. The world's most powerful nation had finally abandoned its self-imposed responsibility to redeem dollars for gold and to make its currency the linchpin for the global monetary system. And, in suspending the convertibility of the dollar into gold or other reserve assets, the United

States had technically violated existing international monetary rules. The effect of Nixon's decision was to give foreign governments a stark choice. Either they could defend existing parities and employ an inconvertible dollar as the basic reserve and vehicle currency, or they could suspend intervention and allow market forces to promote a new currency alignment.

In fact, other major governments had elected to discard the Bretton Woods system before Nixon delivered his fatal blow. Earlier Canada, Germany, and the Netherlands permitted their currencies to float in violation of existing obligations. Furthermore, in continuing to accumulate reserves and in maintaining a mercantilistic trade policy, both Germany and Japan demonstrated little long-term concern for the continuation of a system that imposed heavy burdens, as well as great privileges, on the dollar.

Nor could American policymakers escape some responsibility for the 1971 breakdown. Since 1965, when the mammoth U.S. economy began to overheat, Washington had neglected its own most important contribution to the survival of a global monetary regime that sought to maintain stable currencies, free convertibility, and national economic autonomy. This was the responsibility of the dominant monetary power to maintain internal price stability.

Officials in the International Monetary Fund, custodians of the fixed-exchange rate system, took Nixon's announcement somberly. A few days later an obituary notice circulated through IMF offices.

> R.I.P. We regretfully announce the not unexpected passing away after a long illness of Bretton Woods, at 9 p.m. last Sunday. Bretton was born in New Hampshire in 1944 and died a few days after his 27th birthday. Although abandoned by some of his parents in infancy, he was a sturdy lad and was expected to survive. Alas, in the early nineteen-sixties liquidity anemia set in.
>
> The fatal stroke occurred this month when parasites called speculators inflated his most important member and caused a rupture of his vital element, dollar-gold convertibility.[62]

In a broader sense, however, the spirit and lessons of Bretton Woods seemed likely to survive the 1971 crisis and its aftermath. Even as they experimented with currency floats, major countries endorsed currency convertibility, international monetary cooperation, and multilateral surveillance more willingly than in 1945. As long as major currencies floated precariously, it is true, the International Monetary Fund could not function as its founders intended. But the fund had resources, an international technical staff, and a wealth of experience that could be redirected to internationally beneficial purposes. Furthermore, the longer currencies gyrated uncertainly, the greater was the likelihood that nations would eventually restore a fixed-rate exchange system that would make use of the Bretton Woods instruments and principles. In the darkest days of 1971 and 1973, the fund's staff could take consolation in the memory that at Bretton Woods delegates conferred a death sentence on the Bank for International Settlements, yet it survived to find a new mission.

Ironically, as inflation and structural changes combined to weaken the Bretton Woods currency arrangements, the World Bank Group acquired a new sense of purpose and direction and emerged as the leading source of development capital for needy nations. This shift to multilateral aid came as support for bilateral assistance eroded in the United States.[63]

In the post-Sputnik 1950's, Africa, Asia, the Middle East, and Latin America offered the principal political battlefields for cold war competition. To counteract Soviet initiatives and to facilitate long-term economic growth, which would in turn dampen the popular appeal of communist-style revolutionaries, Presidents Dwight Eisenhower and John F. Kennedy inaugurated a long-term bilateral assistance program. Foreign aid doctrine, as it developed in this period, was aimed at far more than buying friends and suppressing guerrillas. President Kennedy, in calling on the United States and other industrialized countries to support the United Nations Decade of Development, stressed the humanitarian objective of moving "more than half the people of the less-developed nations into self-sustaining economic growth while the rest move substantially closer to the day when they, too, will no longer have to depend upon outside assistance." The fundamental task of American aid policy, Kennedy said, was to "help make a historical demonstration that . . . economic growth and political democracy can develop hand in hand." Committed to global economic development for political, economic, and humanitarian reasons, American economic assistance increased from an annual average of $2.5 billion between 1956 and 1960 to over $4 billion annually between 1961 and 1963. In 1963 the United States supplied 60 percent of all official development capital. And, as a consequence, the United States Agency for International Development became not only the chief source of development capital but also the principal coordinator of international assistance efforts.[64]

But, congressional support for foreign aid waned in the mid-1960's, when racial unrest at home and exhaustion from a costly war in Indochina forced reconsideration of budgetary priorities and stirred discussion of U.S. global responsibilities. Frustrated with wide-ranging commitments and skeptical about the results of bilateral aid, Congress slashed appropriations, and this cutback encouraged official efforts to shift the assistance burden to other affluent donors, especially Germany and Japan, and to rely on multilateral institutions, such as the World Bank.[65]

Although the Agency for International Development once dwarfed other aid-giving institutions, the World Bank Group swiftly expanded its lending and by mid-1969 was providing as large a volume of assistance as the primary American agency. Former investment banker George Woods, who served as World Bank President from 1959 to 1968, encouraged this trend. During his administration the international institution doubled its lending and also exhibited a broader interest in the entire constellation of problems thwarting economic and social development. His successor, Robert McNamara, a businessman and former secretary of defense in the Kennedy and Johnson administrations, continued these policies and added a sense of urgency and activism to the staid World Bank.[66]

The first nonbanker to head the global financial group, McNamara surprised some tradition-minded governors of the bank, shortly after he took charge in 1968, by announcing an ambitious five-year plan. To offset sagging bilateral aid, he proposed that the World Bank Group lend twice as much as it had in the previous five years, and he said a higher proportion of this capital would go to Latin America, Africa, Indonesia, and the United Arab Republic than had in the past. Previously, while the United States took special interest in the Alliance for Progress, the bank and its affiliates concentrated their energies and resources on the South Asian subcontinent. And, in the five-year target period, McNamara did achieve his lending goal. World Bank commitments rose to $13.4 billion, a sum exceeding total operations in the preceding twenty-three years.[67]

McNamara also introduced qualitative changes intended to involve World Bank experts and funds in seeking solutions to such urgent development problems as overpopulation, underemployment, disease, and income maldistribution. This more elastic conception of the institution's development mission marked the beginning of a third distinct phase in the evolution of the bank's thinking. At first, when Eugene Black set priorities, the financial institution presumed that borrowing countries had only a limited capacity to absorb outside capital for productive uses. Consequently, it restricted lending to the foreign-exchange costs of capital infrastructure, primarily public power and transportation facilities, and this cautious approach satisfied bond underwriters, who, after all, helped raise capital for multilateral loans. Later, during the Woods era, bilateral aid programs mushroomed and the bank itself gradually accepted the premise that less-developed countries had greater need for outside assistance. Adopting a more flexible approach to development, the bank gave attention to education, industry, and agriculture; also, it made soft loans through the IDA and experimented with program loans and local-expenditure financing. McNamara resolved to expand these activities, increasing lending for education threefold and capital for agriculture 400 percent in the five-year planning period.[68]

In addition, the World Bank president proposed greater efforts to control population growth, create jobs, and redistribute income to benefit the poorest 40 percent of people living in developing countries. This emphasis implied a different conception of development, one designed as much to support the capacity of bank members to satisfy their own social preferences as to achieve economic development measured in more conventional terms of increasing gross national product, or rising per capita income. Previously many experts, including some bank staff members, had seen an irreconcilable conflict between income redistribution and rapid growth, partly because preoccupation with social equity was thought to reduce entrepreneurial incentives, discourage high rates of saving, and deter introduction of modern technology required to compete effectively on world markets. In urging reconsideration of these relationships, the new World Bank leader emphasized that social justice had a political, as well as a humanitarian, rationale. Believing, as others in the Kennedy administration had, that poverty and political instability were closely related, McNamara anticipated that a widening income gap between a privileged elite and the disadvantaged masses would incite violence, disrupting the development process that was the only permanent solution for poverty in a backward country.[69]

Critics wondered if McNamara's preoccupation with welfare problems—such as income redistribution, family planning, and employment—would lead the international agency along a perilous course that could jeopardize its effectiveness in less controversial areas. Progress against inequitable income distribution, excessive population growth rates, and similar barriers would require more staff than conventional project lending. And, in doubling the bank group's size, the new president was not only creating a large bureaucracy of professional development experts with an institutional perspective, but also enhancing the World Bank's ability to impose its own public policy objectives on clients in ways that could touch sensitive political nerves. For, if the agency proffered or withheld aid to induce a member to adopt an optimal income-distribution pattern or a different population profile, nationalists could accuse it of playing God with a member's future. Previously, while the international institution sometimes applied leverage to assure that a borrower adopted internal economic policies conducive to creditworthiness, it had little occasion to judge sensitive social questions.[70]

As the World Bank metamorphosed into an active development institution, concerned with stimulating economic growth and promoting social justice, money remained a serious constraint on future activities. The parent International Bank for Reconstruction and Development, established as an intermediary for conventional financing, depended on private financial markets, as it always had, for bond sales. But, with higher world interest rates and mounting debts burdening the poorest countries, the International Bank relied increasingly on its soft-loan affiliate for concessionary aid. As useful as the IDA was in helping the poorest underdeveloped nations, its funds required periodic replenishment from the legislatures of affluent donor countries; thus, the future of multilateral development efforts, such as bilateral programs, rested precariously on the shifting sands of public opinion in Western Europe, Japan, and particularly the United States.[71]

To remove development assistance from the scrutiny of financial markets and national legislatures, and to give it a more predictable volume, many experts, including Robert McNamara, favored a permanent link between monetary reserves and development assistance.

According to one version, if Special Drawing Rights became the principal reserve asset of a post–Bretton Woods currency system, the founders might earmark an automatic allocation of SDRs for the IDA's development finance program.

Thus, as the curtain fell on the Bretton Woods era, the second successful experiment with economic internationalism, the future looked bleak not only for the International Monetary Fund and the World Bank Group but also for the international economic cooperation needed to help underdeveloped nations, to promote an orderly procedure for removing payments imbalances, and to encourage the removal of trade-and-currency restrictions inhibiting an efficient international division of labor.

Epilogue

Origins, conduct, and consequences of great wars usually spark titanic historical controversies among the victors as well as the vanquished. World War II was no exception.

Until the mid-1960's most academic debate centered on familiar military and diplomatic themes—including reasons for American involvement in the war, conflict among members of the United Nations coalition, and differences about the postwar treatment of Germany. As a result, Pearl Harbor, Teheran, Yalta, and Potsdam, remote geographic place names, acquired the notoriety and attention that Bretton Woods avoided.[1]

Preoccupation with the cold war, which shattered hopes for great-power harmony, prompted revisionist historians to assert that President Roosevelt and his advisers won the war but lost the peace. According to them, Roosevelt, determined to defeat the Axis challenge speedily and inexpensively in terms of American lives, blithely ignored the long-term political implications of his military strategy and naïvely appeased an expansionist Soviet Union with unwarranted concessions. The president, claimed conservative revisionists, cavalierly sacrificed loyal allies and American national interests to appease Soviet dictator Joseph Stalin. At Yalta the dying American leader reportedly sold China down the river and consented to the Red rape of Poland and Eastern Europe in order to elicit Soviet support for military operations against Japan and to ensure collaboration in the United Nations peace structure.

Epilogue

Some who denounced the pro-Soviet tilt in Roosevelt's wartime policies attributed later setbacks to more than misplaced idealism, personal miscalculation, or the inevitable breakup of wartime alliances. They accused administration officials, including Assistant Secretary of the Treasury Harry Dexter White, of betraying American interests and contributing to this country's postwar diplomatic distress. Allegedly the leader of a Soviet spy ring in the Treasury, White reportedly withheld critical economic assistance from Nationalist China and contributed to the Chinese Communist triumph. Also, revisionists claimed White transferred secret currency plates to Russian authorities and thus helped to undercut German occupation policy. Finally, White reportedly sponsored the much-publicized Morgenthau Plan for "pastoralizing" Germany, a scheme that seemed designed to prepare the way for Russian dominance of Central Europe.[2]

The search for scapegoats and individual conspirators no longer occupies a generation of historians generally skeptical of great-demon theories and more prone to emphasize bureaucratic structures, ideologies, and national interests. Moreover, the appeal of individual conspiracies faded as the early revisionists died without training successors and as government archives failed to provide evidence that would corroborate the charges against White, Alger Hiss, and others.

This study does not attempt to rehabilitate or refute the charges that rocked Washington in the first postwar decade, but it does confirm the often-neglected pro-Soviet stance of Treasury policy. At Bretton Woods, White and Morgenthau did concede the Soviet government drawing rights in the International Monetary Fund and a position in the new monetary system that could not be justified on economic criteria alone. White may have had private motives—this point is arguable—but it is still possible to view Treasury strategy as a component of Roosevelt's own policy of weaning Russia away from autarky toward international collaboration and interdependence. Ironically, a generation later President Richard Nixon, who as a young congressman interrogated White about his pro-Soviet sympathies, also offered the Russian government concessions to secure assistance in winding down another Asian land war and to integrate a self-sufficient Soviet Union into the world economy. It was arguable, however, that Nixon's reconciliation with Russia was based on a more realistic understanding of mutual interests and objectives.

Economic dimensions of World War II peacemaking received more scholarly attention as the wheel of historical interpretation revolved in the early 1960's. As dissent mounted against the Vietnam War, a new generation of revisionists—this time, the radical left—assailed American policies from another perspective. The New Left revisionists blamed Washington for asserting an expansionist Pax Americana that forced Moscow to adopt an aggressive policy in self-defense.[3]

Interpretations vary, but a strong current of revisionist thought borrows heavily from the Marxist-Hobson critique of capitalism. The inherent contradictions of the free-enterprise system prompted the United States to design an open world economy for investing surplus capital, selling excess production, and obtaining raw materials. By temporarily establishing United States preponderance, World War II gave U.S. decision makers a long-sought opportunity to impose a laissez faire capitalist design on vanquished enemies and exhausted allies alike. From this perspective, Bretton Woods marked the triumph of predatory Anglo-American finance capitalism and represented a successful initiative to cast the economy of politics of other countries in a procapitalist mold. Internationalist rhetoric, emphasizing equal access to raw materials, nondiscriminatory trade, and currency convertibility, concealed the classic pursuit of national self-interest.

This line of discussion has the merit of shifting discussion away from great individual conspiracies, often an exercise in futility, and refocusing debate on fundamental economic issues. But the modern revisionist argument has several fundamental fallacies. First, economic determinists, in their quest for synthesis, magnify economic factors at the expense of other policy objectives and thus wrench history out of perspective. One goal of wartime diplomacy was to create an international order compatible with free enterprise, but this was not the only, or even the most compelling, objective. Americans also sought peace, global political stability, and a measure of political and economic integration that would restrain recidivistic nationalism from again plunging the world into war.[4]

Second, there is an unfortunate tendency in some revisionist writings to telescope issues into an epic confrontation between open-door expansionism and revolutionary nationalism. This dichotomy, while it simplifies discussion, obscures the significant differences about ends and means that separated Treasury planners from orthodox bankers in the Bretton Woods debate. Both sides agreed that the United States had a responsibility and interest in reshaping the international economy, and not simply to save the capitalist system. Generally, Keynesians worried about the instability of the free-enterprise system, and they saw planning and global interdependence, achieved under the auspices of international institutions, as the only sensible way to assure a maximum and efficient utilization of world resources. Even the Keynesian stagnationists agreed, however, that macroeconomic policies could arrest a postwar depression. Traditionalists, on the other hand, distrusted economic planning, especially when it involved government management, and they generally feared inflation far more than depression. For bankers and orthodox economists, supranational institutions were unnecessary to protect the American economy from stagnation or to cushion the world from a global depression. They tended to think in terms of economic efficiency and of the salutary webs of political interdependence that resulted from private trade.[5]

The most serious shortcoming of open-door expansionist formulations is the tacit assumption that all economic contact between capitalist and underdeveloped nations is necessarily a zero-sum game in which the former invariably prosper as the latter countries languish. This interpretation stems in part from the Marxist view that capitalist nations export surplus production in order to sustain domestic employment without a more equitable distribution of income at home. But recent international economic experience suggests that the vent-for-surplus thesis is a deficient model for explaining events in the real world. In the late 1960's, it is true, such nominally capitalist nations as Germany and Japan did export surplus production to bolster domestic employment and to accumulate monetary reserves in a mercantilistic fashion. However, socialist countries, like the Soviet Union, also exported surplus lumber, natural gas, and other materials to acquire foreign exchange. Perhaps the most damaging evidence against the radical formulation emerged when a cartel of oil-exporting nations successfully turned the tables on rich, industrial countries and quadrupled oil prices in 1973. This episode demonstrated how countries poor in human resources and underdeveloped by conventional standards could effectively utilize their own power to influence the foreign policies and living patterns of technologically advanced powers.

Preoccupied with the vent-for-surplus argument and how the capitalist nations presumably exploit the Third World, revisionists often overlook two other important justifications for international exchange. First, commerce permits a global distribution of labor along the lines of comparative, or absolute, advantage and, as international economists know, permits the most efficient utilization of world resources. Second, trade-and-capital flows permit less-developed countries to buy or borrow goods and technology to short-cut national development. In this circumstance, trade is a device not for exploitation but for promoting economic development. When these reasons for interchange are computed, international exchange emerges as a positive-sum game. All players benefit, though not all benefit equally at any point in the continuing game.

Bretton Woods monetary planners rationally adopted the broad view that national interest corresponded to global interest. They had little doubt that all countries could benefit from expanding trade, though some, including White and Keynes, had reservations about the relative advantages of capital movements. They wondered whether capital flows benefited exporting nations, quite the reverse of Marxist concerns that capital flows decapitalize underdeveloped countries to enrich capitalists in the metropolises.

The vision of a mutually beneficial economic order was one impulse to Bretton Woods; the ghost of the 1930's was another. What monetary experts feared most was a relapse into economic nationalism and warfare with each country attempting to "slough off its economic troubles onto its neighbors." Economic warfare, it seemed obvious to those familiar with the 1930's, was a negative-sum game that harmed every nation.[6]

Economically, this country had less to lose from autarky than any nation, except the Soviet Union. The United States did import heavily, but it was less dependent on outside supplies than the United Kingdom, Japan, Germany, or smaller countries. And, since the United States produced 32 percent of the total raw material output of the fifteen richest countries before World War II, a unilateral decision for self-sufficiency would probably have harmed U.S. trading partners more than the United States. Economist Eugene Staley reflected the prevailing view among knowledgeable American experts when he wrote in 1939 that this country could stand a "descent into 'autarchy' or self-sufficiency better than other countries." Admittedly this course would have caused temporary disruption and lowered American living standards briefly, but these internal effects were less important to policymakers than the global consequences of American economic isolation. Another withdrawal from responsibility would sharpen the global conflict for markets and raw materials among have-not nations, and this rivalry and instability would likely precipitate another major war and eventually involve the United States in peacekeeping.[7]

Given these premises, the relevant policy issue was not whether to construct an integrated economic system but how. Basically, two options appealed to postwar planners. The first, associated with Lord Keynes but also an integral component of Harry Dexter White's early formulations, involved an abrupt departure from prewar practices. Governments would establish a highly structured international monetary system with a supranational authority authorized to create its own currency and act as a world central bank. Keynes, in fact, thought this clearing union should assume the functions of a world economic government. The other alternative was more consonant with prewar practices under the Tripartite Agreement and involved little more than creating an international stabilization fund and a set of rules to guide each member's monetary behavior. Approval of the first would have involved a revolutionary attack on national sovereignty and monetary autonomy. Acceptance of the second would be little more than a halfway house to international monetary integration. Or, viewed differently, it would offer the monetary world a system of traffic control to prevent crashes, such as occurred in the 1930's, but not a city council or government authority to enforce provisions on sovereign nations.[8]

Keynes's followers, disappointed that the clearing union was rejected by Washington, claim that the Cambridge economist lost the battle but won the war. A short verse captured their misgivings at sacrificing the clearing union.

> In Washington Lord Halifax
> Once whispered to Lord Keynes:
> "It's true *they* have the money bags
> But we have all the brains."

Persistent problems with international adjustment, liquidity, and confidence have confirmed initial opinions that Keynes was prescient and his American opponents myopic in rejecting the British plan. English historian Roy Jenkins, a member of Parliament, reflected this sentiment when he wrote on the twenty-fifth anniversary of Keynes's death that wartime planners were "perhaps foolish, in the long run" to accept the American scheme. "They and the world might have been better off with Keynes's Clearing Union." Financial analyst Eliot Janeway blames a quarter-century of currency ills on "the failure of American imagination at Bretton Woods." While Keynes sagaciously suggested "modernization," White insisted on his own "reactionary standpatism." Basically, advocates of the clearing union think that it would gradually have replaced gold as a reserve instrument with a new managed unit, bancor, for settling international accounts. The clearing union, too, would have promoted automatic adjustment with symmetrical pressures on creditors and debtors and permitted an expansion of international liquidity to satisfy world requirements.[9]

Certainly Keynes's plan did combine technical elegance and simplicity of operation, and in these respects surpassed the system actually approved at Bretton Woods. Technical considerations aside, the clearing union was still an inappropriate and imprudent approach to postwar monetary problems. For one thing, it was politically premature. The clearing union assumed a wider and more durable consensus on monetary integration than existed at that time or later. Opposition to Keynesian-type economic management existed in American business and banking circles, and it crystallized in the monetary deliberations and later congressional debate on the Bretton Woods agreements and full-employment legislation. Available evidence confirms Alvin Hansen's conclusion that "no one familiar with the political realities of the time is likely to argue that a more ambitious scheme could have been approved."[10]

The clearing union had other serious disadvantages. Designed, as it was, to prevent a postwar depression, the scheme had an inflationary bias. Very likely the overdraft system would have placed additional pressure on world resources, compounded postwar transitional problems in the United States, and accelerated international transmission of inflationary impulses. Critics recognized this deficiency at the time. As George Halm wrote, the union contained "enough dynamite to endanger gravely the post-war world which it sets out to save from contraction."[11]

Also, it is doubtful that Keynes's plan could have functioned effectively without enforcement provisions requiring the backing of a world government. Despite widespread discussion of international organization among postwar planners, confidence in internationalism had not then developed to the extent necessary if nations were to surrender voluntarily sovereignty over such sensitive matters as currency values, employment, and production.

Idiosyncratic factors, such as the relative skill and imagination of Keynes and White, had less impact on monetary planning than did underlying realities of national power. London hoped for a dual monarchy in economic planning, but Washington soon established the dominant role that accurately reflected its real economic strength. For, as the war closed, the United States produced 50 percent of the industrialized world's gross national product and held two-thirds of monetary gold. Britain, however, emerged with only about 10 percent of total GNP and heavy liabilities. Its monetary debts exceeded $12 billion. Also, the United Kingdom had damaged industrial facilities and a depleted merchant marine, both necessary if it were to boost exports to meet international obligations. London, with its acute economic and financial weaknesses, played an active part in monetary negotiations largely because the war temporarily concealed the significance of this power transition and because negotiators on both sides of the Atlantic overestimated Britain's recuperative powers, assuming London would continue as a durable pillar of international finance.

Prewar statistics as well as the effects of World War II on the global system also help to explain why the two Anglo-Saxon countries sponsored monetary rehabilitation and identified their national interests with global collaboration. In the interwar period, sterling and the dollar were the major transaction currencies, financing the bulk of international trade. Also, the United Kingdom was the world's leading importer, buying about 17 percent of total imports. Conversely, the United States was the primary exporter, selling about 14 percent of international trade goods. Furthermore, other partners in the United Nations coalition could not be expected to assume responsibility for rehabilitating the world economy. France, China, and the Soviet Union were exhausted, and the latter two had never asserted international economic leadership. Historically, the Soviet Union avoided economic entanglements that might compromise a policy of self-sufficiency.

Accusations that in the exuberance of victory the United States and Britain dictated a monetary settlement that relegated less-powerful countries to a client status in an open-world empire distort the reality of Bretton Woods. It is true that Britain and the United States retained working control of the new international monetary institutions, but this was not a permanent arrangement. Weakness of the dollar and pound and corresponding strength of the German mark and Japanese yen would bring a redistribution of power in the 1960's. At Bretton Woods the legitimate alternative was a League of Nations–type distribution of power that equated sovereign nations without distinguishing among relative economic positions. This threatened to substitute the tyranny of the weak for the dominance of the strong, and most certainly this formula would not have passed the U.S. Congress.

Actually, the United States gave sympathetic consideration to the views of smaller countries and modified the accords when possible. Renewed consideration of the international bank late in 1943 can be interpreted as a concession to smaller countries who desired long-term credit instruments for reconstruction and development purposes.

Moreover, in underwriting the Bretton Woods system, American policymakers voluntarily assumed responsibilities restricting future freedom of action. The scarce-currency clause, for instance, bound the United States to correct a dollar shortage, growing out of postwar deflation, with full employment, contracyclical lending, or liberalized import policies. Otherwise, foreign countries might discriminate against American exports. Also, in unilaterally pledging to maintain two-way convertibility of dollars and gold, Harry White and his aides adopted a position that made the dollar the anchor of the gold-exchange system. As a consequence, the United States could no longer choose the composition of its reserve assets nor could it devalue or revalue the dollar without the acquiescence of other countries who intervened in exchange markets to defend existing parities. Unable to devalue unilaterally, Washington also ceded the right to inflate its domestic economy with the unregulated minting of money, for other parties to the Bretton Woods agreements could, if they wished, redeem unwanted dollars and draw down American gold reserves. The long-term stability of the Bretton Woods system depended in the last analysis on Washington's commitment to greater price stability than existed in other nations.[12]

Retrospectively, the modes of monetary cooperation approved in 1944 are vulnerable to some legitimate criticism. First, reliance on the universal approach to monetary reconstruction preserved the fiction of national equality and produced bold statements of principles that were difficult to implement in the transitional period. A more limited initiative, specifically John Williams's key-currency approach, would at least have avoided the disillusionment and delay that resulted from inflated expectations and limited achievements. Attractive as the key-currency option was to experienced currency experts, it presented serious negotiating problems. Like the sphere-of-influence concept, implicit in Roosevelt's talk of four great postwar policemen—China, the Soviet Union, the United Kingdom, and the United States—this alternative trampled on democratic ideals and aroused popular fear of great-power dominance. Nevertheless, a more realistic assessment presented forthrightly in public statements might have avoided some of the disillusionment that later flourished when other governments were unable to achieve early convertibility.

Second, the International Monetary Fund's provisions for exchange-rate adjustments were technically cumbersome and rigid. Preoccupied with the lessons of the 1930's and overly sensitive to congressional opinion, White rejected proposals from his own technicians for wider margins, which might have allowed currencies to float 2 percent above and below official parities, and from Keynes, who favored more elastic adjustment provisions. As a result, the final accords bound members to support exchange values within 1 percent of declared par values and discouraged frequent and timely exchange-rate variations to correct disequilibria.[13]

Third, at Bretton Woods the negotiators made inadequate provision for the orderly expansion of international reserves. As it turned out, the growth of liquidity depended on such fortuitous factors as the efficiency of gold mining and the persistence of an American balance-of-payments deficit. In the 1960's, fearful that the world faced a shortage of reserves, not a surfeit, experts finally agreed to create a new synthetic reserve asset, Special Drawing Rights, but by then the liquidity problem had reversed. Too much, not too little, paper currency impaired confidence in reserve assets.

Finally, among the familiar criticisms is the charge that Bretton Woods unwarrantedly prolonged the gold standard. Actually, it did not. The agreements carefully circumscribed the use of gold and removed the automaticity and autonomy that characterized operations of the pre–World War I gold standard, at least as it was commonly understood. Gold, it is true, remained as the *numéraire*, or unit of account, and as a medium of reserve settlements, but there, too, its use was carefully hedged. Bretton Woods bound no nation to buy and sell gold; any member could satisfy the fund's convertibility requirements by purchasing and selling other currencies. From this standpoint, then, Bretton Woods loosened the golden knot and permitted a gradual movement away from metallic toward fiduciary reserves. But it is possible to argue that the monetary architects, in loosening the discipline gold once imposed on national authorities, surrendered to national autonomy and failed to create another device to discipline national economic policies, thus jeopardizing international economic equilibrium.[14]

In short, distance suggests that wartime planners, haunted by the disruptions of the 1930's and overly dependent on Keynesian macroanalysis, permitted a fundamental asymmetry to emerge in their work. Fearful of depression, they erected defense mechanisms that strengthened national autonomy, but they neglected parallel restraints on inflation. There was nothing to protect the system from the export of American inflation. Ultimately, this flaw proved fatal.

From December 1958, when Europeans assumed most convertibility obligations, until the mid-1960's, when inflation spiraled, Bretton Woods functioned reasonably well. Major countries simultaneously enjoyed the advantages of stable exchange rates, convertibility, and independent monetary policies. The incompatibility of that trinity emerged in 1965, when the American economy began to overheat and the United States transmitted homemade inflation to other countries. As a result, what some have termed the "imperialism of inflation" distorted exchange values, encouraged private speculation, and eventually forced a series of disruptive adjustments culminating on August 15, 1971, with President Nixon's decision to abandon gold convertibility.[15]

The breakdown of monetary arrangements occurred, as monetarists anticipated a quarter-century earlier, from differential rates of inflation. The same phenomena contributed to the collapse of the gold standard during World War I and its aftermath, and it thwarted attempts to inaugurate the Bretton Woods system after World War II. A generation later, Vietnam, not a great war by most standards, distorted the dollar and precipitated the demise of a Bretton Woods system already in need of basic reforms to promote more efficient adjustments and to protect against disruptive short-term capital flows.

Epilogue

Imperfections in the Bretton Woods accords and short-sighted national behavior should not obscure the salutary impact of Bretton Woods on postwar economic history. Rules devised in 1944 guided international monetary conduct for nearly a generation, and during that interval the world achieved many of its economic objectives. Major currencies remained relatively stable and became increasingly convertible for capital as well as for current transactions. Currency stability and convertibility almost certainly facilitated the extraordinary expansion of global trade and production that made the Bretton Woods generation a golden era. Exports jumped from $48.2 billion in 1947 to $350 billion in 1971. On a historical yardstick these figures show an astounding fourfold increase in trade volume. In the century before World War II, commerce increased only about 4 percent annually, but in the years after 1945 it advanced 7 percent annually. This performance, along with a parallel surge in world production from $300 billion to $3.6 trillion yearly, invited favorable comment. As President Nixon's international economic report concluded, "By any quantitative measure the post–World War II era has been the most successful in international economic history."[16]

Bretton Woods also gave the stamp of respectability to international development efforts, and, in establishing a permanent financial institution for reconstruction and development purposes, it created the first multinational mechanism for supervising capital flows and coordinating a long-term aid effort. Although sensitivity to domestic political considerations kept the founding fathers from endowing the International Bank with a quasi-automatic facility for financing resource transfers, as initial Keynes and White drafts suggested, the World Bank played an important and beneficial role in promoting sound projects and in providing valuable technical assistance.

In the final analysis Bretton Woods inaugurated an economic Pax Americana, but it also achieved an economist's peace consonant with traditional doctrines heralding the advantages of economic interdependence and monetary cooperation. Had Washington and its London surrogate not sponsored this limited experiment in financial internationalism and assumed the burdens of maintaining this novel system, the world might well have witnessed a repetition of dysfunctional economic nationalism that thwarted hopes for material improvement and political stability during the turbulent interwar era.

Notes

Preface

1. U.S., Department of State, *Proceedings and Documents of the United Nations Monetary and Financial Conference, Bretton Woods, New Hampshire, July 1–22, 1944*, I, 1117 (hereafter cited as *Bretton Woods Documents*).
2. Ibid., I, 1120.
3. Ibid., I, 1121–1122.
4. Ibid., I, 1110.
5. Richard S. Kirkendall, "Franklin D. Roosevelt and the Service Intellectual," *Mississippi Valley Historical Review* 49 (December 1962): 456–471.

1. The Quest for a Durable Global Monetary System

1. George Santayana, *The Life of Reason*, I, 284; John L. Gaddis, *The United States and the Origins of the Cold War, 1941–1947*, pp. 1–31; Roosevelt speech to the International Student Assembly, September 3, 1942, in *The Public Papers and Addresses of Franklin D. Roosevelt*, ed. Samuel I. Rosenman, XI, 353. On Roosevelt's obsession with the lessons of World War I peacemaking, see James MacGregor Burns, *Roosevelt: The Soldier of Freedom*, pp. 361–365; and Ernest R. May, *"Lessons" of the Past*, pp. 3–18.
2. On the United Nations, see Robert A. Divine, *Second Chance*.
3. For statistics consult W. S. and E. S. Woytinsky, *World Commerce and Governments*, pp. 32–40, 189–191. On the emergence of an international economy, read William Ashworth, *A Short History of the International Economy since 1850*, pp. 182–217; Norman S. Buchanan and Friedrich A. Lutz, *Rebuilding the World Economy*, pp. 3–37; and William Woodruff, *The Emergence of an International Economy 1700–1914*.
4. On the contributions of the early economists to international trade theory, examine John B. Condliffe, *The Commerce of Nations*; and John Pincus, *Trade, Aid and Development*, pp. 89–146.
5. Adam Smith, *The Wealth of Nations*, II, 422, quotation on p. 183.
6. David Ricardo, *On the Principles of Political Economy and Taxation*, pp. 146–185. For a more complete discussion of theoretical issues, see Paul T. Ellsworth, *The International Economy*, pp. 59–70; Condliffe, *Commerce of Nations*, pp. 169–202;

and Pincus, *Trade, Aid and Development*, pp. 92–110.

7. John Stuart Mill, *Principles of Political Economy*, p. 582.

8. Condliffe, *Commerce of Nations*, pp. 169–202.

9. General references on the pre–World War I gold standard include Leland Yeager, *International Monetary Relations*, pp. 251–265; Condliffe, *Commerce of Nations*, pp. 360–400; and Edwin Kemmerer, *Gold and the Gold Standard*.

10. On the standard's mystique, note Benjamin Anderson, *Economics and the Public Welfare*, p. 1; and John Maynard Keynes, *The Economic Consequences of the Peace*, p. 1. Yeager summarizes changing interpretations in *International Monetary Relations*, pp. 258–265. Among the views that influenced World War II policymakers are William Adams Brown, Jr., *The International Gold Standard Reinterpreted, 1914–1934*, II, 774–806; Gustav Cassel, *The Downfall of the Gold Standard*, pp. 1–19; and League of Nations, Economic, Financial and Transit Department, *International Currency Experience*, pp. 66–68, 100, 231. Readers interested in more modern analyses should consult Robert Triffin, *The Evolution of the International Monetary System* and *Our International Monetary System*. Also, Arthur I. Bloomfield's two monographs *Monetary Policy under the International Gold Standard, 1880–1914* and *Short-Term Capital Movements under the Pre-1914 Gold Standard*.

11. Quotations from Herbert Feis, *The Changing Pattern of International Economic Affairs*, p. 130. For Cordell Hull's understanding of trade issues, see William R. Allen, "Cordell Hull and the Defense of the Trade Agreements Program, 1934–1940," in *Isolation and Security*, ed. Alexander DeConde, pp. 107–132. H. W. Arndt, *The Economic Lessons of the Nineteen-Thirties*, pp. 220–224.

12. For the impact of World War I on the monetary system, see Yeager, *International Monetary Relations*, pp. 266–269; Ashworth, *International Economy*, pp. 218–246; Buchanan and Lutz, *Rebuilding the World Economy*, pp. 3–37; and Ralph George Hawtrey, *The Gold Standard in Theory and Practice*, pp. 107–122.

13. League of Nations, Economic, Financial and Transit Department, *The Course and Control of Inflation*, p. 88.

14. League of Nations, *International Currency Experience*, pp. 27, 232.

15. Yeager, *International Monetary Relations*, pp. 268–274; Ellsworth, *International Economy*, pp. 393–409. On the war-debt problem, see Harold G. Moulton and Leo Pasvolsky, *War Debts and World Prosperity*. Melvyn P. Leffler shows that American economic and business leaders recognized that reparations and war debts were the crux of the postwar international financial problem. These issues required resolution before European debtor nations could stabilize their currencies and liberalize trade restrictions. See Leffler, "The Origins of Republican War Debt Policy, 1921–1933: A Case Study in the Applicability of the Open Door Interpretation," *Journal of American History* 59 (December 1972): 585–601.

16. W. Arthur Lewis, *Economic Survey, 1919–1939*, pp. 156–164; and Ashworth, *International Economy*, pp. 218–246. Both Lester Chandler, in *Benjamin Strong*, pp. 264–266; and Benjamin Anderson, in *Economics and the Public Welfare*, pp. 87–89, discuss aspects of the debate over a postwar American foreign economic policy.

17. Especially useful in this context are William Diamond, *The Economic Thought of Woodrow Wilson*, pp. 183–185; and Ray Stannard Baker, *Woodrow Wilson and the World Settlement*, III, 332–334, 352–358, and quotation on pp. 275–276. Also, Lawrence F. Gelfand, *The Inquiry*, pp. 290–312; and Seth Tillman, *Anglo-American Relations at the Paris Peace Conference of 1919*, pp. 255–274.

18. N. Gordon Levin, *Woodrow Wilson and World Politics*, p. 143; Paul P. Abrahams, "American Bankers and the Economic Tactics of Peace: 1919," *Journal of American History* 56 (December 1969): 572–583. Benjamin D. Rhodes discusses political resistance to debt cancellation in "Reassessing 'Uncle Shylock': The United States and the French War Debt, 1917–1929," *Journal of American History* 55 (March 1969): 787–803.

19. Dean E. Traynor, *International Monetary and Financial Conferences in the Interwar Period*, pp. 42–87, quotation on p. 76.

20. Ibid.; Ray B. Westerfield, *Money, Credit and Banking*, pp. 570–571; Brown, *Gold Standard*, I, 342–346.

21. For American central banker Benjamin Strong's assessment of the Genoa proposals, see Stephen V. O. Clarke, *Central Bank Cooperation, 1924–31*, pp. 36–40.

22. Chandler, *Strong*, p. 291. Clarke, in *Central Bank Cooperation*, pp. 40–44, 71–107; and Richard Meyer, in *Banker's Diplomacy*, pp. 1–15, analyze the stabilization efforts.

23. Lewis, *Economic Survey*, pp. 41, 74–89; Donald Edward Moggridge, *The Return to Gold, 1925*, pp. 9–90; and Alfred E. Kahn, *Great Britain in the World Economy*, pp. 158–178.

24. Brown, *Gold Standard*, I, 386; Chandler, *Strong*, pp. 285–286.

During the 1920's John Maynard Keynes tried to thwart restoration of the gold standard, which he considered incompatible with the requirements of an independent monetary policy (note Seymour E. Harris, ed., "International Economics: Introduction," *The New Economics*, pp. 245–263; Robert Lekachman, *The Age of Keynes*, pp. 58–77).

25. Woytinsky and Woytinsky, *World Commerce*, pp. 71–79; Ellsworth, *International Economy*, p. 407; Lewis, *Economic Survey*, pp. 46–47; Lionel Robbins, *The Great Depression*, pp. 7–8.

26. Lewis, *Economic Survey*, p. 49; Woytinsky and Woytinsky, *World Commerce*, p. 205; Ellsworth, *International Economy*, pp. 404–405; United States, Department of Commerce, Bureau of Foreign and Domestic Commerce, *The United States in the World Economy*, pp. 21, 167–169; Herbert Feis, *Diplomacy of the Dollar*, pp. 61–63. For comprehensive discussions of investments, see Cleona Lewis, *America's Stake in International Investments*; John T. Madden et al., *America's Experience as a Creditor Nation*; and Sir Arthur Salter, *Foreign Investment*, pp. 10–28. Also, Robert W. Oliver, "The Origins of the International Bank for Reconstruction and Development," pp. 115–139.

27. Lewis, *Economic Survey*, pp. 74–81, 46–48; Brown, *Gold Standard*, I, 385–390; League of Nations, *International Currency Experience*, pp. 116–117.

28. League of Nations, *International Currency Experience*, pp. 26–46, 217, 234–235; John Parke Young, *International Trade and Finance*, pp. 368–381; Westerfield, *Money, Credit and Banking*, pp. 554–571. League of Nations experts found that in 1913 fifteen European central

banks held about 12 percent of their total reserves in foreign exchange (see *International Currency Experience*, p. 29). Peter Lindert discusses the emergence of the gold-exchange standard before World War I in *Key Currencies and Gold, 1900–1913*.

29. League of Nations, *International Currency Experience*, p. 217; Lewis, *Economic Survey*, p. 47; Clarke, *Central Bank Cooperation*, pp. 27–44, 201–221. Also helpful on Britain's interwar economic difficulties is Derek H. Aldcroft, *The Inter-War Economy*, pp. 242–294.

30. League of Nations, *International Currency Experience*, pp. 27–46; Westerfield, *Money, Credit and Banking*, pp. 570–575; Ellsworth, *International Economics*, pp. 398–399; A. C. L. Day, *Outline of Monetary Economics*, pp. 494–496.

31. Lewis, *Economic Survey*, pp. 159–160; League of Nations, *International Currency Experience*, pp. 202–205; Feis, *Diplomacy of the Dollar*, pp. 61–63; U.S., Department of Commerce, *The United States in the World Economy*, pp. 173–176. Economic historians continue to debate the depression's origins. Charles P. Kindleberger surveys principal issues and explains the deep, widespread and prolonged contraction in terms of Britain's inability and the United States' unwillingness to stabilize the international economic system. Consult his *The World in Depression, 1929–1939*, pp. 291–292.

32. This discussion draws on Frank Costigliola, "The Other Side of Isolationism: The Establishment of the First World Bank, 1929–1930," *Journal of American History* 59 (December 1972): 602–620; Leon Fraser, "The International Bank and Its Future," *Foreign Affairs* 54 (April 1936): 453–464; and Melvyn Paul Leffler, "The Struggle for Stability: American Policy Toward France, 1921–1933," pp. 377–378. Also, Eleanor Lansing Dulles, *The Bank for International Settlements at Work*, pp. 1–19; and Henry H. Schloss, *The Bank for International Settlements*, pp. 24–36.

33. Woytinsky and Woytinsky, *World Commerce*, p. 42; League of Nations, Report of the Delegation on Economic Depression, *The Transition from War to Peace Economy*, pp. 20–21.

34. U.S., Department of Commerce, *United States in the World Economy*, pp. 5–6, 53–54. On the tariff, see Woytinsky and Woytinsky, *World Commerce*, pp. 252–253; Joseph Jones, *Tariff Retaliation*, pp. 1–33, 300–319; Arndt, *Economic Lessons*, pp. 17–19, 71–72.

35. U.S., Department of Commerce, *United States in the World Economy*, pp. 5–6; Woytinsky and Woytinsky, *World Commerce*, p. 205.

36. Yeager, *International Monetary Relations*, pp. 294–295; League of Nations, Economic, Financial and Transit Department, *Commercial Policy in the Interwar Period*, pp. 136–138; Ellsworth, *International Economy*, pp. 414–415.

37. Robbins, *Great Depression*, pp. 112–118; Clarke, *Central Bank Cooperation*, p. 218.

38. Ellsworth, *International Economy*, pp. 413–417; Clarke, *Central Bank Cooperation*, pp. 168–171; Yeager, *International Monetary Relations*, pp. 296–299; Condliffe, *Commerce of Nations*, p. 497; League of Nations, *Commercial Policy*, pp. 136–149.

39. Arthur M. Schlesinger, Jr., *The Age of Roosevelt: The Coming of the New Deal*, pp. 195–212.

40. Yeager, *International Monetary Relations*, pp. 301–307; Herbert Feis, *1933*, p. 232; Schlesinger, *Coming*

of the *New Deal*, pp. 221–222.
Quotation from Edgar B. Nixon, ed.,
*Franklin D. Roosevelt and Foreign
Affairs*, I, 24. For special emissary
Raymond Moley's account of the
London conference, see his *The First
New Deal*, pp. 393–496.

41. On Roosevelt as an economist, read
James MacGregor Burns, *Roosevelt:
The Lion and the Fox*, pp. 328–336.
A recent assessment of Roosevelt's
gold-purchase program is Elmus
Wicker, "Roosevelt's 1933 Monetary
Experiment," *Journal of American
History* 57 (March 1971): 864–879.
See also John Morton Blum, *From
the Morgenthau Diaries: Years of
Crisis, 1928–1938*, pp. 61–77.

42. Schlesinger, *Coming of the New
Deal*, pp. 244, 248.

43. Blum, *Years of Crisis*, pp. 61–77;
Wicker, "Roosevelt's 1933 Monetary
Experiment," pp. 864–879.

44. Westerfield, *Money, Credit and
Banking*, pp. 802–810; League of
Nations, *International Currency
Experience*, pp. 129–130.

45. U.S., Department of Commerce,
*United States in the World
Economy*, p. 136; League of Nations,
International Currency Experience,
p. 240.

46. Blum, *Years of Crisis*, pp. 72–74. On
the stabilization fund, see Arthur I.
Bloomfield, "Operations of the
American Exchange Stabilization
Fund," *The Review of Economic
Statistics* 26 (May 1944): 69–87.
For a critical account of Roosevelt's
monetary policies, consult James
Daniel Paris, *Monetary Policies of
the United States*, pp. 12–41.

47. Blum, *Years of Crisis*, pp. 1–34,
61–75.

48. *New York Times*, November 16,
1933; John T. Flynn, *The Roosevelt
Myth*, p. 55; Eugene A. Kelly,
"Morgenthau's Rise to Glory,"
American Mercury 34 (January
1935): 13–21; quotation from
Arthur Krock, *The Consent of the

Governed and Other Deceits*, p. 64.
Developments in Treasury administration during the New Deal are
discussed in Arthur Macmahon and
John D. Millett, *Federal Administrators*, pp. 93–115. Edwin Nourse
reflects on the appearance of economic consultants in *Economics in
the Public Service*, pp. 76–93.

49. Blum, *Years of Crisis*, pp. 159–182;
J. Keith Horsefield, *The International
Monetary Fund*, I, 8–10
(hereafter cited as *IMF*); Young,
International Trade, pp. 192–195;
Westerfield, *Money, Credit and
Banking*, p. 813.

50. Bloomfield, "Operations of the
American Exchange Stabilization
Fund," pp. 69–87.

51. Westerfield, *Money, Credit and
Banking*, p. 813.

52. Blum, *Years of Crisis*, pp. 179–182.
For an analysis of French currency
problems, see Martin Wolfe, *The
French Franc between the Wars,
1919–39*.

53. On the reciprocal trade program,
note Allen, "Cordell Hull and the
Defense of the Trade Agreements
Program," pp. 107–132.

54. John H. Williams, "International
Monetary Organization, and Policy,"
in *The Lessons of Monetary Experience*, ed. A. D. Gayer, pp. 23–49.

55. Support for either more frequent
depreciations and appreciations or
floating rates appears in Milton Gil-
bert, *Currency Depreciation*, p. 164;
Seymour E. Harris, *Exchange De-
preciation*; Charles R. Whittlesey,
International Monetary Issues.
Opposition to flexibility appears in
League of Nations, *International
Currency Experience*, pp. 210–212.

56. Bertil Ohlin argued for moderate
exchange controls in "Mechanisms
and Objectives of Exchange Control," *American Economic Review*
28 (March 1937): 141–150. See also
League of Nations, *International
Currency Experience*, p. 183; League

of Nations, Economic Intelligence Service, *The Network of World Trade*, pp. 8–10; James E. Meade, *The Economic Basis of a Durable Peace*, pp. 114–140.

57. League of Nations, *International Currency Experience*, p. 230. See also Arthur I. Bloomfield, "Foreign Exchange Rate Theory and Policy," in *The New Economics*, ed. Seymour E. Harris, pp. 302–303. Earlier but similar opinions appeared in Joint Committee of the Carnegie Endowment for International Peace and the International Chamber of Commerce, *International Economic Reconstruction*, pp. 179–188; James W. Gantenbein, *Financial Questions in United States Foreign Policy*, pp. 52–65.

58. Quotation from League of Nations, *International Currency Experience*, p. 230.

2. America's Global Monetary Design

1. Council on Foreign Relations, "Economic War Aims: General Considerations; the Position as of April 1, 1941," in *Studies of American Interests in the War and the Peace*, No. E-B 32, pp. 9–15.

2. *Documents on American Foreign Relations*, III, 26–34; quotation in *New York Times*, April 9, 1941.

3. Herbert Feis, *The Changing Pattern of International Economic Affairs*, p. 130.

4. Cordell Hull, *The Memoirs of Cordell Hull*, I, 81.

5. Hull, *Memoirs*, II, 1303–1304; Harley Notter, *Postwar Foreign Policy Preparation, 1939–1945*, pp. 2–8; Morgenthau Diaries, Henry Morgenthau, Jr., Papers, Roosevelt Library, 256:253 (hereafter cited as MD).

6. Dean Acheson, *Present at the Creation*, pp. 8–20, 55; U.S., Senate, Committee on the Judiciary, *Interlocking Subversion in Government Departments (The Harry Dexter White Papers), Hearings before the Subcommittee to Investigate the Administration of the Internal Security Act and Other Internal Security Laws*, 84th Cong., 1st sess., August 30, 1955, 30:2339–2341, 2664–2692; IMF, I, 10–11. Adolf Berle credits Harry White with much of the work in Beatrice Bishop Berle and Travis Beal Jacobs, *Navigating the Rapids 1918–1971*, p. 291.

7. Robert A. Divine, *Second Chance*, pp. 6–46. On efforts of elite groups to mold policy, consult Gabriel Almond, *The American People and Foreign Policy*, pp. 136–157. James Rosenau discusses how leaders mobilize public support in his *National Leadership and Foreign Policy*, pp. 3–41.

8. Otto T. Mallery, "Economic Union and Enduring Peace," *Annals* 216 (July 1941): 125–134; quotations on p. 125. Other popular accounts include Lewis Lorwin, *Economic Consequences of the Second World War*, pp. xiii–xvii.

9. Divine, *Second Chance*, pp. 31–33. Economists A. Eugene Staley, Charles W. Cole, Alvin Hansen, and Walter Lichtenstein prepared papers for the Commission to Study the Organization of the Peace, published in *International Conciliation* (April 1943).

10. Council on Foreign Relations, *Studies*, E-B 32, pp. 13–15, and E-B 36, pp. 1–2; quotations from E-B 36, p. 1.

11. Quotations from Samuel I. Rosenman, ed., *The Public Papers and Addresses of Franklin D. Roosevelt*, 1941 vol., pp. 314–315; Theodore A. Wilson, *The First Summit*.

12. Hull, *Memoirs*, II, 975.

13. On Hull's trade policies, consult William R. Allen, "Cordell Hull and the Defense of the Trade Agreements Program, 1934–1940," in *Isolation and Security*, ed. Alexander

DeConde, pp. 107–132, and Arthur W. Schatz, "The Anglo-American Trade Agreement and Cordell Hull's Search for Peace, 1936–1938," *Journal of American History* 57 (June 1970): 85–103.

14. Roy F. Harrod, *The Life of John Maynard Keynes*, p. 512; *IMF*, I, 14–15.

15. Hawkins to Hull, August 4, 1941, Cordell Hull Papers, Box 86; Pasvolsky to Hull, December 12, 1941, Pasvolsky Papers, Leo Pasvolsky Office Files, State Department Records, National Archives, Record Group 59. Hereafter records in the National Archives will be cited as NA, followed by the record group (RG) number. U.S., Department of State, *Bulletin*, February 28, 1942, p. 192; Hull, *Memoirs*, II, 1151–1153, quotation on p. 1153.

16. On executive agreements, the following proved helpful: Elmer Plischke, *Conduct of American Diplomacy*, pp. 409–442; and Louis Henkin, *Foreign Affairs and the Constitution*, pp. 173–188.

17. U.S., Department of State, *Foreign Relations of the United States: 1942*, I, 163–168 (hereafter cited as *FR*); Ernest F. Penrose, *Economic Planning for the Peace*, pp. 32–40; quotation from *Fortune (Supplement: Relations with Britain)* 26 (May 1942): 16.

18. *FR: 1942*, I, 166, 170–171.

19. Notter, *Postwar Policy*, pp. 81–88; Acheson, *Present at the Creation*, pp. 15–16, 38–47.

20. Henry A. Wallace, "Foundations of the Peace," *Atlantic Monthly* 169 (January 1942): 34–41. On conflict with the State Department, consult John Morton Blum, ed., *The Price of Vision*, pp. 53–67.

21. Divine, *Second Chance*, p. 80; Fred Israel, ed., *The War Diary of Breckinridge Long*, pp. 294, 307–310.

22. John M. Blum, *From the Morgen-thau Diaries: Years of War, 1941–1945*, pp. 229, 474.

23. Treasury order No. 43, December 15, 1941, Box 172, NA, RG 59; U.S., Senate, Committee on the Judiciary, *Interlocking Subversion*, 28:2297–2299, quotation on p. 2298; MD, 470:83 and 473:16.

24. Nathan White, *Harry Dexter White*, pp. 267–272; and David Rees, *Harry Dexter White*, pp. 19–40.

25. White, *Harry Dexter White*, pp. 267–272.

26. Blum, *Years of War*, pp. 89–90; MD, 447:23.

27. Ibid.

28. *Life*, November 23, 1953, pp. 29–35.

29. Herbert Feis, *1933*, p. 107; Notes, October 7, 1941, Emanuel Alexandrovich Goldenweiser Papers, Library of Congress, Box 7. On November 1, 1941, White had forty economic analysts on his staff, including Solomon Adler, E. M. Bernstein, Lauren Casaday, V. Frank Coe, Irving S. Friedman, Virgil Salera, Delbert Snider, Frank Southard, Henry Tasca, and William L. Ullmann (U.S., Treasury Department, Division of Monetary Research, November 1, 1941, Box 191, NA, RG 56).

30. Blum, *Years of War*, p. 90. An excellent survey of this controversial episode is Earl Latham, *The Communist Controversy in Washington*. Also helpful are White, *Harry Dexter White*, pp. 54–64; Elizabeth Bentley, *Out of Bondage*, pp. 164–165; Whittaker Chambers, *Witness*, pp. 28–29. Ralph de Toledano reviews the matter in his *J. Edgar Hoover*, pp. 238–256.

31. Columnist Ernest Lindley quoted an unidentified "reliable" source as admitting the government never substantiated its case against White (*Newsweek*, November 30, 1953, p. 36). White's associate Ansel Luxford told me on March 26, 1970, that the late Chief Justice Fred Vinson

reviewed Federal Bureau of Investigation files and concluded that the government lacked proof to support the Bentley-Chambers allegations. On liberal enthusiasm for Soviet Russia in the 1930's, consult Frank Warren, *Liberals and Communism*, pp. 63–68. On White's interest in Soviet planning, see *Life*, November 23, 1953, pp. 29–35; undated letter from White to Frank Taussig, U.S., Senate, Committee on the Judiciary, *Interlocking Subversion*, 30:2570. White's comments on social reform appear in MD, 442:25. In a recent biography David Rees also has difficulty assessing White, but he concludes that the Treasury aide was most likely a sentimental, indiscreet fellow traveler, not a Communist. See Rees, *Harry Dexter White*, pp. 424–426.

32. *Life*, November 23, 1953, pp. 29–35, quotation on p. 32; Chambers, *Witness*, pp. 383–384.

33. White's Keynesian sympathies attracted comment in Herbert Stein, *The Fiscal Revolution in America*, p. 102; Harrod, *Keynes*, p. 538; and Robert Lekachman, *The Age of Keynes*, p. 124.

34. *IMF*, I, 11–12; Robert W. Oliver, *Early Plans for a World Bank*, p. 24; MD, 743:16; Robert Asher, Walter M. Kotschnig, and William Adams Brown, Jr., *United Nations and Economic and Social Cooperation*, p. 36.

35. An April 1942 draft of both institutions appears in *FR: 1942*, I, 171–190. Horsefield reprints portions relating to the fund in his *IMF*, III, 37–82. Edward Bernstein recalls having inserted the word *development* in the bank's title (interview, March 26, 1970). Quotation from *FR: 1942*, I, 177.

36. *FR: 1942*, I, 174.

37. Ibid., pp. 178–184.

38. *IMF*, III, 41–82, quotation on p. 50.

39. Ibid., quotation on p. 76.

40. Ibid., quotations on pp. 48, 64, 43.

41. Ibid., quotation on p. 74.

42. MD, 526:196, 202.

43. *IMF*, III, 41–82, quotation on p. 46.

44. Ibid. For a brief survey of the gold debate, note William Adams Brown, Jr., "Gold: Master or Servant?" *Foreign Affairs* 19 (July 1941): 828–841; also Frank Graham and Charles R. Whittlesey, *Golden Avalanche*; Fritz Machlup, "Eight Questions on Gold," *American Economic Review (Papers and Proceedings)* 30 (February 1941): 30–37.

45. *IMF*, III, 41–82, quotations on pp. 55, 47.

46. Ibid., quotation on p. 63.

47. MD, 526:231. Oliver discusses the background of international lending in *World Bank*, pp. 6–33.

48. MD, 526:271.

49. Ibid., 526:271–272.

50. Ibid., 526:269; *FR: 1942*, I, 184–185, quotation on p. 184.

51. *FR: 1942*, I, 184–186.

52. Ibid., I, 187–188.

53. Ibid., I, 188–189; MD, 526:300.

54. *FR: 1942*, I, 185.

55. Ibid.

56. Ibid.; MD, 526:281–286.

57. If members redeemed banknotes for gold, thus expressing lack of confidence, the bank might have created as little as $2.5 billion. For an analysis of these possibilities, see Oliver, *World Bank*, pp. 30–33.

58. MD, 526:295.

59. MD, 526:111 and 528:296–303; *FR: 1942*, I, 171–177.

60. MD, 528:296–303.

61. *FR: 1942*, I, 171–177, quotation on p. 172.

62. Roosevelt to Morgenthau, May 16, 1942, Harry Dexter White Papers, Firestone Library, Item 24.

63. Ibid.

3. America and Britain: Divergent Approaches to a Common Goal

1. *Time*, March 2, 1942, p. 9; Hadley

Cantril and Mildred Strunk, *Public Opinion, 1935–1946*, pp. 1188–1189.

2. Goldenweiser notes, May 27, 1942, Emanuel Alexandrovich Goldenweiser Papers, Library of Congress, Box 7.

3. MD, 667:86–96.

4. The specialists were Benjamin Cohen, White House; William Adams Brown, Jr., Emilio Collado, Frederick Livesey, Leo Pasvolsky, and John Parke Young, State Department; Elting Arnold, Edward M. Bernstein, Henry J. Bittermann, Ansel F. Luxford, Raymond F. Mikesell, and Harry White, Treasury; William L. Clayton, Hal B. Lary, and August Maffry, Commerce; Alice Bourneuf, Walter Gardner, and E. A. Goldenweiser, Federal Reserve; Walter C. Louchheim, Securities and Exchange Commission; Hawthorne Arey and Walter Lee Pierson, Export-Import Bank; James Angell and V. Frank Coe, Foreign Economic Administration; and Alvin Hansen, National Resources Planning Board.

5. MD, 545:19.

6. Ibid.

7. Walter Gardner memorandum, July 10, 1942, Federal Reserve Papers, Board of Governors of the Federal Reserve System.

8. Leo Pasvolsky memorandum, July 10, 1942, No. 800.515/555, NA, RG 59.

9. MD, 552:142–143 and 552:141.

10. *FR: 1942*, I, 196–202; Cordell Hull, *The Memoirs of Cordell Hull*, I, 103–106; *FR: 1942*, I, 191–192.

11. Roy F. Harrod, *The Life of John Maynard Keynes*, pp. 540–541; *FR: 1942*, I, 191–192.

12. "British and American Incomes," *The Economist*, September 5, 1942, pp. 299–301; "A Comparison with America," *The Economist*, May 1, 1943, pp. 544–545.

13. "The Importance of Exports," *The Economist*, December 12, 1944, p.

725. See also William Ashworth, *A Short History of the International Economy since 1850*, pp. 257–264; H. W. Arndt, *The Economic Lessons of the Nineteen-Thirties*, pp. 94–134; Alfred E. Kahn, *Great Britain in the World Economy*, p. 275; and W. Arthur Lewis, *Economic Survey, 1919–1939*, pp. 74–89.

14. Lionel Robbins, *Autobiography of an Economist*, pp. 190–195; W. M. Scammell, *International Monetary Policy*, p. 120. London Chamber of Commerce embraced the restrictionist alternative (see *The Economist*, January 2, 1943, p. 7). Beaverbrook's imperial position appears in A. J. P. Taylor, *Beaverbrook*, pp. 556–557.

15. *The Economist*, January 23, 1943, p. 99. In reviewing the League of Nations, Economic Intelligence Service, *The Network of World Trade*, this periodical conceded that bilateralism might be necessary for a "shortlived" period. "Bilateralism, as a permanent policy of trade, is the economic nonsense of suicidal politicians."

16. Robbins, *Autobiography*, pp. 192–195, quotation on p. 94; Harrod, *Keynes*, pp. 505–513.

17. *IMF*, III, 1–18, quotations on pp. 17–18.

18. Ibid., quotation from I, 5.

19. Ibid., quotation from p. 3.

20. Ibid., quotation from p. 13.

21. Ibid.

22. Ibid. See also the 1943 version in ibid., III, 19–36.

23. Ibid., III, 1–18, quotation on p. 13.

24. Ibid., quotation from p. 9.

25. Ibid., quotations from pp. 33 and 15.

26. Ibid., quotation from p. 11.

27. Ibid., quotations from p. 15.

28. Ibid.

29. Ibid., quotations from pp. 17–18.

30. Sir Frederick Phillips to White, August 28, 1942, Harry Dexter

White Papers, Firestone Library, Item 24.

31. *FR: 1942*, I, 222–226, quotations on p. 223.

32. Harrod, *Keynes*, pp. 539–541, quotations on p. 539; Ernest F. Penrose, *Economic Planning for the Peace*, pp. 47–49; *IMF*, I, 30.

33. John Morton Blum, *From the Morgenthau Diaries: Years of War, 1941–1945*, pp. 236–237; Richard N. Gardner, *Sterling-Dollar Diplomacy*, pp. 30–35.

34. White urged haste in his initial draft (*FR: 1942*, I, 172).

35. *New Republic*, November 16, 1942, p. 627; *Time*, November 16, 1942, p. 16; "Luce in Tenebris," *The Economist*, November 7, 1942, p. 572; Robert A. Divine, *Second Chance*, p. 73.

36. Joseph Jones to Leo Pasvolsky, November 25, 1942, Pasvolsky Papers, Leo Pasvolsky Office Files, State Department Records, NA, RG 59.

37. Penrose memorandum, December 19, 1942, Pasvolsky Papers, NA, RG 59; *FR: 1942*, I, 230.

38. Walter Gardner to Governor Szymczak, January 29, 1943, Federal Reserve Papers; *FR: 1942*, I, 227–228; MD, 596:197.

39. Harrod, *Keynes*, p. 541.

40. On Anglo-American technical exchanges, see Gardner, *Sterling-Dollar Diplomacy*, pp. 71–100; *IMF*, I, 28–48.

41. *IMF*, I, 28–48.

42. Ibid.

43. Harrod, *Keynes*, pp. 543–545; Blum, *Years of War*, p. 237; Robbins, *Autobiography*, p. 199.

44. *FR: 1943*, I, 1055; *Bretton Woods Documents*, II, 1536; *FR: 1943*, I, 1055–1059. On March 4 the Treasury sent invitations and drafts of White's stabilization fund to the following governments: Australia, Belgium, Brazil, Canada, China, Costa Rica, Cuba, Czechoslovakia, the Dominican Republic, El Salvador, Ethiopia, Great Britain, Greece, Guatemala, Haiti, Honduras, India, Iraq, Luxembourg, Mexico, the Netherlands, New Zealand, Nicaragua, Norway, Panama, Poland, South Africa, the Union of Soviet Socialist Republics, Yugoslavia, Bolivia, Colombia, Chile, Ecuador, Paraguay, Peru, Uruguay, and Venezuela.

45. *FR: 1943*, I, 1059–1061; quotation from Berle memorandum, March 15, 1943, Pasvolsky Papers, NA, RG 59.

46. MD, 617:338–339, 617:153 and 622:2.

47. *FR: 1943*, I, 1064–1070; MD, 625:56–71, 625:83 and 622:246; quotations from MD, 625:83 and 622:246.

4. Consultation and Consensus

1. Samuel I. Rosenman, ed., *The Public Papers and Addresses of Franklin D. Roosevelt*, XII, 32–33.

2. Ibid. H. Bradford Westerfield surveys the politics of postwar planning in *Foreign Policy and Party Politics*, pp. 129–183. Sumner Welles also considers this in *Seven Decisions That Shaped History*, pp. 133–135.

3. Folke Hilgerdt, "The Case for Multilateral Trade," *American Economic Review (Papers and Proceedings)* 33 (March 1943): 393–407; Paul T. Ellsworth, "The Bases of an Economic Foreign Policy," in *Problems of the Postwar World*, ed. Thomas C. T. McCormick, pp. 139–150.

4. Hilgerdt, "Multilateral Trade," pp. 393–407, quotations on pp. 401, 405; League of Nations, Delegation on Economic Depressions, *The Transition from War to Peace Economy*, p. 13; U.S., Senate, Banking and Currency Committee, *Participation of the United States in the*

International Monetary Fund and the International Bank for Reconstruction and Development, 79th Cong., 1st sess., 1945, S. Rept. 452, pp. 2–9. The literature on this topic is voluminous, and I have discussed the rationale more extensively in "Open Door Expansionism Reconsidered: The World War II Experience," *Journal of American History* 59 (March 1973): 909–924.

5. Liberal attacks on bankers appear in *New Republic*, July 3, 1944, p. 6, and July 10, 1944, p. 28, and in various issues of the newspaper *New York PM*, especially July 5 and 10, 1944. Brown's testimony appears in U.S., House, Committee on Banking and Currency, *Bretton Woods Agreements Act, Hearings on H.R. 2211*, 79th Cong., 1st sess., 1945, I, 188–189. *Commercial and Financial Chronicle*, September 30, 1943, p. 1340.

6. MD, 526:232–234.

7. Richard N. Gardner shows that White thought economic expansion more important than tariff reduction (*Sterling-Dollar Diplomacy*, p. 15). Alvin Hansen's paper "International Adjustment of Exchange Rates" appears in the Council on Foreign Relations, *Studies of American Interests in the War and the Peace*, April 6, 1943, No. E-B 64, quotation on p. 7. See also Hansen, "World Institutions for Stability and Expansion," *Foreign Affairs* 22 (January 1944): 148–155; Hansen, "The Importance of Anti-Depression Policy in the Establishment and Preservation of Sound International Relations," *International Conciliation* 369 (April 1941): 424–427. Charles P. Kindleberger provided an early analysis of the "chronic world shortage of dollars" in "International Monetary Stabilization," in *Postwar Economic Problems*, ed. Seymour E. Harris, pp. 375–395.

8. Hansen, "International Adjustment of Exchange Rates"; Alvin Hansen and Charles P. Kindleberger, "The Economic Task of the Postwar World," *Foreign Affairs* 20 (April 1942): 466–476. The League of Nations took a similar approach in League of Nations, *Economic Stability in the Post-War World*, pp. 190–192, 228.

9. *New Republic*, May 3, 1943, p. 589, quotation on p. 590; *Nation*, November 24, 1943, p. 643; *Time*, June 7, 1943, pp. 105–108; *Fortune* 28 (August 1943): 138; Davenport to Charles S. Dewey, June 16, 1943, Charles Dewey Papers, Chicago Historical Society, Box 6.

10. *Commercial and Financial Chronicle*, April 8, 1943, p. 1304; *New York Times*, December 4, 1943; *Newsweek*, April 19, 1943, p. 52. Similar opinions appear in *Wall Street Journal*, March 30, 1943; and *Commercial and Financial Chronicle*, May 20, 1943, p. 1881.

11. Carr to Harry Hawkins, October 25, 1943, No. 800.515/866, NA, RG 59; *Commercial and Financial Chronicle*, September 30, 1943, p. 1315.

12. State Department economist William A. Brown found that only New York bankers had a strong interest in stabilization proposals (Brown memorandum, September 23, 1943, No. 800.515/856, NA, RG 59).

13. Benjamin Anderson, "Free Exchange Stabilization," *Vital Speeches*, June 1, 1943, pp. 487–496. Some British Keynesians thought the gold standard deflationary. Note Thomas Balogh and E. F. Schumacher, "An International Monetary Fund," *Oxford Institute of Statistics Bulletin*, April 29, 1944, pp. 81–93; Joan Robinson, "The International Currency Proposals," *Economic Journal* 53 (June–September 1943): 161–175.

14. John H. Williams, "Currency Stabilization: The Keynes and White

Plans," *Foreign Affairs* 21 (July 1943): 645–658. This essay and others appear in John H. Williams, *Postwar Monetary Plans.*

15. Williams to Federal Reserve Board of Governors, June 28, 1943, Federal Reserve Papers, Board of Governors.

16. The New York Federal Reserve Bank urged a key-currency approach in June 15 and October 7, 1943, memoranda. These are summarized in New York Federal Reserve Bank to Board of Governors, December 21, 1944, Emanuel Alexandrovich Goldenweiser Papers, Library of Congress, Box 4.

17. Ibid.

18. *Bretton Woods Documents*, I, 1573–1574; Winant to Hull, May 1, 1943, No. 800.515/642, NA, RG 59; *FR: 1943*, I, 1068.

19. *Bretton Woods Documents*, I, 1575–1596.

20. John Tuthill memorandum, June 24, 1943, Pasvolsky Papers, Leo Pasvolsky Office Files, State Department Records, NA, RG 59; memorandum, August 2, 1943, Harry Dexter White Papers, Firestone Library.

21. Australian memoranda, May 4 and 15, 1943; and Coombs to White, June 12, 1943, White Papers.

22. *FR: 1943*, I, 1071–1075; Hervé Alphand to White, January 21, 1943, White Papers. See also J. W. Beyen, *Money in a Maelstrom*, pp. 148–152, 160; and Andre Istel, "The Reconstruction of France," *Foreign Affairs* 22 (October 1943): 114–125.

23. *FR: 1943*, I, 1070–1074, 1078–1089.

24. Hermann Max, "Los planes monetarios internacionales," *Boletín del Banco Central de Venezuela* 10 (October 1943): 56–69; Víctor L. Urquidi, "Los proyectos monetarios de la postguerra," *Trimestre Económico* 5 (October–December 1943): 539–557. For background on

Latin American attitudes, consult Samuel Inman, "Some Latin American Views on Postwar Reconstruction," *Foreign Policy Reports*, March 15, 1944, pp. 2–11; and Sanford Mosk, "Main Currents of Economic Thought," in *Inter-American Affairs, 1944*, ed. Arthur P. Whitaker, pp. 140–141.

25. Brazilian memorandum, August, 1943, White Papers.

26. *FR: 1943*, I, 1082–1083.

27. Walter Gardner memorandum, March 24, 1943, Federal Reserve Papers; memorandum, April 21, 1943, Goldenweiser Papers, Box 4.

28. Walter Gardner memorandum, March 24, 1943, Federal Reserve Papers.

29. Ibid. See also *IMF*, I, 39–40.

30. Walter Gardner memorandum, March 24, 1943, Federal Reserve Papers.

31. Memorandum, June 12, 1943, Goldenweiser Papers, Box 7.

32. *New York Times*, August 20, 1943. For a discussion of technical features, see *IMF*, I, 40–48; the July 10, 1943, draft appears in III, 83–96.

33. Goldenweiser memorandum, August 18, 1943, Goldenweiser Papers, Box 2; quotation from Winant to Hull, September 14, 1943, No. 800.515/813, NA, RG 59.

34. Quotation from MD, 657:5–6; *New York Times*, August 14, 1943; Henry Edmiston, "Post-War International Currency Stabilization," *Arkansas Banker* 27 (October 1943): 19–22.

35. U.S., Department of State, *Bulletin*, November 13, 1950, p. 782.

36. *IMF*, I, 48, quotations from I, 53; *FR: 1943*, I, 1081–1082. China also accepted American conditions (*FR: 1943*, I, 1081–1082; memorandum, July 16, 1943, White Papers).

37. Lionel Robbins, *Autobiography of an Economist*, p. 200.

38. *FR: 1943*, I, 1106–1111; Ernest F. Penrose, *Economic Planning for the*

Peace, pp. 47–49, or his memorandum, September 3, 1943, No. 800.50/9–343, NA, RG 59.

39. Roy F. Harrod, *The Life of John Maynard Keynes*, pp. 559–560; Gardner, *Sterling-Dollar Diplomacy*, pp. 111–112.

40. Harrod, *Keynes*, pp. 111–112; *IMF*, I, 57.

41. *Bretton Woods Documents*, II, 1597–1600, quotation on p. 1599; *FR: 1943*, I, 1084–1092; *IMF*, I, 53.

42. *FR: 1943*, I, 1084–1090, quotation on p. 1084; *IMF*, I, 57–77.

43. *IMF*, I, 61–62; Harrod, *Keynes*, pp. 560–564; Gardner, *Sterling-Dollar Diplomacy*, pp. 110–121.

44. Harrod, *Keynes*, pp. 560–564; quotation from *IMF*, I, 66.

45. Harrod, *Keynes*, pp. 560–564; quotation from *IMF*, I, 74.

46. Quotations from Introduction to September 3, 1943, Treasury proposal for the Bank for Reconstruction and Development of the United and Associated Nations, Federal Reserve Papers. See also *Bretton Woods Documents*, II, 1616–1619.

47. Comment on April 30, 1943, draft of Bank for Reconstruction and Development, Federal Reserve Papers; *Bretton Woods Documents*, II, 1617; MD, 667:86–96.

48. Memorandum, August 31, 1943, White Papers.

49. Berle to White, September 4, 1943, White Papers. State Department economist John P. Young also completed a plan for an international investment agency. For details consult U.S., Department of State, *Bulletin*, November 13, 1950, pp. 778–790.

50. *FR: 1943*, I, 1092–1096. Among American technicians Goldenweiser thought that creditor countries rarely recovered the equivalent of their loans (see his notes, January 6, 1943, Goldenweiser Papers, Box 7).

51. *FR: 1943*, I, 1092–1096, quotation on p. 1094.

52. Ibid.; memorandum, August 31, 1943, White Papers.

53. MD, 638:160; U.S., Senate, Committee on the Judiciary, *Morgenthau Diary (Germany)*, I, 362–363; MD, 670:20, and 686:173, 211.

54. Averell Harriman to Hull, December 10, 1943, No. 800.515/913, NA, RG 59.

55. *IMF*, I, 77–78; MD, 724:158–167.

56. MD, 707:59–70, quotation on p. 62.

5. Prelude to Bretton Woods

1. James MacGregor Burns, *Roosevelt: The Soldier of Freedom*, pp. 513–521. Burns emphasizes the president's own preoccupation with Soviet-American collaboration. On the emergence of postwar plans, see Ruth B. Russell, *A History of the United Nations Charter*; and Robert Asher et al., *The United Nations and Promotion of the General Welfare*.

2. *FR: 1944*, II, 10–34; Winant to Morgenthau, January 6, 1944, No. 800.515/925, NA, RG 59.

3. *Congressional Record*, March 7, 1944, pp. 2299–2300.

4. Quotation from *Commercial and Financial Chronicle*, March 9, 1944, p. 986; John Morton Blum, *From the Morgenthau Diaries: Years of War, 1941–1945*, p. 246.

5. *Congressional Record*, December 21, 1943, pp. 19069–19070, and February 1, 1944, p. 1035.

6. MD, 719:36; Dewey to Edwin Kemmerer, April 13, 1944, Edwin Kemmerer Papers, Firestone Library.

7. Collado to Hull, March 20, 1944, Pasvolsky Papers, Leo Pasvolsky Office Files, State Department Records, NA, RG 59.

8. MD, 712:223–224 and quotations from 722:10, 180.

9. MD, 722:186; White memorandum, April 3, 1944, Harry Dexter White

Papers, Firestone Library; Roosevelt to Hull, April 3, 1944, No. 800.515/4–344, NA, RG 59; MD, 717:63, 65, 66.

10. MD, 712:223–225 and 717:186; FR: 1944, II, 107; quotation from MD, 720:222. The Bank of England also strongly opposed the agreement (Winant to Hull, April 12, 1944, White Papers).

11. MD, 720:232; FR: 1944, II, 108–112; Redvers Opie to Harry White, April 15, 1944, Federal Reserve Papers, Board of Governors of the Federal Reserve System.

12. MD, 722:31–37, 48; Blum, Years of War, pp. 246–250; Federal Reserve Bulletin 30 (May 1944): 436–441; Bretton Woods Documents, II, 1629; MD, 723:37, 232. Quotations from FR: 1944, II, 126, and MD, 723:232.

13. Bretton Woods Documents, II, 1629.

14. Ibid., II, 1631.

15. IMF, III, 128, 130, 131.

16. Notes, April 25, 1944, Emanuel Alexandrovich Goldenweiser Papers, Library of Congress, Box 7.

17. Blum, Years of War, pp. 250–251.

18. MD, 724:162 and 167.

19. Ibid., 724:165.

20. FR: 1944, II, 129–130; Winant to Hull, April 28, 1944, White Papers. Public resistance prevented participation of a British Cabinet leader (see FR: 1944, II, 41–44).

21. FR: 1944, II, 132.

22. Roy F. Harrod, The Life of John Maynard Keynes, pp. 573–574; Richard N. Gardner, Sterling-Dollar Diplomacy, p. 124; FR: 1944, II, 131–132; Blum, Years of War, pp. 250–251.

22. "Preparations for Drafting Committee," May 25, 1944, Pasvolsky Papers; MD, 746:124 and 759:135.

23. Quotation from MD, 735:152; FR: 1944, II, 132–133; President's Secretary's File, folder 4-44, Franklin D. Roosevelt Papers, Roosevelt Library; MD, 735:152.

24. Emilio Collado to Dean Acheson, June 3, 1944, No. 800.515/6-344, NA, RG 59.

25. New York Times, June 10, 1944.

26. Arthur Vandenberg, Jr., ed., The Private Papers of Senator Vandenberg, pp. 109–110; MD, 723:232; Dean Acheson, Present at the Creation, p. 82; Dean Acheson, Sketches from Life of Men I Have Known, pp. 137–138; Roosevelt to Byrnes, June 14, 1944, President's Secretary's File, Roosevelt Papers.

27. Quotation from MD, 744:82–83; Bretton Woods Documents, I, 111; Commercial and Financial Chronicle, July 6, 1944, p. 67; quotation from Acheson, Sketches, pp. 139–140.

28. Criticism of the delegation appears in New York Times, June 27, 1944.

29. Commercial and Financial Chronicle, June 15, 1944, p. 2499; U.S., Senate, Committee on the Judiciary, Interlocking Subversion in Government Departments (The Harry Dexter White Papers), Hearings before the Subcommittee to Investigate the Administration of the Internal Security Act and Other Internal Security Laws, 84th Cong., 1st sess., August 30, 1955, 30:2594; quotation from Blum, Years of War, p. 474. Meetings with bankers had occurred intermittently since 1943 (Harold Stonier to Winthrop Aldrich, July 28, 1943, Winthrop Aldrich Papers, Harvard Graduate School of Public Administration, Box 17).

30. Seymour E. Harris, ed., The New Economics, pp. 368–379; Pasvolsky memorandum of conversation with Keynes, June 24, 1944, No. 800.515/BWA-6-2444, NA, RG 59; MD, 746:139; Burgess to White, June 9, 1944, Federal Reserve Papers. Keynes later indicated that he "felt it absolutely necessary to say the things he had said." Before his speech "there was an almost

universal conviction in parliamentary circles that the . . . stabilization fund was dead as far as Britain was concerned" (Memorandum of conversation between Keynes and Pasvolsky, June 24, 1944, No. 800.515/BWA 6-2444, NA, RG 59).

31. MD, 746:139. General Leonard Ayres, an American Bankers Association official, had similar comments (June 23, 1944, Leonard Ayres Papers, Library of Congress, Box 4). Other criticisms appear in *Commercial and Financial Chronicle*, May 11, 1944, p. 1947, or can be found in Chamber of Commerce of the United States, Finance Department, *World Currency Stabilization Proposals*, p. 42.

32. Cited in memorandum, December 12, 1944, Goldenweiser Papers, Box 4.

33. "The International Monetary Plan," June 6, 1944, Federal Reserve Papers.

34. *New York Times*, June 23, 1944.

35. *Congressional Record*, August 11, 1944, p. A 3581; *New York Times*, June 30, 1944.

36. *Boletín de la Sociedad Nacional de Mineria*, February 4, 1944, pp. 61–70; George Messersmith to White, May 29, 1944, No. 800.515/1136, and Orme Wilson to Hull, June 22, 1944, No. 800.515/1346, NA, RG 59; Messersmith to Hull, June 12, 1944, No. 800.515/6-1944, and William Busser to Hull, June 12, 1944, No. 800.515/1160, NA, RG 59; *New York Times*, June 30, 1944. Bimetallism had no appeal to the New York financial community. Criticisms appear in *Commercial and Financial Chronicle*, June 1, 1944, p. 2250.

37. *FR: 1944*, II, 132–135; MD, 746:133.

38. Atlantic City Conversations, June 24, 1944, No. 800.515/BWA 6-2444, NA, RG 59. For a detailed analysis of issues, see *IMF*, I, 82–87.

39. Atlantic City Conversations, June

24, 1944, No. 800.515/BWA 6-2444, NA, RG 59. Harrod comments in *Keynes*, pp. 575–577.

40. Atlantic City Conversations, June 24, 1944, No. 800.515/BWA 6-2444, NA, RG 59.

41. Ibid.

42. Ibid.

43. Ibid. Henry J. Bittermann, "Negotiation of the Articles of Agreement of the International Bank for Reconstruction and Development," *International Lawyer* 5 (January 1971): 59–88. "Memorandum of U. K. Experts on the Bank for Reconstruction and Development," April 20, 1944, No. 800.516/88a, NA, RG 59. Also, memorandum, May 9, 1944, White Papers. Keynes's attitude appears in *FR: 1944*, II, 46–47.

44. *FR: 1944*, II, 134–135.

45. MD, 749:159–160.

46. MD, 749:20, 23.

47. MD, 749:29–34, quotation on p. 31.

48. MD, 753:6 and 749:159.

49. MD, 749:30.

50. MD, 749:45.

51. MD, 749:11.

52. MD, 749:2–9; "Questions at Issue on the Fund," undated, No. 800.515/6-2844, NA, RG 59.

53. "Questions at Issue on the Fund."

54. Ibid.

55. Ibid.

56. MD, 749:24–25.

57. MD, 749:15–18. For Keynes's critique of Churchill, see John Maynard Keynes, *Essays in Persuasion*, pp. 244–270.

58. MD, 749:34–38, 145–146.

59. Quotations from MD, 753:2–3. See also, MD, 749:176.

60. MD, 753:4–5.

61. MD, 749:173–175 and 753:7–8.

62. "Questions at Issue on the Bank," undated, No. 800.515/6-2844, NA, RG 59.

63. MD, 749:232–241.

64. MD, 749:2, quotation from *Commercial and Financial Chronicle*, September 28, 1944, p. 1355.

6. Bretton Woods

1. The following forty-four governments sent delegations: Australia, Belgium, Bolivia, Brazil, Canada, Chile, China, Colombia, Costa Rica, Cuba, Czechoslovakia, the Dominican Republic, Ecuador, Egypt, El Salvador, Ethiopia, France, Greece, Guatemala, Haiti, Honduras, Iceland, India, Iran, Iraq, Liberia, Luxembourg, Mexico, the Netherlands, New Zealand, Nicaragua, Norway, Panama, Paraguay, Peru, the Philippine Commonwealth, Poland, the Union of South Africa, the Union of Soviet Socialist Republics, the United Kingdom, the United States of America, Uruguay, Venezuela, and Yugoslavia. The Danish minister to the United States attended in his personal capacity (Warren Kelchner to White, May, 1944, container 1309/54/D/82, State Department Conference Records, NA, RG 59).
2. Elmer Munson Hunt, *New Hampshire Town Names and Whence They Came*, p. 205.
3. Third-person circular, June 22, 1944, No. 800.515/1385a, NA, RG 59; F. Allen Burt, *The Story of Mount Washington*, p. 105; John Anderson and Stearns Morse, *The Book of the White Mountains*, p. 177; *Christian Science Monitor*, July 6, 1944; *IMF*, I, 89.
4. *Bretton Woods Documents*, I, 71.
5. Ibid., I, 75–83, quotations on pp. 81, 82, 80.
6. Ibid., I, 60–68.
7. Ibid., I, 294–306, quotation on p. 299.
8. Roy F. Harrod, *The Life of John Maynard Keynes*, p. 581; memorandum, July 31, 1944, Emanuel Alexandrovich Goldenweiser Papers, Library of Congress, Box 4.
9. Memorandum, July 31, 1944, Goldenweiser Papers, Box 4.
10. *Time*, July 17, 1944, pp. 79–82; *New York Post*, July 14, 1944.
11. J. Keith Horsefield offers the most complete discussion of technical issues in his official history, *IMF*, I, 93–113.
12. "Questions and Answers on the International Monetary Fund," June 10, 1944, Robert Wagner Papers, Georgetown University; *Bretton Woods Documents*, I, 635–640, quotation on p. 639.
13. See chapter 4, pp. 103–105; and chapter 5, p. 113.
14. *Bretton Woods Documents*, I, 70–79.
15. MD, 752:212. For participants' views of Soviet negotiators and their bargaining positions, see also Raymond F. Mikesell, "Negotiating at Bretton Woods," in *Negotiating with the Russians*, ed. Raymond Dennett and Joseph E. Johnson, pp. 101–116; J. W. Beyen, *Money in a Maelstrom*, p. 171; and Harrod, *Keynes*, p. 582.
16. On other Soviet negotiations, see Dennett and Johnson, eds., *Negotiating with the Russians*; memorandum, July 31, 1944, Goldenweiser Papers, Box 4; and Goldenweiser's statement, November 2, 1944, Federal Reserve Papers, Board of Governors of the Federal Reserve System.
17. *IMF*, I, 77–78, 94–98; quotation from John Morton Blum, *From the Morgenthau Diaries: Years of War, 1941–1945*, p. 260; Acheson to W. A. Harriman, July 5, 1944, No. 800.515/7–544, NA, RG 59.
18. MD, 750:109–110, 113–116, 124, quotations on pp. 115–116.
19. Ibid., 750:124.
20. Ibid., 750:274, quotation on p. 282; Blum, *Years of War*, p. 164, quotation on p. 262.
21. MD, 752:203, 750:295, and quotation from 752:203.
22. Ibid., 752:212–216, quotations on

pp. 202, 216. Harry White's proposal for a $5 billion credit is in MD, 707:59–70.

23. *New York Journal-American*, July 8, 1944. See also *New York Times*, July 14 and 15, 1944; Blum, *Years of War*, p. 164.

24. Blum, *Years of War*, pp. 264–265; *Bretton Woods Documents*, I, 648–649, 53, quotation on p. 877; MD, 754:122, 124.

25. *New York Times*, July 14, 1944; *IMF*, I, 94–98; Harrod, *Keynes*, p. 579; memorandum, July 29, 1944, Goldenweiser Papers, Box 4; memorandum of meeting with Chilean delegation, July 9, 1944, container 1308/54/D/82, State Department Conference Records.

26. Harrod, *Keynes*, p. 579; Blum, *Years of War*, pp. 269–270; Hull to Winant, July 15, 1944, No. 800.515/7–1544, NA, RG 59; *IMF*, III, 202; MD, 753:125–126.

27. *IMF*, III, 202.

28. Memorandum, July 29, 1944, Goldenweiser Papers, Box 4. Compare Clause IV of the joint statement in *IMF*, III, 133, and Article IV (Sec. 5, 6) of the articles of agreement in ibid., III, 190.

29. Memorandum, July 29, 1944, Goldenweiser Papers, Box 4; Article XII (Sec. 8) in *IMF*, III, 202.

30. MD, 749:34–36; quotation from *Bretton Woods Documents*, I, 893.

31. *Bretton Woods Documents*, I, 135, and II, 1181. See also B. K. Maddan, "Echoes of Bretton Woods," *Finance and Development* 6 (June 1969): 33; memorandum, July 31, 1944, Goldenweiser Papers, Box 4.

32. MD, 749:14, 19, 160, 175, quotation on p. 14. In 1944 American officials still assumed lend-lease would meet a large portion of Britain's reconstruction needs in the period between V-E Day and V-J Day (note Robert W. Oliver, *Early Plans for a World Bank*, p. 37).

33. *Bretton Woods Documents*, I, 971–975, quotation on p. 975.

34. MD, 749:146–151, 750:109–112 and 749:33, quotations from 749:146 and 749:151. On problems of beginning exchange transactions in an economically distorted world, examine *IMF*, I, 159–161.

35. *Bretton Woods Documents*, I, 284, 326.

36. Beyen, *Money*, pp. 137–140, 176–177; *Bretton Woods Documents*, I, 330. On the origins of the Bank for International Settlements (BIS), note Frank Costigliola, "The Other Side of Isolationism: The Establishment of the First World Bank, 1929–1930," *Journal of American History* 59 (December 1972): 602–620.

37. MD, 756:133–136 and 755:171–178, quotation from 755:178. Fraser's speech on November 16, 1943, is cited in Chamber of Commerce of the United States, Finance Department, *World Currency Stabilization Proposals*, pp. 18–19.

38. *New York PM*, July 16, 1944.

39. MD, 755:210–212; *Bretton Woods Documents*, I, 939. In his *The Bank for International Settlements*, pp. 102–121, Henry Schloss cites a letter from the United States Treasury dated October 13, 1950, indicating that Washington attempted to implement this resolution, but European governments opposed it. Apparently they saw the BIS as a mechanism for facilitating central bank cooperation at a time when European nations experienced similar reconstruction problems. Additional discussion appears in Roger Auboin, *The Bank for International Settlements, 1930–1955*.

40. David L. Gordon and Royden Dangerfield, *The Hidden Weapon*, pp. 164–180; *FR: 1944*, II, 213–251; *Bretton Woods Documents*, I, 329, 862, 920, 939.

41. *Bretton Woods Documents*, I, 227,

327–329, 939, II, 1206, I, 731, 739, 941, and II, 1205.

42. Ibid., I, 330, 834, quotation on p. 279.

43. Interview with Luis Machado, July 9, 1968; *New York Times*, July 14, 1944; quotation from MD, 752:1–40; Dorothy Adelson, "World Agreement at Bretton Woods," *Pan American*, October 15, 1944, pp. 35–39; Lewis Clark to Hull, August 31, 1944, No. 800.515/8-3144, NA, RG 59.

44. *Bretton Woods Documents*, I, 84–88, quotations on pp. 88, 84, 85. Henry J. Bittermann, "Negotiation of the Articles of Agreement of the International Bank for Reconstruction and Development," *International Lawyer* 5 (January 1971): 59–88.

45. Memorandum, July 31, 1944, Goldenweiser Papers, Box 4.

46. Warren Kelchner to Larson, July 18, 1944, container 1309/54/D/82, State Department Conference Records; *New York Times*, July 18, 1944; *New Yorker*, August 5, 1944, pp. 12–14; MD, 755:74.

47. *Bretton Woods Documents*, I, 367–368, 485–486, 488, quotation on p. 1053.

48. Ibid., I, 365–400; memorandum, July 29, 1944, Goldenweiser Papers, Box 4.

49. *Bretton Woods Documents*, I, 374, 543–544.

50. MD, 752:221, 255–256, quotation on p. 221.

51. Ibid., 753:2–18.

52. Ibid., 756:13–14.

53. Ibid., 753:2–18, quotation on p. 18.

54. *Bretton Woods Documents*, I, 1020–1021. On the latitude allowed bank administrators by the articles of agreement, see David A. Baldwin, "The International Bank in Political Perspective," *World Politics* 18 (October 1965): 68–81.

55. *Bretton Woods Documents*, I, 1027; Baldwin, "International Bank," pp.

68–81. A trenchant Marxist criticism of the bank's political leverage appears in Teresa Hayter, *Aid as Imperialism*, pp. 46–87. More recently Michael Hudson has taken a similar approach in *Super Imperialism*, pp. 90–128.

56. *Bretton Woods Documents*, I, 1061–1077, quotation on p. 1076. Early bank practices are described in the bank's own publication, *International Bank for Reconstruction and Development, 1946–1953*.

57. *Bretton Woods Documents*, I, 86–87.

58. Ibid., I, 1108–1109, quotation on p. 1119; memorandum, July 31, 1944, Goldenweiser Papers, Box 4.

59. First three quotations from MD, 759:5–6, and the rest from 759:15–16. Keynes was also optimistic about the prospects for continued great-power cooperation (Harrod, *Keynes*, p. 582).

60. *Bretton Woods Documents*, I, 1100–1101.

61. Ibid., quotation on p. 1119; memorandum, July 31, 1944, Goldenweiser Papers, Box 4.

62. *Bretton Woods Documents*, I, 731, 739–748, and II, 1194–1196, quotation from II, 1195.

63. Ibid., I, 1045, and II, 1197–1198, quotation from II, 1197.

64. Ibid., I, 1088–1091; Mikesell, "Negotiating at Bretton Woods," pp. 113–114. Mikesell, a participant, considered none of the Russian reservations sufficiently important to explain later refusal to join the two institutions. Edward M. Bernstein said, in an interview March 26, 1970, that American technicians found their Soviet counterparts generally receptive to the arrangements. Negotiators had no indication that the Soviets thought membership in the world institutions would require a capitulation of national interests and security concerns, a claim that some historians have advanced more recently. See,

for instance, Thomas G. Paterson, "The Abortive American Loan to Russia and the Origins of the Cold War, 1943–1946," *Journal of American History* 56 (June 1969): 87, 91. Actually, the Bretton Woods arrangements were generous to the Russians. They could borrow up to 200 percent of their quota—perhaps $2.4 billion altogether—in foreign currencies, and this was little more than a concealed loan.

At the conference Soviet negotiators did not regard the requirement that members divulge economic details an insurmountable obstacle, though Moscow was traditionally secretive. To "avoid all these disagreements," the Soviets consented to supply information on newly mined gold, prices, and income (MD, 754:118), and they registered no objections on this issue in the minutes of Commission I. There the Russians merely reiterated their request for a reduction in gold payments for members whose home areas had suffered extensive war damage. Other alterations or interpretations concerned technical details or definitions, and none seemed sufficiently important to warrant an autarkic postwar economic policy (see *Bretton Woods Documents*, I, 1090–1091).

65. Quotations from *Bretton Woods Documents*, I, 1109–1110; Harrod, *Keynes*, p. 584; Maddan, "Echoes of Bretton Woods," p. 33.

66. *Bretton Woods Documents*, I, 1116–1120, quotations on pp. 1116, 1117, 1119–1120.

67. Memorandum, July 31, 1944, Goldenweiser Papers, Box 4.

7. Selling the "Magnificent Blueprint"

1. *Bretton Woods Documents*, I, 1110.
2. Ibid.
3. MD, 764:89–90. Morgenthau also told the House Committee on Bank-

ing and Currency that other nations were awaiting the American decision, in *Bretton Woods Agreement Acts, Hearings on H.R. 2211*, 79th Cong., 1st sess., March 7–April 11, 1945, I, 10–15.

4. Nelson Rockefeller to Roosevelt, July 9, 1944, Official File 5549, Franklin D. Roosevelt Papers, Roosevelt Library; quotation from Morgenthau to Roosevelt, June 29, 1944, President's Secretary's File, Roosevelt Papers; *Wall Street Journal*, July 1, 1944; *New York Times*, July 1, 1944; *Chicago Tribune*, July 2, 1944; MD, 763:138; *Chicago Tribune*, July 9, 11, and 15, 1944; *New York Journal-American*, July 7 and 8, 1944; *Chicago Journal of Commerce*, July 6 and 8, 1944.

5. Quotation from MD, 749:165; *Washington Evening Star*, July 9, 1944.

6. MD, 749:165–170; quotation from *New York Times*, July 12, 1944. Memorandum, July 18, 1944, Emanuel Alexandrovich Goldenweiser Papers, Library of Congress, Box 4; *Magazine of Wall Street*, July 22, 1944, p. 380, and August 19, 1944, p. 492; *Time*, July 24, 1944, p. 73, and July 10, 1944, p. 79; *Fortune* 30 (September 1944): 118–119; MD, 773:31.

7. Memorandum, July 31, 1944, Goldenweiser Papers, Box 4.

8. Memorandum, July 26, 1944, Harry Dexter White Papers, Firestone Library, Item 35.

9. MD, 763:219–220 and quotations from 752:277; *Commercial and Financial Chronicle*, August 3, 1944, p. 486.

10. MD, 768:42, 813:226–227, and quotations from 819:90–92. Promotional techniques used during the Bretton Woods campaign resembled those used in behalf of the Employment Act of 1946. Stephen Kemp Bailey's *Congress Makes a Law* is a helpful guide. For other broad-

ranging discussions of propaganda and pressure as employed by government agencies, consult Bertram M. Gross, *The Legislative Struggle—A Study in Social Combat*, pp. 242–264; Daniel M. Berman, *In Congress Assembled*, pp. 91–94; and Abraham Holtzman, *Legislative Liaison*.

11. MD, 819:93.
12. Quotation from MD, 768:42; *New York Times*, February 27, 1945; *Congressional Record*, March 15, 1945, p. 10; *Commercial and Financial Chronicle*, February 15, 1945, p. 719, quotation from p. 742.
13. Copies of Bernstein's speech, October 25, 1944, and Luxford's speech, October 27, 1944, were found among the papers of Edwin W. Kemmerer, Firestone Library, Princeton University.
14. MD, 820:49, 839:308–311, and 845:385–387; Feltus to White, February 23, 1945, Ansel Luxford Papers, International Bank Law Library, International Bank for Reconstruction and Development; MD, 839:311; Frank Gervasi, "Bretton Woods or World War III," *Collier's*, June 2, 1945, p. 18.
15. MD, 768:42 and quotations from 805:219.
16. *Southern Banker* 83 (September 1944): 25. Among the many articles prepared by participants are Edward M. Bernstein, "A Practical International Monetary Policy," *American Economic Review* 34 (December 1944): 840–847; Edward E. Brown, "The International Monetary Fund," *Journal of Business* 17 (October 1944): 199–208; Harry Dexter White, "The Monetary Fund," *Foreign Affairs* 23 (January 1945): 195–210.
17. MD 774:91; *New York Times*, February 19, 1945; Walter E. Spahr to Frederick C. Smith, February 19, 1945, Kemmerer Papers; U.S., Senate, Banking and Currency Committee, *Bretton Woods Agreements Act, Hearings on H.R. 3314*, 79th Cong., 1st sess., 1945, pp. 459–460; John Morton Blum, *From the Morgenthau Diaries: Years of War, 1941–1945*, p. 430.
18. Senate, *Bretton Woods Hearings*, pp. 639, 642, 645.
19. Henry C. Simons, "The U.S. Holds the Cards," *Fortune* 30 (September 1944): 157. Recent comment on Simons's position appears in Harry G. Johnson, "Political Economy Aspects of International Monetary Reform," *Journal of International Economics* 2 (September 1972): 401–423.
20. *Chicago Tribune*, September 24, 1944.
21. Letter from Charles S. Dewey, September 8, 1968. Also undated radio address, Charles Dewey Papers, Chicago Historical Society, Box 8; *Congressional Record*, August 14, 1944, pp. 6926–6927. Irving Fisher to Dewey, August 18, 1944; Dewey to Fisher, August 25, 1944; and Dewey to a citizen, August 19, 1944, all in Dewey Papers, Box 9.
22. See chapter 4, pp. 86–90.
23. MD, 773:31; Winthrop W. Aldrich, "Some Aspects of American Foreign Economic Policy," *Vital Speeches*, October 15, 1944, pp. 20–26, quotation on p. 26. Note also Arthur M. Johnson, *Winthrop W. Aldrich*, pp. 285–291.
24. Aldrich, "Some Aspects of American Foreign Economic Policy," p. 21.
25. *The Economist*, September 23, 1944, pp. 423–424.
26. *Congressional Record*, September 21, 1944, pp. 8059–8060; MD, 773:31.
27. Memorandum, September 16, 1944, Goldenweiser Papers, Box 4.
28. Collado memorandum, August 15, 1944, No. 800.515/8-1544, NA, RG 59. Also helpful are notes, November 1, 1944, Goldenweiser Papers, Box 7; and John H. Williams's

article "International Monetary Plans: After Bretton Woods," *Foreign Affairs* 23 (October 1944): 38–56.

29. Memorandum, October 7, 1944, Goldenweiser Papers, Box 4; Collado memorandum, August 15, 1944, No. 800.515/8-1544, NA, RG 59; MD, 773:31.

30. Notes, January 6, 1945, Goldenweiser Papers, Box 4.

31. Ibid.

32. Ibid.

33. *New York Times*, February 5, 1945.

34. Ibid.

35. *New York Times*, February 6, 1945; *Commercial and Financial Chronicle*, February 8, 1945, pp. 644–645.

36. *New York Post*, February 15, 1945, and February 9, 1945.

37. MD, 819:187.

38. Samuel I. Rosenman, ed., *The Public Papers and Addresses of Franklin D. Roosevelt*, 1944–1945 vol., pp. 457–482, quotation on pp. 516–517.

39. Ibid., p. 516.

40. Rosenman, ed., *Public Papers*, 1944–1945 vol., pp. 457–482, quotation on p. 457.

41. Ibid., p. 476. For additional discussion of the political, economic, and diplomatic obstacles facing Roosevelt early in 1945, consult James MacGregor Burns, *Roosevelt: The Soldier of Freedom*, pp. 557–597; and Robert A. Divine, *Second Chance*, pp. 243–278.

42. U.S., Department of State, *Bulletin*, February 18, 1945, pp. 220–222.

43. Hadley Cantril and Mildred Strunk, *Public Opinion, 1935–1946*, pp. 209, 908–909; Henry Morgenthau, "Bretton Woods and International Cooperation," *Foreign Affairs* 23 (January 1945): 184–185.

44. Atlantic City conversations, June 24, 1944, No. 800.515/BWA/6-2444, NA, RG 59; Ansel Luxford to Robert Wagner, February 10, 1945, Bill file 37 for S. 540, NA, RG 46; and

Senate, *Bretton Woods Hearings*, pp. 529–562.

45. House, *Bretton Woods Hearings*, I, 5–15, quotations on pp. 5, 11–12.

46. Ibid., pp. 167, 176.

47. "Battle of Bretton Woods," *Fortune* 32 (July 1945): 122–123.

48. These conclusions emerge in the House and Senate hearings. Analysis draws heavily on the testimony of W. Randolph Burgess, Allan Sproul, and John H. Williams, as well as Harry Dexter White and Edward Bernstein.

49. Senate, *Bretton Woods Hearings*, pp. 300–307; House, *Bretton Woods Hearings*, I, 345; Senate, *Bretton Woods Hearings*, pp. 319–325, quotation on p. 325.

50. House, *Bretton Woods Hearings*, I, 221. For criticisms, consult U.S., Senate, *Participation of the United States in the International Monetary Fund and the International Bank for Reconstruction and Development*, Rept. 452, 2 parts, 79th Cong., 1st sess., 2:16.

51. Taft's comment appears in *Congressional Record*, July 16, 1945, p. 7573.

52. U.S., House of Representatives, *Participation of the United States in the International Monetary Fund and the International Bank for Reconstruction and Development*, Rept. 629, 79th Cong., 1st sess., p. 52; House, *Bretton Woods Hearings*, I, 106–107.

53. Sproul's testimony, Senate, *Bretton Woods Hearings*, p. 305; Senate, Rept. 452, 2:11.

54. House, Rept. 629, p. 56.

55. Senate, Rept. 452, 2:14.

56. Quotations from House, Rept. 629, p. 58; and Senate, *Bretton Woods Hearings*, pp. 618–619. White, "The Monetary Fund"; Keynes's speech reprinted in Senate, *Bretton Woods Hearings*, p. 211.

57. FR: *1946*, I, 1391–1411.

58. Keynes's speech reprinted in Senate,

Bretton Woods Hearings, p. 209. White cited in Richard N. Gardner, *Sterling-Dollar Diplomacy,* pp. 195, 241; Blum, *Years of War,* p. 316.

59. Edward Bernstein and Henry Bittermann discussed their policy differences with White in interviews on March 26, 1970, and June 20, 1968. See also Blum, *Years of War,* pp. 307, 326; and George C. Herring, Jr., "The United States and British Bankruptcy, 1944–1945: Responsibilities Deferred," *Political Science Quarterly* 86 (June 1971): 260–280. Quotation from Blum, *Years of War,* p. 447.

60. House, *Bretton Woods Hearings,* I, 222.

61. Senate, Rept. 452, 1:19; interview with Edward M. Bernstein, March 26, 1970; *FR: 1945,* VI, 54–56; Frederick J. Dobney, ed., *Selected Papers of Will Clayton,* pp. 146–149; Gardner, *Sterling-Dollar Diplomacy,* pp. 178–187.

62. Feltus to White, June 16, 1945, Luxford Papers.

63. House, *Bretton Woods Hearings,* I, 506, II, 720.

64. Ibid., II, 1257–1262. Among the prominent individuals who helped prepare the report were Ralph Flanders, president of the Boston Federal Reserve Bank; Chester Davis, president of the St. Louis Federal Reserve Bank; Paul Hoffman, president of the Studebaker Corporation; Eric A. Johnston, president of the United States Chamber of Commerce; and R. Gordon Wasson, vice-president, J. P. Morgan & Company. For sympathetic accounts of CED activities, read Karl Schriftgiesser, *Business Comes of Age,* pp. 122–124, and *Business and Public Policy,* p. 115.

65. Schriftgiesser, *Business and Public Policy,* p. 117; House, *Bretton Woods Hearings,* I, 352.

66. Undated memorandum, Goldenweiser Papers, Box 4.

67. House, *Bretton Woods Hearings,* I, 352–358; MD, 831:4 and 832: 48–49.

68. MD, 831:85; Americans United for World Organization, *Capitol Hill Views the World,* March 22, 1945; *New York Post,* March 27 and April 5, 1945.

69. MD, 832:48–49 and 834:108.

70. Ibid., 834:227–233.

71. Ibid., 834:231.

72. Ibid., 834:227–233, 835:1–5, quotation on p. 4, and 837:10.

73. Ibid., 834:4 and 837:10, 12–13, 16, 35–36, quotation from 835:C.

74. Allen Drury, *A Senate Journal, 1943–1945,* pp. 414–415; Ansel Luxford to Morgenthau, April 16, 1945, Official File 85-E, Harry S. Truman Papers, Truman Library; MD, 837:27. In discussing the impact of Roosevelt's death on preparations for the United Nations, Robert A. Divine comments that "to the very end Roosevelt proved to be the master of timing, providing in his death a final boost to a movement he had so often ignored" (*Second Chance,* p. 278). This judgment could apply to Bretton Woods as well.

75. MD, 839:308–311 and 845:385–387; Congress of Industrial Organizations, *5,000,000 Jobs in World Trade;* Joseph Gaer, *Bretton Woods Is No Mystery;* quotation from Joy Hume Falk, *The Story of Bretton Woods.*

76. Americans United for World Organization, *Capitol Hill Views the World,* May 16, 1945; Cantril and Strunk, *Public Opinion, 1935–1946,* p. 209; *Congressional Record,* July 16, 1945, pp. 7576–7584, quotation on p. 7576.

77. Wolcott quotation from Joseph O'Connell and Luxford to Morgenthau, April 21, 1945, Luxford Papers; MD, 839:100–104 and 845:378; Luxford to Morgenthau, May 12, 1945, Luxford Papers; quotations

from unsigned memorandum, May 16, 1945, Official File 85-E, Truman Papers. The State Department wanted to take control of the council, but Morgenthau, recognizing that the Treasury's position in monetary matters was at stake, gained President Truman's approval for his position (MD, 847:271–281, 289–292).

78. Dean Acheson, *Present at the Creation*, p. 107; quotation from MD, 849:14; Truman to Spence, June 1, 1945, Official File 85-E, Truman Papers.

79. *Congressional Record*, June 5, 1945, pp. 5542, 5569–5570.

80. Ibid., p. 5540.

81. Acheson, *Present at the Creation*, p. 108; McNaughton to Bermingham, June 8, 1945, Frank McNaughton Papers, Truman Library; MD, 854:53–54.

82. Blum, *Years of War*, pp. 434–436; Acheson, *Present at the Creation*, pp. 107–109; quotation from MD, 820:38.

83. MD, 856:7–9 and 856:148.

84. James T. Patterson, *Mr. Republican*, pp. 41–42, 291–295; Senate, Rept. 452, 2:1–16, quotation on p. 1.

85. Patterson, *Mr. Republican*, pp. 291–295, quotation on p. 293; second quotation from Blum, *Years of War*, p. 430.

86. Senate, Rept. 452, 2:2–9, quotations on pp. 8–9. Taft's criticisms of foreign investments have earned him sympathetic treatment from revisionist historians who have rehabilitated the Ohio senator as a "conservative nationalist" understanding "the imperialist implications of American economic investment in the underdeveloped world" (Read, for instance, Henry W. Berger, "Senator Robert A. Taft Dissents from Military Escalation," in *Cold War Critics*, ed. Thomas G. Paterson, pp. 167–204, quotation on pp. 194–195). Taft's biographer, James

T. Patterson, also praises his "perceptive conclusion concerning economic exploitation," which sounds "prophetic in the 1960's" (*Mr. Republican*, p. 294). However, from a more orthodox perspective it is arguable that neither Taft nor his revisionist defenders fully understood the process of international investment or the advantages of multilateral lending over bilateral government or private loans. In a world where economic backwardness jeopardized the fulfillment of human aspirations for both improvement and political stability, it is arguable that some form of international assistance was preferable to reliance on scarce domestic resources to stimulate economic growth. And, if outside capital is accepted as necessary or desirable, it follows that potential recipients have a wider range of choice—hence more independence of action—when there are international aid mechanisms, not just bilateral government programs or private capital.

87. Senate, Rept. 452, 2:9–19; Senate, *Bretton Woods Hearings*, p. 55.

88. Drury, *Senate Journal*, p. 465.

89. *Congressional Record*, July 18, 1945, p. 7690.

90. *Congressional Record*, July 18, 1945, pp. 7672, 7699.

91. M. Connelly to Truman, July 2, 1945, Official File 85-E, Truman Papers; Americans United for World Organization, *Capitol Hill Views the World*, July 30, 1945; quotation from Drury, *Senate Journal*, p. 466.

92. *IMF*, I, 116.

93. Gardner, *Sterling-Dollar Diplomacy*, p. 224.

94. Hugh Dalton, *High Tide and After*, pp. 68–89, quotation on p. 73. Standard accounts of the extended loans negotiations include Gardner's excellent analysis in *Sterling-*

Dollar Diplomacy as well as the firsthand accounts of Roy F. Harrod, *The Life of John Maynard Keynes*, pp. 587–623; and Lionel Robbins, *Autobiography of an Economist*, pp. 205–211.

95. For Keynes's views on a credit, see *FR: 1945*, VI, 83, 132–134.

96. Documents in *Foreign Relations* show quite clearly that, although Washington held out for sterling convertibility, Keynes initially suggested this course. Richard Gardner did not have access to these documents when he concluded that the "American negotiators proposed a rigid commitment" while "Keynes strongly resisted the idea of a fixed deadline" (*Sterling-Dollar Diplomacy*, p. 204).

97. *FR: 1945*, VI, 188–189, 190–193.

98. Keynes's speech to the House of Lords on December 18, 1945, is reprinted in Seymour E. Harris, ed., *The New Economics*, pp. 380–395, quotation on p. 386. See also Gardner, *Sterling-Dollar Diplomacy*, pp. 201–212.

99. Harrod agreed that the Americans correctly viewed sterling convertibility as "the first indispensable step towards a satisfactory reconstruction of the international economy" (*Keynes*, p. 606). *The Economist*, June 28, 1947, pp. 1032–1033, quotation from July 19, 1947, p. 118. Administration testimony on the British loan appears in U.S., Senate, Banking and Currency Committee, *Anglo-American Financial Agreement, Hearings on S. J. Res. 138*, 79th Cong., 2d sess., 1946; and U.S., House of Representatives, Committee on Banking and Currency, *Anglo-American Financial Agreement, Hearings on H. J. Res. 311 and S. J. Res. 138*, 79th Cong., 2d sess., 1946. Quotations from U.S., National Advisory Council on International Monetary and Financial Policies, *Report* (August

1945–February 1946), p. 17.

Although the loan reflected a key-currency approach, John Williams criticized its terms. He favored a grant, not a loan, and thought the current-account convertibility provision an unduly stringent requirement designed to satisfy Congress, which wanted a "good commercial bargain" (see John H. Williams, *Economic Stability in a Changing World*, pp. 84–85). But a recent British interpretation takes objection to standard criticisms that the Americans demanded too much and loaned too little. Susan Strange says in her *Sterling and British Policy* that British officials misused the American loan. She concludes that "the strings attached by the United States to the loan were so weak or so insecurely tied that unless they confirmed decisions already made by Britain they did little to change British policy either at home or abroad" (pp. 269–274, quotation on p. 274).

100. *New York Times*, December 29, 1945.

101. Harriman's comment appears in *FR: 1944*, IV, 951. This section draws heavily on John L. Gaddis, *The United States and the Origins of the Cold War, 1941–1947*, pp. 189–194, 216–224; George C. Herring, Jr., *Aid to Russia, 1941–1946*, pp. 144–178; and Eugene V. Rostow, *Peace in the Balance*, pp. 105–131.

102. Herring, *Aid to Russia*, pp. 167–223, 290–291.

103. Thomas G. Paterson, a revisionist, presents the argument that a handsome, unconditional loan might have served "as a peace potion for easing increasingly bitter Soviet-American relations" (see his "The Abortive American Loan to Russia and the Origins of the Cold War, 1943–1946," *Journal of American History* 56 [June 1969]: 70–92. A revised version appears in

Soviet-American Confrontation, pp. 33–56). Rostow surveys a portion of the literature on this issue and seeks to rebut revisionist claims in *Peace in the Balance*, pp. 105–131. Herring, while critical of American policymakers for handling the reconstruction assistance issue poorly, criticizes some of the revisionist arguments in *Aid to Russia*, pp. 208–210, 234–236, 287. Gaddis shows how difficulties with unconditional wartime assistance convinced some American officials that postwar aid should be linked to political concessions in *The United States and the Origins of the Cold War*, pp. 80–88, 189–197.

104. Rostow, *Peace in the Balance*, p. 128.

105. *FR: 1946*, I, 1387–1388.

106. *IMF*, I, 117; *FR: 1946*, I, 1313–1317, 1355–1366, quotation on p. 1355. To say that membership in the Bretton Woods institutions would have required the Soviet Union to provide information about sensitive economic matters is not to argue, as some revisionist historians have done, that membership obligations would have restricted Soviet domestic economic policies or required a capitulation of national security interests. If these considerations were important, the Soviet negotiators did not allow them to stand in the way at Bretton Woods. While it is difficult, without access to Soviet archives, to grasp Moscow's perceptions or calculations, American technicians saw no irreconcilable conflict between the needs of a centrally planned economy and the requirements of international economic cooperation. Edward Bernstein made this point in an interview on March 26, 1970, and it is substantiated in Raymond Frech Mikesell's "Negotiating at Bretton Woods," in *Negotiating with the Russians*, ed. Raymond Dennett and Joseph E. Johnson, pp. 101–116. Mikesell correctly points out there and in "The Role of International Monetary Agreements in a World of Planned Economies," *Journal of Political Economy* 55 (December 1947): 497–498, that these "agreements do not require that trade be conducted by private enterprise, nor do they provide for the elimination of state controls. . . . Developments affecting the patterns of economic controls . . . are generally unaffected by the platitudes and the vague and well-hedged obligations of international conventions." For the hypothesis that Soviet decision makers may have anticipated a second depression and expected to obtain outside assistance without undertaking formal commitments, see Charles Prince, "The USSR's Role in International Finance," *Harvard Business Review* 25 (Autumn 1946): 111–128. George F. Kennan, determined to deflate Treasury optimism, responded to a request for information about Soviet attitudes toward international economic cooperation with his seminal analysis of Soviet policy interests in February 1946. Autarky, he argued, was consistent with Russian fears of contact with the capitalist West (see his *Memoirs 1925–1950*, pp. 256, 292–293, 561–565).

107. Quotations from U.S., Department of State, *Bulletin*, December 30, 1945, pp. 1058–1059; *New York Times*, December 28, 1945. See also *FR: 1946*, I, 1384–1387.

108. *New York Times*, December 28, 1945.

8. The Protracted Transition

1. Criticisms of postwar monetary planning appear in Richard N. Gardner, *Sterling-Dollar Diplomacy*, pp. 381–385; Ernest F. Penrose,

Economic Planning for the Peace, pp. 347–375; and Raymond Frech Mikesell, *United States Economic Policy and International Relations,* pp. 121–127.

2. U.S., Department of State, *Bulletin,* March 16, 1947, pp. 481–485, quotation on p. 482, and second quotation from April 19, 1954, p. 602. The United States' mission to assume the economic responsibilities of a great power elicits comment in Raymond Frech Mikesell, "America's Economic Responsibilities as a Great Power," *American Economic Review (Papers and Proceedings)* 72 (1959): 258; and Woodrow Wilson Foundation and the National Planning Association, *The Political Economy of American Foreign Policy,* pp. 201–234.

3. IMF, *First Annual Meeting of the Board of Governors: Report of the Executive Directors and Summary Proceedings (September 27 to October 3, 1946),* pp. 33–34.

4. Jack N. Behrman, "Political Factors in U.S. International Financial Cooperation, 1945–1950," *American Political Science Review* 47 (June 1953): 431–460; *IMF,* I, 121–135; Roy F. Harrod, *The Life of John Maynard Keynes,* pp. 624–639, quotation on p. 632.

5. IMF, First Annual Meeting, *Report,* p. 34; Gardner, *Sterling-Dollar Diplomacy,* pp. 291–292; *FR: 1946,* I, 1435–1436.

6. U.S., Department of State, *Bulletin,* March 10, 1946, pp. 380–384; *FR: 1946,* I, 1391–1435. Foreign assistance stimulated the American economy and created jobs, but economic policymakers did not sponsor the program primarily to avert a domestic depression. The Council of Economic Advisers rebutted this assertion in *The Economic Situation at Midyear 1948,* p. 36: "The foreign aid program is not designed to put props under our current business boom. The unfilled demands of the American market, with its enormous purchasing power, would sustain our prosperity for the present even if foreign markets were sharply reduced. We are deliberately subjecting ourselves to inflationary pressure on the domestic economy in the short-run in order to contribute to international security and economic stabilization in the long-run." See also Lester Chandler, *Inflation in the United States, 1940–1948,* pp. 226–230.

7. On the politics of foreign lending, consult *FR: 1946,* I, 1391–1438 and VI, 133–193. The views of Fred Vinson and Will Clayton appear in ibid., V, 441 and I, 1434.

8. On politics of the bilateral lending program, note documents in *FR: 1945,* VI, 99; *FR: 1946,* I, 1391–1428 and V, 399–478.

9. Radical revisionists often see multilateralism as a cause of the cold war. My own interpretation takes the more traditional view that the cold war disrupted economic designs, in "Open Door Expansionism Reconsidered: The World War II Experience," *Journal of American History* 59 (March 1973): 909–924.

10. Leland Yeager, *International Monetary Relations,* pp. 339–340; Robert Triffin, *Europe and the Money Muddle,* pp. 31–87, 318–322.

11. U.S., Department of State, *Bulletin,* May 11, 1947, p. 919; Clayton's comments from *FR: 1947,* III, 230–232.

12. Gardner discusses the consequences of the British loan in *Sterling-Dollar Diplomacy,* rev. ed., pp. 313–336. Susan Strange draws on this analysis for her *Sterling and British Policy,* pp. 269–276. On Britain's economic conditions in 1947, see *FR: 1947,* III, 62; and Hugh Dalton, *High Tide and After,* pp. 254–267. Criticisms of Labour government policy in-

clude "The Planner's Last Chance," *The Economist*, August 2, 1947, pp. 177–178; and "Monetary Disorder," *The Banker's Magazine* 164 (August 1947): 61–65.

13. Raymond Frech Mikesell, *Foreign Exchange in the Postwar World*, pp. 42–46; Dalton, *High Tide*, pp. 254–267; quotations from U.S., National Advisory Council on International Monetary and Financial Policies, *Annual Report*, 1948, p. 22.

14. *Documents on American Foreign Relations*, IX, 423.

15. Quotation from *FR: 1947*, III, 237–239; quotation from Dalton, *High Tide*, p. 89; Mikesell, *Economic Policy*, pp. 264–266. On the Marshall Plan itself, consult William Adams Brown, Jr., and Redvers Opie, *American Foreign Assistance*; and Harry B. Price, *The Marshall Plan and Its Meaning*. William F. Diebold, Jr., considers it in the broader context of international economic policy in *The United States and the Industrial World*, pp. 23–26.

16. W. S. and E. S. Woytinsky, *World Commerce and Governments*, p. 223; Clarence B. Randall, in U.S., Commission on Foreign Economic Policy, *Report to the President and the Congress*, p. 6; Gordon Gray, *Report to the President on Foreign Economic Policies*, p. 3.

17. Richard Gardner speculates about how the Keynes Plan might have enabled the United States to finance its deficit more easily in *Sterling-Dollar Diplomacy*, pp. 1–11. See also Brian Johnson, *The Politics of Money*, p. 143.

18. See Treasury Secretary John Snyder's comment to the first annual meeting in IMF, First Annual Meeting of the Board of Governors, *Report of the Executive Directors and Summary Proceedings*, p. 34; and Gardner, *Sterling-Dollar Diplomacy*, pp. 291–292.

19. Discussion of the International Bank draws on the following: David A. Baldwin, *Economic Development and American Foreign Policy, 1943–1962*, pp. 8–51; Antonin Basch, "International Bank for Reconstruction and Development, 1944–1949: A Review," *International Conciliation* 455 (November 1949): 791–827; Alec Cairncross, *The International Bank for Reconstruction and Development*; International Bank for Reconstruction and Development (IBRD), *The International Bank for Reconstruction and Development, 1946–1953*, pp. 3–37; Edward S. Mason and Robert E. Asher, *The World Bank since Bretton Woods*, pp. 36–61; Mikesell, *Economic Policy*, pp. 216–242; and W. M. Scammell, *International Monetary Policy*, pp. 226–241.

20. Mason and Asher, *World Bank*, pp. 36–61; IBRD, *Second Annual Report of the Board of Governors, 1946–1947*, Proceedings, p. 15.

21. Basch, "International Bank," p. 799; Mason and Asher, *World Bank*, p. 105.

22. Baldwin, *Economic Development*, pp. 30–32; Mason and Asher, *World Bank*, p. 107; Mikesell, *Economic Policy*, p. 199. On difficulties with bank bonds, see *Business Week*, November 1, 1947, p. 75; and "Slowdown of World Bank," *U.S. News and World Report*, January 30, 1948, pp. 51–52.

23. On the bank's management problems, see *New York Times*, December 5, 6, 7, and 17, 1946. Quotation from *Bretton Woods Documents*, I, 1119.

24. Mason and Asher, *World Bank*, p. 49; "Making Policy," *U.S. News and World Report*, May 23, 1947, pp. 20–21. McCloy and his successor Eugene Black successfully projected the image of no-nonsense, hard-boiled bankers. Portraits of McCloy appear as follows: Kermit Roosevelt, "Handy Man Goes

Banker," *Saturday Evening Post*, November 1, 1947, pp. 24–25; and Edward B. Lockett, "Banker to a Promised Land," *Nation's Business* 36 (June 1948): 39. On Black, see *Business Week*, June 4, 1949, p. 6.

25. Quotation from Mason and Asher, *World Bank*, p. 61; quotation from IBRD, *Fourth Annual Report, 1948–1949*, p. 5; Baldwin, *Economic Development*, p. 50; Basch, "International Bank," p. 826.

26. On changing bank policies, see "Slowdown of World Bank," *U.S. News and World Report*, January 30, 1948, pp. 51–52; and John J. McCloy, "The Lesson of the World Bank," *Foreign Affairs* 27 (July 1949): 551–560, quotation on p. 552.

27. Mikesell, *Economic Policy*, p. 204; Basch, "International Bank," p. 800; and Mason and Asher, *World Bank*, pp. 155–157.

28. Mason and Asher, *World Bank*, pp. 155–157.

29. Basch, "International Bank," pp. 791–827; IBRD, *International Bank*, pp. 68–83; Royal Institute of International Affairs, *The Problem of International Investment*, p. 170.

30. IBRD, *International Bank*, pp. 68–83; Woytinsky and Woytinsky, *World Commerce and Governments*, pp. 223, 229; IBRD, *Annual Report, 1971*, p. 62.

31. IBRD, *Third Annual Report*, pp. 4–5.

32. The fund's official history, documents, and perspective on economic and technical issues is indispensable for students of that institution (see *IMF*, I–III). Other important accounts are Raymond Frech Mikesell, "The International Monetary Fund, 1944–1949: A Review," *International Conciliation* 455 (November 1949): 828–874; Mikesell, *Economic Policy*, pp. 128–170; Scammell, *International Monetary Policy*, pp. 171–225; Brian Tew, *International Monetary Cooperation*,

1945–1967, pp. 75–99; and Yeager, *International Monetary Relations*, pp. 347–358. The quotation appears in Mikesell, "IMF," p. 138.

33. *IMF*, I, 161, 187–194; Mikesell, *Economic Policy*, pp. 157–161; Mikesell, "IMF," pp. 862–865.

34. *IMF*, II, 559–560; Fred Hirsch, *Money International*, pp. 198–199; Mikesell, *Economic Policy*, pp. 149–152. Correspondence regarding the U.S. commitment to buy and sell gold is printed in U.S., Congress, Joint Economic Committee, *The Balance-of-Payments Mess, Hearings before the Subcommittee on International Exchange and Payments*, 92d Cong., 1st sess., June 16–23, 1971, p. 417; *IMF*, I, 156 and II, 44–53; Mikesell, *Economic Policy*, pp. 134–136; Mikesell, "IMF," pp. 848–850.

35. *IMF*, I, 161, 187–194, quotation on p. 161; Mikesell, *Economic Policy*, pp. 157–161; Mikesell, "IMF," pp. 862–865.

36. *IMF*, I, 187–194, quotation on p. 194.

37. IMF, *Annual Report, 1952*, p. 31.

38. *IMF*, I, 193 and II, 586–588; Mikesell, "IMF," p. 836; Scammell, *International Monetary Policy*, p. 165.

39. *IMF*, I, 297. Criticisms of the fund appear in "The Fund's Decline," *New Republic*, September 17, 1951, pp. 7–8; *Time*, September 24, 1951, pp. 101–102; "Bretton Woods: The Road Ahead," *Business Week*, September 22, 1951, p. 176.

40. *IMF*, I, 297–298 and II, 25–35; "Gutt of the Fund," *Fortune* 37 (April 1948): 113; "IMF Comes to Life," *Business Week*, September 25, 1954, p. 200. Marxist criticisms of the fund include Michael Hudson, *Super Imperialism*; and Teresa Hayter, *Aid as Imperialism*, pp. 33–46. For an introduction to the structuralist critique, consult Albert

O. Hirschman, ed., *Latin American Issues.*

41. Mikesell, *Economic Policy*, pp. 171–191; Gardner Patterson, *Survey of United States International Finance, 1949*, pp. 114–116, 128–134; Mikesell, *Foreign Exchange in the Postwar World*, pp. 138–151.

42. Tew, *International Monetary Cooperation*, pp. 175–180; Robert Triffin, *The World Money Maze*, pp. 179–200; Yeager, *International Monetary Relations*, pp. 378–384; *IMF*, I, 234–242.

43. Triffin, *Money Maze*, p. 195.

44. Bank for International Settlements (BIS), *Twentieth Annual Report*, p. 260; Randall Hinshaw, *Toward European Convertibility*, pp. 12–22.

45. Scammell, *International Monetary Policy*, pp. 288–311; U.S., Commission on Foreign Economic Policy, *Report to the President and the Congress*, pp. 72–75; *IMF*, I, 353–355; *Wall Street Journal*, January 25, 1954; U.S., Department of State, *Bulletin*, April 19, 1954, pp. 602–607.

46. Peter G. Peterson, *The United States in the Changing World Economy*, II, 3–8; Per Jacobsson, "Toward More Stable Money," *Foreign Affairs* 37 (April 1959): 378–393.

47. *New York Times*, December 28–29, 1958.

48. U.S., House of Representatives, *Bretton Woods Agreements Act, Hearings before Subcommittee No. 1 of the Committee on Banking and Currency*, 86th Cong., 1st sess., March 3–6, 1959, pp. 42–43.

49. Scammell, *International Monetary Policy*, pp. 397–402; Richard N. Cooper, *The Economics of Interdependence*, pp. 43–45; *IMF*, II, 381–467.

50. Edwin L. Dale, "Global Success Story: The World Fund," *New York Times Magazine*, September 7, 1958, p. 16; "The Influential Fund," *Fortune* 60 (August 1959): 57.

51. *Time*, January 12, 1959, p. 23; Jacobsson, "Stable Money," pp. 378–393, quotation on p. 378. Other favorable commentary includes *Business Week*, January 3, 1959, pp. 17, 68; *U.S. News and World Report*, January 9, 1959, p. 36; "An Act of Bravery?" *The Economist*, January 3, 1959, p. 13; BIS, *Twenty-Ninth Annual Report*, pp. 241–243.

52. Raymond Frech Mikesell, "The Emergence of the World Bank as a Development Institution," in *Bretton Woods Revisited*, by A. L. K. Acheson, J. F. Chant, and M. F. J. Prachowny, pp. 70–84. On the World Bank's coordinating role, see John White, *Pledged to Development*, pp. 171–180.

53. James Morris, *The Road to Huddersfield*, pp. 54–61; Mason and Asher, *World Bank*, pp. 96–98, 148.

54. Mikesell, "Emergence of the World Bank," pp. 70–84, quotation on pp. 819–820; Raymond Frech Mikesell, *The Economics of Foreign Aid*, pp. 256–282.

55. Mason and Asher, *World Bank*, pp. 380–419. On the origins of IDA, see James H. Weaver, *The International Development Association*, pp. 1–224; and Baldwin, *Economic Development*, pp. 219–236.

56. Mason and Asher, *World Bank*, pp. 350–359.

9. "Death of Bretton Woods"

1. On the importance of a "dominant currency," consult Robert Triffin, "International Monetary Collapse and Reconstruction in April 1972," *Journal of International Economics* 2 (September 1972): 375–400; Susan Strange, *Sterling and British Policy*, pp. 1–73.

2. Peter G. Peterson, *The United States in the Changing World Economy*, II, 3–6; U.S., President,

International Economic Report of the President, p. 92.

3. Peterson, *Changing World Economy*, II, 3–10; U.S., President, *International Economic Report*, p. 65.

4. Peterson, *Changing World Economy*, II, 3.

5. Ibid., II, 10; U.S., President, *International Economic Report*, pp. 1–2. Richard N. Cooper develops the implications of this trend in his *The Economics of Interdependence*.

6. Peterson, *Changing World Economy*, II, 43–45; Cooper, *Economics of Interdependence*, pp. 112–173; U.S., Senate, Committee on Finance, *Implications of Multinational Firms for World Trade and Investment and for U.S. Trade and Labor*, pp. 453–549.

7. An excellent analysis of the "inconsistent trinity" was presented by economist Henry C. Wallich, "The Monetary Crisis of 1971—the Lessons to be Learned," to the 1972 lecture meeting of the Per Jacobsson Foundation, September 24, 1972, during the annual meetings of the International Monetary Fund and World Bank Group.

8. Henry C. Wallich, "Government Action," in *The Dollar in Crisis*, ed. Seymour E. Harris, pp. 97–113; Per Jacobsson, "Toward More Stable Money," *Foreign Affairs* 37 (April 1959): 378–393; BIS, *Twenty-Fifth Annual Report*, pp. 28–29. The dollar deficit was discussed in terms of a world dollar shortage in U.S., Commission on Foreign Economic Policy, *Staff Papers*, pp. 6–22.

9. Harris, ed., *Dollar in Crisis*, pp. 1–45, 295–309, quotation on p. 296; BIS, *Forty-Second Annual Report*, pp. 3–33.

10. Harris, ed., *Dollar in Crisis*, pp. 1–45.

11. This and subsequent sections draw heavily on Lawrence B. Krause, *Sequel to Bretton Woods*, pp. 17–31. Also extremely useful is IMF,

Reform of the International Monetary System.

12. Krause, *Bretton Woods*, pp. 17–31.

13. Ibid.; U.S., President, *International Economic Report*, pp. 15–17; U.S., President, *Economic Report of the President, 1972*, pp. 121–122.

14. U.S., President, *International Economic Report*, p. 15–17, quotation on p. 15. On Eisenhower's economic policies, see Harris, ed., *Dollar in Crisis*, p. 5, and Wallich in ibid., pp. 97–113; Herbert Stein, *The Fiscal Revolution in America*, pp. 346–371; BIS, *Thirty-First Annual Report*, p. 181; and Richard M. Nixon, *Six Crises*, pp. 309–311.

15. U.S., President, *International Economic Report*, pp. 15–17; Krause, *Bretton Woods*, pp. 17–31.

16. *IMF*, II, 111–113; Franz Pick, *Pick's Currency Yearbook 1972*, p. 9.

17. Implications of dollar devaluation are considered in Robert Z. Aliber, "The Costs and Benefits of the U.S. Role as a Reserve Currency Country," *The Quarterly Journal of Economics* 77 (August 1964): 442–457; Robert Z. Aliber, *The Future of the Dollar as an International Currency*; and Peter B. Kenen, "The International Position of the Dollar in a Changing World," *International Organization* 23 (Summer 1969): 705–718.

18. Krause, *Bretton Woods*, pp. 29–31; Robert Z. Aliber, *Choices for the Dollar*, pp. 5–14.

19. Krause, *Bretton Woods*, pp. 8–9.

20. Robert Triffin, *Gold and the Dollar Crisis*, pp. 3–20.

21. Robert Triffin, "The International Monetary Position of the United States," in Harris, ed., *Dollar in Crisis*, pp. 223–242.

22. Triffin, *Gold and the Dollar Crisis*, pp. 3–20, quotation on p. 9.

23. Ibid., pp. 60–61.

24. Harris, ed., *Dollar in Crisis*, pp. 1, 295–307.

25. Ibid., pp. 1–45; Robert V. Roosa,

The Dollar and World Liquidity, pp. 3–4; quotations from BIS, Forty-Second Annual Report, p. 17.

26. New York Times, February 5, 1965; Stephen D. Cohen, International Monetary Reform, 1964–1969, pp. 53–60.

27. Aliber, Choices for the Dollar, pp. 31–50. Michael Hudson, Super Imperialism, pp. 208–230, claims that the dollar standard allowed the United States to finance its wars "with other people's money."

28. Susan Strange notes the coincidence of monetary and military considerations in Sterling and British Policy, pp. 17–21. Aliber considers political, economic, and security dimensions in Choices for the Dollar.

29. Lawrence B. Krause discusses the implications of declining monetary sovereignty in an interdependent world in his essay "Private International Finance," in Transnational Relations and World Politics, ed. Robert O. Keohane and Joseph S. Nye, Jr., pp. 173–190. Richard N. Cooper assesses some economic aspects in The Economics of Interdependence, pp. 227–256.

30. The range of monetary plans is presented in Herbert G. Grubel, ed., World Monetary Reform; quotation on p. 330. For Rueff and Heilperin, see ibid., pp. 320–342. Also, note Fritz Machlup, Plans for Reform of the International Monetary System.

31. Milton Friedman, Capitalism and Freedom, pp. 67–71, quotation on p. 71.

32. Triffin, Gold and the Dollar Crisis, pp. 102–120. Triffin faces a critic in Harris, ed., Dollar in Crisis, pp. 223–294. Roosa's comment appears in Grubel, ed., World Monetary Reform, p. 268.

33. Edward M. Bernstein, "Proposed Reforms in the International Monetary System," in World Monetary Reform, ed. Herbert G. Grubel, pp. 187–202; Robert Triffin,

The World Money Maze, pp. 258–272; Edward M. Bernstein, "The International Monetary Fund as a Monetary Authority," pp. 12–13.

34. Harris, ed., Dollar in Crisis, pp. 35, 41, 295–307; Roosa, Dollar and World Liquidity, pp. 3–39; Gottfried Haberler and Thomas D. Willett, U.S. Balance-of-Payments Policies and International Monetary Reform, pp. 11–38.

35. BIS, Forty-Second Annual Report, pp. 5–6.

36. Ibid., pp. 3–27; U.S., President, International Economic Report, pp. 18–25, 82–85.

37. U.S., President, International Economic Report, p. 86; U.S., President, Economic Report of the President, 1973, p. 299.

38. These developments are summarized in BIS, Forty-Second Annual Report, pp. 1–27; Robert A. Mundell, "The Collapse of the Gold Exchange Standard," in U.S., Congress, Joint Economic Committee, Next Steps in International Monetary Reform, Hearings before the Subcommittee on International Exchange and Payments, 90th Cong., 2d sess., September 9, 1968, pp. 38–45; Roosa, Dollar and World Liquidity, pp. 3–39, 215–261; Fred Hirsch, Money International, pp. 219–256.

39. Roosa, Dollar and World Liquidity, pp. 3–39; U.S., Treasury Department, Maintaining the Strength of the United States Dollar in a Strong Free World Economy, pp. 22–23; Robert Z. Aliber, The Management of the Dollar in International Finance, pp. 1–61; quotation from Hirsch, Money International, p. 262; Strange, Sterling and British Policy, p. 278; Stephen D. Cohen, International Monetary Reform, 1964–1969, pp. 28–29.

40. Triffin, Gold and the Dollar Crisis,

pp. 3–14; U.S., Treasury, *Maintaining the Strength*, p. 37.

41. IMF, *Annual Report, 1968*, pp. 83–84; BIS, *Forty-Second Annual Report*, pp. 18–19; *New York Times*, March 19, 1968.

42. Cohen traces the evolution of liquidity negotiations in *International Monetary Reform, 1964–1969*. See also the summary in U.S., Treasury, *Maintaining the Strength*, pp. 39–45. Paul Einzig criticizes excessive, not inadequate, liquidity in "Too Much Aid?—Too Little Discipline?" *Euromoney*, September 1971, pp. 94–96.

43. U.S., Treasury, *Maintaining the Strength*, p. 44.

44. *New York Times*, April 26, 1971.

45. Senate, Committee on Finance, *Implications of Multinational Firms*, pp. 532–533.

46. BIS, *Thirty-Eighth Annual Report*, pp. 18–19; *Business Week*, November 25, 1967, pp. 31–38; Henry Brandon, *In the Red*, pp. 1–114.

47. Quotation from *New York Times*, November 22, 1967; *Wall Street Journal*, April 4, 1968. Lyndon B. Johnson suggests in his *The Vantage Point*, p. 426, that the likelihood of obtaining a tax increase, which he considered vital to the "stability of the dollar and the economic health of the nation and the world," would be "close to zero" if he were a presidential candidate.

48. BIS, *Forty-Second Annual Report*, pp. 24–27; IMF, *1971 Annual Report*, pp. 88–102; U.S., President, *Economic Report of the President, 1972*, pp. 143–164.

49. The Council of Economic Advisers displayed enthusiasm for this approach. See U.S., President, *Economic Report of the President, 1971*, pp. 151–152. Economic support appears in Gottfried Haberler and Thomas D. Willett, *A Strategy for U.S. Balance of Payments Policy*; and Lawrence B. Krause, "A Passive Balance-of-Payments Strategy for the United States," *Brookings Papers on Economic Activity*, no. 3 (1970), p. 339. See also *New York Times*, February 16, 1971; and Fred Hirsch, "The Dollar: Unbenign Neglect," *The Economist*, August 5, 1972, pp. 62–63.

50. U.S., Congress, Joint Economic Committee, *The Balance-of-Payments Mess*, Hearings before the Subcommittee on International Exchange and Payments, 92d Cong., 1st sess., June 16–23, 1971, p. 412.

51. Hirsch, "Unbenign Neglect," pp. 62–63; Joint Economic Committee, *Balance-of-Payments Mess*, pp. 409–411; *New York Times*, April 28 and May 19, 1971; BIS, *Forty-First Annual Report*, p. 194. Treasury Secretary Connally and the Federal Reserve opposed "benign neglect" (*New York Times*, April 28 and May 19, 1971).

52. BIS, *Forty-Second Annual Report*, pp. 25–26; *New York Times*, May 19, 1971.

53. Joint Economic Committee, *Balance-of-Payments Mess*, pp. 214–242.

54. Hirsch, "Unbenign Neglect," pp. 62–63; *New York Times*, May 19, 1971; BIS, *Forty-Second Annual Report*, p. 26; U.S., President, *Economic Report of the President, 1972*, p. 148. However, former National Security Council staff economist C. Fred Bergsten questions whether creditors were demanding to redeem gold in "The New Economics and U.S. Foreign Policy," *Foreign Affairs* 50 (January 1972): 201. Henry Brandon shows how Britain helped to bring down the Bretton Woods system it helped create by activating a currency swap facility with the New York Federal Reserve Bank that enabled London to obtain $750

million on August 13, 1971—a sum that helped cushion Britain's official dollar holdings against devaluation. See Brandon, *The Retreat of American Power*, pp. 224–226.

55. U.S., Treasury, *1972 Report of the Secretary of the Treasury*, pp. 46–48.

56. Ibid., pp. 44–50; U.S., President, *Economic Report of the President, 1972*, pp. 142–164; U.S., National Advisory Council on International Monetary and Financial Policies, *Annual Report, July 1, 1971–June 30, 1972*, pp. 3–5.

57. U.S., Secretary of State, *United States Foreign Policy in 1971*, pp. 430–433.

58. *New York Times*, April 28, 1971; *Wall Street Journal*, August 27, 1971; William F. Diebold, Jr., *The United States and the Industrial World*, p. 431.

59. Diebold, *Industrial World*, pp. 423–445; Bergsten, "New Economics and U.S. Foreign Policy," pp. 200–222; *New York Times*, September 5, 1971.

60. Diebold, *Industrial World*, pp. 423–445; U.S., Treasury, *1972 Annual Report of the Secretary of the Treasury*, p. 431.

61. *New York Times*, August 18, 1971; *The Economist*, August 21, 1971, p. 60; *New York Times*, October 30, 1971; *Business Week*, August 28, 1971, p. 64.

62. *New York Times*, September 22, 1971.

63. On the World Bank's expanding role as a development agency, read Escott Reid, "McNamara's World Bank," *Foreign Affairs* 51 (July 1973): 794–810; Raymond F. Mikesell, "The Emergence of the World Bank as a Development Institution," in *Bretton Woods Revisited*, by A. L. K. Acheson, J. F. Chant, and M. F. J. Prachowny, pp. 70–84.

64. John F. Kennedy, *Public Papers of the Presidents of the United States: Containing the Public Messages, Speeches, and Statements of the President, January 20 to December 31, 1961*, pp. 203–205; Robert A. Packenham, *Liberal America and the Third World*, p. 60; Walt Whitman Rostow, *The Diffusion of Power*, pp. 86–93, 185–188. On American aid, see Joan M. Nelson, *Aid, Influence and Foreign Policy*, pp. 1–18.

65. Rostow, *Diffusion of Power*, p. 403. Also, Robert Asher, *Development Assistance in the Seventies*, pp. 11–68.

66. Edward S. Mason and Robert E. Asher, *The World Bank since Bretton Woods*, pp. 96–101.

67. Robert S. McNamara, *One Hundred Countries, Two Billion People*, pp. 7–28; Martin Shivnan, "The Bank Group Meeting," *Finance and Development* 10 (December 1973): 34–35.

68. McNamara, *One Hundred Countries*, pp. 7–28.

69. Mason and Asher, *World Bank*, pp. 457–487, 722–755; "World Banking McNamara-Style," *Business Week*, November 27, 1969, pp. 96–97; "Why McNamara's Aid Policy is Under Fire," *Business Week*, May 6, 1972, p. 88.

70. Reid, "McNamara's World Bank."

71. Mason and Asher, *World Bank*, pp. 723–755.

10. Epilogue

1. Robert A. Divine, ed., *Causes and Consequences of World War II*, provides a brief historiographical survey.

2. Important conservative revisionist accounts include George N. Crocker, *Roosevelt's Road to Russia*; and J. Anthony Kubek,

How the Far East Was Lost. On Harry Dexter White, see Kubek's comments in U.S., Senate, Committee on the Judiciary, *Morgenthau Diary (Germany)*, I, 1–81.

3. Divine, ed., *Causes and Consequences*, pp. 3–44. Revisionists differ among themselves nearly as much as they do with orthodox interpreters. Radical accounts emphasizing economic factors include Lloyd C. Gardner, *Economic Aspects of New Deal Diplomacy*; Michael Hudson, *Super Imperialism*; Gabriel Kolko, *The Politics of War*; and William Appleman Williams, *The Tragedy of American Diplomacy*. Critiques include Benjamin J. Cohen, "On United States 'Imperialism,' " in *Modern Political Economy*, ed. James H. Weaver, pp. 338–347; Alfred E. Eckes, Jr., "Open Door Expansionism Reconsidered: The World War II Experience," *Journal of American History* 59 (March 1973): 909–924; and Robert W. Tucker, *The Radical Left and American Foreign Policy*. A more general criticism of radical historians and their use of sources is Robert James Maddox, *The New Left and the Origins of the Cold War*.

4. John L. Gaddis, *The United States and the Origins of the Cold War, 1941–1947*, pp. 353–361.

5. Eckes, "Open Door Expansionism," pp. 909–924.

6. Fred Hirsch, "The Development and Functioning of the Postwar International Monetary System," *Finance and Development* 9 (June 1972): 48–52, quotation on p. 48.

7. A. Eugene Staley, *World Economy in Transition*, pp. 315–333, quotation on p. 316; Charles K. Leith, J. W. Furness, and Cleona Lewis, *World Minerals and World Peace*, p. 46.

8. Hirsch, "Development and Functioning," pp. 48–52.

9. Richard N. Gardner, *Sterling-Dollar Diplomacy*, p. xvii; *London Times*, March 21, 1972; Eliot Janeway, *The Economics of Crisis*, pp. 200–201.

10. Hirsch, "Development and Functioning," pp. 48–52; Alvin Hansen, *The Dollar and the International Monetary System*, p. 177.

11. See chapter 3, p. 72; George Halm, *International Monetary Cooperation*, p. 121.

12. Peter B. Kenen, "The International Position of the Dollar in a Changing World," *International Organization* 23 (Summer 1969): 705–718.

13. Edward M. Bernstein recalls discussion of wider margins in Randall Hinshaw, ed., *The Economics of International Adjustment*, pp. 168–170.

14. Hirsch, "Development and Functioning," pp. 48–52.

15. Paul Einzig discusses the "imperialism of inflation" in *The Destiny of the Dollar*, pp. 78–88. Otmar Emminger assesses the impact of inflation in his 1973 Per Jacobsson lecture, *IMF Survey*, June 25, 1973, p. 177; and comments appear in *IMF Survey*, July 9, 1973, p. 195. Randall Hinshaw has edited a round table on *Inflation as a Global Problem*. The monetarist emphasis on American price stability as the key to satisfactory functioning of the Bretton Woods system appears in Harry G. Johnson, "Political Economy Aspects of International Monetary Reform," *Journal of International Economics* 2 (September 1972): 412–413; and in his *Inflation and the Monetarist Controversy*, pp. 75–93.

16. U.S., President, *International Economic Report of the President*, p. 1. Fritz Machlup disputes the view that fixed exchange rates promoted trade in "Nationalism, Provincialism, Fixed Exchange

Rates and Monetary Union," in *Convertibility, Multilateralism and* *Freedom*, ed. Wolfgang Schmitz, pp. 267–269.

.

Bibliography

Manuscript Collections

Agriculture Department. National Archives, Record Group 16.
Winthrop Aldrich Papers. Harvard Graduate School of Public Administration, Boston, Massachusetts.
Leonard Ayres Papers. Library of Congress.
Bernard Baruch Papers. Firestone Library, Princeton, New Jersey.
John W. Bricker Papers. Ohio Historical Society, Columbus, Ohio.
Commerce Department. National Archives, Record Group 40.
Tom Connally Papers. Library of Congress.
Oscar Cox Papers. Roosevelt Library, Hyde Park, New York.
Charles Dewey Papers. Chicago Historical Society, Chicago, Illinois.
Federal Reserve Papers. Board of Governors of the Federal Reserve System.
Herbert Gaston Papers. Roosevelt Library, Hyde Park, New York.
Emanuel Alexandrovich Goldenweiser Papers. Library of Congress.
House Banking and Currency Committee. National Archives, Record Group 233.
Cordell Hull Papers. Library of Congress.
Jesse Jones Papers. Library of Congress.
Edwin Kemmerer Papers. Firestone Library, Princeton, New Jersey.
Breckinridge Long Papers. Library of Congress.
Ansel Luxford Papers. International Bank Law Library, International Bank for Reconstruction and Development.
Frank McNaughton Papers. Truman Library, Independence, Missouri.
Henry Morgenthau, Jr., Papers. Roosevelt Library, Hyde Park, New York.
Leo Pasvolsky Office Files. State Department Records, National Archives, Record Group 59.
Franklin D. Roosevelt Papers. Roosevelt Library, Hyde Park, New York.
Senate Banking and Currency Committee. National Archives, Record Group 46.
Frederick C. Smith Papers. Ohio Historical Society, Columbus, Ohio.
Brent Spence Papers. University of Kentucky, Lexington, Kentucky.
State Department Conference Files. State Department.
State Department Records. National Archives, Record Group 59.
Treasury Department. National Archives, Record Group 56.
Harry S. Truman Papers. Truman Library, Independence, Missouri.

Bibliography

Robert Wagner Papers. Georgetown University, Washington, D.C.
Harry Dexter White Papers. Firestone Library, Princeton, New Jersey.

Dissertations

Birnbaum, Philip. "Economic Nationalism and International Monetary Cooperation." Ph.D. dissertation, Harvard University, 1960.

Eckes, Alfred E. "Bretton Woods: America's New Deal for an Open World." Ph.D. dissertation, University of Texas, 1969.

Leffler, Melvyn Paul. "The Struggle for Stability: American Policy Toward France, 1921–1933." Ph.D. dissertation, Ohio State University, 1972.

Lehman, Ernest D. "The Attitudes of Selected Business Groups toward American Foreign Economic Policy, 1945–1955." Ph.D. dissertation, University of Chicago, 1961.

Mansfield, Lawrence F. "The Origins of the International Monetary Fund." Ph.D. dissertation, University of North Carolina, 1960.

Oliver, Robert W. "The Origins of the International Bank for Reconstruction and Development." Ph.D. dissertation, Princeton University, 1957.

Peacock, Leslie Clark. "Policies and Operations of the International Monetary Fund: 1947–1956." Ph.D. dissertation, University of Texas, 1958.

Pritchard, Ross Joseph. "Will Clayton: A Study of Business-Statesmanship in the Formulation of United States Economic Foreign Policy." Ph.D. dissertation, Fletcher School of Law and Diplomacy, 1955.

Official Documents

Bank for International Settlements. *Annual Report*. Basle: Bank for International Settlements, 1945–1972.

Documents on American Foreign Relations. Vols. I–XI (1938–1949). Boston and Princeton: World Peace Foundation, 1939–1950.

Gray, Gordon. *Report to the President on Foreign Economic Policies*. Washington: Government Printing Office, 1950.

Horsefield, J. Keith. *The International Monetary Fund: Twenty Years of International Monetary Cooperation, 1945–1965*. 3 vols. Washington: International Monetary Fund, 1969.

International Bank for Reconstruction and Development. *Annual Report of the Board of Governors, Proceedings*. Washington: International Bank for Reconstruction and Development, 1946–1972.

——. *The International Bank for Reconstruction and Development, 1946–1953*. Baltimore: Johns Hopkins University Press, 1954.

——. *Policies and Operations: The World Bank, IDA, and IFC*. Washington: World Bank Group, 1971.

——. *World Bank Operations*. Baltimore: Johns Hopkins University Press, 1972.

International Monetary Fund. *Annual Report*. Washington: International Monetary Fund, 1946–1972.

——. *Finance and Development*. Washington: International Monetary Fund and International Bank for Reconstruction and Development, 1969–1973.

——. *Reform of the International Monetary System: A Report by the Executive Directors to the Board of Governors*. Washington: International Monetary Fund, 1972.

———. *Summary Proceedings*. Washington: International Monetary Fund, 1946–1972.

Kennedy, John F. *Public Papers of the Presidents of the United States: Containing the Public Messages, Speeches, and Statements of the President, January 20 to December 31, 1961*. Washington: Government Printing Office, 1962.

League of Nations. Economic, Financial and Transit Department. *Commercial Policy in the Interwar Period*. Geneva: League of Nations, 1942.

———. ———. *The Course and Control of Inflation*. Geneva: League of Nations, 1946.

———. ———. *International Currency Experience*. Geneva: League of Nations, 1944.

———. Economic Intelligence Service. *The Network of World Trade*. Geneva: League of Nations, 1942.

———. Report of the Delegation on Economic Depressions. *Economic Stability in the Post-War World*. Geneva: League of Nations, 1945.

———. ———. *The Transition from War to Peace Economy*. Geneva: League of Nations, 1943.

Notter, Harley. *Postwar Foreign Policy Preparation, 1939–1945*. Washington: Government Printing Office, 1949.

Peterson, Peter G. *The United States in the Changing World Economy*. 2 vols. Washington: Government Printing Office, 1971.

U.S. Commission on Foreign Economic Policy. *Report to the President and the Congress*. Washington: Government Printing Office, 1954.

———. *Staff Papers*. Washington: Government Printing Office, 1954.

U.S. Congress. *Congressional Record*. 78th–79th Cong. (1943–1946).

———. Joint Economic Committee. *The Balance-of-Payments Mess, Hearings before the Subcommittee on International Exchange and Payments*. 92d Cong., 1st sess., June 16–23, 1971.

———. ———. *Next Steps in International Monetary Reform, Hearings before the Subcommittee on International Exchange and Payments*. 90th Cong., 2d sess., September 9, 1968.

U.S. Department of Commerce. Bureau of Foreign and Domestic Commerce. *The United States in the World Economy*. Washington: Government Printing Office, 1943.

U.S. Department of State. *Bulletin*. Vols. 1–66 (1939–1972).

———. *Foreign Relations of the United States*. Annual volumes 1941–1947. Washington: Government Printing Office, 1958–1971.

———. *Proceedings and Documents of the United Nations Monetary and Financial Conference, Bretton Woods, New Hampshire, July 1–22, 1944*. 2 vols. Washington: Government Printing Office, 1948.

———. Secretary of State. *United States Foreign Policy in 1971*. Washington: Government Printing Office, 1972.

U.S. House of Representatives. Committee on Banking and Currency. *Anglo-American Financial Agreement, Hearings on H.J. Res. 311 and S.J. Res. 138*. 79th Cong., 2d sess., May 14–June 7, 1946.

———. ———. *Bretton Woods Agreements Act, Hearings before Subcommittee No. 1 of the Committee on Banking and Currency*. 86th Cong., 1st sess., March 3–6, 1959.

———. ———. *Bretton Woods Agreements Act, Hearings on H.R. 2211*. 2 vols. 79th Cong., 1st sess., March 7–April 11, 1945.

———. ———. *Participation of United States in the International Monetary Fund*

Bibliography

and the International Bank for Reconstruction and Development. Rept. 629. 79th Cong., 1st sess. Washington: Government Printing Office, 1945.

——. Committee on Foreign Affairs. Reconstruction Fund in Joint Account with Foreign Governments for Rehabilitation, Stabilization of Currencies, and Reconstruction, Hearings on H.J. Res. 226. 78th Cong., 2d sess., April 25–May 17, 1944.

U.S. National Advisory Council on International Monetary and Financial Policies. Annual Report. Washington: Government Printing Office, 1946–1972.

U.S. President. Council of Economic Advisers. The Economic Situation at Midyear 1948. Washington: Government Printing Office, 1948.

——. ——. Economic Report of the President. Washington: Government Printing Office, 1947–1973.

——. ——. International Economic Report of the President. Washington: Government Printing Office, March 1973.

U.S. Senate. Banking and Currency Committee. Anglo-American Financial Agreement, Hearings on S.J. Res. 138. 79th Cong., 2d sess., March 5–20, 1946.

——. ——. Bretton Woods Agreements Act, Hearings on H.R. 3314. 79th Cong., 1st sess., June 12–28, 1945.

——. Committee on Finance. Implications of Multinational Firms for World Trade and Investment and for U.S. Trade and Labor. Washington: Government Printing Office, February, 1973.

——. Committee on the Judiciary. Interlocking Subversion in Government Departments (The Harry Dexter White Papers), Hearings before the Subcommittee to Investigate the Administration of the Internal Security Act and Other Internal Security Laws. 84th Cong., 1st sess. 30 pts. August 30, 1955.

——. ——. Morgenthau Diary (China). 2 vols. Washington: Government Printing Office, 1965.

——. ——. Morgenthau Diary (Germany). 2 vols. Washington: Government Printing Office, 1967.

——. Participation of the United States in the International Monetary Fund and the International Bank for Reconstruction and Development, Rept. 452. 79th Cong., 1st sess. 2 pts. Washington: Government Printing Office, 1945.

U.S. Treasury Department. Annual Report of the Secretary of the Treasury. Washington: Government Printing Office, 1939–1972.

——. Maintaining the Strength of the United States Dollar in a Strong Free World Economy. Washington: Government Printing Office, January, 1968.

Books and Articles

Abrahams, Paul P. "American Bankers and the Economic Tactics of Peace: 1919." Journal of American History 56 (December 1969): 572–583.

Acheson, A. L. K.; Chant, J. F.; and Prachowny, M. F. J. Bretton Woods Revisited. Toronto: University of Toronto Press, 1972.

Acheson, Dean. Present at the Creation: My Years in the State Department. New York: Norton, 1969.

——. Sketches from Life of Men I Have Known. New York: Harper, 1961.

Adelson, Dorothy. "World Agreement at Bretton Woods." Pan American, October 15, 1944, pp. 35–39.

Aldcroft, Derek H. The Inter-War Economy: Britain, 1919–1939. New York: Columbia University Press, 1970.

Aldrich, Winthrop W. "Some Aspects of American Foreign Economic Policy." *Vital Speeches*, October 15, 1944, pp. 20–26.

Aliber, Robert Z. *Choices for the Dollar: Costs and Benefits of Possible Approaches to the Balance-of-Payments Problem*. Washington: National Planning Association, 1969.

———. "The Costs and Benefits of the U.S. Role as a Reserve Currency Country." *Quarterly Journal of Economics* 77 (August 1964): 442–457.

———. *The Future of the Dollar as an International Currency*. New York: Praeger, 1966.

———. *The International Money Game*. New York: Basic Books, 1973.

———. *The Management of the Dollar in International Finance*. Princeton Studies in International Finance, no. 13. Princeton: Department of Economics, Princeton University, 1964.

Almond, Gabriel. *The American People and Foreign Policy*. New York: Harcourt, Brace, 1950.

Anderson, Benjamin. *Economics and the Public Welfare*. New York: Van Nostrand, 1949.

———. "Free Exchange Stabilization." *Vital Speeches*, June 1, 1943, pp. 487–496.

Anderson, John, and Morse, Stearns. *The Book of the White Mountains*. New York: Minton, Balch & Company, 1930.

Arkes, Hadley. *Bureaucracy, the Marshall Plan, and the National Interest*. Princeton: Princeton University Press, 1972.

Arndt, H. W. *The Economic Lessons of the Nineteen-Thirties*. London: Oxford University Press, 1944.

Asher, Robert. *Development Assistance in the Seventies: Alternatives for the United States*. Washington: Brookings Institution, 1970.

———; Kotschnig, Walter M.; and Brown, William Adams, Jr. *United Nations and Economic and Social Cooperation*. Washington: Brookings Institution, 1957.

———; Kotschnig, Walter M.; Brown, William Adams, Jr.; Green, James Frederick; Sady, Emil J.; and others. *The United Nations and Promotion of the General Welfare*. Washington: Brookings Institution, 1957.

Ashworth, William. *A Short History of the International Economy since 1850*. 2d ed. London: Longmans, 1962.

Auboin, Roger. *The Bank for International Settlements, 1930–1955*. Essays in International Finance, no. 22. Princeton: Department of Economics, Princeton University, 1955.

Bailey, Stephen Kemp. *Congress Makes a Law*. New York: Columbia University Press, 1950.

Baker, Ray Stannard. *Woodrow Wilson and the World Settlement*. 3 vols. Garden City, N.Y.: Doubleday, Page, 1922.

Baldwin, David A. *Economic Development and American Foreign Policy, 1943–1962*. Chicago: University of Chicago Press, 1966.

———. "The International Bank in Political Perspective." *World Politics* 18 (October 1965): 68–81.

Balogh, Thomas, and Schumacher, E. F. "An International Monetary Fund." *Oxford Institute of Statistics Bulletin*, April 29, 1944, pp. 81–93.

Basch, Antonin. "International Bank for Reconstruction and Development, 1944–1949: A Review." *International Conciliation* 455 (November 1949): 791–827.

Behrman, Jack N. "Political Factors in U.S. International Financial Cooperation, 1945–1950." *American Political Science Review* 47 (June 1953): 431–460.

Bibliography

Bellush, Bernard. *He Walked Alone: A Biography of John Gilbert Winant*. The Hague: Mouton, 1968.

Bentley, Elizabeth. *Out of Bondage: The Story of Elizabeth Bentley*. New York: Devin-Adair, 1951.

Berger, Henry W. "Senator Robert A. Taft Dissents from Military Escalation." In *Cold War Critics*, edited by Thomas G. Paterson, pp. 167–204. Chicago: Quadrangle Books, 1971.

Bergsten, C. Fred. "The New Economics and U.S. Foreign Policy." *Foreign Affairs* 50 (January 1972): 199–222.

————. *Reforming the Dollar: An International Monetary Policy for the United States*. New York: Council on Foreign Relations, 1972.

Berle, Beatrice Bishop, and Jacobs, Travis Beal. *Navigating the Rapids 1918–1971: From the Papers of Adolf A. Berle*. New York: Harcourt Brace Jovanovich, 1973.

Berman, Daniel M. *In Congress Assembled: The Legislative Process in National Government*. New York: Macmillan, 1964.

Bernstein, Edward M. "The International Monetary Fund as a Monetary Authority." Unpublished paper. Washington: E M B Ltd., January 15, 1970.

————. "A Practical International Monetary Policy." *American Economic Review* 34 (December 1944): 840–847.

Beyen, J. W. *Money in a Maelstrom*. New York: Macmillan, 1949.

Bittermann, Henry J. "Negotiation of the Articles of Agreement of the International Bank for Reconstruction and Development." *International Lawyer* 5 (January 1971): 59–88.

Black, Eugene. *The Diplomacy of Economic Development*. Cambridge: Harvard University Press, 1960.

Bloomfield, Arthur I. *Monetary Policy under the International Gold Standard, 1880–1914*. New York: Federal Reserve Bank of New York, 1959.

————. "Operations of the American Exchange Stabilization Fund." *The Review of Economic Statistics* 26 (May 1944): 69–87.

————. *Short-Term Capital Movements under the Pre-1914 Gold Standard*. Princeton Studies in International Finance, no. 11. Princeton: Department of Economics, Princeton University, 1963.

Blum, John Morton. *From the Morgenthau Diaries: Years of Crisis, 1928–1938*. Boston: Houghton Mifflin, 1959.

————. *From the Morgenthau Diaries: Years of Urgency, 1938–1941*. Boston: Houghton Mifflin, 1965.

————. *From the Morgenthau Diaries: Years of War, 1941–1945*. Boston: Houghton Mifflin, 1967.

————, ed. *The Price of Vision: The Diary of Henry A. Wallace, 1942–1946*. Boston: Houghton Mifflin, 1973.

Boyle, Andrew. *Montagu Norman*. New York: Weybright and Talley, 1967.

Brandon, Henry. *In the Red: The Struggle for Sterling, 1964–1966*. Boston: Houghton Mifflin, 1967.

————. *The Retreat of American Power*. New York: Dell, 1972.

Brown, Edward E. "The International Monetary Fund." *Journal of Business* 17 (October 1944): 199–208.

Brown, William Adams, Jr. "Gold: Master or Servant?" *Foreign Affairs* 19 (July 1941): 828–841.

————. *The International Gold Standard Reinterpreted, 1914–1934*. 2 vols. New York: National Bureau of Economic Research, 1940.

————. *The United States and the Restoration of World Trade.* Washington: Brookings Institution, 1950.

————, and Opie, Redvers. *American Foreign Assistance.* Washington: Brookings Institution, 1953.

Buchanan, Norman S., and Lutz, Friedrich A. *Rebuilding the World Economy.* New York: Twentieth Century Fund, 1947.

Burns, James MacGregor. *Roosevelt: The Lion and the Fox.* New York: Harcourt, Brace, 1956.

————. *Roosevelt: The Soldier of Freedom.* New York: Harcourt Brace Jovanovich, 1970.

Burt, F. Allen. *The Story of Mount Washington.* Hanover, N.H.: Dartmouth Publications, 1960.

Cairncross, Alec. *The International Bank for Reconstruction and Development.* Essays in International Finance, no. 33. Princeton: Department of Economics and Sociology, Princeton University, 1959.

Calleo, David P., and Rowland, Benjamin M. *America and the World Political Economy.* Bloomington: Indiana University Press, 1973.

Cantril, Hadley, and Strunk, Mildred. *Public Opinion, 1935–1946.* Princeton: Princeton University Press, 1951.

Cassel, Gustav. *The Downfall of the Gold Standard.* London: Clarendon Press, 1936.

Chalmers, Eric. *International Interest Rate War.* London: St. Martin's Press, 1972.

Chamber of Commerce of the United States. Finance Department. *World Currency Stabilization Proposals.* Washington: Chamber of Commerce, 1944.

Chambers, Whittaker. *Witness.* New York: Random House, 1952.

Chandler, Lester. *American Monetary Policy, 1928–1941.* New York: Harper and Row, 1971.

————. *Benjamin Strong: A Central Banker.* Washington: Brookings Institution, 1958.

————. *Inflation in the United States, 1940–1948.* New York: Harper, 1951.

Clarke, Stephen V. O. *Central Bank Cooperation, 1924–31.* New York: Federal Reserve Bank of New York, 1967.

Cohen, Benjamin J. *The Future of Sterling as an International Currency.* London: Macmillan Press, 1971.

————. "On United States 'Imperialism.' " In *Modern Political Economy: Radical and Orthodox Views on Crucial Issues,* edited by James H. Weaver, pp. 338–347. Boston: Allyn and Bacon, 1973.

Cohen, Stephen D. *International Monetary Reform, 1964–1969.* New York: Praeger, 1970.

Cole, Charles Woolsey. "International Economic Interdependence." *International Conciliation* 369 (April 1941): 240–245.

Cole, George Douglas Howard. *Great Britain in the Post-War World.* London: V. Gollancz, 1942.

Commission of Inquiry into National Policy in International Economic Relations. *International Economic Relations.* Minneapolis: University of Minnesota Press, 1935.

Condliffe, John B. *Agenda for a Postwar World.* New York: Norton, 1942.

————. *The Commerce of Nations.* New York: Norton, 1950.

————. *The Reconstruction of World Trade.* New York: Norton, 1941.

Congress of Industrial Organizations. *5,000,000 Jobs in World Trade: The Promise of Bretton Woods.* Washington: CIO, 1945.

Bibliography

Cooper, Richard N. *The Economics of Interdependence: Economic Policy in the Atlantic Community.* New York: McGraw-Hill, 1968.

Costigliola, Frank. "The Other Side of Isolationism: The Establishment of the First World Bank, 1929–1930." *Journal of American History* 59 (December 1972): 602–620.

Council on Foreign Relations. "Economic War Aims: General Considerations; the Position as of April 1, 1941." In *Studies of American Interests in the War and the Peace,* No. E-B 32. New York: Council on Foreign Relations, April 17, 1941.

———. "Economic War Aims: Main Lines of Approach: Preliminary Statement." In *Studies of American Interests in the War and the Peace,* No. E-B 36. New York: Council on Foreign Relations, June 22, 1941.

———. *The Smithsonian Agreement and Its Aftermath: Several Views.* New York: Council on Foreign Relations, 1972.

Crocker, George N. *Roosevelt's Road to Russia.* Chicago: H. Regnery Co., 1959.

Curzon, Gerard. *Multilateral Commercial Diplomacy.* New York: Praeger, 1966.

Dale, Edwin L. "Global Success Story: The World Fund." *New York Times Magazine,* September 7, 1958, p. 16.

Dalton, Hugh. *High Tide and After: Memoirs, 1945–1960.* London: Muller, 1962.

Day, A. C. L. *Outline of Monetary Economics.* Oxford: Clarendon Press, 1957.

DeConde, Alexander, ed. *Isolation and Security: Ideas and Interests in Twentieth-Century American Foreign Policy.* Durham, N.C.: Duke University Press, 1957.

Dennett, Raymond, and Johnson, Joseph E., eds. *Negotiating with the Russians.* Boston: World Peace Foundation, 1951.

De Toledano, Ralph. *J. Edgar Hoover.* New Rochelle, N.Y.: Arlington House, 1973.

Dewey, Charles S. *As I Recall It.* Washington: Williams and Heintz Lithograph, 1957.

Diamond, William. *The Economic Thought of Woodrow Wilson.* Baltimore: Johns Hopkins University Press, 1943.

Diebold, William F., Jr. *Trade and Payments in Western Europe.* New York: Harper, 1952.

———. *The United States and the Industrial World.* New York: Praeger, 1972.

Divine, Robert A. *Roosevelt and World War II.* Baltimore: Johns Hopkins University Press, 1969.

———. *Second Chance: The Triumph of Internationalism in America during World War II.* New York: Atheneum, 1967.

———, ed. *Causes and Consequences of World War II.* Chicago: Quadrangle Books, 1969.

Dobney, Frederick J., ed. *Selected Papers of Will Clayton.* Baltimore: Johns Hopkins University Press, 1971.

Drury, Allen. *A Senate Journal, 1943–1945.* New York: McGraw-Hill, 1963.

Dulles, Eleanor Lansing. *The Bank for International Settlements at Work.* New York: Macmillan, 1932.

Eccles, Marriner. *Beckoning Frontiers: Public and Personal Recollections.* New York: Knopf, 1951.

Eckes, Alfred E., Jr. "Open Door Expansionism Reconsidered: The World War II Experience." *Journal of American History* 59 (March 1973): 909–924.

Edmiston, Henry. "Post-War International Currency Stabilization." *Arkansas Banker* 27 (October 1943): 19–22.

Einzig, Paul. *The Destiny of the Dollar.* London: Macmillan & Co., 1972.

———. "Too Much Aid?—Too Little Discipline?" *Euromoney,* September 1971, pp. 94–96.

Bibliography

Ellsworth, Paul T. *The International Economy*. 4th ed. New York: Macmillan, 1969.

Everest, Allan Seymour. *Morgenthau, the New Deal, and Silver*. New York: King's Crown Press, 1950.

Falk, Joy Hume. *The Story of Bretton Woods*. Washington: National League of Women Voters, April, 1945.

Feis, Herbert. *The Changing Pattern of International Economic Affairs*. New York: Harper, 1940.

————. *Diplomacy of the Dollar*. Baltimore: Johns Hopkins University Press, 1950.

————. *1933: Characters in Crisis*. Boston: Little, Brown, 1966.

————. *Sinews of Peace*. New York: Harper, 1944.

Flynn, John T. *The Roosevelt Myth*. New York: Devin-Adair Co., 1938.

Fraser, Leon. "The International Bank and Its Future." *Foreign Affairs* 54 (April 1936): 453–464.

Friedman, Milton. *Capitalism and Freedom*. Chicago: University of Chicago Press, 1969.

Gaddis, John L. *The United States and the Origins of the Cold War, 1941–1947*. New York: Columbia University Press, 1972.

Gaer, Joseph. *Bretton Woods Is No Mystery*. New York: CIO Political Action Committee, 1945.

Gantenbein, James W. *Financial Questions in United States Foreign Policy*. New York: Columbia University Press, 1939.

Gardner, Lloyd C. *Architects of Illusion: Men and Ideas in American Foreign Policy, 1941–1949*. Chicago: Quadrangle Books, 1970.

————. *Economic Aspects of New Deal Diplomacy*. Madison: University of Wisconsin Press, 1964.

Gardner, Richard N. *Sterling-Dollar Diplomacy: The Origins and the Prospects of Our International Economic Order*. Rev. ed. New York: McGraw-Hill, 1969.

Garwood, Ellen Clayton. *Will Clayton: A Short Biography*. Austin: University of Texas Press, 1968.

Gayer, A. D. *The Lessons of Monetary Experience*. New York: Farrart & Rinehart, Inc., 1937.

Gelfand, Lawrence F. *The Inquiry: American Preparations for Peace, 1917–1919*. New Haven: Yale University Press, 1963.

Gervasi, Frank. "Bretton Woods or World War III." *Collier's*, June 2, 1945, p. 18.

Gilbert, Milton. *Currency Depreciation*. Philadelphia: University of Pennsylvania Press, 1939.

Gordon, David L., and Dangerfield, Royden. *The Hidden Weapon: The Story of Economic Warfare*. New York: Harper, 1947.

Graham, Benjamin. *World Commodities and World Currency*. New York: McGraw-Hill, 1944.

Graham, Frank, and Whittlesey, Charles R. *Golden Avalanche*. Princeton: Princeton University Press, 1940.

Green, David. *The Containment of Latin America*. Chicago: Quadrangle Books, 1971.

Gross, Bertram M. *The Legislative Struggle—A Study in Social Combat*. New York: McGraw-Hill, 1953.

Grubel, Herbert G., ed. *World Monetary Reform*. Stanford: Stanford University Press, 1963.

Haberler, Gottfried, and Willett, Thomas D. *A Strategy for U.S. Balance of Payments Policy*. Washington: American Enterprise Institute for Public Policy Research, 1971.

329

Bibliography

————. U.S. Balance-of-Payments Policies and International Monetary Reform: A Critical Analysis. Washington: American Enterprise Institute for Public Policy Research, 1968.

Halm, George. International Monetary Cooperation. Chapel Hill: University of North Carolina Press, 1945.

Hansen, Alvin. America's Role in the World Economy. New York: Norton, 1945.

————. The Dollar and the International Monetary System. New York: McGraw-Hill, 1965.

————. "The Importance of Anti-Depression Policy in the Establishment and Preservation of Sound International Relations." International Conciliation 369 (April 1941): 424–427.

————. "International Adjustment of Exchange Rates." In Studies of American Interests in the War and the Peace, No. E-B 64. New York: Council on Foreign Relations, April 6, 1943.

————. "World Institutions for Stability and Expansion." Foreign Affairs 22 (January 1944): 148–155.

————, and Kindleberger, Charles P. "The Economic Task of the Postwar World." Foreign Affairs 20 (April 1942): 466–476.

Harris, Seymour E. Exchange Depreciation. Cambridge, Mass.: Harvard University Press, 1936.

————, ed. The Dollar in Crisis. New York: Harcourt, Brace and World, 1961.

————, ed. The New Economics. New York: Knopf, 1947.

————, ed. Postwar Economic Problems. New York: McGraw-Hill, 1943.

Harrod, Roy F. The Life of John Maynard Keynes. New York: Harcourt Brace, 1951.

Hawtrey, Ralph George. The Gold Standard in Theory and Practice. 4th ed. London: Longmans, Green, 1939.

Hayter, Teresa. Aid as Imperialism. Harmondsworth, Eng.: Penguin, 1971.

Heilperin, Michael A. The Trade of Nations. New York: Knopf, 1946.

Henkin, Louis. Foreign Affairs and the Constitution. Mineola, N.Y.: The Foundation Press, Inc., 1972.

Herring, George C., Jr. Aid to Russia, 1941–1946. New York: Columbia University Press, 1973.

————. "The United States and British Bankruptcy, 1944–1945: Responsibilities Deferred." Political Science Quarterly 86 (June 1971): 260–280.

Heymann, Hans. Plan for Permanent Peace. New York: Harper, 1941.

Hilgerdt, Folke. "The Case for Multilateral Trade." American Economic Review (Papers and Proceedings) 33 (March 1943): 393–407.

Hill, Martin. The Economic and Financial Organization of the League of Nations. Washington: Carnegie Endowment for International Peace, 1946.

Hinshaw, Randall. Toward European Convertibility. Essays in International Finance, no. 31. Princeton: Department of Economics and Sociology, Princeton University, November, 1958.

————, ed. The Economics of International Adjustment. Baltimore: Johns Hopkins University Press, 1971.

————, ed. Inflation as a Global Problem. Baltimore: Johns Hopkins University Press, 1972.

Hirsch, Fred. "The Development and Functioning of the Postwar International Monetary System." Finance and Development 9 (June 1972): 48–52.

————. "The Dollar: Unbenign Neglect." The Economist, August 5, 1972, pp. 62–63.

————. Money International. London: Penguin, 1967.

Bibliography

Hirschman, Albert O., ed. *Latin American Issues: Essays and Comments*. New York: The Twentieth Century Fund, 1961.

Holtzman, Abraham. *Legislative Liaison: Executive Leadership in Congress*. Chicago: Rand McNally, 1970.

Horie, Shigeo. *The International Monetary Fund*. New York: St. Martin's Press, 1964.

Hudson, Michael. *Super Imperialism: The Economic Strategy of American Empire*. New York: Holt, Rinehart and Winston, 1972.

Hull, Cordell. *The Memoirs of Cordell Hull*. 2 vols. New York: Macmillan, 1948.

Hunt, Elmer Munson. *New Hampshire Town Names and Whence They Came*. Peterborough, N.H.: Noone House, 1970.

Huthmacher, J. Joseph. *Senator Robert F. Wagner*. New York: Atheneum, 1968.

Inman, Samuel. "Some Latin American Views on Postwar Reconstruction." *Foreign Policy Reports*, March 15, 1944, pp. 2–11.

Israel, Fred, ed. *The War Diary of Breckinridge Long: Selections from the Years 1939–1944*. Lincoln: University of Nebraska Press, 1966.

Istel, Andre. "The Reconstruction of France." *Foreign Affairs* 22 (October 1943): 114–125.

Iugov, Aron. *Russia's Economic Front for War and Peace*. New York: Harper, 1942.

Jacobsson, Per. "Toward More Stable Money." *Foreign Affairs* 37 (April 1959): 378–393.

Janeway, Eliot. *The Economics of Crisis*. New York: Weybright and Talley, 1968.

Johnson, Arthur M. *Winthrop W. Aldrich: Lawyer, Banker, Diplomat*. Boston: Graduate School of Business Administration, Harvard University, 1968.

Johnson, Brian. *The Politics of Money*. New York: McGraw-Hill, 1970.

Johnson, Gove Griffith. *The Treasury and Monetary Policy, 1933–38*. Cambridge: Harvard University Press, 1939.

Johnson, Harry G. *Inflation and the Monetarist Controversy*. Amsterdam: North-Holland, 1972.

———. "Political Economy Aspects of International Monetary Reform." *Journal of International Economics* 2 (September 1972): 401–423.

Johnson, Lyndon B. *The Vantage Point: Perspectives of the Presidency, 1963–1969*. New York: Holt, Rinehart and Winston, 1971.

Joint Committee of the Carnegie Endowment for International Peace and the International Chamber of Commerce. *International Economic Reconstruction*. Paris: International Chamber of Commerce, 1936.

Jones, Jesse. *Fifty Billion Dollars: My Thirteen Years with the RFC, 1932–1945*. New York: Macmillan, 1951.

Jones, Joseph. *Tariff Retaliation: Repercussions of the Hawley-Smoot Bill*. Philadelphia: University of Pennsylvania Press, 1934.

Kahn, Alfred E. *Great Britain in the World Economy*. New York: Columbia University Press, 1946.

Kelly, Eugene A. "Morgenthau's Rise to Glory." *American Mercury* 34 (January 1935): 13–21.

Kemmerer, Edwin. *Gold and the Gold Standard*. New York: McGraw-Hill, 1944.

Kenen, Peter B. "The International Position of the Dollar in a Changing World." *International Organization* 23 (Summer 1969): 705–718.

Kennan, George F. *Memoirs 1925–1950*. Boston: Little, Brown, 1967.

Keohane, Robert O., and Nye, Joseph S., Jr., eds. *Transnational Relations and World Politics*. Cambridge: Harvard University Press, 1972.

331

Bibliography

Keynes, John Maynard. *The Economic Consequences of the Peace.* New York: Harcourt, Brace and Howe, 1920.

————. *Essays in Persuasion.* New York: Harcourt, Brace and Company, 1932.

Kimball, Warren F. *The Most Unsordid Act: Lend-Lease, 1939–1941.* Baltimore: Johns Hopkins University Press, 1969.

Kindleberger, Charles P. *The World in Depression, 1929–1939.* Berkeley, Calif.: University of California Press, 1973.

Kirkendall, Richard S. "Franklin D. Roosevelt and the Service Intellectual." *The Mississippi Valley Historical Review* 49 (December 1962): 456–471.

Kolko, Gabriel. *The Limits of Power: The World and United States Foreign Policy, 1945–1954.* New York: Harper and Row, 1972.

————. *The Politics of War: The World and United States Foreign Policy, 1943–1945.* New York: Random House, 1968.

————. *The Roots of American Foreign Policy: An Analysis of Power and Purpose.* Boston: Beacon Press, 1969.

Kranold, Herman. *The International Distribution of Raw Materials.* London: Routledge, 1938.

Krause, Lawrence B. "A Passive Balance-of-Payments Strategy for the United States." *Brookings Papers on Economic Activity,* no. 3 (1970).

————. "Private International Finance." In *Transnational Relations and World Politics,* edited by Robert O. Keohane and Joseph S. Nye, Jr., pp. 173–190. Cambridge, Mass.: Harvard University Press, 1972.

————. *Sequel to Bretton Woods.* Washington: Brookings Institution, 1971.

Krock, Arthur. *The Consent of the Governed and Other Deceits.* New York: Little, Brown and Co., 1971.

Kubek, J. Anthony. *How the Far East Was Lost: American Policy and the Creation of Communist China, 1941–1949.* Chicago: H. Regnery Co., 1963.

Kuklick, Bruce. *American Policy and the Division of Germany: The Clash with Russia over Reparations.* Ithaca, N.Y.: Cornell University Press, 1972.

Latham, Earl. *The Communist Controversy in Washington.* Cambridge: Harvard University Press, 1966.

Leffler, Melvyn P. "The Origins of Republican War Debt Policy, 1921–1933: A Case Study in the Applicability of the Open Door Interpretation." *Journal of American History* 59 (December 1972): 585–601.

Leith, Charles K.; Furness, J. W.; and Lewis, Cleona. *World Minerals and World Peace.* Washington: Brookings Institution, 1943.

Lekachman, Robert. *The Age of Keynes.* New York: Random House, 1968.

Levin, N. Gordon. *Woodrow Wilson and World Politics: America's Response to War and Revolution.* New York: Oxford University Press, 1968.

Lewis, Cleona. *America's Stake in International Investments.* Washington: Brookings Institution, 1938.

————. *The United States and Foreign Investment Problems.* Washington: Brookings Institution, 1948.

Lewis, W. Arthur. *Economic Survey, 1919–1939.* London: Allen and Unwin, 1949.

Lichtenstein, Walter. "International Financial Organization." *International Conciliation* 369 (April 1941): 428–434.

Lindert, Peter. *Key Currencies and Gold, 1900–1913.* Princeton Studies in International Finance, no. 24. Princeton: International Finance Section, Princeton University, 1969.

Lockett, Edward B. "Banker to a Promised Land." *Nation's Business* 36 (June 1948): 39.

Lorwin, Lewis. *Economic Consequences of the Second World War.* New York: Random House, 1941.

McCloy, John J. "The Lesson of the World Bank." *Foreign Affairs* 27 (July 1949): 551–560.

McCormick, Thomas C. T., ed. *Problems of the Postwar World.* New York: McGraw-Hill, 1945.

Machlup, Fritz. "Eight Questions on Gold." *American Economic Review (Papers and Proceedings)* 30 (February 1941): 30–37.

———. *Plans for Reform of the International Monetary System.* Special Papers in International Economics, no. 3. Rev. ed. Princeton: Department of Economics, Princeton University, 1964.

Macmahon, Arthur, and Millett, John D. *Federal Administrators.* New York: Columbia University Press, 1939.

McNamara, Robert S. *One Hundred Countries, Two Billion People: The Dimensions of Development.* New York: Praeger, 1973.

McNeill, William H. *America, Britain and Russia: Their Co-operation and Conflict, 1941–1946.* London: Oxford University Press, 1953.

Maddan, B. K. "Echoes of Bretton Woods." *Finance and Development* 6 (June 1969): 33.

Madden, John T.; Nadler, Marcus; and Sauvain, Harry. *America's Experience as a Creditor Nation.* New York: Prentice-Hall, 1937.

Maddox, Robert James. *The New Left and the Origins of the Cold War.* Princeton: Princeton University Press, 1973.

Mallery, Otto T. *Economic Union and Durable Peace.* New York: Harper, 1943.

———. "Economic Union and Enduring Peace." *Annals* 216 (July 1941): 125–134.

Mason, Edward S., and Asher, Robert E. *The World Bank since Bretton Woods.* Washington: Brookings Institution, 1973.

Max, Hermann. "Los planes monetarios internacionales." *Boletín del Banco Central de Venezuela* 10 (October 1943): 56–69.

May, Ernest R. *"Lessons" of the Past: The Use and Misuse of History in American Foreign Policy.* New York: Oxford University Press, 1973.

Meade, James E. *The Economic Basis of a Durable Peace.* New York: Oxford University Press, 1940.

———. *The Theory of International Economic Policy.* 2 vols. New York: Oxford University Press, 1951–1955.

Meyer, Richard. *Banker's Diplomacy: Monetary Stabilization in the Twenties.* New York: Columbia University Press, 1970.

Mikesell, Raymond Frech. "America's Economic Responsibilities as a Great Power." *American Economic Review (Papers and Proceedings)* 72 (1959): 258–270.

———. *The Economics of Foreign Aid.* Chicago: Aldine Pub. Co., 1968.

———. *Foreign Exchange in the Postwar World.* New York: Twentieth Century Fund, 1954.

———. "The International Monetary Fund, 1944–1949: A Review." *International Conciliation* 455 (November 1949): 828–874.

———. "Negotiating at Bretton Woods." In *Negotiating with the Russians,* edited by Raymond Dennett and Joseph E. Johnson, pp. 101–116. Boston: World Peace Foundation, 1951.

———. "The Role of International Monetary Agreements in a World of Planned Economies." *Journal of Political Economy* 55 (December 1947): 497–498.

———. *United States Economic Policy and International Relations.* New York: McGraw-Hill, 1952.

Bibliography

Mill, John Stuart. *Principles of Political Economy*. 1871. Reprint, New York: D. Appleton and Company, 1965.

Moggridge, Donald Edward. *British Monetary Policy, 1924–1931: The Norman Conquest of $4.86*. Cambridge: At the University Press, 1972.

—————. *The Return to Gold, 1925: The Formulation of Economic Policy and Its Critics*. Cambridge: At the University Press, 1969.

Moley, Raymond. *The First New Deal*. New York: Harcourt, Brace & World, 1966.

Morgenthau, Henry. "Bretton Woods and International Cooperation." *Foreign Affairs* 23 (January 1945): 182–194.

Morris, James. *The Road to Huddersfield: A Journey to Five Continents*. New York: Pantheon, 1963.

Morton, Walter A. *British Finance 1930–1940*. Madison, Wis.: University of Wisconsin Press, 1943.

Mosse, Robert. *Le système monétaire de Bretton Woods et les grands problèmes de l'après-guerre*. Paris: Recueil Sirey, 1948.

Moulton, Harold G., and Pasvolsky, Leo. *War Debts and World Prosperity*. Washington: Brookings Institution, 1932.

Myrdal, Gunnar. *An International Economy: Problems and Prospects*. New York: Harper, 1956.

Nelson, Joan M. *Aid, Influence and Foreign Policy*. New York: Macmillan, 1968.

Nixon, Edgar B., ed. *Franklin D. Roosevelt and Foreign Affairs*. 3 vols. Cambridge: Harvard University Press, 1969.

Nixon, Richard M. *Six Crises*. Garden City, N.Y.: Doubleday, 1962.

Norton, Hugh S. *The Role of the Economist in Government*. Berkeley, Cal.: McCutchan, 1969.

Nourse, Edwin. *Economics in the Public Service*. New York: Harcourt, Brace, 1953.

Ohlin, Bertil. "Mechanisms and Objectives of Exchange Control." *American Economic Review* 28 (March 1937): 141–150.

Oliver, Robert W. *Early Plans for a World Bank*. Princeton Studies in International Finance, no. 29. Princeton: International Finance Section, Princeton University, 1971.

Packenham, Robert A. *Liberal America and the Third World: Political Development Ideas in Foreign Aid and Social Science*. Princeton: Princeton University Press, 1973.

Palyi, Melchior. *The Twilight of Gold, 1914–1936*. Chicago: Henry Regnery, 1972.

Paris, James Daniel. *Monetary Policies of the United States*. New York: Columbia University Press, 1938.

Parrini, Carl P. *Heir to Empire: United States Economic Diplomacy, 1916–1923*. Pittsburgh: University of Pittsburgh Press, 1969.

Paterson, Thomas G. "The Abortive American Loan to Russia and the Origins of the Cold War, 1943–1946." *Journal of American History* 56 (June 1969): 70–92.

—————. *Soviet-American Confrontation: Postwar Reconstruction and the Origins of the Cold War*. Baltimore: Johns Hopkins University Press, 1973.

Patterson, Gardner. *Discrimination in International Trade: The Policy Issues, 1945–1965*. Princeton: Princeton University Press, 1966.

—————. *Survey of United States International Finance, 1949*. Princeton: Princeton University Press, 1950.

Patterson, James T. *Mr. Republican: A Biography of Robert A. Taft*. Boston: Houghton Mifflin, 1972.

Penrose, Ernest F. *Economic Planning for the Peace*. Princeton: Princeton University Press, 1953.

334

Bibliography

Pick, Franz. *Pick's Currency Yearbook 1972.* New York: Pick's World Currency Report, 1972.

Pincus, John. *Trade, Aid and Development.* New York: McGraw-Hill, 1967.

Pink, Louis H. *Freedom from Fear.* New York: Harper, 1944.

Plischke, Elmer. *Conduct of American Diplomacy.* 2d ed. New York: Van Nostrand, 1961.

Price, Harry B. *The Marshall Plan and Its Meaning.* Ithaca: Cornell University Press, 1955.

Prince, Charles. "The USSR's Role in International Finance." *Harvard Business Review* 25 (Autumn 1946): 111–128.

Rees, David. *Harry Dexter White: A Study in Paradox.* New York: Coward, McCann & Geoghegan, 1973.

Reeve, Joseph E. *Monetary Reform Movements: A Survey of Recent Plans and Panaceas.* Washington: American Council on Public Affairs, 1943.

Reid, Escott. "McNamara's World Bank." *Foreign Affairs* 51 (July 1973): 794–810.

———. *Strengthening the World Bank.* Chicago: Adlai Stevenson Institute, 1973.

Rhodes, Benjamin D. "Reassessing 'Uncle Shylock': The United States and the French War Debt, 1917–1929." *Journal of American History* 55 (March 1969): 787–803.

Ricardo, David. *On the Principles of Political Economy and Taxation.* London: J. Murray, 1817.

Robbins, Lionel. *Autobiography of an Economist.* London: St. Martin's Press, 1971.

———. *The Great Depression.* London: Macmillan and Company, Ltd., 1934.

Robinson, Joan. "The International Currency Proposals." *Economic Journal* 53 (June–September 1943): 161–175.

Roll, Erich. *The World after Keynes.* New York: Praeger, 1968.

Roosa, Robert V. *The Dollar and World Liquidity.* New York: Random House, 1967.

Roosevelt, Kermit. "Handy Man Goes Banker." *Saturday Evening Post,* November 1, 1947, pp. 24–25.

Rosenau, James. *National Leadership and Foreign Policy.* Princeton: Princeton University Press, 1963.

Rosenman, Samuel I., ed. *The Public Papers and Addresses of Franklin D. Roosevelt.* 13 vols. New York: Random House, 1938–1950.

Rostow, Eugene V. *Peace in the Balance: The Future of American Foreign Policy.* New York: Simon and Schuster, 1972.

Rostow, Walt Whitman. *The Diffusion of Power: An Essay in Recent History.* New York: Macmillan, 1972.

———. *The United States in the World Arena.* New York: Simon and Schuster, 1960.

Royal Institute of International Affairs. *The Problem of International Investment.* London: Oxford University Press, 1937.

Russell, Ruth B. *A History of the United Nations Charter: The Role of the United States, 1940–1945.* Washington: Brookings Institution, 1958.

Salter, Sir Arthur. *Foreign Investment.* Essays in International Finance, no. 12. Princeton: Department of Economics and Social Institutions, Princeton University, 1951.

Santayana, George. *The Life of Reason: Reason in Common Sense.* 5 vols. New York: C. Scribner's Sons, 1905.

Sayers, Richard S. *Financial Policy 1939–1945.* London: H. M. Stationery Office, 1956.

Scammell, W. M. *International Monetary Policy.* 2d ed. London: St. Martin's Press, 1961.

Schapsmeier, Edward L., and Schapsmeier, Frederick H. *Prophet in Politics: Henry*

Bibliography

A. Wallace and the War Years, 1940–1945. Ames: Iowa State University Press, 1970.

Schatz, Arthur W. "The Anglo-American Trade Agreement and Cordell Hull's Search for Peace, 1936–1938." *Journal of American History* 57 (June 1970): 85–103.

Schlesinger, Arthur M., Jr. *The Age of Roosevelt: The Coming of the New Deal.* Boston: Houghton Mifflin, 1958.

Schloss, Henry. *The Bank for International Settlements: An Experiment in Central Bank Cooperation.* Amsterdam: North-Holland, 1958.

Schmitz, Wolfgang, ed. *Convertibility, Multilateralism and Freedom.* Vienna: Springer, 1972.

Schneider, Wilbert M. *The American Bankers Association: Its Past and Present.* Washington: Public Affairs Press, 1956.

Schriftgiesser, Karl. *Business and Public Policy: The Role of the Committee for Economic Development, 1942–1967.* New York: Prentice-Hall, 1967.

————. *Business Comes of Age: The Story of the Committee for Economic Development and Its Impact upon the Economic Policies of the United States, 1942–1960.* New York: Harper, 1960.

Sherwood, Robert E. *Roosevelt and Hopkins: An Intimate History.* Rev. ed. New York: Harper, 1950.

Shivnan, Martin. "The Bank Group Meeting." *Finance and Development* 10 (December 1973): 34–35.

Simons, Henry C. "The U.S. Holds the Cards." *Fortune* 30 (September 1944): 157.

Smith, Adam. *The Wealth of Nations.* 7th ed. 3 vols. London: A. Strahan and T. Cadell, 1793.

Smith, Gaddis. *Dean Acheson.* New York: Cooper Square Publishers, 1972.

Staley, A. Eugene. "The Economic Organization of Peace." *International Conciliation* 369 (March 1941): 394–423.

————. *World Economy in Transition.* New York: Council on Foreign Relations, 1939.

Stein, Herbert. *The Fiscal Revolution in America.* Chicago: University of Chicago Press, 1969.

Stern, Siegfried. *The U.S. in International Banking.* New York: Columbia University Press, 1951.

Stokvis, H. *Bretton Woods en het internationaal monetair bestel.* Leiden: Stenfert Kroese, 1948.

Strange, Susan. *Sterling and British Policy.* London: Oxford University Press, 1971.

Taft, Robert A. "A Post-War Peace Organization of Nations." *Vital Speeches,* June 1, 1944, pp. 492–495.

Taylor, A. J. P. *Beaverbrook.* New York: Simon and Schuster, 1972.

Tew, Brian. *International Monetary Cooperation, 1945–1967.* 9th ed. London: Hutchinson, 1967.

Tillman, Seth. *Anglo-American Relations at the Paris Peace Conference of 1919.* Princeton: Princeton University Press, 1961.

Tinbergen, Jan. *Shaping the World Economy: Suggestions for an International Economic Policy.* New York: Twentieth Century Fund, 1962.

Tompkins, C. David. *Senator Arthur H. Vandenberg: The Evolution of a Modern Republican, 1884–1945.* East Lansing: Michigan State University Press, 1970.

Traynor, Dean E. *International Monetary and Financial Conferences in the Interwar Period.* Washington: Catholic University of America Press, 1949.

Bibliography

Triffin, Robert. *Europe and the Money Muddle: From Bilateralism to Near-Convertibility, 1947–1956.* New Haven: Yale University Press, 1967.
————. *The Evolution of the International Monetary System: Historical Reappraisal and Future Perspective.* Princeton Studies in International Finance, no. 12. Princeton: Department of Economics, Princeton University, 1964.
————. *Gold and the Dollar Crisis: The Future of Convertibility.* New Haven: Yale University Press, 1960.
————. "International Monetary Collapse and Reconstruction in April 1972." *Journal of International Economics* 2 (September 1972): 375–400.
————. *Our International Monetary System: Yesterday, Today, and Tomorrow.* New York: Random House, 1968.
————. *The World Money Maze: National Currencies in International Payments.* New Haven: Yale University Press, 1966.
Truman, Harry S. *Memoirs: Year of Decisions.* Garden City, N.Y.: Doubleday, 1955.
Tucker, Robert W. *The Radical Left and American Foreign Policy.* Baltimore: Johns Hopkins University Press, 1971.
Ulam, Adam B. *Expansion and Coexistence: The History of Soviet Foreign Policy, 1917–1967.* New York: Praeger, 1968.
Urquidi, Víctor L. "Los proyectos monetarios de la postguerra." *Trimestre Económico* 5 (October–December 1943): 539–557.
Vandenberg, Arthur, Jr., ed. *The Private Papers of Senator Vandenberg.* Boston: Houghton Mifflin, 1952.
Viner, Jacob. *International Economics: Studies.* Glencoe, Ill.: Free Press, 1951.
Wallace, Henry A. "Foundations of the Peace." *Atlantic Monthly* 169 (January 1942): 34–41.
Warren, Frank. *Liberals and Communism: The "Red Decade" Revisited.* Bloomington: Indiana University Press, 1966.
Weaver, James H. *The International Development Association: A New Approach to Foreign Aid.* New York: Praeger, 1965.
Welles, Sumner. *Seven Decisions That Shaped History.* New York: Harper, 1951.
Werth, Alexander. *Russia at War: 1941–1945.* New York: Dutton, 1965.
Westerfield, H. Bradford. *Foreign Policy and Party Politics.* New Haven: Yale University Press, 1955.
Westerfield, Ray B. *Money, Credit and Banking.* Rev. ed. New York: Ronald Press, 1947.
Whitaker, Arthur P., ed. *Inter-American Affairs, 1944.* New York: Columbia University Press, 1945.
White, Harry Dexter. *The French International Accounts, 1880–1913.* Cambridge: Harvard University Press, 1933.
————. "The Monetary Fund." *Foreign Affairs* 23 (January 1945): 195–210.
White, John. *Pledged to Development.* London: Overseas Development Institute, 1967.
White, Nathan. *Harry Dexter White: Loyal American.* Waban, Mass.: B. W. Bloom, 1956.
Whittlesey, Charles R. *International Monetary Issues.* New York: McGraw-Hill, 1937.
Wicker, Elmus. "Roosevelt's 1933 Monetary Experiment." *Journal of American History* 57 (March 1971): 864–879.
Williams, Benjamin. *Economic Foreign Policy of the United States.* New York: McGraw-Hill, 1929.
Williams, John H. "Currency Stabilization: The Keynes and White Plans." *Foreign Affairs* 21 (July 1943): 645–658.

Bibliography

———. *Economic Stability in a Changing World.* New York: Oxford University Press, 1953.

———. "International Monetary Plans: After Bretton Woods." *Foreign Affairs* 23 (October 1944): 38–56.

———. *Postwar Monetary Plans.* 3d ed. New York: Knopf, 1947.

Williams, William Appleman. *The Tragedy of American Diplomacy.* Cleveland: World Publishing, 1959.

Wilson, Joan Hoff. *American Business and Foreign Policy, 1920–33.* Lexington: University of Kentucky Press, 1971.

Wilson, Theodore A. *The First Summit: Roosevelt and Churchill at Placentia Bay 1941.* Boston: Houghton Mifflin, 1969.

Wolfe, Martin. *The French Franc between the Wars, 1919–39.* New York: Columbia University Press, 1951.

Woodrow Wilson Foundation and the National Planning Association. *The Political Economy of American Foreign Policy.* New York: Holt, 1955.

Woodruff, William. *The Emergence of an International Economy 1700–1914.* London: Fontana, 1971.

Woytinsky, W. S., and Woytinsky, E. S. *World Commerce and Governments: Trends and Outlook.* New York: Twentieth Century Fund, 1955.

Yeager, Leland. *International Monetary Relations.* New York: Harper and Row, 1966.

Young, John Parke. *International Trade and Finance.* New York: Ronald Press, 1938.

Young, Roland. *Congressional Politics in the Second World War.* New York: Columbia University Press, 1956.

Periodicals

American Banker.
American Economic Review.
Arkansas Banker.
Bankers' Magazine (London), 1944–1949.
Boletín de la Sociedad Nacional de Mineria (Lima, Peru), 1944.
Boletín del Banco Central de Venezuela.
Boston Globe.
Business Week, 1947–1972.
Capitol Hill Views the World, 1945.
Chicago Journal of Commerce, 1944.
Chicago Tribune.
Christian Science Monitor.
Columbus Dispatch.
Commercial and Financial Chronicle, 1943–1945.
Economic Journal.
Economist (London), 1939–1971.
Euromoney.
Federal Reserve Bulletin, 1944–1945.
Foreign Affairs.
Foreign Policy Reports.
Fortune, 1942–1959.
Guaranty Survey, 1944.
Harvard Business Review.
IMF Survey, 1971–1972.

International Conciliation, 1940–1945.
Journal of American History.
Journal of Business.
Journal of International Economics.
Journal of Political Economy.
Littleton (N.H.) *Courier.*
Magazine of Wall Street, 1943–1949.
Manchester (N.H.) *Union.*
Nation, 1943.
New Republic, 1942–1951.
Newsweek, 1943–1953.
New York Journal-American, 1944.
New York PM, 1944.
New York Post, 1944–1945.
New York Times, 1933–1971.
New Yorker, 1944.
Oxford Institute of Statistics Bulletin.
Quarterly Journal of Economics.
Southern Banker, 1944.
Time, 1942–1959.
Trimestre Economico (Mexico City).
Vital Speeches.
Wall Street Journal, 1943–1971.
Washington Evening Star, 1944.
Washington Post.

Bibliography

Interviews

Edward M. Bernstein, Henry J. Bittermann, Ansel F. Luxford, and William L. Ullmann, all former associates of Harry Dexter White, discussed monetary planning from the American perspective. Others, including Emilio Collado, Charles S. Dewey, Herbert Feis, and John Parke Young, responded to written queries. Sr. Luis Machado also recalled activities of the Latin American delegations at Bretton Woods.

Many other bankers, diplomats, economists, and public officials responded anonymously to queries about more recent monetary developments. They were interviewed in Buenos Aires, Jerusalem, London, Mexico City, Rio de Janeiro, and Washington between 1971 and late 1973, or at annual meetings of the International Monetary Fund and World Bank Group in Washington.

339

Index

Index

Index

standard, 2–5; suspension of, during World War I, 7; sterling, in 1925, 12–13; and expansion of trade in 1920's, 14; and gold-exchange standard, 16; suspension of, in 1931, 21; and Tripartite Agreement, 26; and White plan, 47–48; and Keynes plan for one-way, 67–68; Federal Reserve experts and gold, 95; Simons's view of, 171–172; loan to achieve sterling, 176, 203–205; as goal of U.S. policy, 212–213; bilateral lending to achieve, 214–215; 1947 British experience with, 217–218; regional approach to, 219, 229; IMF seeks current-account, 226–229; U.S. pledge to gold, 226–227, 250; gradualism as approach to current-account, 231–233; and non-redeemable dollar, 250–252; Nixon suspends gold, 260–261, 265–266; in retrospect, 281. *See also* Bretton Woods system; Confidence problem; Gold-exchange standard

Coombs, H. C., 91

Costa Rica, 146

Council of Economic Advisers, U.S., 260–262

Council on Foreign Relations, 37–38, 168

Crimea Conference (Yalta), 180, 206, 273

Crowley, Leo T., 115

Crowther, Samuel, 144–145

CRU. *See* Composite Reserve Unit

Cuba, 43, 121, 233, 250; at Bretton Woods Conference, 141, 145, 153–154

Currency: floating rates of, 20–22, 28; controls on, 20–22, 29; realignment of, in Great Depression, 24; stability of, and Tripartite Agreement, 26–27; stability of, and White plan, 50, 99–100, 111–112; stability of, under IMF, 121–122, 130, 146–147, 186–187, 225–228, 243–246, 283. *See also* Convertibility; Currency, international; Gold-exchange standard; Parities; Payments adjustment, balance of

Currency, international: in White plan, 54–55; in Keynes plan, 65–69; in technical discussions, 76. *See also* Gold; Gold-exchange standard; Special Drawing Rights

Czechoslovakia, 121, 123, 132, 141, 151, 156

Dalton, Hugh, 203, 217–218

Danaher, John, 116

Davenport, Russell, 85

Dawes Plan, 12

De Gaulle, Charles, 232, 250–251, 255

DeMille, Cecil B., 139

Denmark, 220

Detroit Economic Club, 168

Dewey, Charles S., 117; and Central Reconstruction Fund, 108–110; and Republican alternative, 119–120; opposition of, to Bretton Woods agreements, 173–175; and support for House of Representatives compromise, 198

Dewey, Thomas E., 74, 109, 152, 176

Diebold, William, 37–38

Dollar (U.S.): shortage of, in Great Depression, 20; devaluation of, 1934, 22–25; and gold-exchange standard under Tripartite Agreement, 26–27; Treasury pledges gold convertibility of, 226–227; dominance of, in post–World War II world, 237–238; shortage of, after World War II, 242; glut of, 242–243, 248–249; and weaknesses of Bretton Woods system, 243–249; difficulties of devaluing, 244–247; and liquidity problem, 247–249; as international monetary standard, 249–250, 251; Kennedy's efforts to protect, 250–255; in deficit, 254–255; efforts to protect, 255–259; devaluation of, 259–266. *See also* Currency; International Monetary Fund; Key currency; Treasury Department, U.S.

Downey, Sheridan, 201

Drury, Allen, 195, 201

DuBois, Ben, 191

Dulles, John Foster, 36, 152

Dumbarton Oaks, 173

Eccles, Marriner, 112, 115, 143

Economic Defense Board, U.S., 41–42

Economic development: as White plan objective, 46, 52–53, 292 n. 35; as Keynes plan objective, 69–71; and Hansen's analysis, 84–85; as goal of

Index

Index

Index

Index

Index

Milton Keynes UK
Ingram Content Group UK Ltd.
UKHW010649211223
434766UK00001B/11